THE HISTORY OF COLOR

NEIL PARKINSON

FOR ROSIE

FRANCES
LINCOLN

THE HISTORY OF COLOR

A universe of chromatic phenomena

ESSAYS

THE COLOR OF

CHAPTERS

INTRO

DUCTION

Color is everywhere we look, but its ubiquity means we often end up not really noticing it at all. It can be objectively measured, yet its subjective effects are incalculable. It can delight or unsettle and has fascinated artists, physicists, and philosophers since antiquity, driving many to the point of obsession. All these paradoxes have spawned thousands of books across hundreds of years that have tried to understand and organize color, to describe its behavior and divine its meaning, to celebrate its iridescent abundance.

Nothing in the world is left untouched by color. It is a phenomenon so interdisciplinary, with a millennium of literature so vast and so richly illustrated, that one could imagine building an entire library of books about its effects. Such a hypothetical collection could even be organized along the principles of classic library science and classified according to the Dewey Decimal system: the 155 section for books about the psychology of color; 744 for the volumes on color and interior design. It could even drill down into niche areas: 658.823 for the small number of publications on color and packaging, perhaps.

In fact, such a resource already exists. The Colour Reference Library, one of the special collections at the Royal College of Art in London, contains nearly 2,000 titles, from the sixteenth century to the present day. It takes in a vertiginous range of subjects, from the psychology and symbolism of color to the history of pigments, from camouflage to synaesthesia. Despite its capacious remit, all the books in the collection, whether by Newton, Kandinsky or Wittgenstein, are united in the seriousness of their approach. Historically, the subject of color has often been dismissed as a frivolity; a gaudy afterthought or footnote to the rules of design or the history of science. By seeking to identify and understand color, to name, organize, contextualize, and master it, the canon of color literature elevates its subject to a status worthy of study.

The drivers for this pursuit of color have differed through the ages. Ancient Greek philosophers wanted to make sense of the world and explain our experience of it. Enlightenment botanists sought a way to represent the natural world in all its dazzle and dirt. *Fin-de-siècle* occultists were convinced the spectrum offered a glimpse of the supernatural. Modern entrepreneurs and corporations wanted to define proprietary ranges of commercial (artificial) color, in order to maximize profits.

This volume offers an overview of many of the key works in the history of color, and in particular those held in the Colour Reference Library, setting them in their historical and aesthetic contexts. It is a book about books about color, in all their beauty and ambition. It charts myriad attempts to establish relationships and hierarchies of color, to understand its rules that create contrast and harmony, or their opposites.

These efforts are not just theoretical but frequently visual, resulting in beautiful illustrations packed with individual tints, shades, and tones and ordered into circles, grids, pyramids, and cubes. While frequently conceived as complex tools for color mixing or specification, these color diagrams resemble works of art in their own right and are often triumphs of information design.

While the core of this book travels from 3000 BCE to the late twentieth century, it is not only a chronology. In keeping with the structure of the Colour Reference Library, and the kaleidoscopic nature of its subject, four historical chapters are supplemented by eight thematic sections, exploring the representation of color in different fields across time. These essays consider a wider range of color literature, the quirky as well as the canonical, and include some obscure publications that nevertheless approach color radically. The blend should encourage the reader to jump around from one discipline to another, like the experience of browsing the Colour Reference Library or the protean nature of color itself.

Color is an enormous subject and no survey can cover all its facets and functions. This is not a book about the history of pigments, or the history of color in art or commerce, although these factors surface throughout the narrative to provide context and motivation to the quest for color knowledge. This book also reflects some of the boundaries and biases of the collection, which does not quite hold everything on the subject, and some of the lacunae typical of Western libraries with their emphasis on male European scholars that dominate the conventional history of science. Nevertheless, the Colour Reference Library has always tried to be a broad church in a narrow field, and to consider all approaches to the subject valid. While it inevitably reflects the reference points of WEIRD societies (Western, Educated, Industrialized, Rich, and Democratic), its open-armed collecting policy means it also contains plenty of plain old weird stuff, including books about optical illusions, auras, chromotherapy, and spiritualism that might otherwise remain in the shadows.

Whether viewing the subject through the lens of physics or aesthetics, what shines through the books celebrated in this volume is the sense of color as a force of nature, the proud main character rather than a supporting role, fundamental to art and science, commerce and design. The scholars we meet in the following pages often anthropomorphized color, endowing it with personality or characterizing it as a primal force that could enrich lives. Their faith in its transformative power links them across the centuries regardless of whether their own approach involved measuring wavelengths, devising decorative schemes for the home, mapping the palette of birds' feathers, or casting spells. Organizing color has been a proxy for ordering the world, and a way to quantify aspects of the human experience within it.

In his classic work *The Art of Color* (1961) painter and former Bauhaus teacher Johannes Itten considered the spectrum and wrote: "Between black and white, there throbs the universe of chromatic phenomena." Happily for us, that universe, in all its glorious permutations, its tints and shades, its lines and circles, also thrives between the covers of a book.

Antiquity

1704

ALL WAS

LIGHT

Color is such a natural, insistent, and ubiquitous quality of everyday life that it feels as if it has always existed, and will endure long after we are gone. But it is all an illusion. Color as we perceive it does not truly exist outside our brains; it is a trick of the light. The world has only appeared colorful for as long as there have been creatures to see it. The sort of sophisticated color vision we possess today first began to emerge around 30 million years ago, when our primate ancestors evolved the ability to distinguish between multiple wavelengths of the visible portion of the electromagnetic spectrum. The light that fell in this band then began to be interpreted as different colors. Color begat color, and evolution accelerated its spread, with the natural world producing ever-more-spectacular displays as it grew itself a living, breathing, growing audience for the palette it could play with. For color to be perceived at all, three things need to interact: a light source, an object that reflects the light that strikes it, and an onlooker. This last component is us, and it is our perception of color that helps bring it into being. Color is dynamic and thrilling, a glorious, generous product of the biology of our bodies and the physics of light. And yet it bears repeating: it does not exist.

Whether despite or because of its illusory nature, color has inspired millennia of thought, tantalizing us with displays of mysterious rainbows and radiant coral reefs. When the poet Robert Frost described how the Northern lights "run like tingling nerves",he evoked the electricity of colorful displays and their profound effect. Its everyday magic has fascinated, perplexed, and infuriated philosophers, scientists, and artists alike, from Aristotle to Isaac Newton to Wassily Kandinsky. The ancient Greeks, the early scientists of the Islamic Golden Age, and the Enlightenment scholars all had parts to play, formulating new models to frame how color should be organized, to explain how we see it, and to understand how color relates to light. This last part is crucial. When Newton demonstrated that white light could be split into a rainbow of hues by channeling a sunbeam through a prism, he proved that color and light are different manifestations of the same thing, the former packed within the latter, ready to be released. To understand color, we also have to understand light and sight.

The earliest episodes of the history of our understanding of color contain all the clichés of scientific endeavor: visionaries imprisoned for heresy, social pariahs toiling in isolation, lone geniuses squinting down tubes to observe phenomena, or drawing the blinds to set the scene for a revelation. Following centuries of philosophical speculation, many of the advances in our understanding of color were eventually confirmed by those who followed an approach that became the scientific method: the formulation of testable hypotheses, and repeatable experiments to prove them correct. The first chapter of this story covers an era in which almost mythological models of the

A woodcut of a cross-section of the human eye, including the optic nerve, in the first printed edition of Opticae Thesaurus *(1572). This seven-volume work by Ibn al-Haytham, originally compiled in 1030, was published under the Latinised name of Alhazen.*

ergo nerui continet medium ſphærę glacialis: & eſt neruus ille concauus deferens in ſe ſpiritum uiſibilem à cerebro ad oculum, & per eius uenas paruas peruenit nutrimentũ ad oculum, & diffunditur in illo per uias nutrimenti: & eſt in interſectiõe huius nerui in anteriori parte cerebri uirtus uiſiua ſentiẽs & dijudicãs omne uiſibile: & conſolidatur uuea cum glaciali in circulo continente foramen rotundum in poſteriori uueæ. Interſecãt quoq; ſe ſphæræ iſtæ duæ, ſcilicet glacialis & uitrea neceſſariò: cum cõuexum unius obuiet cõuexo alterius: ſicut enim ſunt diuerſę naturę & diaphanitatis, ſic ſunt portiões diuerſarum ſphærarum ſe ſecantium: cõmunis itaq; ſectio illarum ſphærarum eſt circulus per 80 t 1 huius. Idem ergo circulus eſt baſis pyramidis nerui optici, & interſectionis eiuſdem pyramidis, & ſphærę cryſtallinæ, & conſolidationis uueæ ſphæræ cum ſphæra cryſtallina, & fortè interſectiònis earundẽ ſphærarũ. Corpus uerò conſolidatiuę continet partẽ pyramidalem nerui, quę eſt intra forã nen oſsis, per quod tranſit neruus, & intra circumferentiam ſphærę glacialis: & continet ſphærã uueam. Ex his itaq; patet humorẽ glacialem propriè eſſe organũ uirtutis uiſiuę: nam huius ſolius diaphanitas eſt receptibilis formarum uiſibiliũ: & eſt in medio omnium & humorũ & tunicarũ collocatus: & ſi alij cuicũq; tunicę uel humori accidat læſio, ſaluo glaciali humore, ſemper auxilio medicinę recipit oculus curationem, & ſanatur ac reſtituitur uiſus: ipſa uerò corrupta, corrumpitur uiſus totus ſine ſpe reſtitutiõis per auxiliũ curę medicinalis. Eſt itaq; humor cryſtallinus uel glacialis principaliter uirtutis uiſiuę organũ: propter quod eſt diligentius conſeruatũ. Et cõſtituit natura duos oculos propter perfectionẽ bonitatis uiſionis, & complementũ eius. Sic ergo patet, quòd humores & tunicę oculi ſphæricè ſe interſecant: & patet declaratio definitionis propoſitæ oculi ſecundũ omniũ eorũ experientiã qui de ipſius anatomia hactenus ſcripſerũt. Hæc aũt omnia, quæ ſcilicet de cõpoſitione oculi in hac quarta propoſitione huius tertij libri noſtræ perſpectiuæ ſunt præmiſſa: nunc ſummatim in figura mathematica ádiecta ſpectanda proponimus.

VERA OCVLI DESCRIPTIO
atq; effigies è recentioribus anatomicis libris deſumpta.

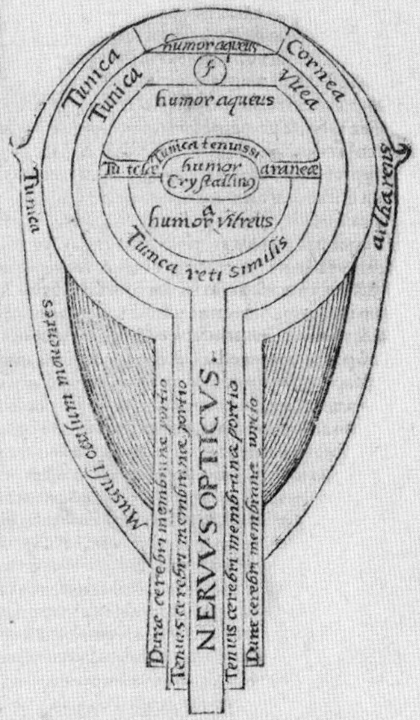

5. *Impoſsibile eſt uiſum rebus uiſis applicari per radios ab oculis egreſſos. Alhazen 23 n 1. item 23 n 2.*

Si enim aliqui radij egrediuntur ab oculis, per quos uirtus uiſiua rebus extra cõiungitur: aut illi radij ſunt corporei, uel incorporei. Si corporei, tũc cum uiſus uiderit ſtellas & cœlum: neceſſarium eſt, ut à uiſu corporeũ exiẽs impleat totũ ſpacium uniuerſi, quod eſt inter uiſum & partẽ cœli uiſam præter diminotionẽ ipſius oculi: quod & impoſsibile eſt fieri, & etiã tam citò fieri (ſubſtãtia & quantitate oculi manente ſalua.) Si uerò detur, quòd radij ſint incorporei, cum ſenſus nõ ſit niſi in re corporali: tunc ipſi radij nõ ſentirent rẽm uiſam: ergo nec oculus corporeus mediante hoc incorporeo non ſentiente poterit ſentire: nec enim talia incorporea reddunt aliquid uiſui, quo uiſus poſſet comprehendere rem uiſam, cum uiſus non fiat, niſi per contactũ uiſus cum forma uiſa: quia ſine cõtactu nõ fit actio. Radij ergo procedentes ab oculo ſi nihil reddunt uiſui: tunc non fiet per ipſos uiſio: ſi uerò aliquid reddunt uiſui, hæc erunt luces uel colores, quę per ſe uidentur, & quæ inter radios multiplicantur ad uiſum. Radij ergo nõ ſunt cauſſa applicationis uiſus cum rebus uiſis, ſed aliquid aliud, quod ſe multiplicat ad uiſum, eſt per ſe cauſſa uiſiõis. Impoſsibile eſt ergo radios per ſe eſſe cauſſam uiſionis, niſi fortè radij dicantur lineæ deſcriptę per puncta formarũ multiplicata à ſuperficiebus rerum uiſarum ad uiſum: quoniam, ut patet per 2 huius, inter quodlibet punctum ſuperficiei rei uiſibilis, & aliquod punctum ſuperficiei uiſus neceſſe eſt poſſe produci lineas rectas, ut res actu uideatur: tales uerò radij ab oculis non egrediuntur. Patet ergo propoſitum.

6. *Viſio ſit ex actione formæ uiſibilis in uiſum, & ex paſsione uiſus ab hac forma. Alhazen 1.2.3.14 n 1.*

Formas uiſibiles agere in uiſum ex 2 & 3 ſuppoſitione patet: lęditur enim uiſus ex forti luce, ut in

world were upended by iconoclasts who applied reason and rigor against symbolism and speculation. It boasts a colorful cast of characters to which history has assigned flamboyant titles: Doctor Mirabilis; the Father of Optics; the Last Magician. Several of these giants eventually ended up on the national banknotes of their birth countries to honor their legacies; another was nearly canonized.

Although some of the discoveries about color would shake the foundations of understanding and overturn centuries of received wisdom, in the earliest days efforts were more modest and color was often approached as the subject of a mapping project. Different scholars attempted to divine a natural sequence of colors and place them along a linear scale, imposing order on the natural world. In ancient Greece, one of the earliest contributors to the field, Aristotle (384–322 BCE), observed color, conducted experiments with colored glass and studied visible hues in natural phenomena such as rainbows and sunsets. This culminated in what is often considered to be the first known book about color, *De colouribus* (or *Peri khromaton*), which is attributed to the followers of Aristotle rather than the man himself, but it explored a theme that recurred throughout his earlier work on wider subjects.

Aristotle thought that all color lay between the extremes of black and white and could be created out of a fusion of darkness and light, an "interpenetration" of both, so altered by their commingling that something entirely new—colors—appeared. He believed black and white could be combined in similar ways to musical ratios, and the most pleasing proportions would produce the most pleasing colors. Aristotle explained in *Peri aistheseos kai aistheton* (*Sense and Sensibilia*) his conviction that gray was a variant of black, while yellow was a variant of white. His thought moved incrementally toward the model of a full spectrum and he eventually defined seven colors in total. These were not, however, the familiar rainbow hues—red, orange, yellow, green, blue, indigo, violet—of later thought. Instead, Aristotle included black and white as colors in their own right, with five chromatic types between them: yellow, crimson, violet, a color translated as "leek green" and blue. The appearance of the oddly specific reference to leeks alerts us to the problem of translation when trying to discern the intended color schemes devised in antiquity. Color names in use simply did not map to objective, universal hues that could be communicated instantly through familiar adjectives, as we might broadly understand "purple" today. Instead, they often referred to materials from the natural world used to extract a color, with all the instability and inconsistency this entailed.

De colouribus was fundamental for its crucial point that color was an inherent property of objects, and that this quality was fixed regardless of how an individual saw them. But the author also understood that the color of things changed depending on the external conditions. Color, the work argued, should properly

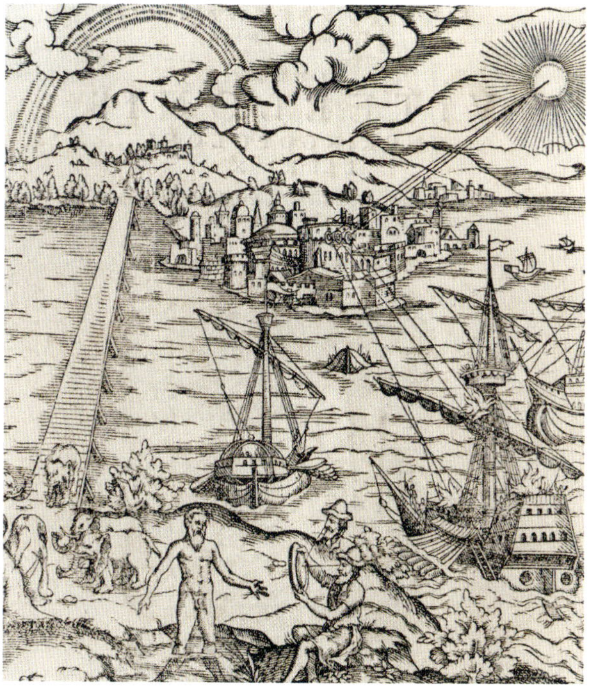

be observed as a phenomenon that is altered by the act of light upon objects and the infinite tints and shades this creates: "We never see a color in absolute purity, but always blended, if not with another color, then with rays of light or with shadows, and so it assumes a tint other than its own." Blue is rarely just blue: it is more likely to be kind of blue, or blue ... ish.

Aristotle's model was adapted and expanded centuries later by Persian polymath Ibn Sina (c.980–1037), more commonly known in the West as Avicenna. As with many of the figures in this story, for Ibn Sina the study of color was a fruitful sideline rather than a life's focus, and he is principally remembered for his far-reaching contributions to the field of medicine. A key figure of the Islamic Golden Age, his work *Kitāb al-Shifā* (or *Book of Healing*) contained sections devoted to vision and color. Ibn Sina expanded Aristotle's scales, believing black could take one of three different paths in its progress to white, via yellow-green, along a path of deepening red, or through a transition from blue-green to indigo. Which path was taken, he conjectured, was dependent on the depth of blackness originally present.

Ibn Sina was focusing on colored light, not color as a property reflected off the surface of physical objects (the two operate very differently, as we shall see), and drew his conclusions from simple observation, including the behavior of flames. Where he departed from Aristotle was in acknowledging the importance of tints and shades—lighter or darker versions of a particular hue, with additions of white or black, respectively—in establishing a graduated color scale. He also believed light to be made up of particles, and in this he anticipated Isaac Newton's seventeenth-century model of "corpuscles" of light (see p.25) by hundreds of years. His comprehension of the rainbow, that persistent source of mystery and marvels, was less enduring, however, and he wrongly posited that its color was simply a subjective experience of the onlooker.

Another figure of the Islamic Golden Age dominated this period. Ibn al-Haytham (965–1039) (much later published under the Latinized name Alhazen) was an Arab astronomer and physicist who would later be considered the father of modern optics. Ibn al-Haytham was the first to explain correctly that sight occurs when light is reflected off objects and enters the eyes, and that vision (and color perception) occurs in the brain, not the eyes themselves. He demonstrated that light travels in straight lines by peering down a cylinder at a flame and realizing that its flickering orange flowed directly to his eyes through the vessel aligned with it (the color went straight down

Engraving from the first printed edition of Ibn al-Haytham's Opticae Thesaurus *(1572). The image incorporates the behavior of light in different contexts, including refraction in water and a rainbow on the horizon. It features a representation of Archimedes using a mirror and the sun to set fire to enemy ships.*

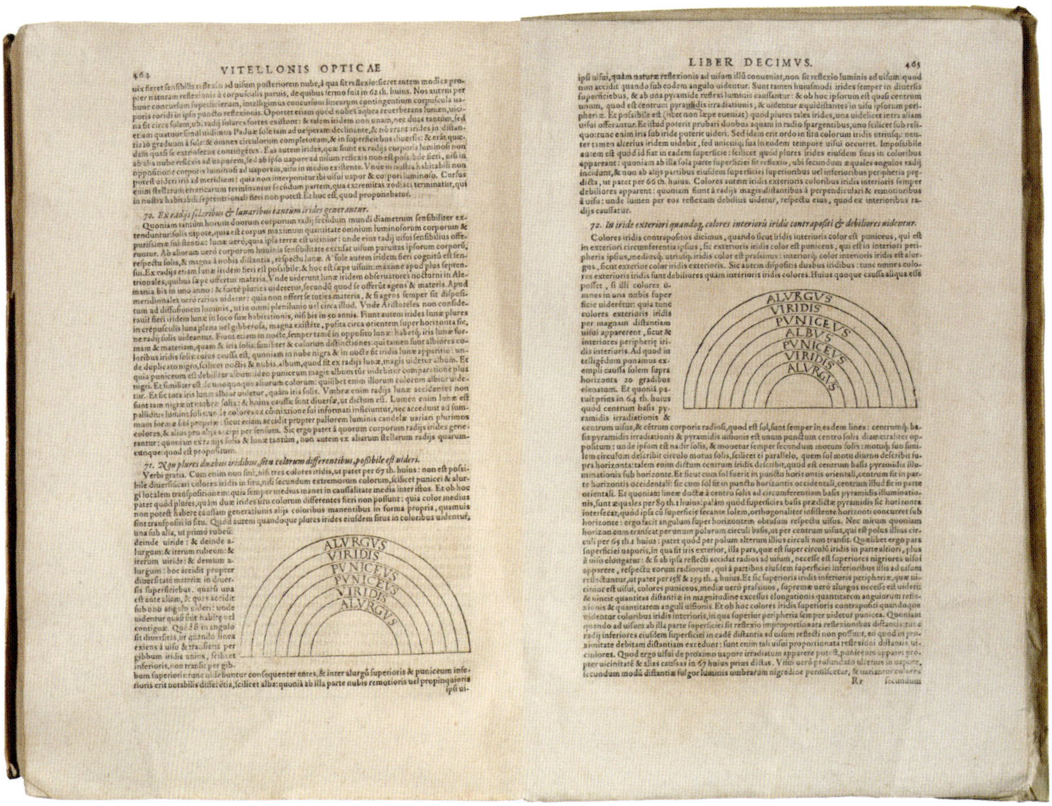

The first published edition of Ibn al-Haytham's Opticae Thesaurus *also included a work by Polish natural philosopher Vitello (c.1230–80), whose own book of optics was based extensively on al-Haytham's findings. In this section, Vitello contemplates the appearance of solar and lunar rainbows.*

the tube, in other words, rather than around it). These were important steps toward increasing understanding, but his most significant contribution to comprehension of sight was his refutation of the so-called emission theory of light. This had originally been advanced by the Greek philosopher Empedocles in the fifth century BCE and later by the mathematician Euclid and astronomer Ptolemy. Emission theory stated that humans saw because their eyes emitted cone-shaped beams of light that illuminated the objects of focus, like flashlights shining wherever anyone turned their gaze. Plato thought fire streamed from the eyes and entered into a kind of conflagration with daylight, creating channels through which the world could be illuminated. To modern sensibilities, the notion of beams blazing from the human eyeballs conjures visions of super-villains or the robots of classic science fiction. It may feel self-evidently wrong but it had common currency a millennium ago, especially as it was developed and used to explain other phenomena. Euclid, for example, believed the rays blasting from everyone's eyes must travel in straight lines, which explained why objects in the distance looked smaller: if a fingertip held up in front of one's face seemed the same height as a column in the distance, then the two objects must lie on the same straight line.

Emission theory seemed to make sense, but Ibn al-Haytham had doubts. He believed it was the duty of anyone who investigated accepted scientific thought to challenge it and "make himself an enemy of all that he reads, [...] attack it from every side." The theory could not explain why one's eyes hurt when staring into the sun, for example, and fell down when trying to describe how we see a glowing moon at night. And could we really see stars because light beams from our eyes were traveling far across the night sky and out across the galaxy? To counter these evident absurdities, Ibn al-Haytham turned to a rival explanation: Aristotle's woollier intromission theory, which posited that sight involved something traveling into the eye rather than flowing out of it. When we look upon a thing, Aristotle believed, a mysterious essence of that object enters our eyes, instantaneously. But Ibn al-Haytham did not like this either, troubled by the absence of any mathematical underpinning. If it did not add up, it failed to convince.

Ibn al-Haytham's genius was to take these two partially correct but deeply flawed theories and combine them, fusing Euclid's model of mathematical rays with Aristotle's intromission theory. By braiding the most convincing elements of both schools of thought, he worked out that rays were reflected from every point of objects. Sight occurs when some of those rays, colored or otherwise, strike the eyes and enter them, and, since rays travel in a straight line, their rigidity creates a point-to-point relationship between the surface of objects being looked at and the image they form on the retina. To demonstrate this, he built what was in effect a pinhole camera: a black box with a tiny aperture that formed images of whatever was in front of it on its back wall as light traveled through the hole. The images, however, were upside down, because the rays traveled in straight lines from multiple points to recreate the image in proportion, crossing over as they entered through the hole and flipping the image by the time they hit the wall. (Our eyes do this, too. Everything we see appears on our retina upside down, but our brains compensate and flip the image back so the world seems the right way up as we move through it.)

In 1030 Ibn al-Haytham compiled his body of work on light, color, and optics into a seven-volume magnum opus: the *Book of Optics* (*Kitāb al-Manāzir*). Some biographies relate that he wrote this while under house arrest, having feigned madness to escape the wrath of the caliph of Cairo when his proposed engineering solution to stop the Nile flooding went spectacularly wrong. There is debate over whether his experiments were conducted under semi-imprisonment or in the more conventional surrounds of

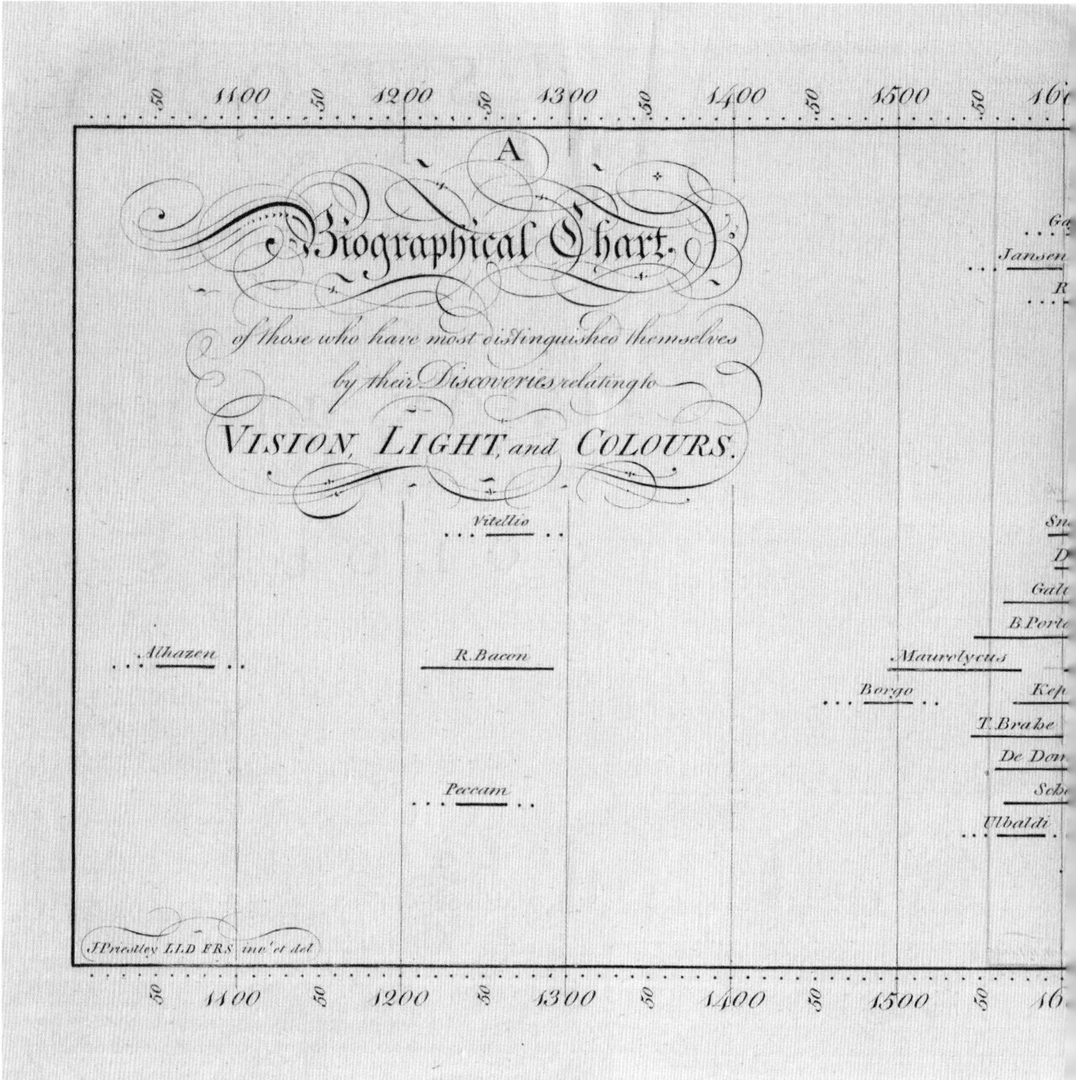

A timeline of the great early scholars of color and optics in Joseph Priestley's The History and Present State of Discoveries Relating to Vision, Light, and Colours (1772). Priestley places Alhazen (Ibn al-Haytham) as the founding father, with a striking gap between his research and the thirteenth-century activities of Roger Bacon. The space between Alhazen and Isaac Newton, separated by 600 years, is even wider.

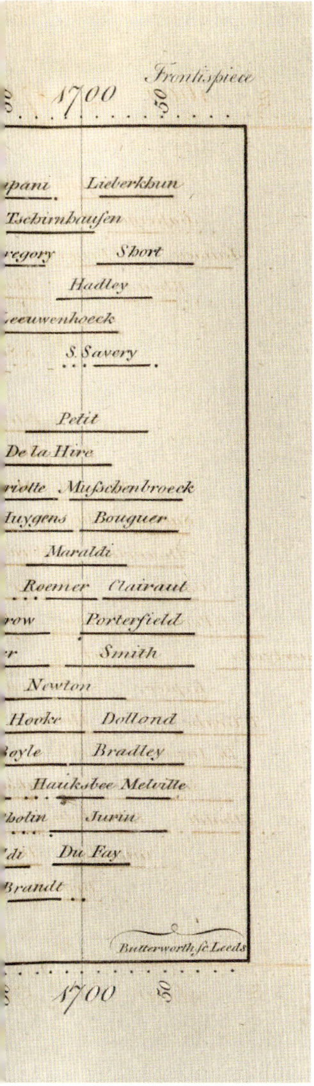

Al-Azhar University in Cairo, but, wherever he made his discoveries, Ibn al-Haytham's conclusions proved more water-tight than his flood barrier, and went on to be popularized by Europeans centuries later. His methods combined physics and mathematics, driven by experimentation and controlled testing, and he knew that independent replication and verification of his findings were fundamental to his authority. Once translated into Latin, the *Book of Optics* was circulated in the late twelfth century in western Europe, where it found an appreciative audience. The readership expanded considerably when it was first published by Friedrich Risner in 1572 under the title *Opticae Thesaurus*, the author's name Latinized to Alhazen. It remains a canonical work in the history of physics, extraordinary for its rigor and perspicacity.

As the writings of the Islamic Golden Age began to be translated into Latin and circulated in Europe, so too was the earlier work of the ancient Greeks. In England, one-time Bishop of Lincoln Robert Grosseteste (c.1170–1253) wrote *De colore* (c.1230), borrowing heavily from Aristotle's color theory. Grosseteste's near-contemporary, the Franciscan philosopher Bartholomeus Anglicus (d.1272), compiled encyclopedias of knowledge and incorporated the theories of both Aristotle and Grosseteste in turn in his own *De proprietatibus rerum (On the Properties of Things*, c.1240). This immensely popular work attempted to encapsulate all human knowledge of the universe, and included musings on colors and the rainbow. It was translated into Middle English by John of Trevisa in the fourteenth century.

In thirteenth-century Europe, the steadfast Aristotelian principles of logic and reason endured, but Ibn al-Haytham's revisionism also found an audience. Grosseteste was a key reader of the *Book of Optics* in England, but it was especially influential on the Franciscan friar Roger Bacon (c.1214–c.1292), who agreed with its author that color and light were separate phenomena that nonetheless modified each other, and that color existed outside of human perception, even in darkness.

Bacon's interests were wide ranging and forward looking. He experimented with lenses, describing the potential use of spectacles before they existed, and also demonstrated how to make gunpowder. His interests were potentially explosive for other reasons, though, and became increasingly esoteric by the standards of the time, even bending toward the heretical. Perhaps inspired by al-Haytham's analyses, Bacon was transfixed by the rainbow and investigated how rays passing through water could create colors. He even devised a portable demonstration, in which he filled his mouth with water, puffed out his cheeks and expelled the spray through his pursed lips. Under the right conditions, wherever the water caught the light, it created miniature rainbows and splashes of color, to the delight of most of the onlookers. Not everyone was impressed. In the dominant teachings of the Catholic church, light was nothing less than an instrument of divinity, while the rainbow, glowing with Old Testament symbolism, was a manifestation of God's miracles on earth. How could it be possible for an ordinary man to recreate one domestically, and in such a grotesque display? This was just one of many "suspected novelties" and irreverent acts that Bacon had introduced into his teaching, and these increasingly angered the authorities. The official response was brutal: he was imprisoned for years. Popularly known as Doctor Mirabilis—the wonderful teacher—history has been kinder to Bacon than the Church.

From around 1500, and into the so-called Age of Discovery, pigments and dyes became increasingly globalized and commodified. European colonialism advanced to the Americas to exploit natural resources and indigenous knowledge alike. Color soon became a lucrative current running through the economy of the Spanish Empire. Cochineal red was obtained from Mexico, extracted from crushed insects and processed in line with the traditional methods of the Aztecs. In the seventeenth century, the British East India Company's ruthless plunder of local labor and expertise opened up supplies of indigo from India. Extracted from the leaves of the *Indigofera tinctoria*, the much loved blue-black dye was so popular and profitable that the British eventually forced local farmers to abandon food production to keep up with demand.

Alongside this international flow of an expanding range of colors, there was a growing audience for recipe books and instruction manuals to help mix paints effectively. The standard was set by painter Cennino Cennini in fifteenth-century Florence. His *Il libro dell'arte* (*The Craftsman's Handbook*) compiled recommended techniques for drawing, painting, printing, and gilding, alongside an encyclopedic survey of pigments and their handling. Cennini described, for example, how verdigris was manufactured by "alchemy" (chemistry) and was beautiful but impermanent. He warned artists off accidentally ingesting the potentially poisonous yellow orpiment: "Beware of soiling your mouth with it, lest you suffer personal injury." The longest description was reserved for the extraordinary deep blue of ultramarine, extracted from lapis lazuli, and Cennini underscored the popular perception of the color as unparalleled in beauty and radiance, not to mention price.

By the time of the Renaissance, and on into seventeenth-century Europe, Catholic institutions were still exercising control over emerging thought about physics and cosmology among natural philosophers (the term scientist was not yet in use). In this, the establishment had a particular champion in the form of French philosopher René Descartes (1596–1650). Descartes' belief system was that the universe, including living things, was a giant machine, or series of machines, that operated like clockwork, with God playing the role of chief engineer. Descartes strove to demonstrate that light and color also operated on mechanical principles, just as the eye's lens resembles a piece of optical equipment. Descartes' explanation of how color arose

A late-fourteenth-century illuminated manuscript of an extract from Bartholomeus Anglicus's De proprietatibus rerum (On the Properties of Things)*. The original work of c.1240 was an anthology of writings from the ancient world and included Aristotle's analysis of the rainbow. Part of the translation reads: "Therefore the bow seemeth coloured, for, as Bede saith, it taketh colour of the four elements. [...] And these colours are more principal than others."*

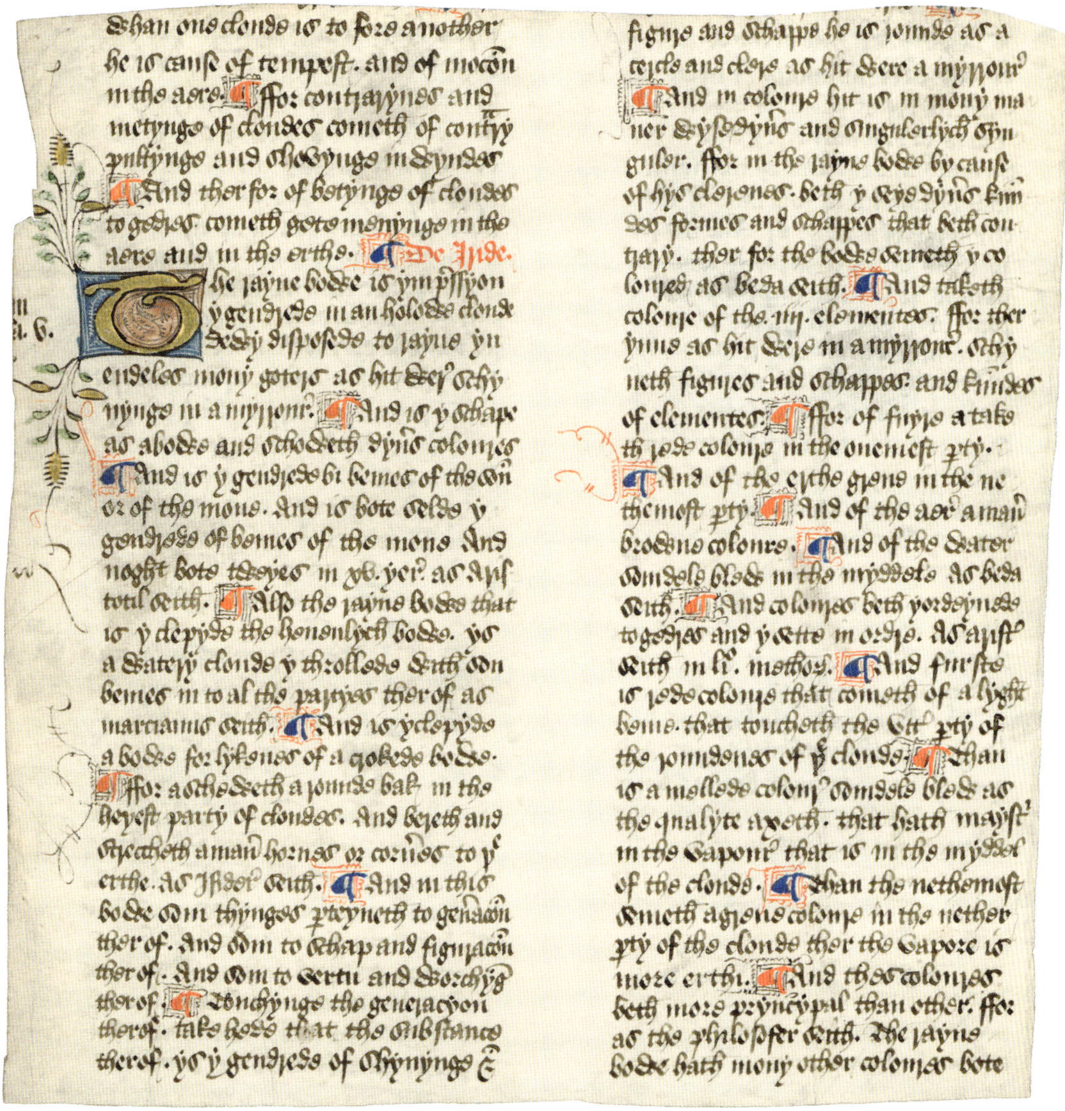

whan one cloude is to fore another
he is cause of tempest. And of mocion
in the aere. ¶ ffor contrarynes and
metynge of cloudes cometh of contry-
pullynge and chowynge in wyndes
¶ And ther for of betynge of cloudes
to gedres cometh grete monynge in the
aere and in the erthe. ¶ De Iride.
The rayne bowe is ymprission
ygendred in an holowe cloude
wery disposed to rayne yn
endeles mony gotes as hit were schy-
nynge in a myrrour. ¶ And is y schape
as a bowe and scheweth dyuers coloures
¶ And is y gendred bi bemes of the son
or of the mone. And is bote selde y-
gendred of bemes of the mone And
nought bote tweyes in .l. yer. as Aris-
totil seith. ¶ Also the rayne bowe that
is y clepyde the heuenlych bowe. ys
a watery cloude y thrilled with son
bemes in to al the partyes ther of as
marcianus seith. ¶ And is y clepyde
a bowe for lyknes of a bowed bowe.
¶ ffor a the weth a rounde bak in the
heyest party of cloudes. And bereth and
streccheth a man hornes or cornes to the
erthe. As Isidor seith. ¶ And in this
bowe som thynges perteyneth to generacion
ther of. And som to schap and figuracion
ther of. And som to vertu and worchyng
ther of. ¶ Touchynge the generacion
ther of. take hede that the substance
ther of. ys y gendred of schynynge &c

figure and schappe he is rounde as a
cercle and cleere as hit were a myrrour
¶ And in coloure hit is in mony ma-
ner wyssedyuers and singulerlych syn-
guler. ffor in the rayne bowe by cause
of hys clerenes. beth y sene dyuers kin-
des formes and schappes that beth con-
trary. ther for the bowe semeth y co-
loured as Beda seith. ¶ And taketh
colour of the .iiij. elementes. ffor ther
ynne as hit were in a myrrour. schy-
neth figures and schappes and kindes
of elementes. ¶ ffor of fyre a take-
th rede coloure in the ouemest party.
¶ And of the erthe grene in the ne-
themost party. ¶ And of the aer a man
browne coloure. ¶ And of the water
somdele blew in the myddele as Beda
seith. ¶ And coloures beth yordeyned
to gedres and y sette in ordre. As arist'
seith in li. methor. ¶ And first
is rede coloure that cometh of a lyght
beme that toucheth the vtter party of
the roundenes of the cloude. ¶ Than
is a mellede colour somdele blew as
the qualyte axeth. that hath mayst'
in the vapour that is in the myddel
of the cloude. ¶ Than the nethemost
semeth a grene coloure in the nether
party of the cloude ther the vapore is
more erthi. ¶ And thes coloures
beth more prynycipal than other. ffor
as the phylosofer seith. The rayne
bowe hath mony other coloures bote

added a new variable to help it fit into his mechanized model: velocity. He believed light was made of spinning particles and that color appeared whenever those particles spun faster and passed through "globules" in the ether. He addressed the well-known prism experiment—in which a triangular block of glass apparently created an array of color as light passed through it—by explaining that the prism was adding to, and modifying, the pure light that struck it, helping to create the color it revealed. Robert Hooke (1635–1703) made the same argument in *Micrographia* (1665), his mammoth study of the miniature world that explored nature as it suddenly appeared through magnifying lenses, revealing all its previously invisible intricacy.

The dominant Protestant faith in England, however, wanted to counter some of the models endorsed by the Catholics of mainland Europe. In opposition to Descartes' analysis of light and color rose one of the greatest figures in the history of science: Isaac Newton (1642–1727). Newton also felt the link between light and divinity, and was intimidated by the prospect of peering into the mind of God. Yet light, color, and vision fascinated and nagged him, pushing him to probe deeper to try to reach more convincing explanations than Descartes, constrained by his clockwork model, had been able to supply. Newton's almost unhealthy obsession with the subject was apparent when he began to experiment with optics as a twenty-something recluse. Musing on whether sight was triggered by the act of something external pressing on the eyes, he decided to push a wooden needle into the space between his eyeball and eye socket to see what happened. To his delight, the pressure on his lens caused colored rainbowlike circles to appear in his peripheral vision. And his eye was still in one piece.

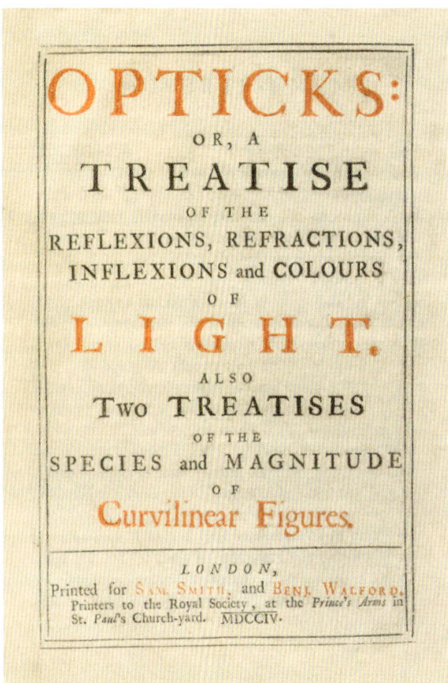

OPTICKS:
OR, A
TREATISE
OF THE
REFLEXIONS, REFRACTIONS,
INFLEXIONS and COLOURS
OF
LIGHT.
ALSO
Two TREATISES
OF THE
SPECIES and MAGNITUDE
OF
Curvilinear Figures.

LONDON,
Printed for SAM. SMITH, and BENJ. WALFORD,
Printers to the Royal Society, at the *Prince's Arms* in
St. *Paul's* Church-yard. MDCCIV.

Ask anyone to recall an image related to Newton's famous findings and many might think first of the apple, feeling gravity's pull and setting Newton's mind whirring as it tumbled to the ground. But asked to name another, it is likely that plenty will also recall his famous prism experiment, one of the most spectacular appearances of color as an object of study in the history of science. Newton drew the blinds in his home, made a hole to allow sunlight to enter in a narrow beam, and positioned a prism carefully in its path. On locating the correct angle at which to hold the prism, the sunbeam traveled through the glass medium and emerged to create a spectacular, glowing array of color on the wall. Newton noted the colors appeared in the same sequence as the rainbow, and called the ghostly colored ring before him a "spectrum", referring to its original meaning of an apparition (or spectre) rather than a fan of colors. This was not an experiment of Newton's own devising—Descartes had already explained it in his own way, as we have seen. But Newton unpicked it differently and concluded the prism was not in fact modifying or adding to the light to create color; quite the opposite. The prism, he correctly surmised, was bending component parts of white light and fanning it out into colors,

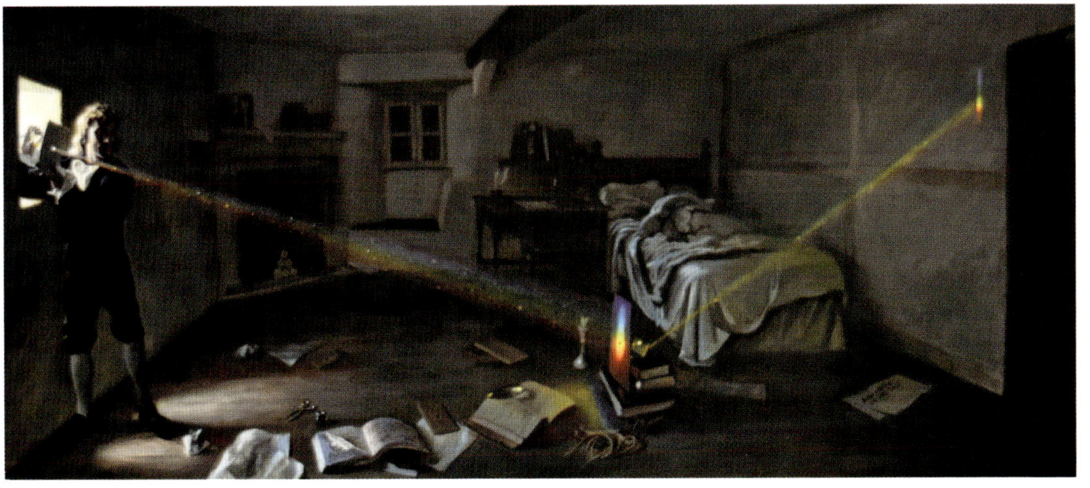

of which the seemingly pure white light had been formed all along. "My observations, though paradoxical, are clear," he wrote. "It is each separate color that is pure. And it is the white light that is the mixture."

Not only was this a new, and counter-intuitive, explanation for the phenomenon, but Newton saw the prism experiment as a starting point that could be adapted to prove his theory correct. His investigations turned on what he later called his "*experimentum crucis*". After splitting the light, he used a further hole in another screen and diverted just the red light of the spectrum through it. What would happen if he then placed another prism in the path of this red light? According to Descartes, the color would be further modified and perhaps split off into yet more colors. But the red light shone on unchanged, irreducible. Newton was right: prisms added nothing to white light, they just stripped it down to its essentials.

Newton bundled his experiments together, ensuring, like Ibn al-Haytham centuries earlier, that they were forensically detailed, clear enough to allow his peers to replicate them and confirm the findings. He sent them to the Royal Society as "a new theory of light and colors" in 1672. By 1703 he was President of that same institution and published his collected works on the subject as *Opticks: or a Treatise of the Reflexions, Refractions, Inflexions and Colours of Light* the following year.

Opticks (1704) was also notable for the inclusion of what is often thought to be the first color wheel—reproduced, of course, in monochrome. Once Newton noticed that the start and end of the visible spectrum, red and violet, were fading in from, and out to, a similar dark purple, he joined the two ends to form a circle. This was a stroke of genius: he had created a reference tool that drove color theory for the next century and beyond, a

OPPOSITE
The title page of Isaac Newton's Opticks *(1704). Newton's many experiments into light and color had been undertaken over the preceding decades but* Opticks *represented the summation of his research and his conclusions.*

ABOVE
An artist's impression of Isaac Newton performing his fundamental prism experiment—the "experimentum crucis"*—in his bedroom. Newton not only split the white sunlight into a colored spectrum with the first of two prisms, but channeled a portion of the resulting hues through the second to see if the color would be modified further.*

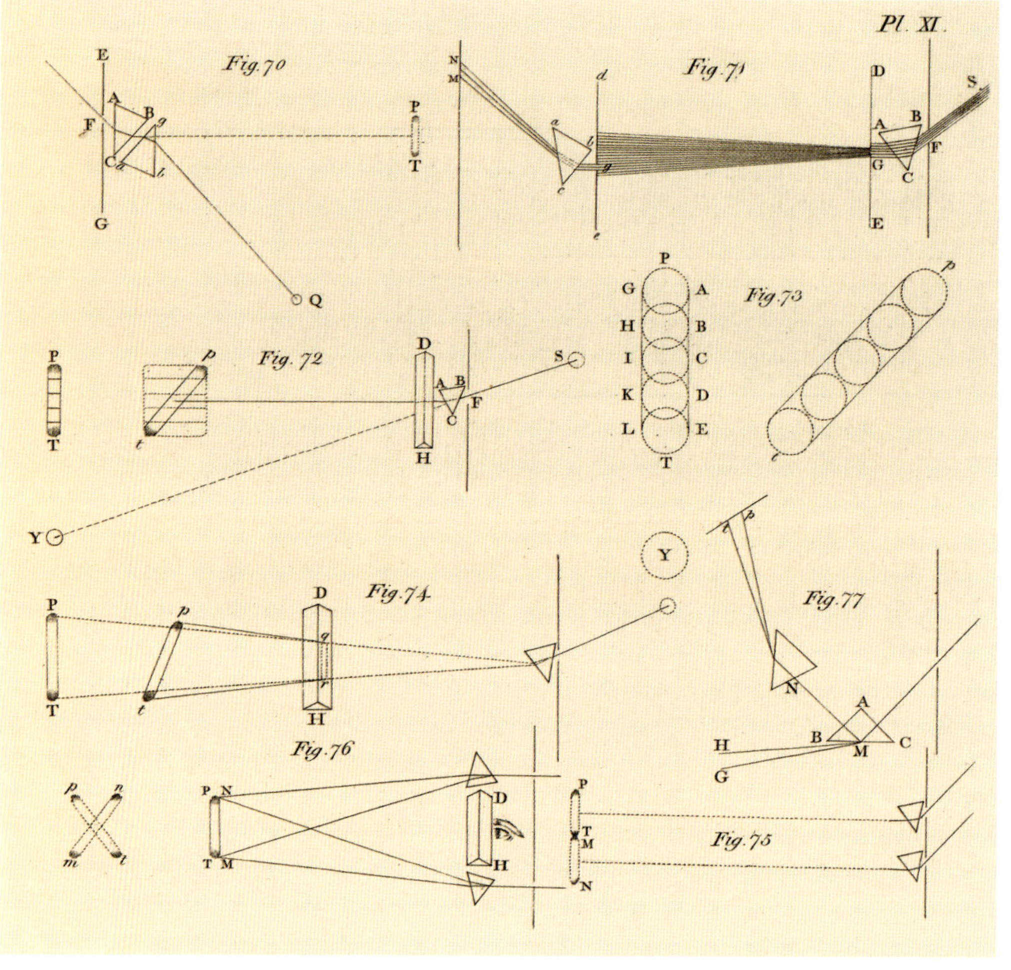

ABOVE
Newton's experimentum crucis in its original diagrammatic form (Fig. 71, top right) as reproduced in Joseph Priestley's The History and Present State of Discoveries Relating to Vision, Light and Colours *(1772).*

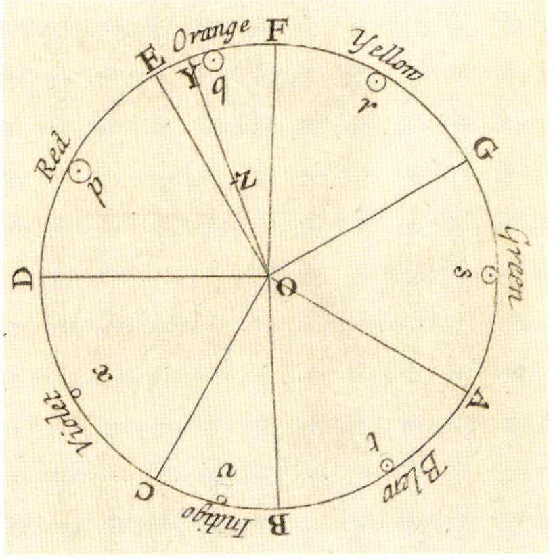

ABOVE
Fig. 11 of Book I of Opticks *(1704) is Newton's famous seven-segment color wheel. He marked points on the circle corresponding to musical notes, and an octave that began and ended with D. The attempt to force the spectrum into seven distinct colors is muddied between blue and indigo, which are closely related in a way that the other color categories are not. The unequal divisions of sections reflect Newton's calculations of their respective wavelengths, and the proportion of the visible spectrum each appeared to occupy.*

visual representation that transformed the linear thinking of Aristotle and demonstrated not just color sequences but color relationships. It was also artificial. The spectrum does not loop like this: it emerges from wavelengths we cannot see before red and fades out beyond violet into the invisible ultraviolet. Newton picked out seven for his wheel not because these were all that he could see but because he wanted to force an analogy with music (see p.208) and the Dorian musical scale, believing sound and light to be inextricably, if mysteriously, linked. Ironically, in this arbitrary and unscientific association, he may have been influenced by Descartes, who produced a similar wheel to show divisions of major and minor tones in his *Compendium musicae* (1618), a work on the mathematics of music. For all its misrepresentation of reality, the seven-segment color wheel—red, orange, yellow, green, blue, indigo, and violet, later recalled through the mnemonic ROY G BIV or "Richard of York Gave Battle in Vain"—has profoundly influenced our understanding of the order and division of color.

Newton's circle was deceptively complex. While it first appeared to depict segments of pure hue, like unfairly divided slices of cake, in fact, the center (marked O) represented pure white, with the colors intended to be visualized as increasing in saturation (richness or depth) as they extended toward the circumference.

Newton's conclusions got so much right that would become fundamental to human comprehension. But his notion that light was composed of corpuscles, rays that resembled a kind of fire that passed through transparent surfaces, was already being challenged. His contemporary, Dutch physicist and astronomer Christiaan Huygens (1629–95), posited a wave theory of light instead, proposing that it might take the form of wavelengths: undulating, periodic disturbances of matter. This was described in his *Traité de la lumière* in 1690, published ahead of *Opticks*. Huygens was later proved correct by the experiments of English polymath Thomas Young (see p.84) but Newton's mis-step did nothing to invalidate the depth of his insight into the relationship between white light and colors.

This survey of the early centuries of color research has covered a lot of ground, geographically and temporally. Evolution in thinking about color was slow, progressing only gradually from speculation and observation to measurement and analysis, sometimes as a by-product of other investigations. The color circle of Newton was an elegant full stop to this phase but also a culmination of the linking of theories, the tying off of loose ends and the creation of a new visualization of color. After centuries of speculation about which colors even existed, Newton had trapped the visible spectrum in a loop, pinning its component colors down for successors to experiment on further, or to try to set them free.

1

THE COLOR OF

BELIEF

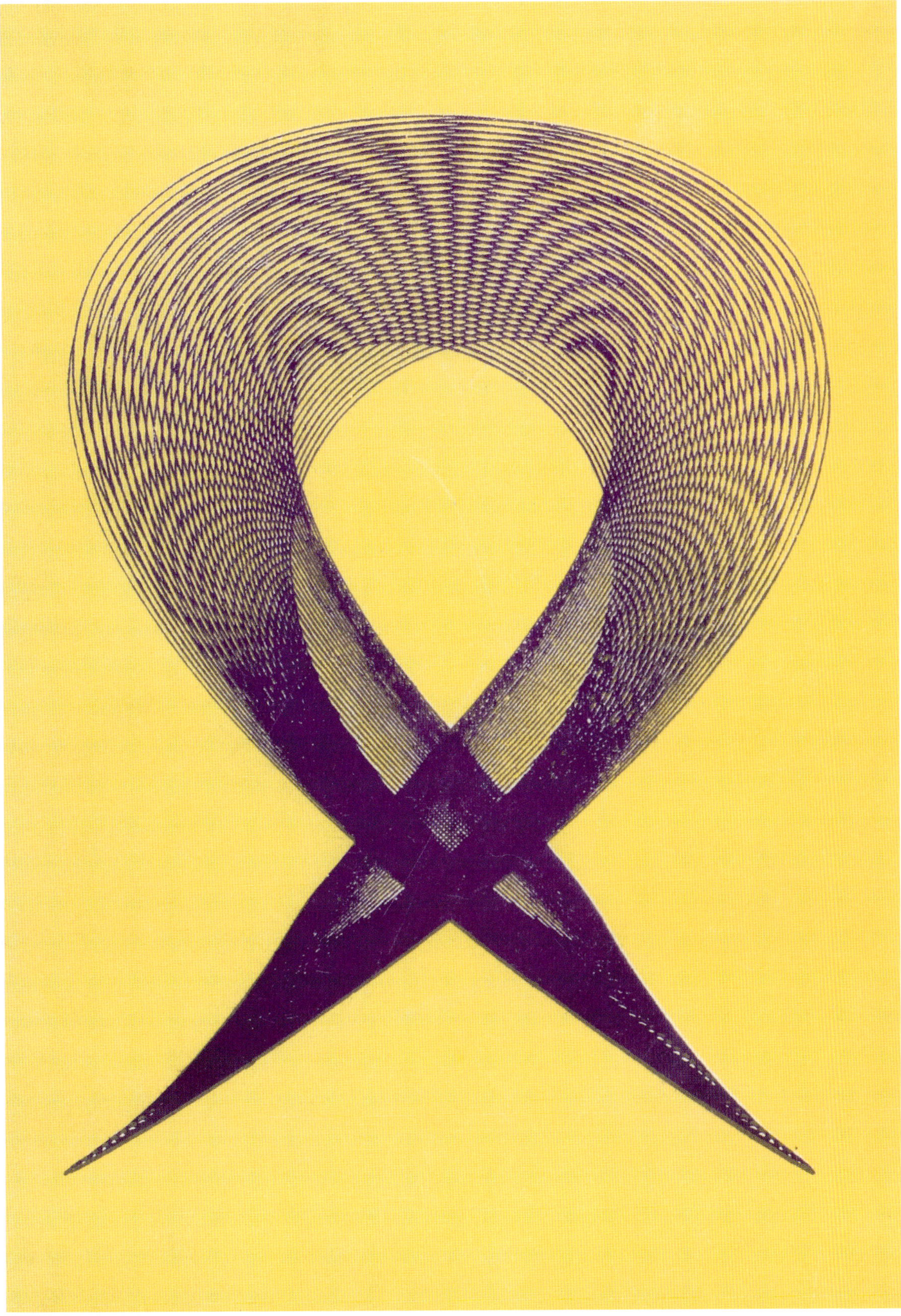

When Newton used a simple block of glass to turn a sunbeam into a ghostly ring of colors, spectators could be forgiven for thinking this was more sorcery than science. After all, color had long been linked with both magic and divinity to signify the numinous. The ancient Egyptians, for example, color-coded their gods to draw parallels with their earthly manifestations (Osiris was represented by green, which also connoted vegetation and rebirth) and used contrasting red ink in the *Book of the Dead* to highlight the names of spells and evil spirits. World religions used color wordlessly to symbolize tenets of faith and convey important concepts. In the Old Testament the rainbow itself represented God's covenant with humanity, while the use of white in Judaism denoted the purity of Noah's dove. Green emerged as central to Islam, resonant of the Prophet's turban and signifying foliage and fertility.

Early scientific investigations into color also maintained a bridge to the occult. Newton himself practiced alchemy during an era in which the bounds of science were not fully established and so-called natural philosophy readily overlapped with the supernatural. As the science of color advanced, along with the understanding of its physical basis, so too did its potential for symbolism. In the 1790s, for example, the Reverend William Jones postulated that the three primary colors of light bore a powerful relation to the Christian Trinity, because they combined to form pure white light. His suggestion may well have influenced another man of faith, pigment manufacturer and color theorist George Field (see p.96), who drew a similar analogy in his *Chromatics* (1817), a work exploring the attainment of perfect harmony.

In the later nineteenth century, a mass-produced ephemeral publication of the evangelical movement provided a more overt expression of color as a metaphor for Christian faith. Originally devised in the 1860s by Baptist preacher Charles Haddon Spurgeon, *The Wordless Book* was a slender pamphlet entirely composed of double-page spreads of solid color. Any text was reserved for the title on the front cover and a key on the back, relating each color to a specific Bible verse. The book's typical sequence moved narratively from the blackness of sin (and its corresponding verse: "we are all as an unclean thing, and all our righteousnesses are as filthy rags"), through the redemptive red blood of Christ,

PREVIOUS PAGE
In their book *Thought Forms* (1905), Charles Leadbeater and Annie Besant of the mystical Theosophical Society claimed human thoughts and feelings took the form of colored etheric shapes and tried to replicate them on the page. This illustration, "An Aspiration to Enfold All", represented the state of a person in meditation, projecting a love of humanity.

OPPOSITE
The Wordless Book, an ephemeral publication of evangelical Christians of the late nineteenth century, consisted of double-page spreads of solid color. The colors were keyed to Bible verses and represented a progression from sin to redemption through the blood of Christ.

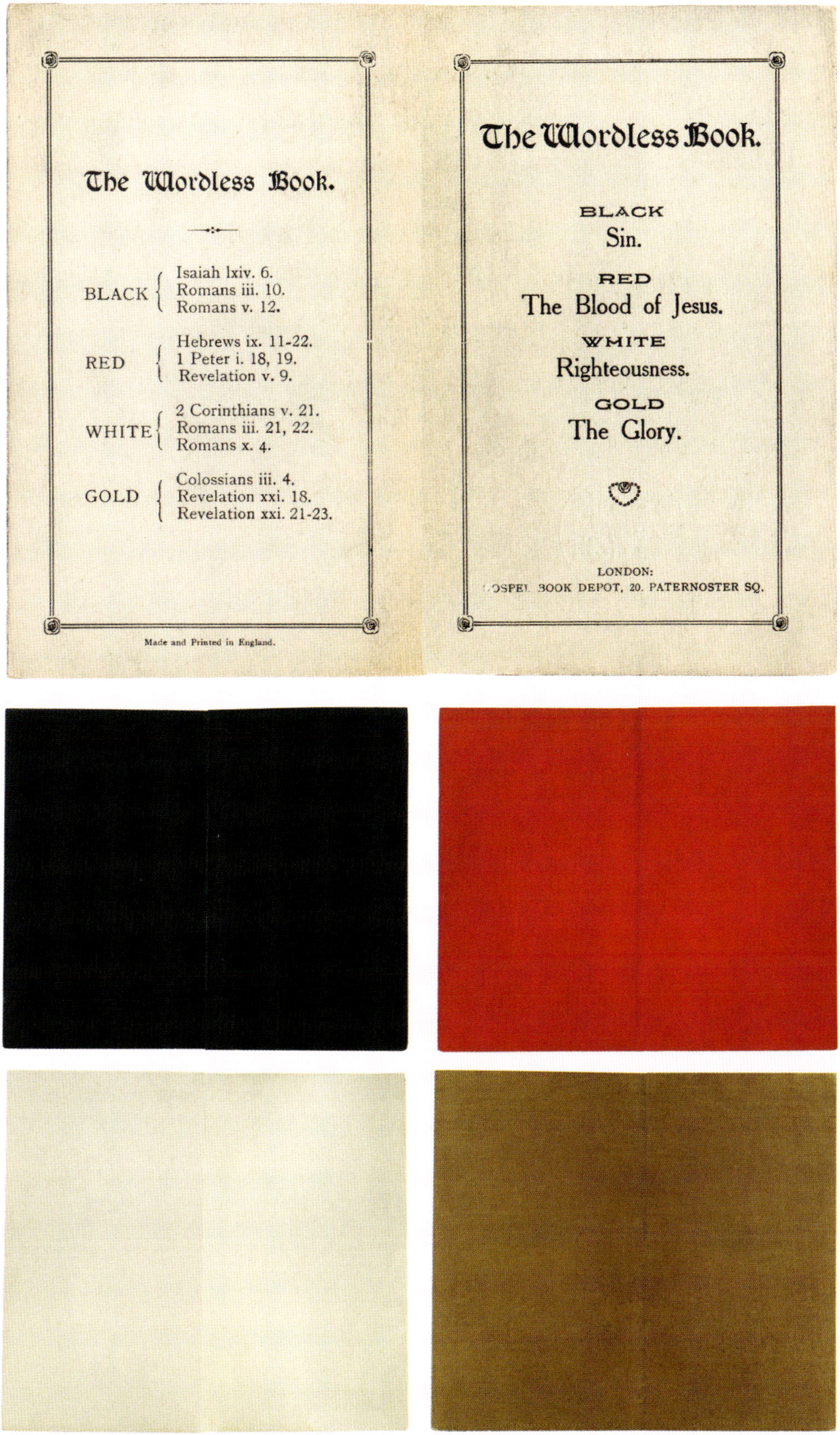

The Wordless Book.

BLACK	Isaiah lxiv. 6. Romans iii. 10. Romans v. 12.
RED	Hebrews ix. 11-22. 1 Peter i. 18, 19. Revelation v. 9.
WHITE	2 Corinthians v. 21. Romans iii. 21, 22. Romans x. 4.
GOLD	Colossians iii. 4. Revelation xxi. 18. Revelation xxi. 21-23.

Made and Printed in England.

The Wordless Book.

BLACK
Sin.

RED
The Blood of Jesus.

WHITE
Righteousness.

GOLD
The Glory.

LONDON:
GOSPEL BOOK DEPOT, 20. PATERNOSTER SQ.

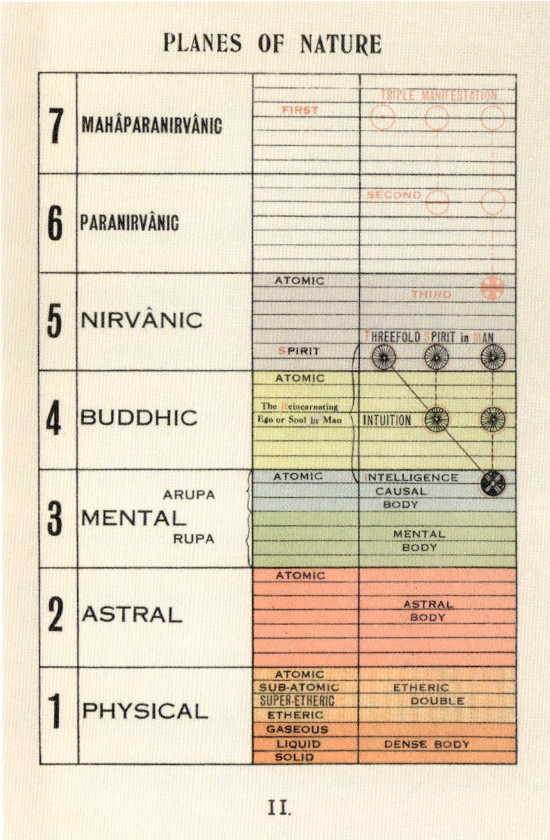

ABOVE
A color-coded plate from Charles Leadbeater's *Man Visible and Invisible* (1902) detailing the planes of human existence and potential experience. In the tenets of the Theosophical Society, to which Leadbeater was attached, six higher planes operated above the physical realm.

OPPOSITE
This "Key to the Meanings of Colours" appeared in both *Thought Forms* and *Man Visible and Invisible*. It acted as a reference chart for those who could "see" these colored emanations, and related colors to the feelings being revealed.

to a state of righteousness embodied by pure white. Some editions took the reader on into the golden "Glory" (ascent to heaven) on the final pages. In effect, *The Wordless Book* was a chromatic catechism: a visualization of the transformative power of faith that was often used as a teaching aid for illiterate adults and young children. Monolithic yet portable, its full-bleed rectangles of allusive color allowed contemplation on the move, helpful for the many Western missionaries who took copies to east Asia to amplify their message. The lack of universal color symbolism may have worked against their efforts in China, however, where red was synonymous with good fortune, and white more commonly associated with funerals.

In the *fin-de-siècle* era, color became increasingly presented as an agent of cosmic power rather than a mere symbol of it, largely through the influential writings of Madame (Helena) Blavatsky (1831–91), the co-founder of the Theosophical Society. Theosophy was a seductive brew of reworked and spliced Buddhist and Hindu thought and maintained that a secret universe of higher planes existed, governed by eternal "masters". In her dense work *The Secret Doctrine* (1888), Blavatsky applied each of Newton's seven colors (or "rays") to these beings. She claimed that the transience of life was a distraction from the permanence of the masters' realm, but that higher planes could be glimpsed through finding "correspondences" or simplified forms in the physical world. Color was often explored by Theosophists as a fundamental example of such a link, interpreted as a powerful coating to all things that could both mask and reveal. When physicist and educator Ogden Rood (see p.168) described the miracle of human color vision as a "magical drapery" cast over the world, he was speaking figuratively, but to Blavatsky and her followers, the magic was real. Color provided not just a rich visual dimension to our world but a glimpse of another one entirely.

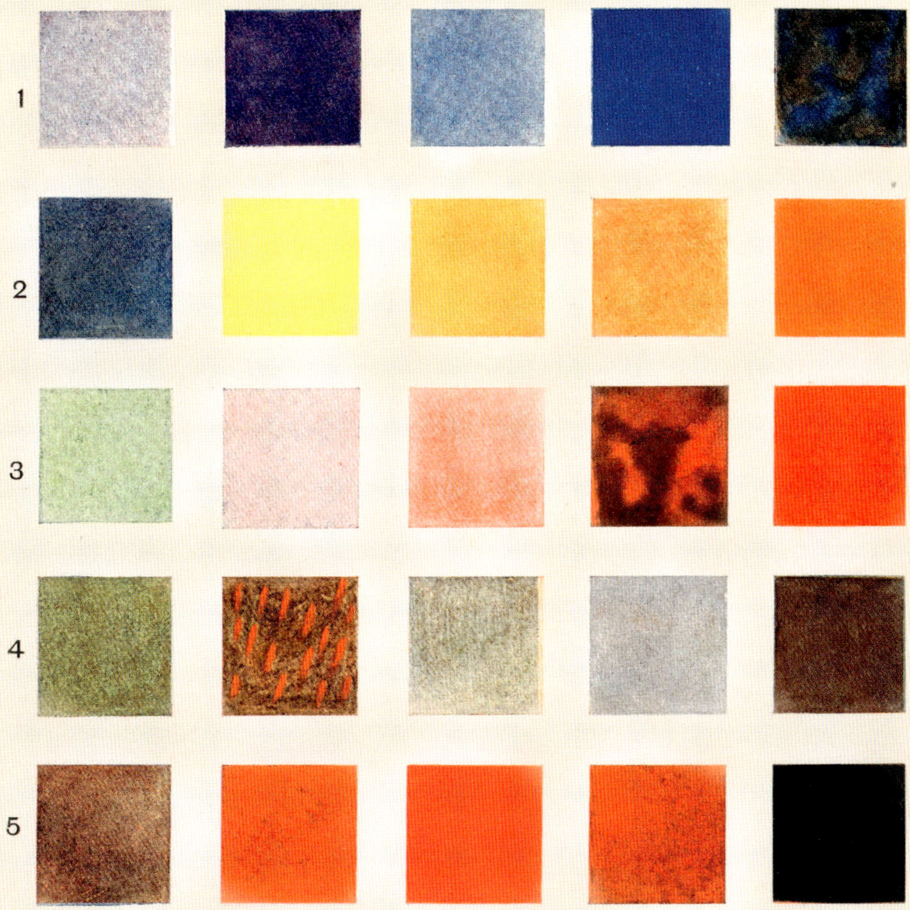

1. High Spirituality.	1. Devotion mixed with Affection.	1. Devotion to a Noble Ideal.	1. Pure Religious Feeling.	1. Selfish Religious Feeling.
2. Religious Feeling, tinged with Fear.	2. Highest Intellect.	2. Strong Intellect.	2. Low type of Intellect.	2. Pride.
3. Sympathy.	3. Love for Humanity.	3. Unselfish Affection.	3. Selfish Affection.	3. Pure Affection.
4 Adaptability.	4. Jealousy.	4. Deceit.	4. Fear.	4. Depression.
5. Selfishness.	5 Avarice.	5. Anger.	5. Sensuality.	5. Malice.

KEY TO THE MEANINGS OF COLOURS.

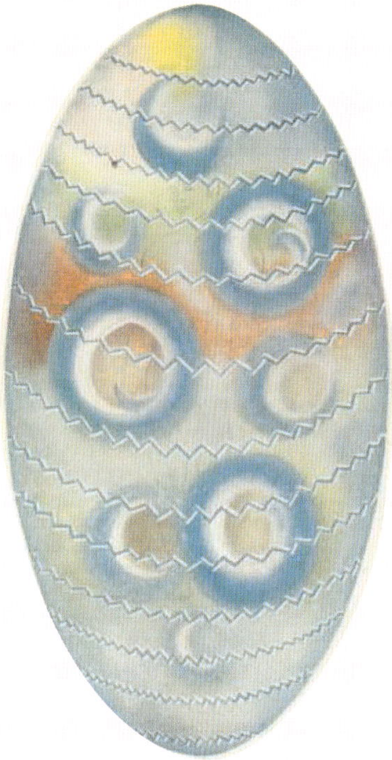

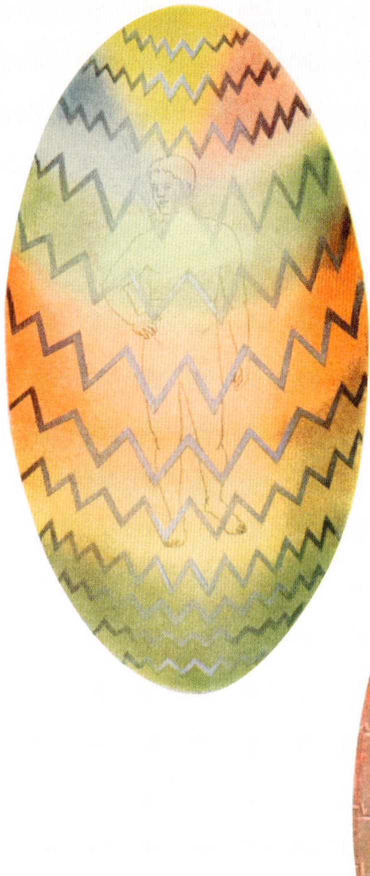

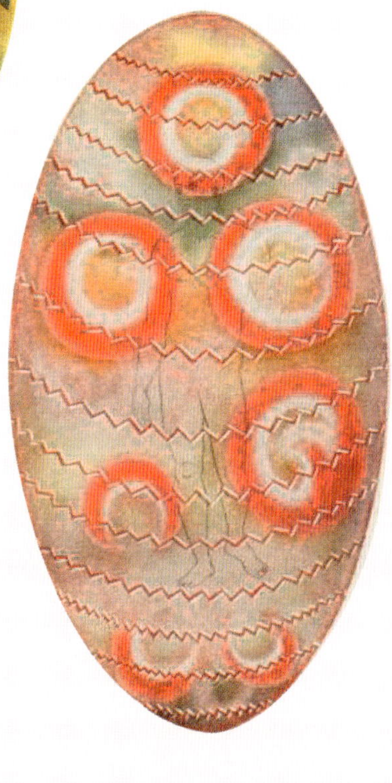

It was not simply visible color that concerned Theosophists. Around 1900, several of their members began to articulate their beliefs around auras, the concept of a cloud of mysterious colors that emanated from all living things as an outward expression of their psyche. Charles Webster Leadbeater (1854–1934) was originally a Church of England priest who became interested in Hinduism and Buddhism after traveling to Burma and Ceylon (Myanmar and Sri Lanka) where he claimed to have acquired clairvoyant powers. In his *Man Visible and Invisible* (1902) he described how the human body contained not just cells but also "etheric matter". A clairvoyant would be able to see this matter appearing as colored emanations around the body, but the colors themselves belonged to the astral plane, set above the physical world. Examples of different auras, which changed shape and color according to the subject's mood, were included throughout the book and could be decoded using the frontispiece key: crimson denoted love, for example, while yellow signified intelligence. Livid gray, meanwhile, "a most hideous and frightful hue", was a sign of fear. These auras had both shape and color. A mother's sudden feeling of love for her child was presented as "coils or vortices of vivid color", and contrasted with formally similar but chromatically different blue coils emanating from the steadfast devotions of a nun.

Leadbeater followed up this work with *Thought Forms* (1905), a collaboration with his friend Annie Besant (1847–1933), who later became president of the Theosophical Society. In more than fifty color illustrations, the pair explored the specific manifestation of thoughts and emotional states. In describing the phenomenon, the authors explained that every thought created "a marvellous play of color, like that in the spray of a waterfall as the sunlight strikes it, raised to the nth degree". Complexity and ambivalence of thoughts resulted in multicolored emanations; the color revealed the quality

Three representations of different emotional states in *Man Visible and Invisible*. Both the top left and bottom right images depict sudden rushes of emotion but are differently colored. The blue coils represent the devotional feelings experienced by a nun, while the red version depicts a mother who "snatches up her baby and covers it with kisses", overwhelmed by love. In the central image, the zig-zags and multicolored bands represent a person in a state of fear and inhabiting "a curious livid grey mist".

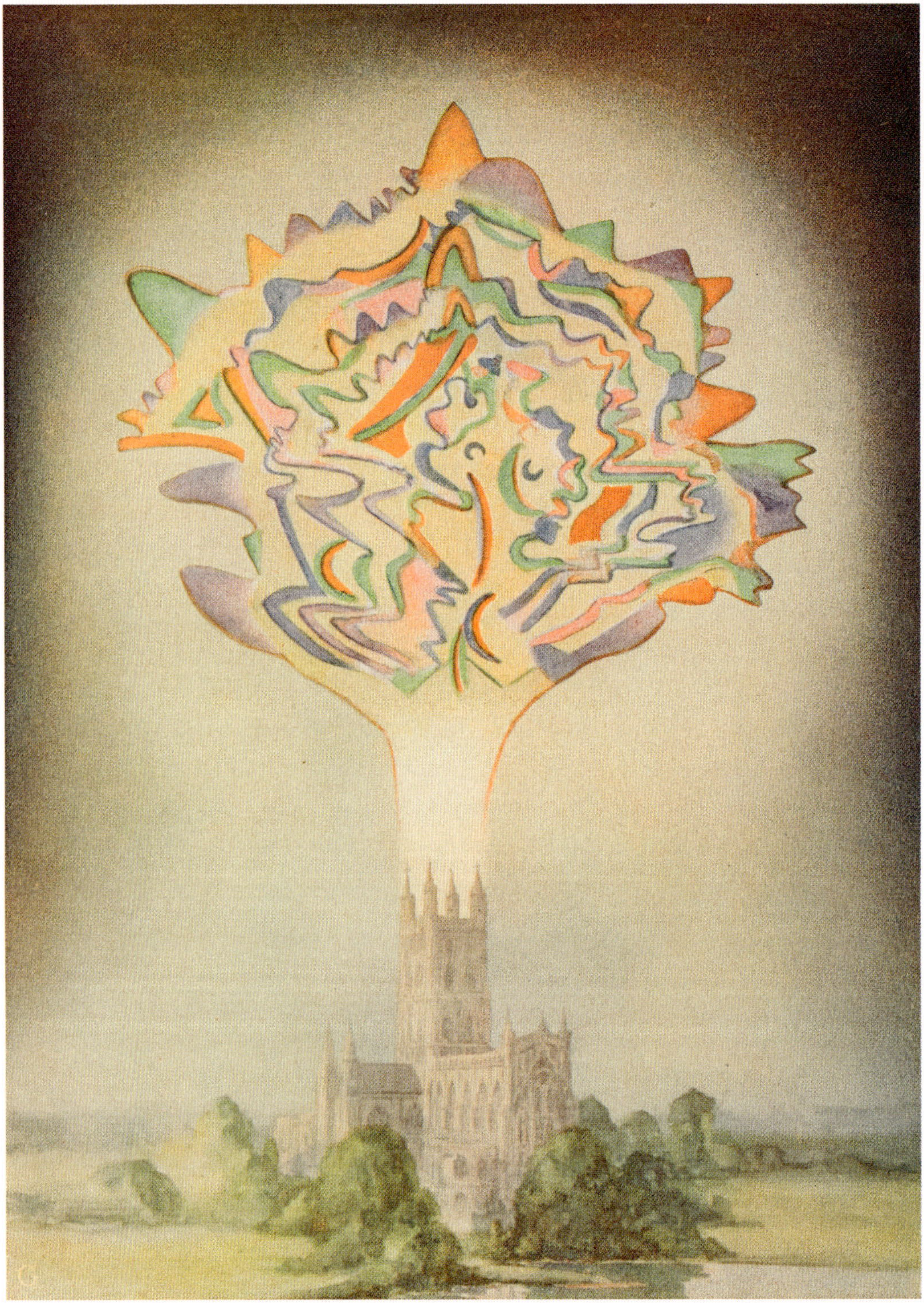

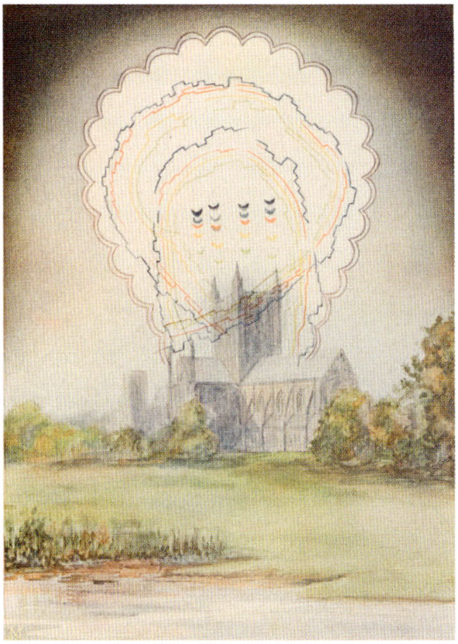

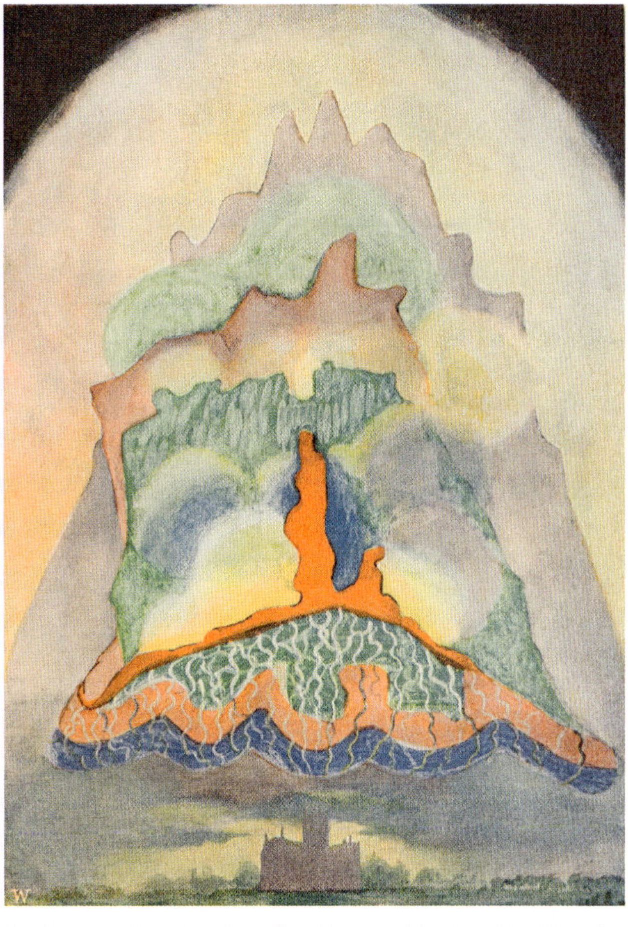

OPPOSITE
Thought Forms (1905) included representations of mystical colored emanations that apparently also manifested wherever music was performed. This visualization is of a piece by Gounod as performed on a church organ.

ABOVE
The shape and colors change significantly for a gentler work by Mendelssohn.

RIGHT
The most overwhelming and complex color forms appear when Wagner is performed. "All the magnificent masses of color are built up of many comparatively small bands ... each mountain peak has its own brilliant hue."

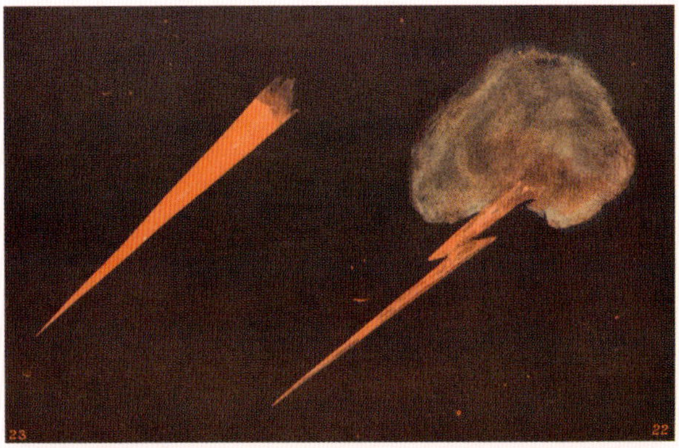

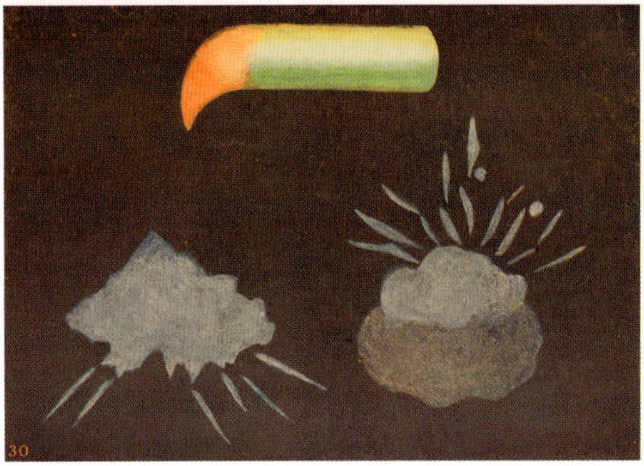

ABOVE LEFT
Representations of a person's "explosive anger" in *Thought Forms*.

LEFT
Expressions of different emotional responses during the chaos of a shipwreck. On the bottom left is a sense of panic, confusion and "the livid grey of fear". The colorful shape at the top represents the stoicism and resolution of the officer in charge, attempting to save the day.

of thoughts, while their nature was reflected in their shape. Thought forms, like auras, were invisible to most of humanity, but Besant and Leadbeater claimed to have seen them with extra-sensory powers and asked artist friends to recreate them from their descriptions. Naturally, it was a challenge "to paint in earth's dull colors the forms clothed in the living light of other worlds' and the visible spectrum was apparently a lot wider in the astral plane. Among the emotions illustrated and colorized were "pure affection", "murderous rage", and "vague sympathy". More pictorial images embodied specific narratives in moments of intensity: "At a Street Accident" visualized the emotions of bystanders on seeing a pedestrian being run over. "At a Funeral" contrasted the experience of two mourners, one a Theosophist and the other a non-believer. The latter's mental state was a doomy gray cloud with a sharp hook or ratlike tail, while the Theosophist's enlightened experience, and certainty that the deceased had just moved to a higher plane, resembled a colorful cone or a sparkly wizard's hat. The pair also argued that live performances of music produced similar emissions and illustrated this by comparing the colorful emanations

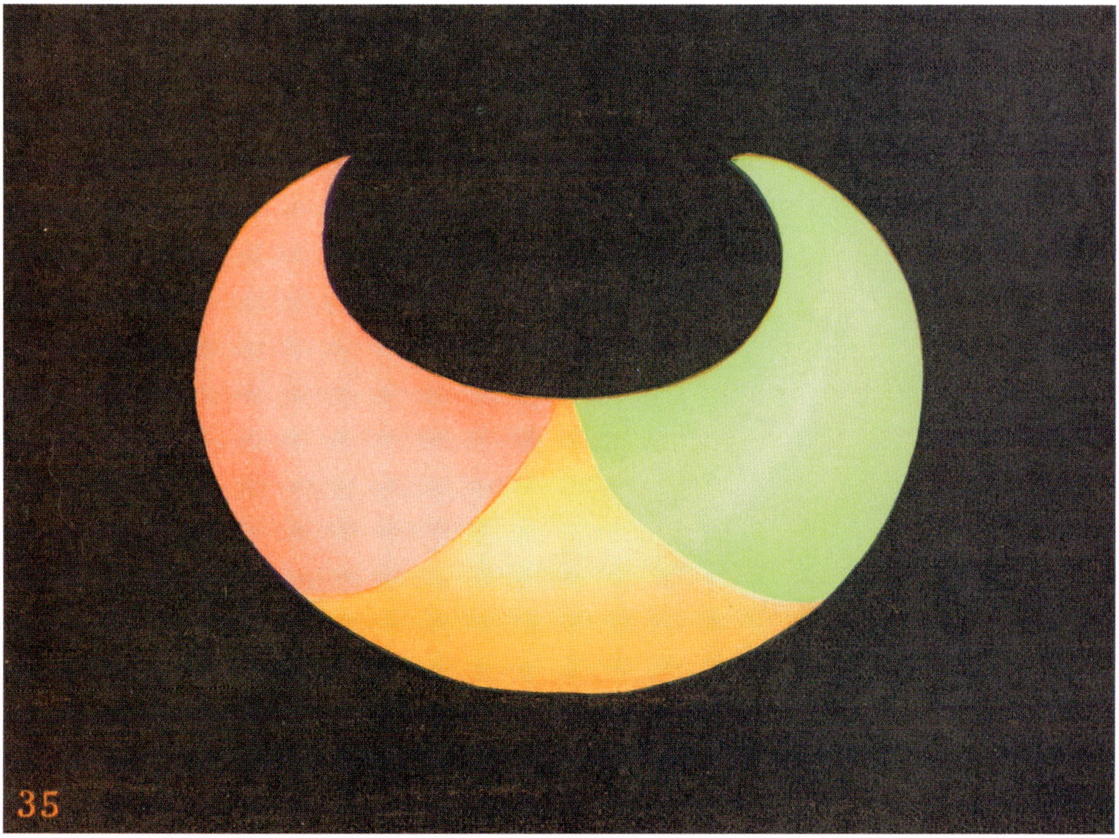

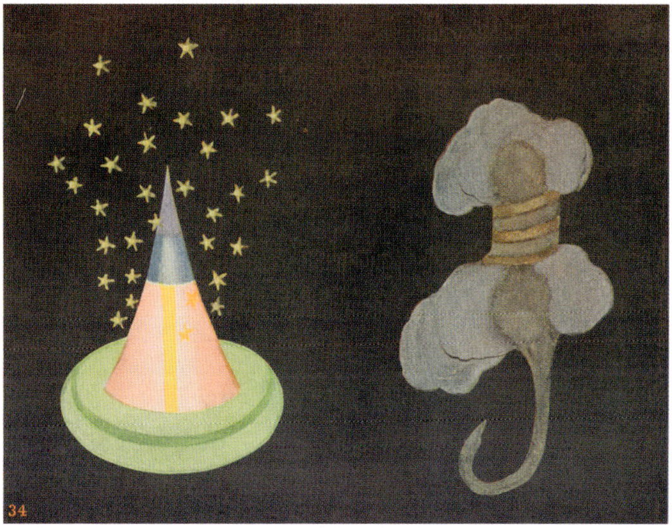

ABOVE
A representation of the experience of meeting a friend from whom one has long been separated. The shape resembles outstretched arms.

RIGHT
Contrasting experiences of two mourners at a funeral. The thoughts of the person on the right are despairing. The colorful, upward-pointing shape on the left reflects one who believes the deceased has ascended to a higher plane.

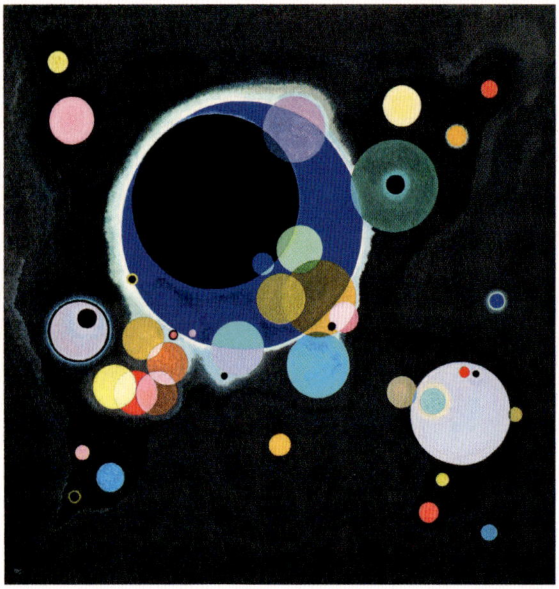

ABOVE
Wassily Kandinsky, *Several Circles* (1926). By the 1920s, Kandinsky's early, bold landscapes had shifted to an intense geometric abstraction as his interest in the mysterious relationship between color and form grew. He believed the circle was complex and powerful, arguing that "of the three primary forms, it points most clearly to the fourth dimension."

OPPOSITE
Mary Sargent Florence's mathematical "Color Square' from her 1940 book *Colour Co-ordination* was a particular influence on Maxwell Armfield and his increasingly mystical quest to link music and color.

from pieces by Mendelssohn, Gounod, and Wagner, each played on the same church organ. In Leadbeater and Besant's resulting visualizations colorful clouds bubbled above an illustration of the church in which the pieces of music were performed. The undulating skybound colors varied according to the temperament of each piece and the concept had obvious links to the synaesthetic experience.

Rudolf Steiner (1861–1925) was a more tentative Theosophist who eventually diverged from the movement but held many views congruent with it. Steiner was a scholar of Goethe (see p.92), but gradually moved from studying the physical behavior of pigments and light into his own examination of spiritual "auric" colors. He delivered three lectures on color in 1921 and these were collected and published. Steiner argued that cosmic forces imbued everyday objects with "etheric" color, distinct from their normal appearance, and believed the primary colors of red, yellow, and blue had a unique and symbolic "lustre" relating to the living, the spirit and the soul, respectively. Color was a gateway: it "descends into the surfaces of physical objects but it also raises us from the purely material and leads us to the spiritual". In Steiner's fervent argument, painters could properly animate their work if they tried to "paint out of the color" and "spiritualize" their palette. Despite the urgency of his phraseology, quite what these actions involved on a practical level remained inscrutable.

Nevertheless, Theosophy influenced the color ranges and modes of expression of artists for decades to come, including Piet Mondrian, Hilma af Klint, Max Beckmann, and Maxwell Armfield. Af Klint joined the Theosophical Society in 1904 and her work was animated by a belief that abstract art had a moral imperative. If it could open minds to new ways of conceptualizing the world, it could pave the way for a kind of utopia. Kandinsky felt a similar moral obligation on the artist to aspire to abstraction and the writings of Leadbeater and Besant were profoundly influential on his own manifesto, *Concerning the Spiritual in Art* (1912, see p.236).

Maxwell Armfield (1881–1972) was a painter and illustrator associated with the Arts and Crafts movement who spent the last decades of his life in search of a hidden "syntax" that could be revealed by color. After the death of his wife, Constance Smedley, in 1941, Armfield plunged into a quest to try to uncover the universal significance behind signs and symbols and to divine a deeper meaning to existence. He later described "an amazing inflow of inspiration ... I now covered a vast field of occult reading in this short interregnum, especially the invaluable books of Madame Blovatsky [*sic*] and [A.P.] Sinnett. My especial study was the Qabalah and its Tree of Life symbol. This filled me with confidence and awe." He was also inspired by the work of one Mary Sargant Florence (1857–1954), whose recently published *Colour Co-ordination* (1940) was an elaborate attempt to link color and music (see p.208). Armfield adapted Sargant Florence's work but could not devise a satisfactory series of correlations, so turned instead to schemes based on the number twelve. Drawing inspiration from "the enigmatic form of the dodecahedron with its twelve faces", he related these to semi-hues, the signs of the zodiac, and the tarot deck.

Although Armfield wrote several books on color, he published these under pseudonyms, usually as Hugh Darval,

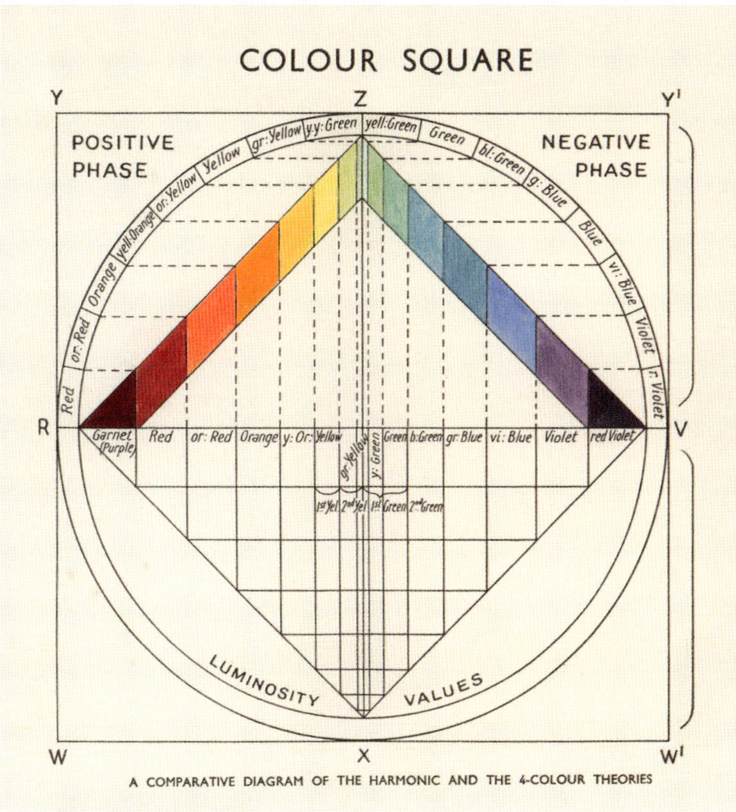

with additional commentary provided by a certain John Moxford. In *Colour: Its Meaning and Use* (1944), Armfield/Darval included a reasonable amount of practical advice, but it was Moxford's interpretations of the color scales that transported the works to another dimension, embroidering Darval's analysis with elaborate symbols and claims of occult significance. Each semi-hue was related to a planetary sigil, a zodiacal sign, and a corresponding musical semi-tone (pillar-box red, for example, apparently responded to C-sharp). In a Nabokovian twist, Moxford himself later turned out to be just another pseudonym for Armfield again, one persona commenting on the work of another, placing a double distance between the author and his esoteric obsessions in public. Yet Armfield was fully committed to his beliefs, and treated color with the utmost seriousness. In his worldview, color was the final piece of a puzzle, the endgame in a dark age that heralded an imminent rebirth. "Being the final factor in art," he claimed, "color is necessarily, from the symbolic angle, at that point where Involution ceases and Evolution begins."

Color studies have often led researchers down paths of pure esoterica. But for every credulous color theorist, there has been a sceptic. Michel Eugène Chevreul, the great nineteenth-century French chemist and researcher of color contrast (see p.135) became fascinated by the paranormal in later life, and even attended seances, but ultimately tried to debunk some of the occultists' more outlandish practices. One delightful book of visual phenomena, J.H. Brown's *Spectropia* (1864), superficially appeared to glorify the ghoulish, with its oddly colored illustrations of prancing skeletons, witches, and disembodied hands. In fact, Brown's aim was to explain the rational and physical basis of optical illusions, including "floaters" and afterimages. Indignantly, he wrote, he intended to expose "the absurd follies of spiritualism … showing some of the many ways in which our senses may be deceived."

Although many have been obsessed with relating color to occult systems and mythologies, all the color schemes that resulted from their efforts were inconsistent and arbitrary, attractive but unscientific. Human nature's drive to find patterns or correlations has driven not just the search for color harmony, but the many attempts to push beyond such schemes, to try to make them mean something profound or supernatural. In a famous essay on the human tendency to find symbolic meanings in the everyday, the Argentinian writer Jorge Luis Borges expressed scepticism of the whole endeavor: "It is doubtful that the world has a meaning … even more doubtful that it has a double or triple meaning." Madame Blavatsky and others would never have agreed but perhaps, given the relativism and subjectivity of color, it is too nebulous to be numinous, better as a source of private pleasures than cosmic answers.

In *The Twelve Primary Colours in the Key System* (1945), Maxwell Armfield (writing as Hugh Darval) mapped out correspondences between colors, musical notes, and zodiacal signs.

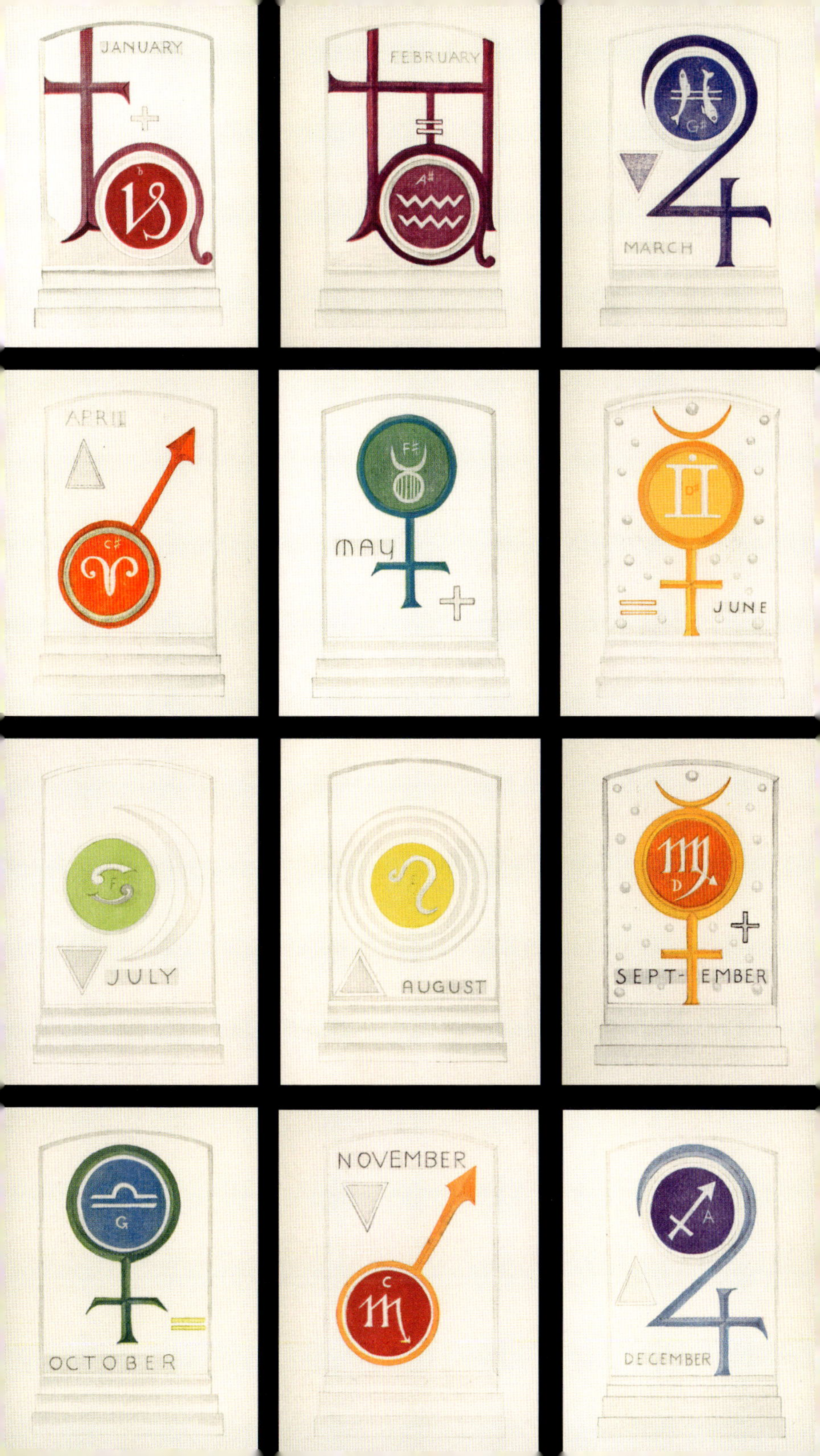
JANUARY
FEBRUARY
MARCH
APRIL
MAY
JUNE
JULY
AUGUST
SEPT-EMBER
OCTOBER
NOVEMBER
DECEMBER

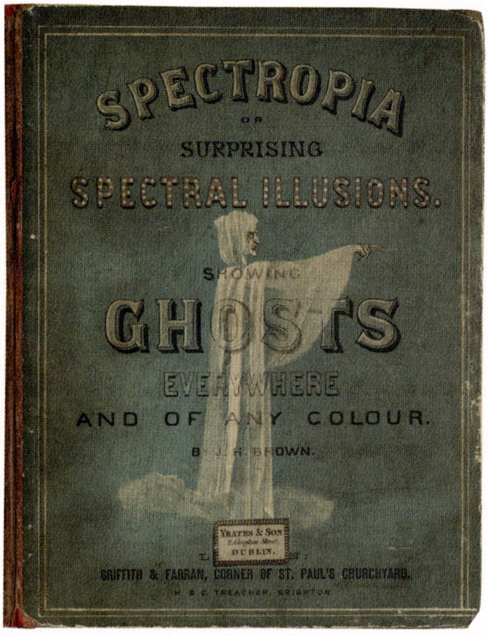
SPECTROPIA
OR
SURPRISING
SPECTRAL ILLUSIONS.
SHOWING
GHOSTS
EVERYWHERE
AND OF ANY COLOUR.
BY J. H. BROWN.
YEATES & SON
DUBLIN.
GRIFFITH & FARRAN, CORNER OF ST. PAUL'S CHURCHYARD.

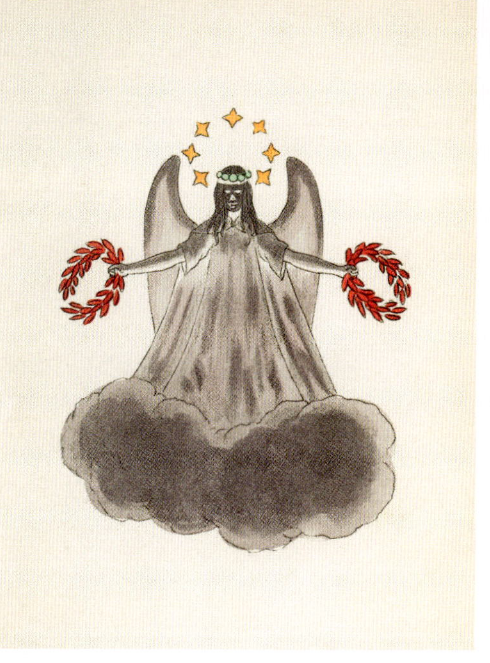

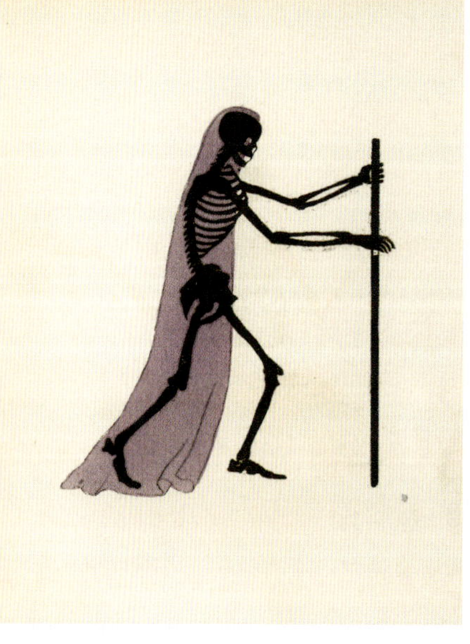

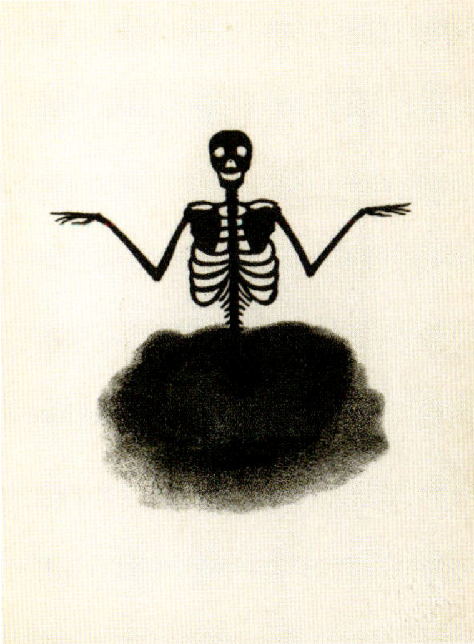

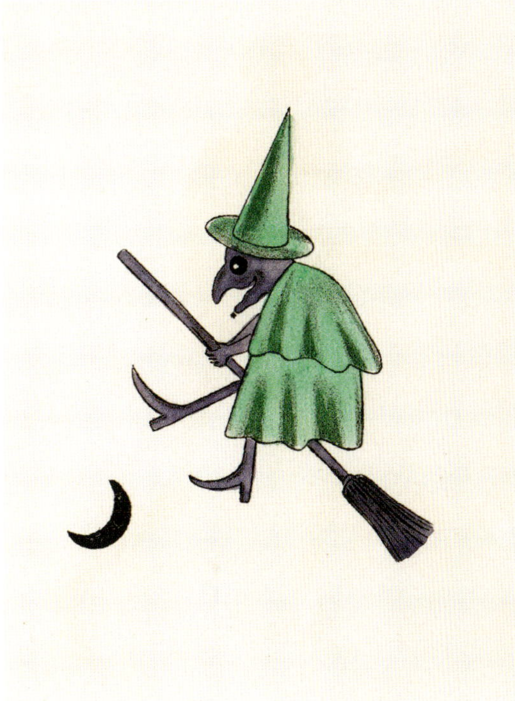

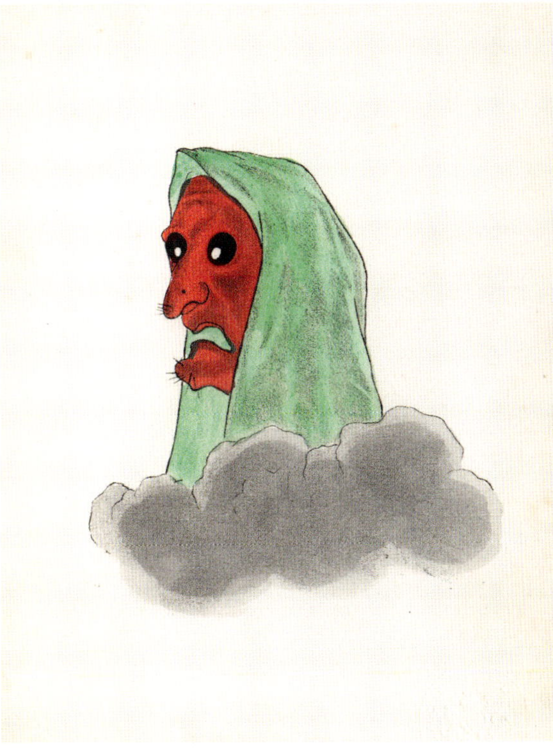

In *Spectropia* (1864) J.H. Brown compiled a range of ghostly images intended to demonstrate how easily "spectres" could be conjured through the simple optical illusion of afterimages. Staring at any of the oddly colored characters would result in the reader experiencing floating versions in opposing (and more "correct") colors as their eyes grew tired. Brown's aim was to debunk the tricks deployed by fraudulent spiritualists.

2

THE COLOR OF

COMMERCE

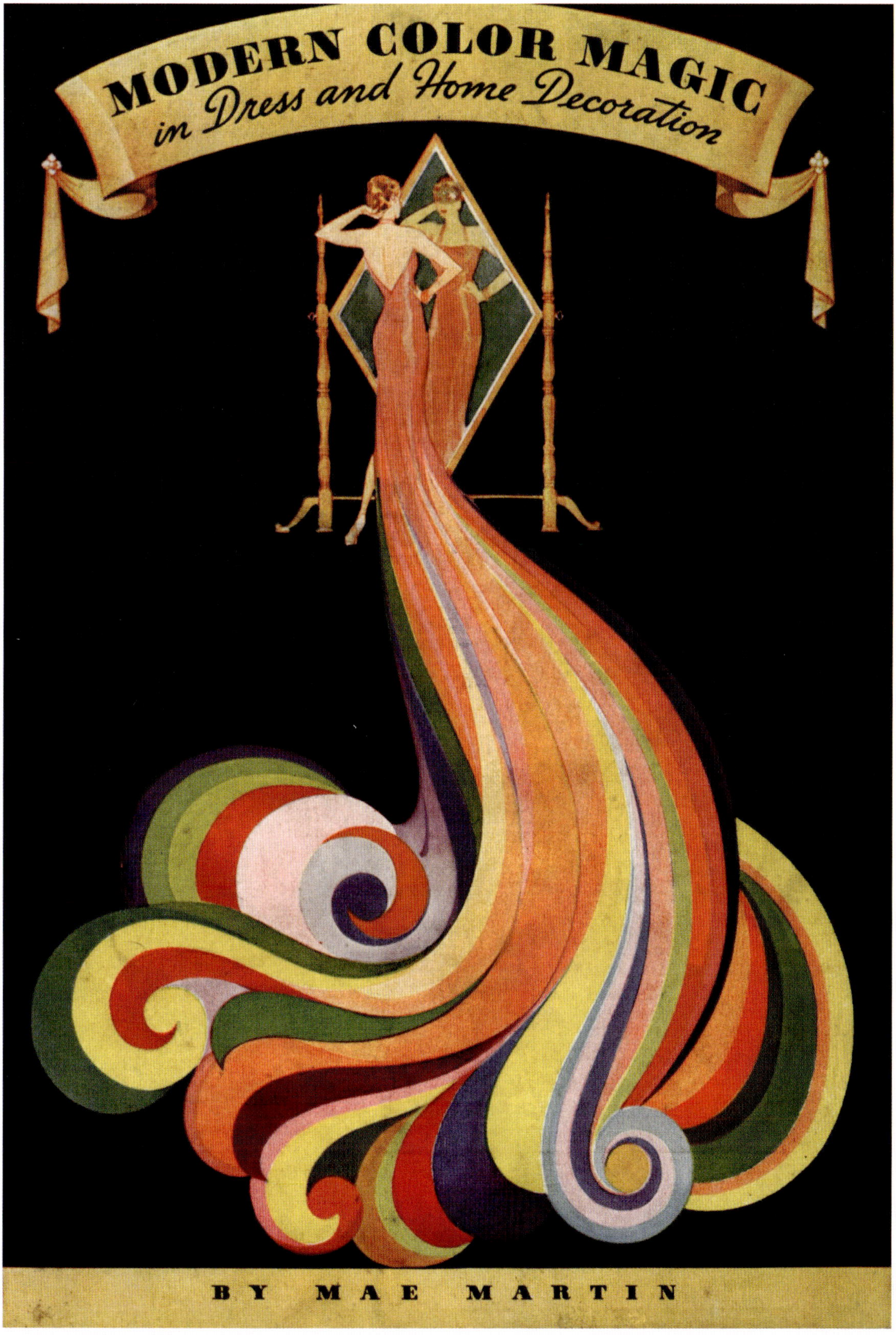
MODERN COLOR MAGIC
in Dress and Home Decoration
BY MAE MARTIN

The long history of purple is a good reminder of the high price of color. The process of extracting the mucus of sea snails in ancient Greece and Rome to make a luxurious dye, Tyrian purple, was so expensive that the color itself became synonymous with wealth. The similarly hued artificial dye chanced upon in 1856 by teenage chemist William Perkin (see p.134), which sent the world mad for mauve, was almost the opposite. The dye itself was easy to produce, and became so ubiquitous in fashion that it was likened to an outbreak of measles, but the innovation was Perkin's intellectual property and quickly made him a millionaire. The value of color as a commercial asset, as a seductive coating of products or something infused in the fibers of fashion, only accelerated thereafter, once thousands of new chemical colors came to market. Taking stock halfway through the twentieth century, in 1956, color consultant Faber Birren wrote of the then-recent "tremendous expansion of color in consumer goods. American homes, inside and out, have been thoroughly refurbished with color. Plastics and synthetic materials of many types have brought color into countless products that were once either colorless or nearly so."

Birren was on the frontline of a brand-new profession comprising a cabal of specialists that advised businesses on the effective use of color to develop appealing products and drive sales. This strategy was made possible by advances in both technology and psychology: more color lines reached the market just as consumers' taste for them became framed in terms of conscious aspirations and subconscious desires. Color in the marketplace had multiple applications. It could be a selling point or a marker of taste, lending sparkle to quotidian objects. It could also be a cynical means to limit the lifespan of purchases. As last year's palette fell out of fashion, the pressure built to buy a replacement wristwatch or radio in this year's hue, even if neither was faulty. The planned obsolescence of consumer goods was unfolding in full color.

Saturation of modern life redoubled with each passing decade as color progressively inhabited the home, coated the printed page, and filled the screen in glorious Technicolor. Printed commercial color standards proliferated and companies produced lustrous pattern books and pamphlets in proprietary rainbow ranges. In booklike formats, these often contained physical samples of wares including silk ribbon, wool, carpet pile, hosiery, strips painted with household paint, and even cakes of soap. Textile samples were presented in multiple finishes to demonstrate how they appeared under different lighting conditions, just as charts of household paints included varieties in matt and gloss. Some samples highlighted the range of chromatic possibilities afforded by improved dyes, selling color as a product in its own right. One especially innovative example used dipdyed bird feathers at a time when the coloring of white feathers for fashion accessories was in vogue. The Bayer Company's *Ausfarbungen auf Federn* (*c.*1920) presented 143 examples of its palette in booklet form, complete with recipes for the colors.

Paint companies pushed color as an empowering fix: anyone could buy some tins and daringly transform their environment overnight, inspired by pamphlets entitled *The Joy of Colour* or *Now You Can Spread Color: Quickly, Easily, and at Low Cost*. Manufacturers did not just rely on technology to create new saleable color lines but actively marketed them in a way that gave a context and backstory to the colors themselves. An early example was a range of themed "Historical Colours" produced by Thomas Parsons & Sons and published under the same title in 1937. Its packaged ranges of complementary colors were designed to evoke eras, locales, and manufacturers, including Pompeian, Moorish, and Gobelins tapestry colors, and the enduring (artificial) Tyrian purple.

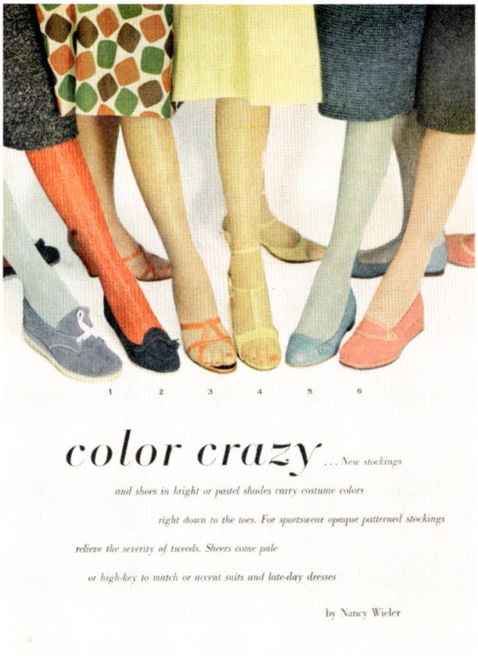

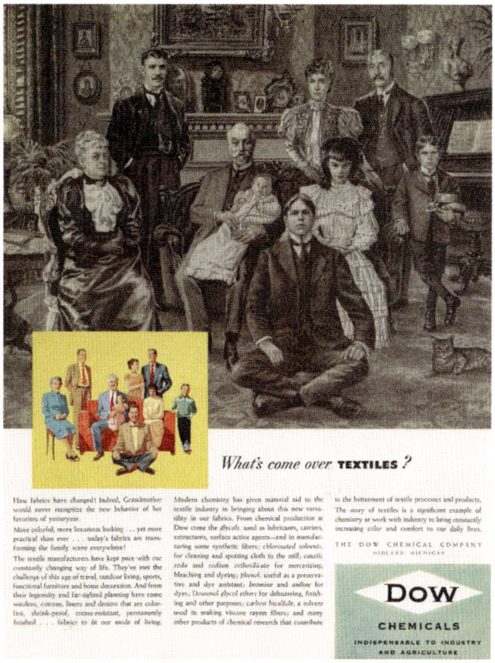

Through canny marketing and a reinvention of color, consumers could tap into the allure of heritage tastes but reclaim them for the modern era.

Proprietary standards were usually tied to particular businesses, but some were industry wide. In the United States, the Textile Color Card Association (TCCA; later the Color Association of the United States) formed in 1915 in response to wartime disruption to the fashion industry that destroyed normal lines of communication with Paris. The TCCA filled the gap, effectively nationalizing trends by producing seasonal sample cards for the home market. Its first "Standard Color Card of America" appeared in 1915 as a concertina-format booklet containing 106 colors in samples of uniquely named skeindyed ribbons, woven to appear half satin and half grosgrain. Over the years, the cards compiled both traditional

PREVIOUS PAGE
Modern Color Magic (1936) by color consultant Mae Martin was a trade catalog produced by Diamond Tints and Dyes that encouraged the reader to experiment with color around the home by dyeing clothes, table linens, and curtains. Martin presented color as a quick change to enliven one's surroundings at low cost.

ABOVE LEFT
An American advertisement for colored stockings and shoes (1955) demonstrated the potential to match and contrast colors in different product lines.

ABOVE RIGHT
Color print advertisement from *The Saturday Evening Post* for Dow Chemical Company. The images not only promoted the revolution in colorful clothing made possible by advances in chemistry but provided an example of the increasing use of color in advertisements themselves.

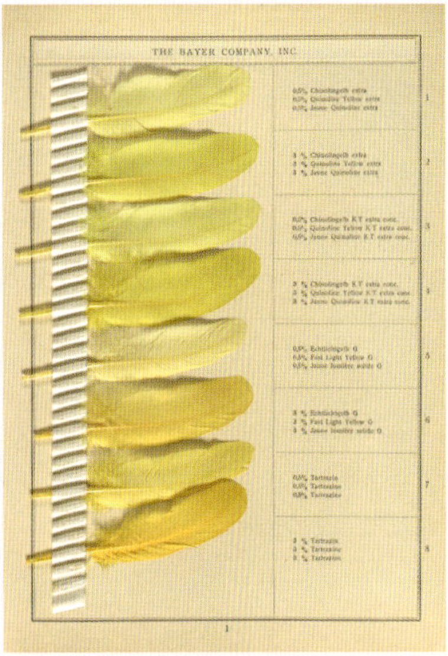
THE BAYER COMPANY, INC.
1

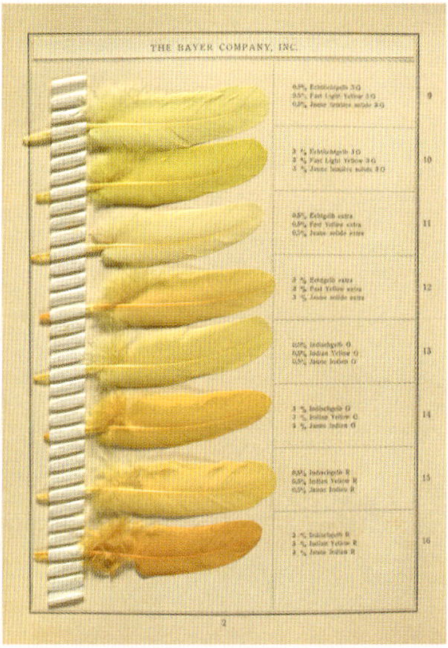
THE BAYER COMPANY, INC.
2

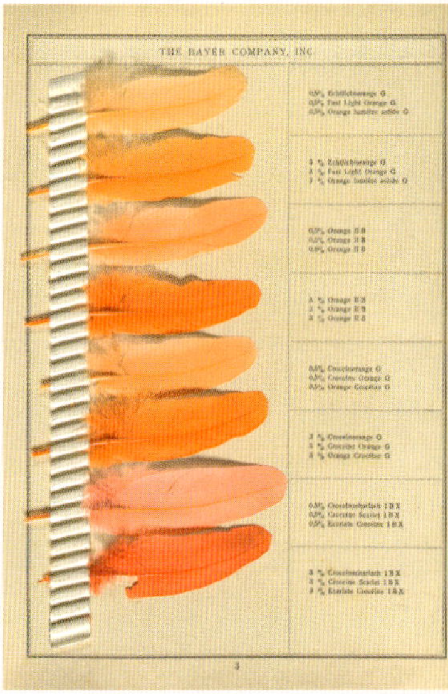
THE BAYER COMPANY, INC.
3

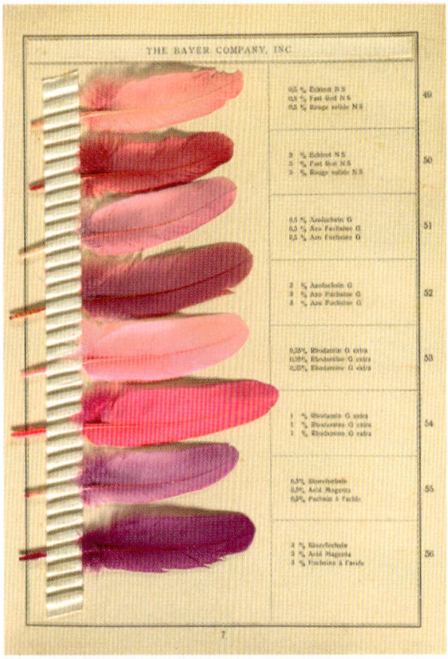
THE BAYER COMPANY, INC.
7

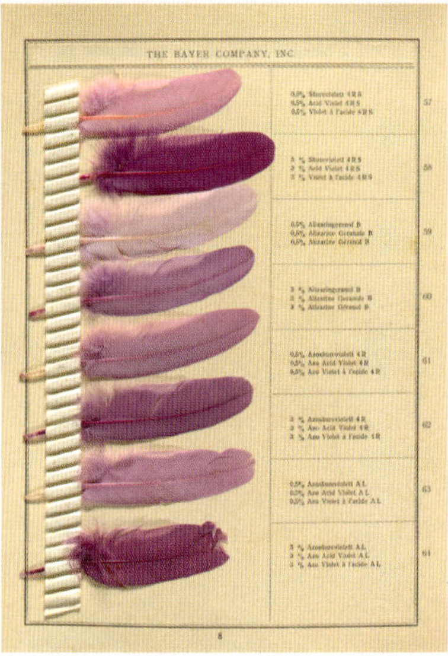
THE BAYER COMPANY, INC.
8

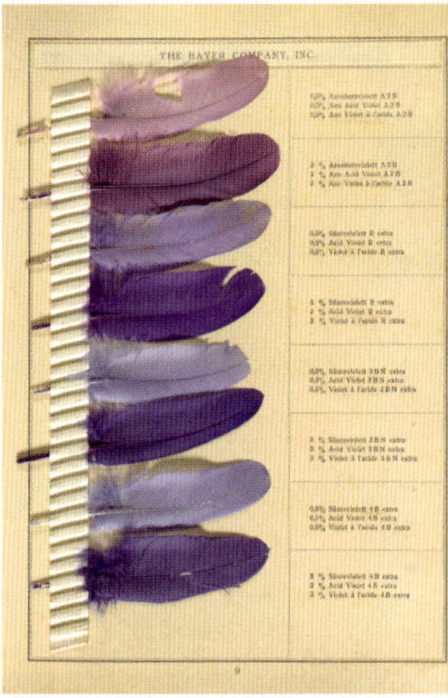
THE BAYER COMPANY, INC.
9

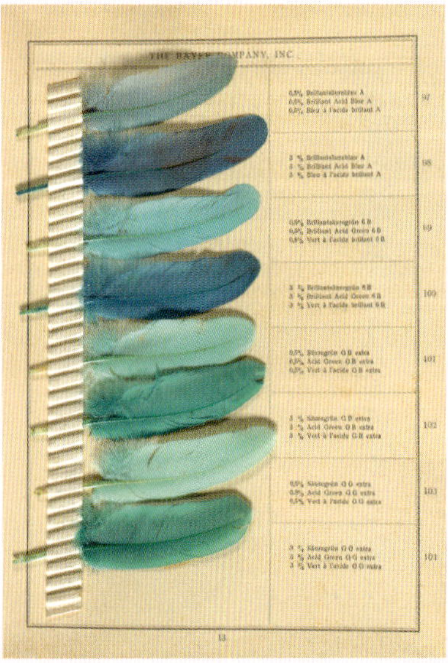
13

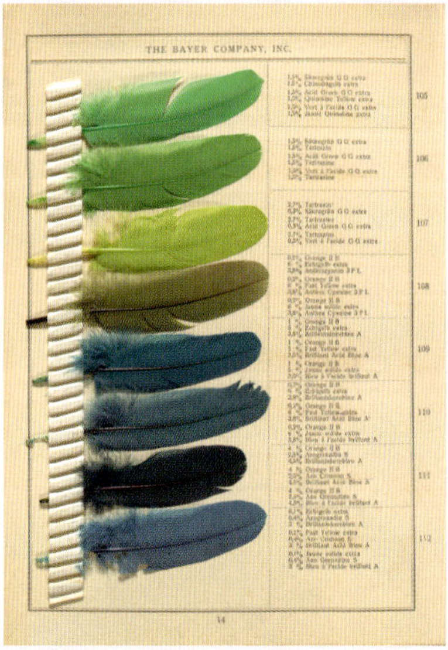
THE BAYER COMPANY, INC.
14

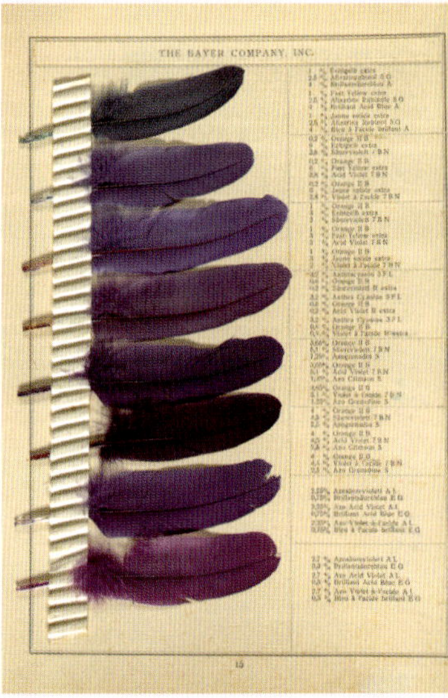
THE BAYER COMPANY, INC.
15

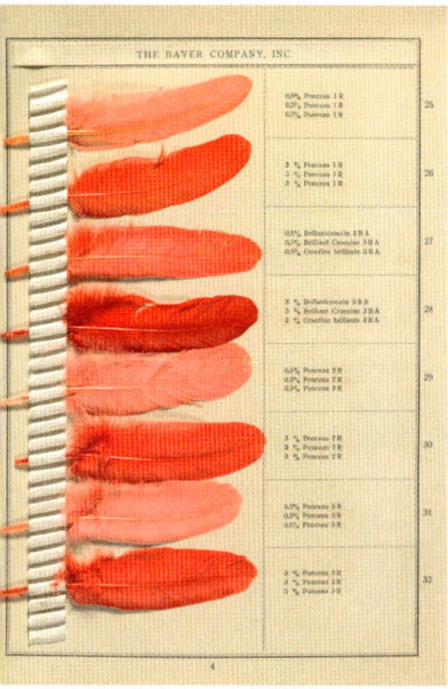
THE BAYER COMPANY, INC.

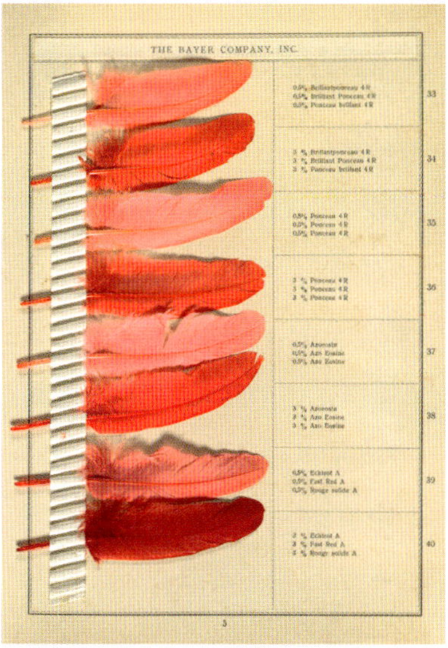
THE BAYER COMPANY, INC.

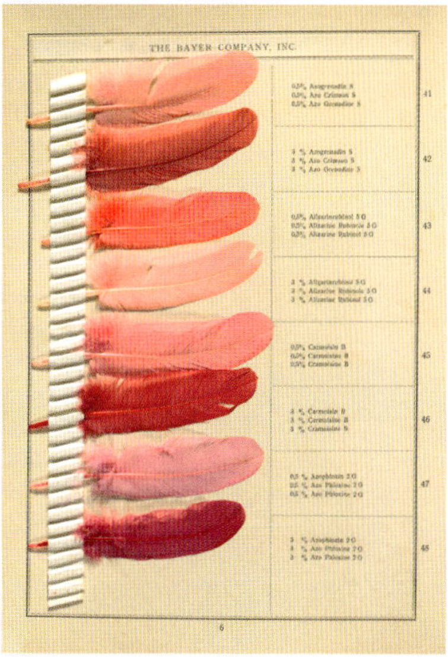
THE BAYER COMPANY, INC.

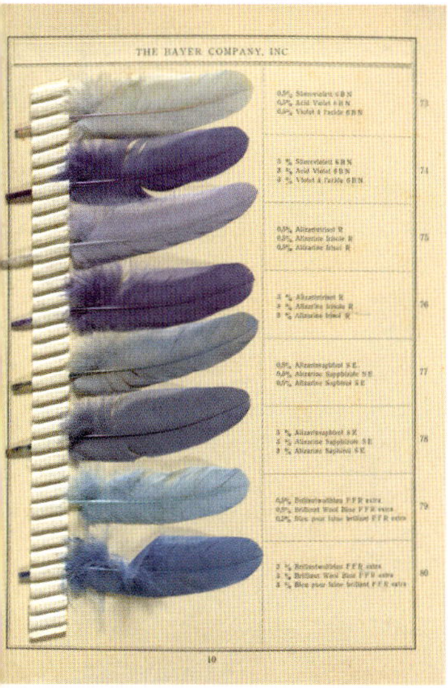
THE BAYER COMPANY, INC.

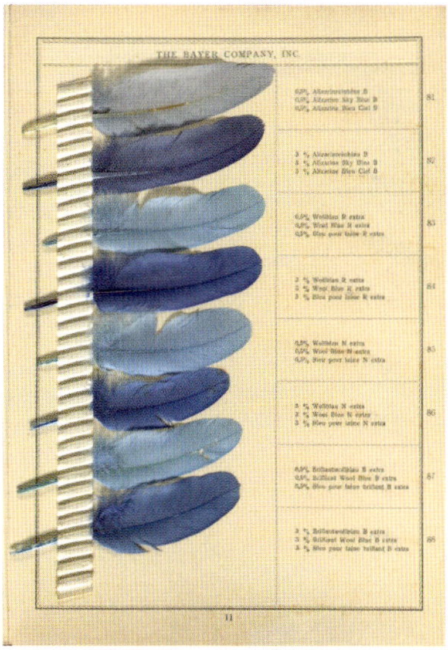
THE BAYER COMPANY, INC.

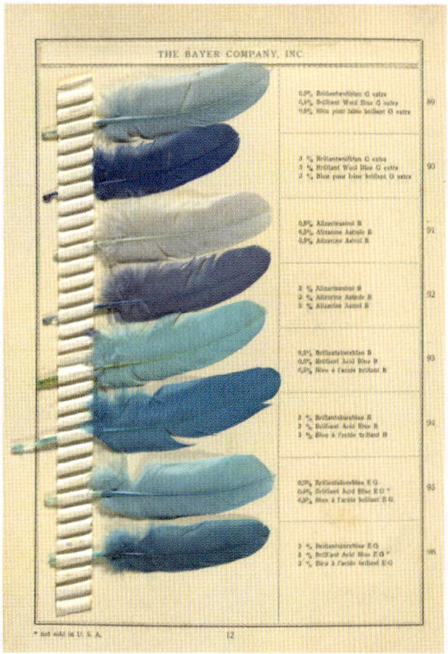
THE BAYER COMPANY, INC.

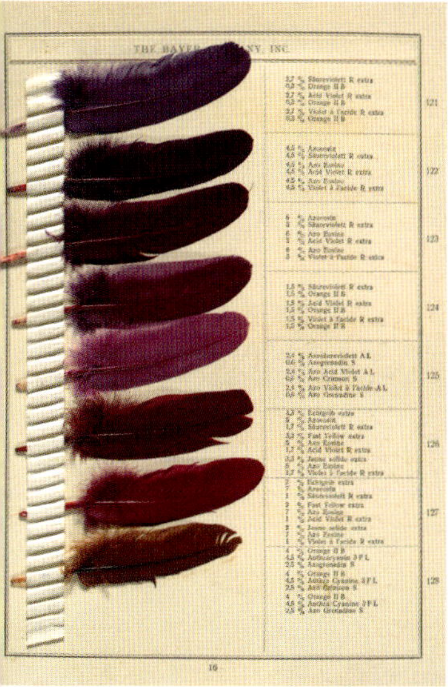

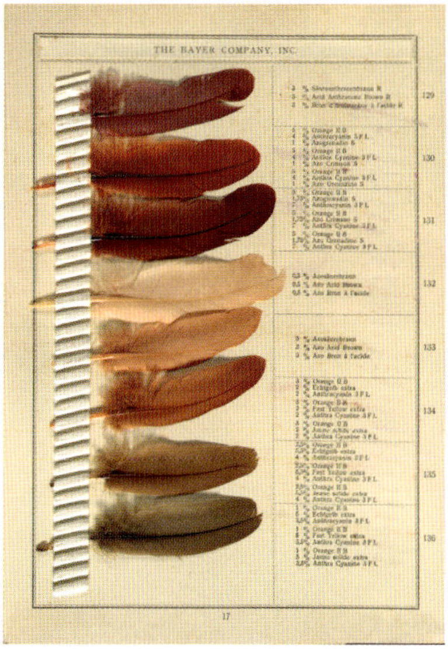
THE BAYER COMPANY, INC.

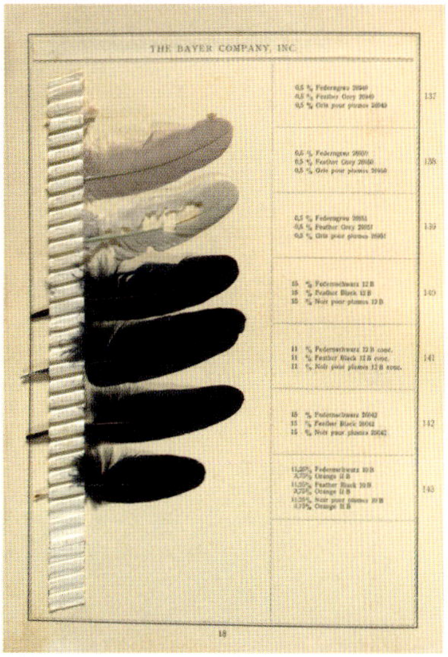
THE BAYER COMPANY, INC.

and innovative color ranges, along with selections on a theme ('Fairy Tales", "Carnival Colors", or "Colours of Gauguin") and ranges for spring and fall. Under the guidance of chief forecaster Margaret Hayden Rorke, described as "America's uncrowned queen of color", these began to influence trends as much as describe them. The Seasonal Card was effectively a collaboration between manufacturers and retailers to coordinate product lines, helping match garments to accessories while maximizing sales of both.

Equivalent bodies sprang up in other corners of the world. In 1927, artist and design professor Sanzō Wada (1883–1967) set up the Japan Standard Color Association (later the Japan Color Research Institute) to establish color standards in industry. It produced numerous publications over the ensuing decades, including an innovative guide to the pigmentation of human skin (see p.182). Sanzō Wada's eleven-volume *Color Schemes* (1934) provided a rigorous analysis of multiple color combinations. The UK equivalent was the British Colour Council (BCC), founded in 1931 under director Robert Wilson, which produced similar directories and dictionaries of color, including a standard for the fashion industry in 1934 that took its cues from the TCCA across the Atlantic. Containing 220 colors, separate editions reproduced the range in both silk and woolen samples. The BCC also aimed to regulate color use in official contexts throughout the British Empire, a remit reflected in its nomenclature and the presence of Post Office Red, Pigeon, RAF Blue-Grey, and Union Jack Blue. Back in the USA, *House & Garden* magazine attempted, from the 1930s onward, to coordinate whole product ranges by carrying out surveys of color preferences and promoting particular hues through a network of department stores, attempting to steal a march on public taste, pushing product lines in colors the masses did not yet know they would love. This insidious march of capitalism was blandly described by Faber Birren as "coordinated merchandizing."

In the arms race of color ranges for the next season's shades, the color consultant became indispensable. Some individuals were tied to specific companies such as Harold Ledyard Towle (1890–1973), who spent the 1920s at the Duco Color Advisory Service within Du Pont Motors. The company had recently perfected a hardwearing paint that could be manufactured in numerous colors, so Towle's job was to devise striking and saleable color combinations for high-end automobiles, a world away from the monotonous black of the Ford Model T. Towle had been a camoufleur in the First World War, using color effects and illusions to hide buildings and objects from enemy detection, and referred to his subsequent career as "reverse camouflage".

Others set themselves up as advisors to industry at large. Matthew Luckiesh (1883–1967) was a physicist who specialized in lighting and color effects, publishing several books on their commercial application. His *Light and Color in Advertising and Marketing* (1923) explored the effective use of color to enhance brand awareness. At that time, it was starting to appear in small quantities on the pages of magazines as an expensive but dramatic

PREVIOUS PAGES
This sample book from the Bayer Company entitled *Ausfarbungen auf Federn* (*Shades on Feathers*) from c.1920 included 143 examples of dyed feathers to represent the range of artificial colors available. The coloring of white feathers to make fashion accessories was a popular activity at the time of the guide's publication.

OPPOSITE
In the early twentieth century, the National Aniline and Chemical Company produced a sample publication containing eighteen dyed soaps, together with recipes and instructions.

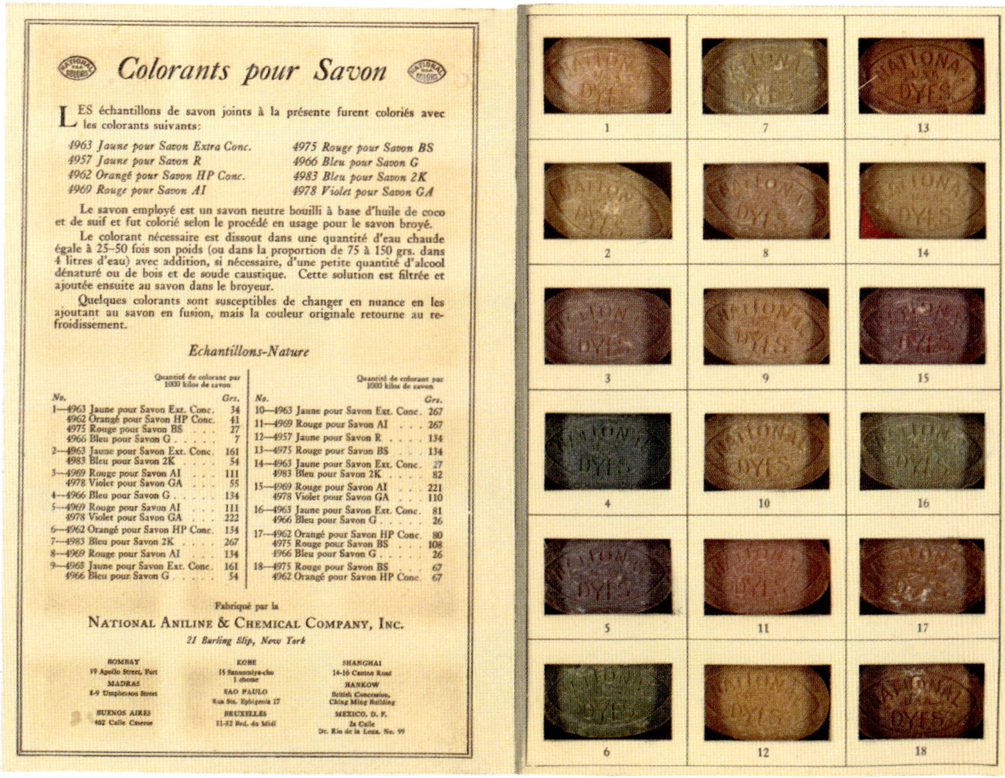

enhancement, deployed in "an appealing and forceful manner to reinforce the selling power." Luckiesh documented the many qualities color brought to the page, listing vividness, realism, and potential symbolism as powerful enhancements to any campaign. He trumpeted the success of a seed catalog from a supplier whose sales increased nine-fold when pages were printed in color. He quickly established red as the reliable go-to color for attention-grabbing layouts but cautioned against its over-use ('For some purposes, it is of ill repute"). Several studies underpinned his pronouncements, such as an experiment that showed test subjects more readily recalled words printed in red than those in black.

Much more consumer research had been undertaken by 1956, when Faber Birren published *Selling Color to People*, and it all informed his US-centered guide to color in marketing and consumer goods. This study offered advice on color in product lines, the psychology of the consumer, and effective advertising. Birren even included a chapter on the potential of color television. He considered his work to be a fact-based approach to color as a quantifiable profit-driver, based on data from sales and surveys, and was unimpressed by designers and architects who dismissed this evidence because they felt they "knew" color better than ordinary people. For Birren, the public was mercurial and could only be understood through psychological insight and consumer research. And things had moved on. Birren engaged with a world transformed by color since Luckiesh's limited and costly splashes of red ink: "The nation is no longer merely color-conscious; it has become almost completely color-minded."

From his evidence base, Birren extrapolated some broad principles. He demonstrated how eccentric and extensive color lines in high fashion gradually became whittled down to a narrow band

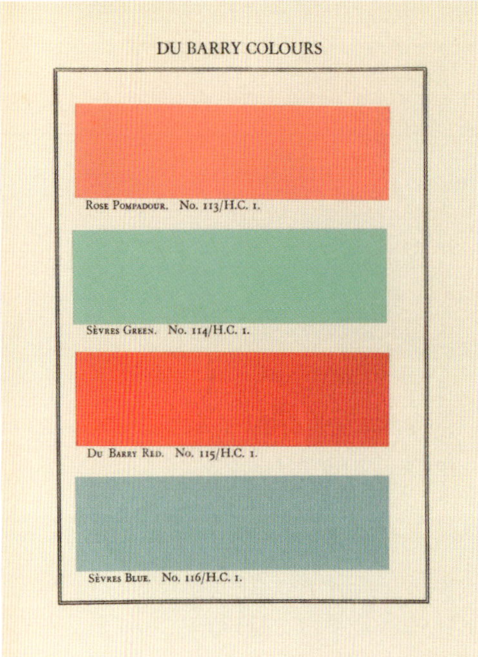

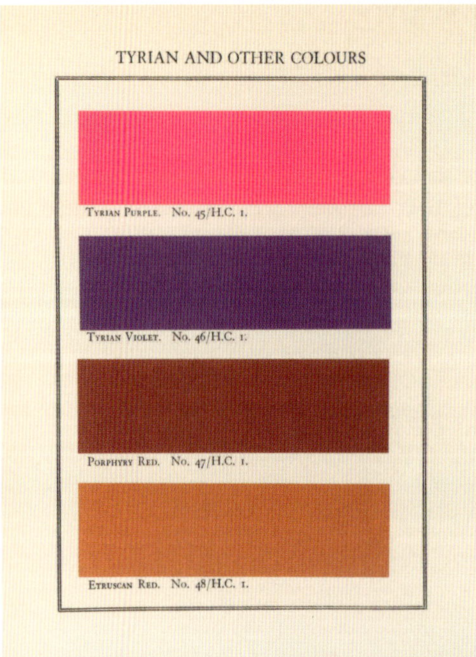

of sensible options as they reached the high street. The public, whom he refused to patronize, liked a small range of simple, bold colors: "[Their] taste in color is good for the mere reason that it is honest and unassuming." He believed people were turned off by "in-between" colors they could not easily name. He also described the predictable phases of color popularity and cited survey results that established a universal preference for the same six colors in a particular order (blue, red, green, violet, orange, yellow). Yet for such a color advocate, he was conscious of its limitations in the marketplace, sceptical of its widespread and sometimes inappropriate use, and argued that providing many options within a product line was a mistake. Using sales data, he demonstrated that, among products available in a wide range of colors, most sales came from a tiny number of predictably popular colors such as deep blue, while second-division options, such as purple, were left on the shelves untouched. It was better, he argued, to offer many patterns in a small number of colors than a few patterns in a wide range of colors. And was color even always necessary? If traditional and dependable utensils had always been made out of wood or metal, Birren cautioned, the public would recoil from colorful plastic versions. He cited his own professional error of creating a brightly colored slide projector, a cutting-edge product for its time, but one where the gaudy finish clashed with consumer expectations of a dependable, precision-engineered piece of equipment.

The book was charmingly illustrated with monochrome drawings, infographics, and photographs in classic midcentury style. The limitations of the spot-color printing method were ingeniously incorporated by placing geometrical blocks of translucent color atop the black and white photography, symbolically rendering color as an abstract, disruptive force, pushing its way into a previously staid world.

All these shortcuts to profit were not without their critics. By the early

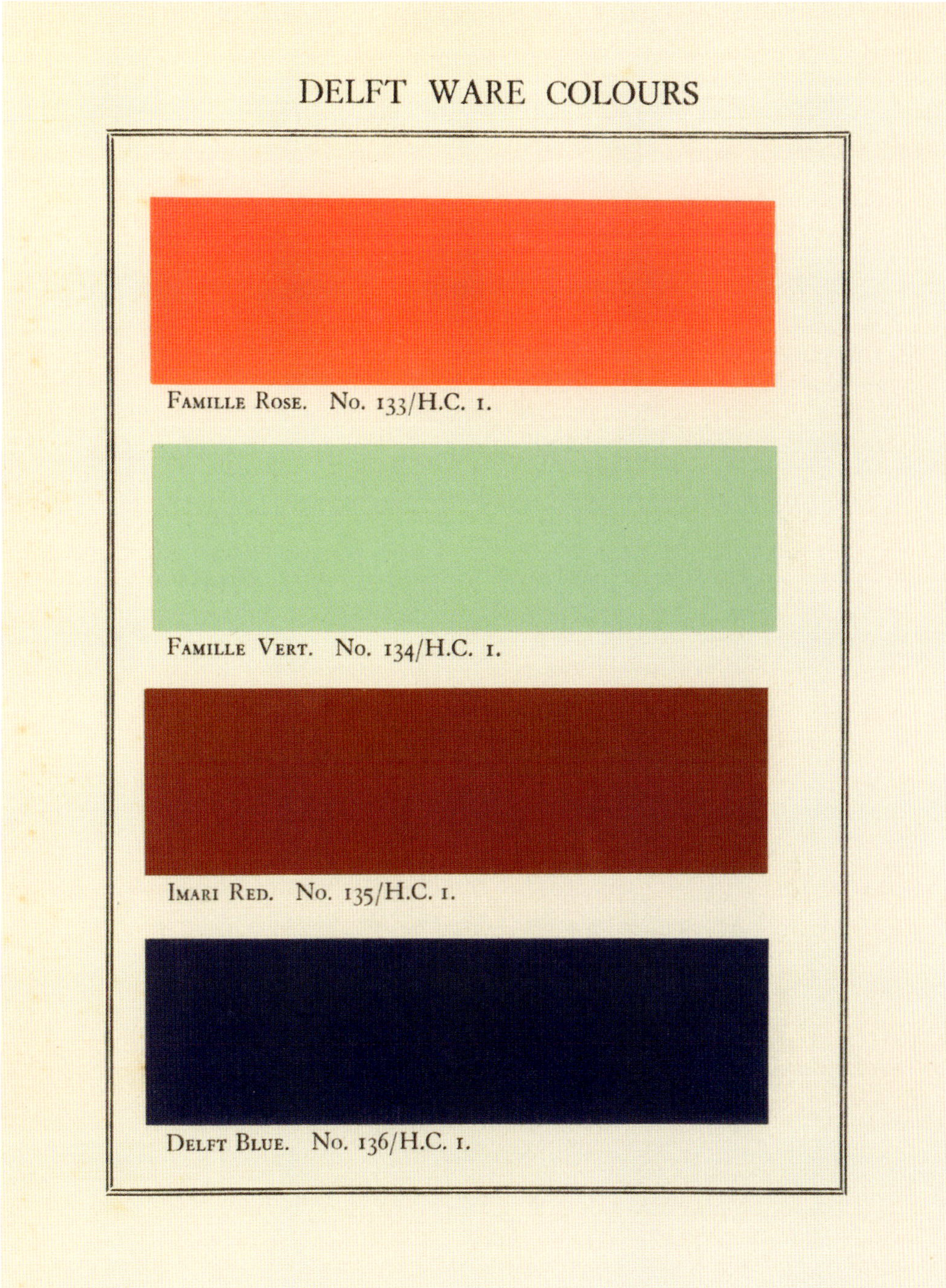

DELFT WARE COLOURS

Famille Rose. No. 133/H.C. 1.

Famille Vert. No. 134/H.C. 1.

Imari Red. No. 135/H.C. 1.

Delft Blue. No. 136/H.C. 1.

Color schemes from *Historical Colours* (est. 1937), a range of household paints inspired by historical eras and other cultures and manufactured by Thomas Parsons & Sons Ltd, London.

1960s, the distractions of pretty and bright domestic goods were being interrogated by writers such as Betty Friedan in *The Feminine Mystique* (1963) and the philosopher Herbert Marcuse in *One-Dimensional Man* (1964), both of whom analyzed the heavy toll that relentless consumerism took on the human psyche. Far from being a medium for self-expression, this line of criticism argued, the modern obsession with buying things was a displacement activity: bread and circuses for the Technicolor age. In fact, this line of attack was established earlier, when Birren was at his zenith as a color guru. In 1957, a year after *Selling Color to People* appeared, journalist Vance Packard wrote *The Hidden Persuaders*, an indignant examination of the subliminal tricks used by marketers to understand consumers' irrational behavior and then cynically monetize it. For Packard, this was not about smart sales techniques but manipulative trickery, pulling the strings of a consumer class whose views of a product could be shaped by the color of its packaging and whose hands could be directed to hover over particular shelves. He cited a study by the Color Research Institute that asked housewives (and it was always housewives) to assess the best-performing washing powder from three differently packaged boxes: one designed in blue, one in yellow, and the third in a combination of the two. Most felt the cleaning power of the product in the blue box was too weak while the powder in yellow packaging was too strong. Many agreed, however, that the variety in the blue and yellow box was just right. Inevitably, all three contained the same product. Packard called it "a startling encounter with [a] proneness to irrationality."

By the end of the 1960s, colors were bolder, more lurid, and fundamental to the confidence of the youthful counter-culture movement. Taking these trends into account, one other color consultant, Eric P. Danger, produced *Using Colour to Sell* (1968), a book indebted to Birren's research but reconceptualized for British industry and youthful sensibilities in a very different age. In the preceding decades, women had always been assumed to be the taste-makers and the natural market for colorful fashions and goods, but things were changing fast. Danger described a world where men were suddenly wearing pink shirts and buying their own toiletries: "The young male of today is often more colorful than his sister." For marketers, this cultural subversion of gender stereotypes was significant only as an opportunity for deeper profits. Color was everywhere, for everyone, especially the "young marrieds", who were now even

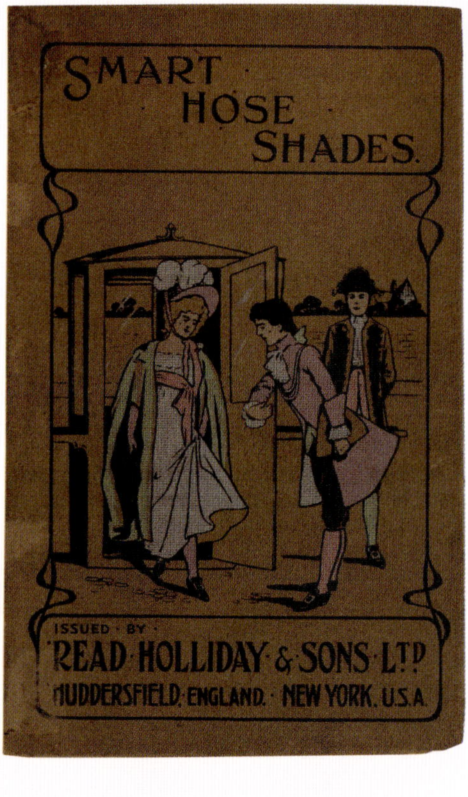

Smart Hose Shades (c.1900) from the transatlantic company Read Holliday contained samples of colors and formulae for dyes to be used in a range of hosiery. The range of colors for stockings is displayed using samples of hosiery glued behind leg-shaped isolating masks.

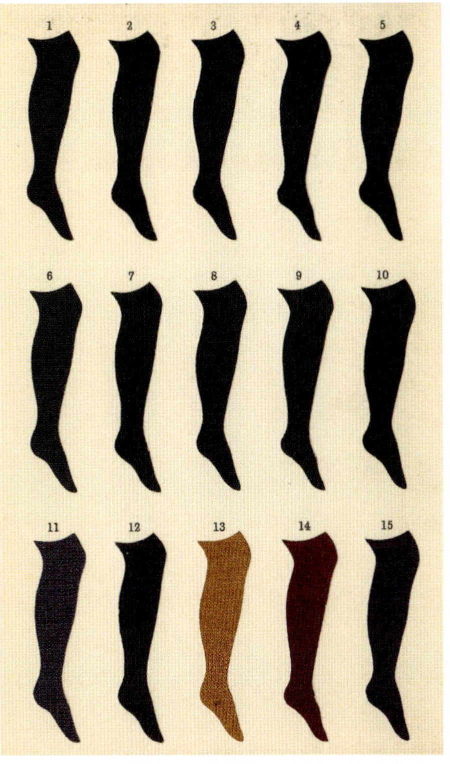
1 2 3 4 5
6 7 8 9 10
11 12 13 14 15

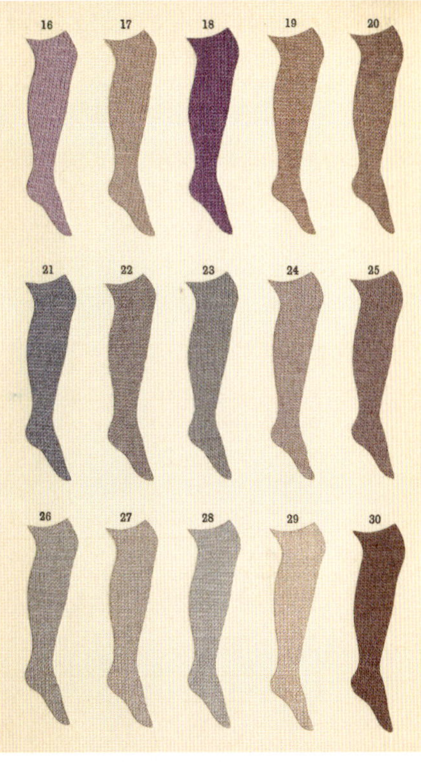
16 17 18 19 20
21 22 23 24 25
26 27 28 29 30

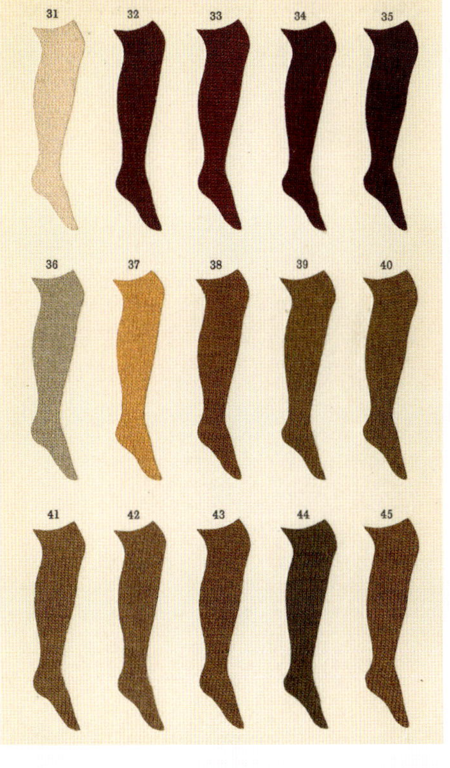
31 32 33 34 35
36 37 38 39 40
41 42 43 44 45

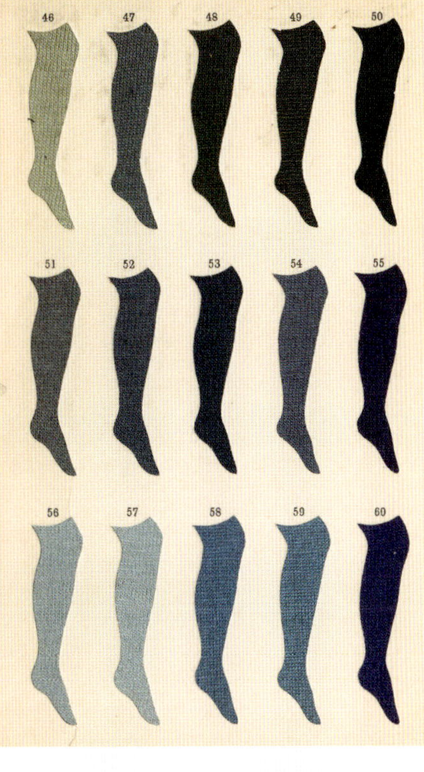
46 47 48 49 50
51 52 53 54 55
56 57 58 59 60

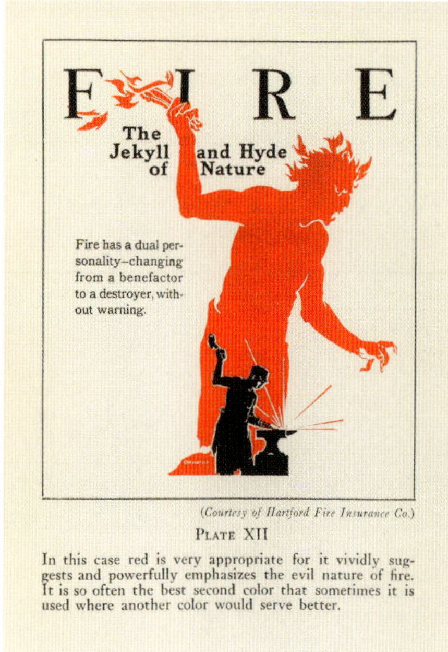

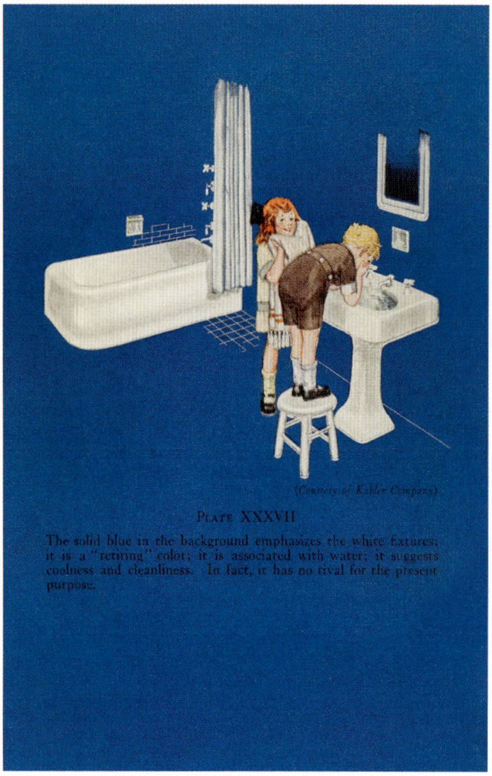

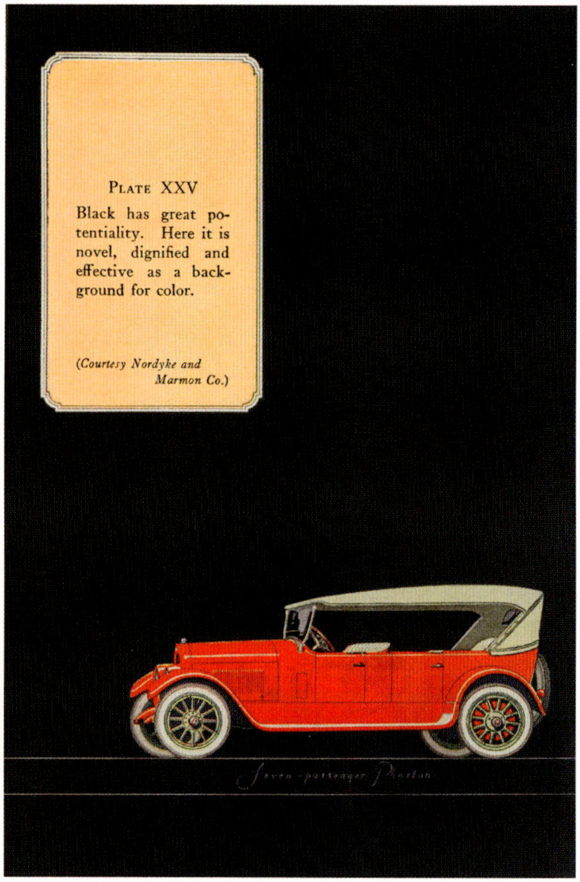

THIS PAGE
Examples of solid spot color in advertising as cited by Matthew Luckiesh in his *Light and Colour in Advertising and Merchandising* (1923). The expanse of flat, single colors reflects the limitations of the printing technology of the time, but Luckiesh demonstrated how to maximize its effects.

OPPOSITE ABOVE
Color consultant Faber Birren used quirky drawings and graphics to convey his advice and conclusions in *Selling Color to People* (1956). This illustration alluded to the multiple sensory effects of color on the consumer.

OPPOSITE BELOW
A photographic representation of cumulative sales records in Birren's *Selling Color to People*. These were visualizations of the waxing and waning popularity of different colors in product lines over time.

drawn to buying furniture in outlandish colors. Disposable products in ephemeral colors encouraged buyers to gamble. As Danger put it, "They know they can change the colour in a comparatively short time and buy something else," and the manufacturers knew it too. But there were limits. Danger recalled how attempts to sell colored bread to match a line of colored sugar had been a commercial disaster, the vibrant slices disturbing purchasers rather than enticing them. Refrigerators, meanwhile, remained stubbornly resistant to the opportunities of color. One manufacturer tried to strike out with a prominent display of a red model. The campaign drove huge sales, catching the eye of passing trade, all of whom went on to purchase it in the original white.

In the late twentieth century, industry standards such as RAL for painted and plastic surfaces, and Pantone® for print materials, had gained currency and brand recognition that extended far beyond their professional fields. Consumers increasingly understood the concepts of proprietary and seasonal colors and the color revolution endured because technology enabled commerce to evolve along with fashion and taste. If color drained from certain lines over the course of the twentieth century, with the car industry in particular reverting to bland neutrals, it surged in others, from kitchen utensils to baby buggies. Even in the world of ultra-chromatic consumerism, broad principles endured. The reliable popularity of basic color families and the public preference for simple, bold colors remained constant. The trick, as ever, was for manufacturers to have the right product available in the right color at the right time, to anticipate what would percolate down, or what might bubble up. Color forecasting and color marketing could make well-informed guesses and try to influence public taste, but it was always a gamble, with a lot more to bet on than red and black.

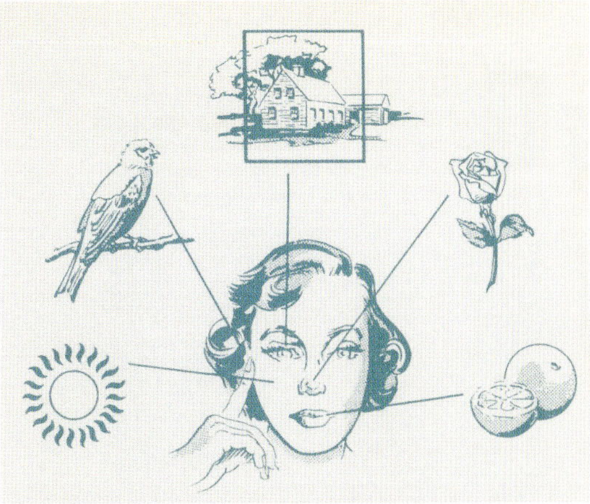

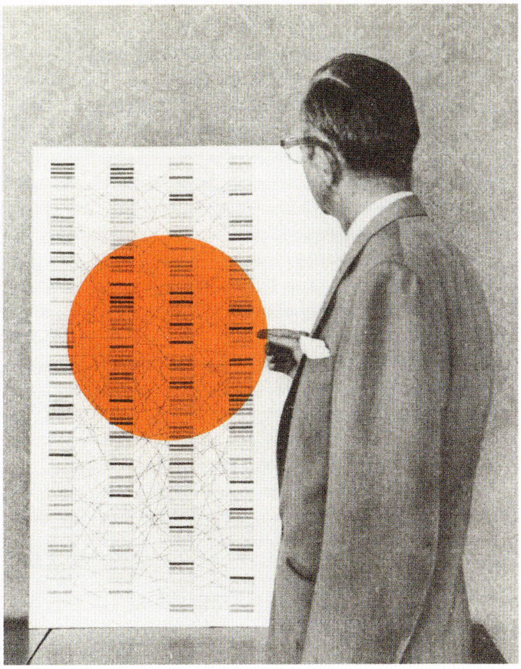

3

THE COLOR OF

LANGUAGE

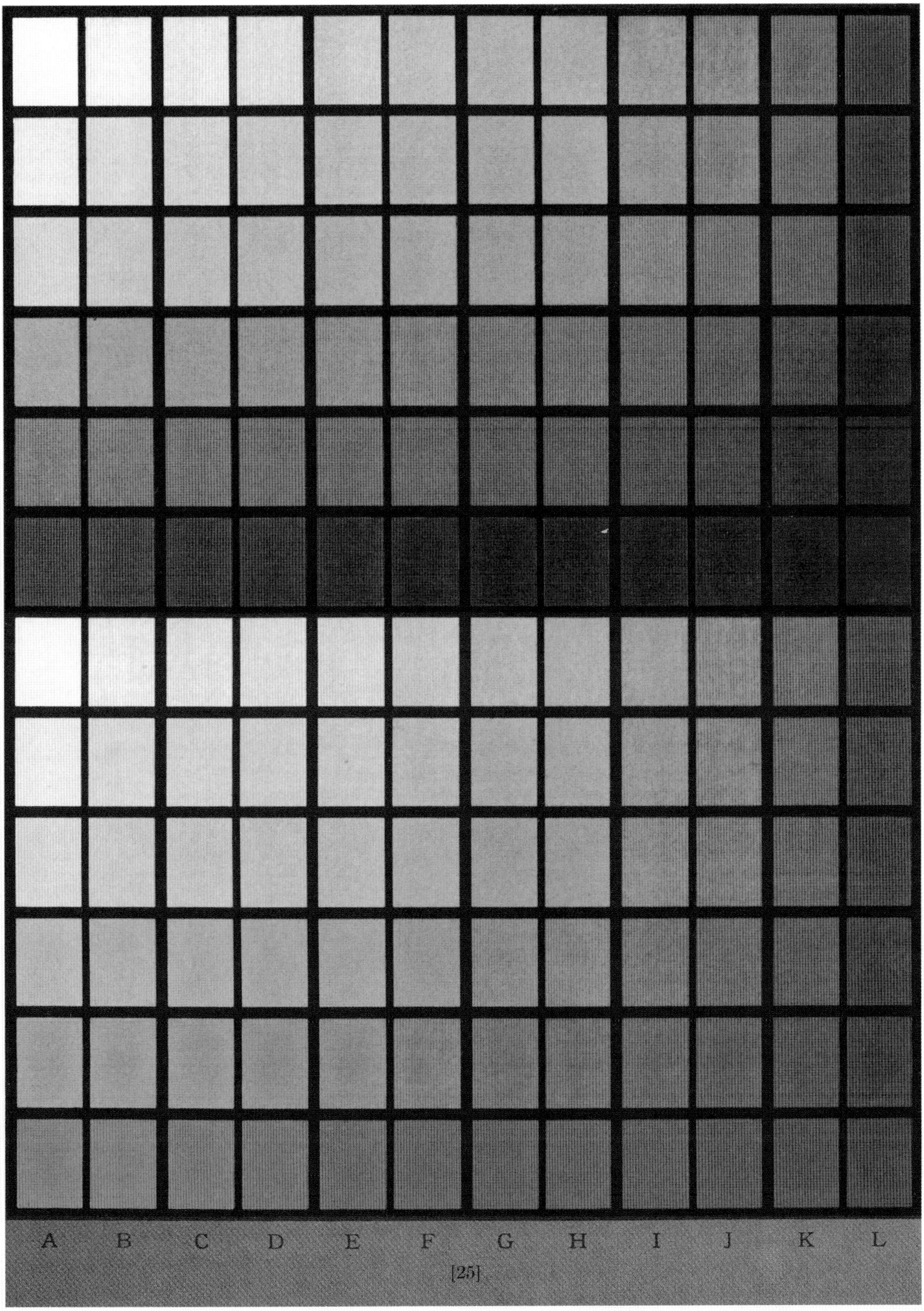
A B C D E F G H I J K L

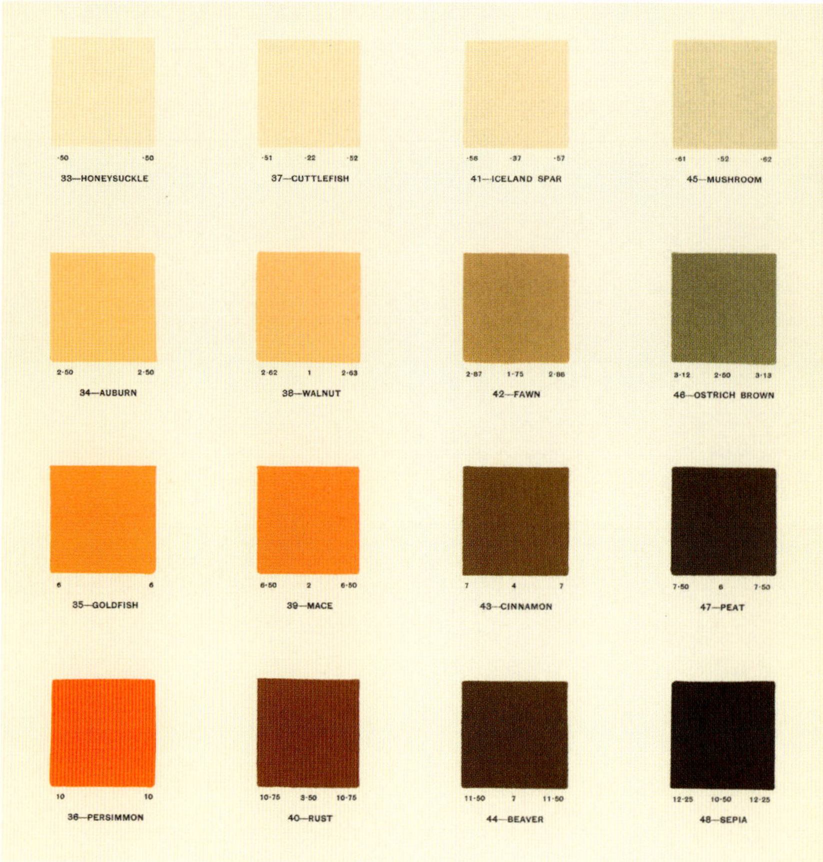

The human eye can perceive over a million different varieties of color, but the human brain has better things to do than name them all. Newton segmented the spectrum into just seven named colors: the classic ROY G BIV divisions. While this might have seemed arbitrary, much later research by anthropologists concluded that most cultures at least have names for black, white, red, green, yellow, and blue: six basic color terms typically named in that order, as if there were an innate hierarchy. Yet the lines are not always drawn in the same place. Early studies in this field revealed that the language of the Chukchi indigenous people of Siberia, for example, had just three words for color categories—black, white, and red—into which all other colors fitted. Some languages have made no distinction between green and blue, while others, including Greek and Russian, have classed light blue and dark blue as two entirely separate colors.

Red is usually top of the color tree, the most basic of the basic color terms, present in most languages, and the first to be named after black and white. But even this simple color contains multitudes. "If one says 'Red,'" wrote artist and teacher Josef Albers, "and there are 50 people listening, it can be expected that there will be 50 reds in their minds. And one can be sure that all these reds will be very different." With a family extending from dusky rose to

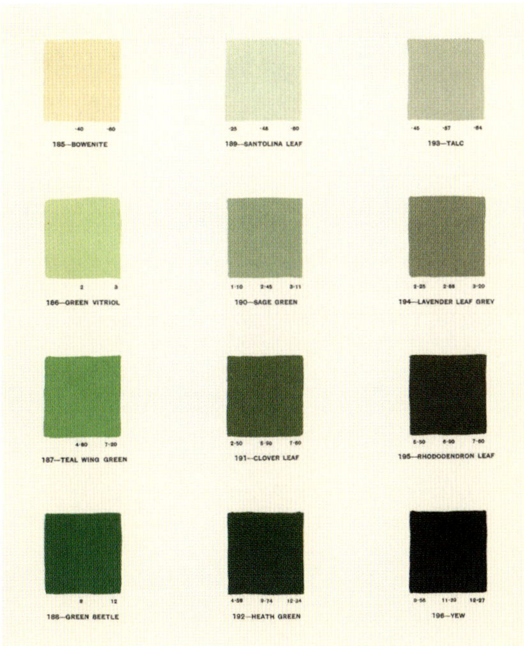

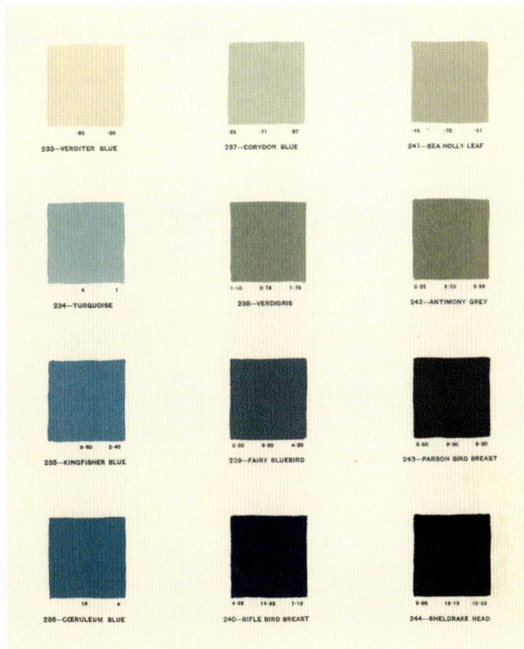

PREVIOUS PAGE
Plate of red-orange color variants in Maerz and Paul's *A Dictionary of Color* (1930).

OPPOSITE, ABOVE AND RIGHT
Plates from E. Fellowes' *Colour: Charted and Catalogued* (1922), a ringbound set of colors with names inspired by nature. Some of the lively nomenclature includes Goldfish, Green Beetle, Wasp Yellow, and Antimony Grey. The numbers below each sample refer to the red, blue, and yellow settings on the Tintometer, a popular color-measuring device.

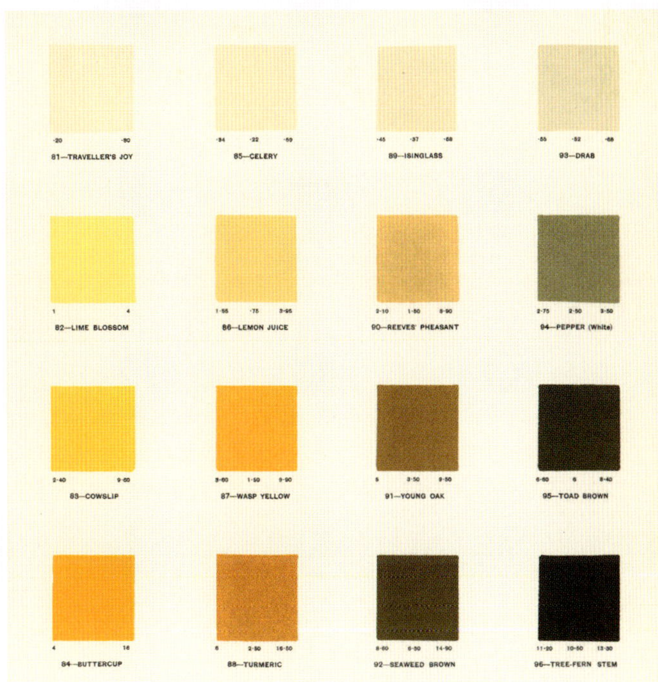

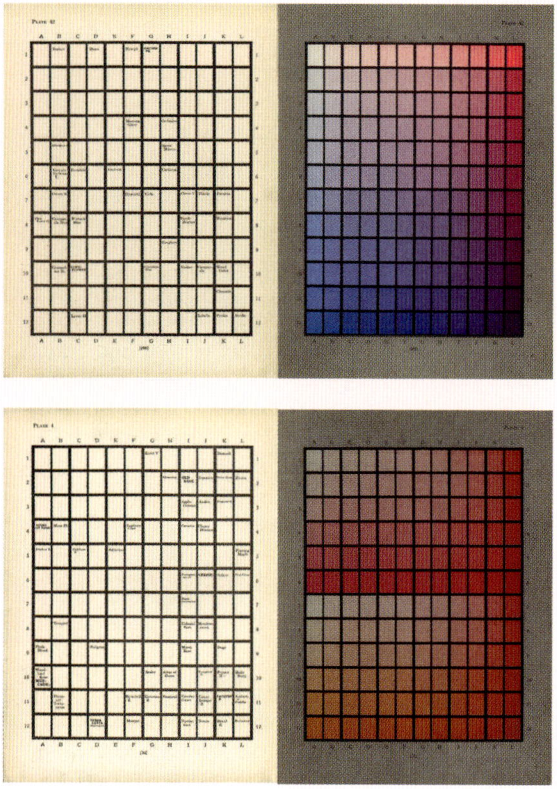

Spreads from Maerz and Paul's *A Dictionary of Color* (1930). The variants on the right could be located in the grid on the left to find the popular name for the tints and shades. The dictionary contained over 7,000 color terms.

deepest scarlet, many words are needed to distinguish between red's multiple siblings and distant cousins. Will Albers's fifty listeners typically imagine cadmium red, so called because of its derivation from cadmium sulphide? How about pillar box red, named after the color of post boxes in the United Kingdom? In other contexts, naming color is another way of classifying it or asserting ownership and control. Color terminology has only grown with our mastery of the spectrum once chemistry unlocked ever more hues and commerce rushed in to monetize them. Language was vital to control the spread. Descriptors added biographical, poetic, and allusive dimensions, giving individual tints and shades a backstory and a personality: yellow can be Naples, lemon or chrome; red can be deep, dark, or purplish. Or all three.

In their many schemes to order color, early scholars sometimes specified particular named pigments but usually kept things simple, labeling sections with red and yellow and blue. Moses Harris, creator of two famous wheels of primary and secondary colors (see p.75), believed that color names should refer solely to hue rather than alluding to the natural world. (He thought oranges were named after the color, rather than the other way round.) He used prosaic hybrid terms for combinations: green-yellow for a yellow with a tinge of green; yellow-green for the inverse. Much later, color educator Albert Munsell used a similar convention for his detailed system of color specification (see p.225), where each color was expressed as one of five principal hues, or a combination thereof, such as blue-green. He excluded the word orange, which he thought too vague, and preferred the hybrid yellow-red (or YR), with origins in the Old English word *geoluhread*. (Chaucer later described the color of a fox as "bitwixe yelow and reed" in his *Canterbury Tales*.) Munsell's unofficial rival, Wilhelm Ostwald, also omitted the word orange from his contemporaneous *Farbenfibel* system (1917, see p.222), but may have done so for political

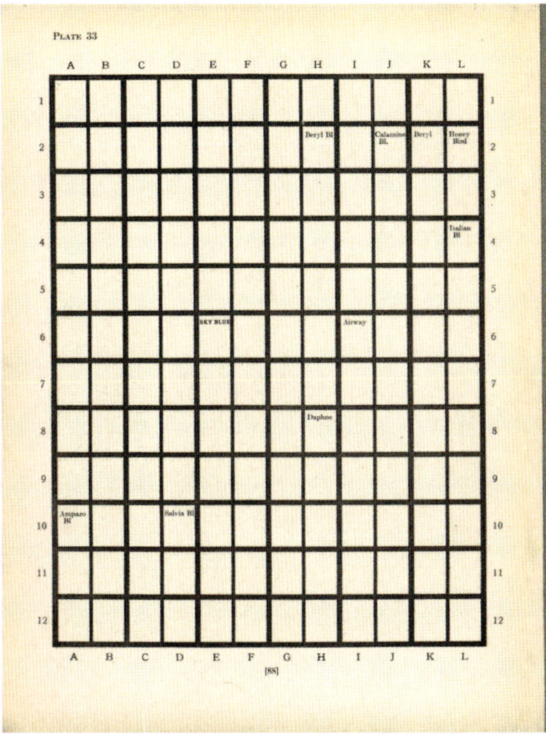

PLATE 33

	A	B	C	D	E	F	G	H	I	J	K	L	
1													1
2								Beryl Bl		Calamine Bl.	Beryl	Honey Bird	2
3													3
4												Italian Bl	4
5													5
6					SKY BLUE				Airway				6
7													7
8								Daphne					8
9													9
10	Amparo Bl			Salvia Bl									10
11													11
12													12
	A	B	C	D	E	F	G	H	I	J	K	L	

[88]

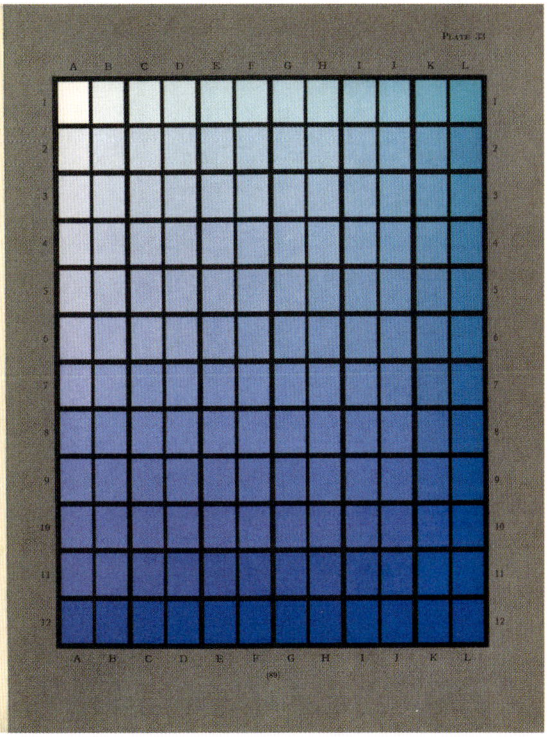

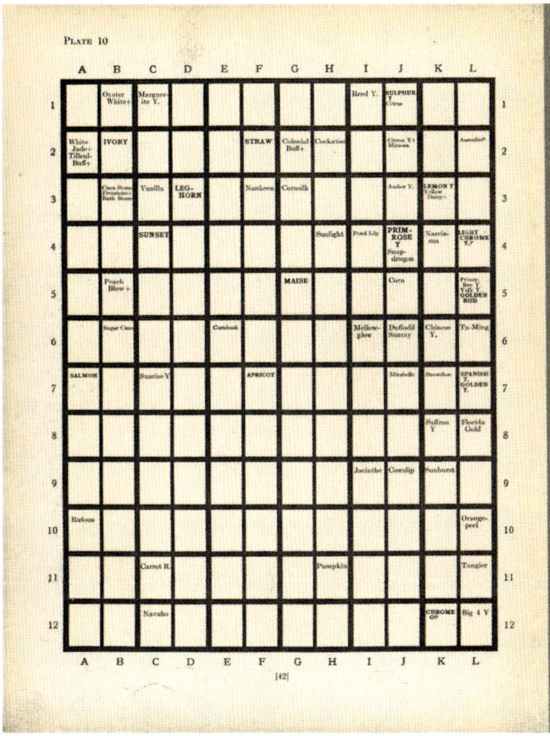

PLATE 10

	A	B	C	D	E	F	G	H	I	J	K	L	
1		Oyster White+	Marguerite Y.						Reed Y.	SULPHUR Y Citrus			1
2	White Jade+ Tilleul-Buff+	IVORY				STRAW	Colonial Buff+	Cockatoo		Citron Y+ Mimosa		Aureolin	2
3		Caen Stone Freestone+ Bath Stone	Vanilla	LEG-HORN		Nankeen	Cornsilk			Amber Y.	LEMON Y Yellow Daisy+		3
4			SUNSET					Sunlight	Pond Lily	PRIMROSE Y Snapdragon	Narcissus	LIGHT CHROME Y.P	4
5		Peach Blow +					MAISE			Corn		Primrose Y Yolk Y GOLDEN ROD	5
6		Sugar Cane			Cornhusk				Mellow-glow	Daffodil Sunray	Chinese Y.	Ta-Ming	6
7	SALMON		Sunrise Y			APRICOT				Mirabelle	[illegible]	SPANISH Y, GOLDEN Y.	7
8											Saffron Y	Florida Gold	8
9									Jacinthe	Cowslip	Sunburst		9
10	Rufous											Orange-peel	10
11			Carrot R.					Pumpkin				Tangier	11
12			Navaho								CHROME OP	Big 4 Y	12
	A	B	C	D	E	F	G	H	I	J	K	L	

[42]

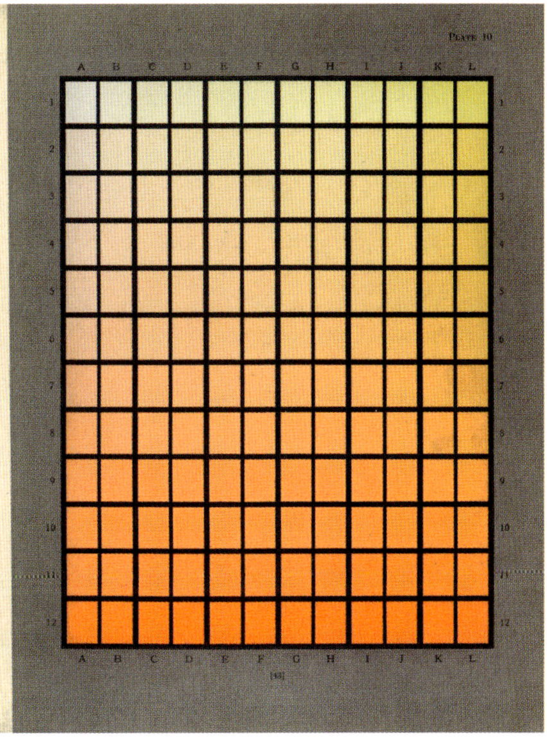

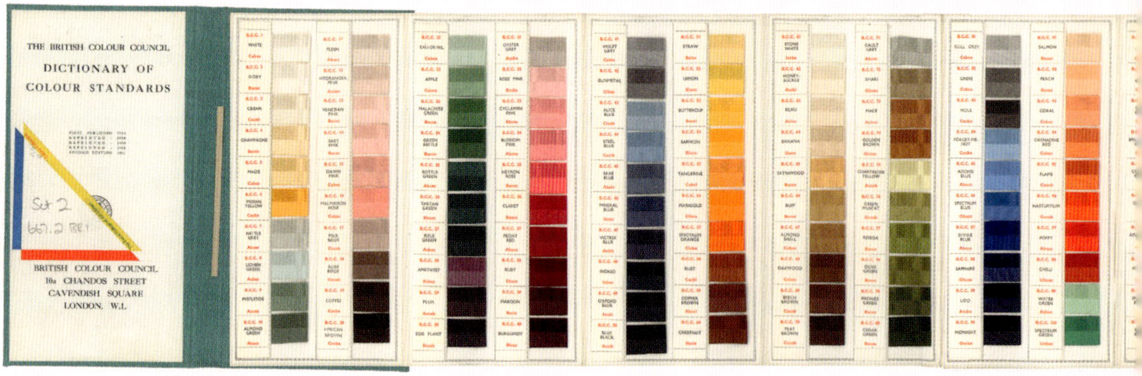

reasons: French terms were verboten during the Great War and so orange was diplomatically replaced with "kress".

Just as Ostwald, Munsell and others were drawing up ways to specify individual colors with alphanumeric codes, marketers of paints and dyes were undoing all their work by inventing wildly misleading names for their ranges. Clearly there was a need for standardization of words alongside color samples, and several attempts were made to simplify and solidify the language of color. With color detached from the natural world and becoming a matter of personal taste, consumers' relationship with it changed, requiring a more detailed, heightened lexicon. Munsell's literalism had its place but factual labels wore thin when commerce looked to the metaphor and allusion of poetry. For the purists, this was a step backward, and they tried to bring the terminology under control. Ornithologist Robert Ridgway (see p.231), compiled two detailed "nomenclatures" of color in 1886 and 1912, identifying and defining over a thousand color variants. In *Color Standards and Color Nomenclature* (1912), he consciously excluded modish trade names from fashion, "as capricious in their meaning as in their origin: among them

The British Colour Council's *Dictionary of Colour Standards* (second edition, 1951) contained 240 named and numbered colored textile samples and was intended to regulate industry. Featured colors included Gull Grey, Squirrel (another gray rather than a red), and Post Office Red.

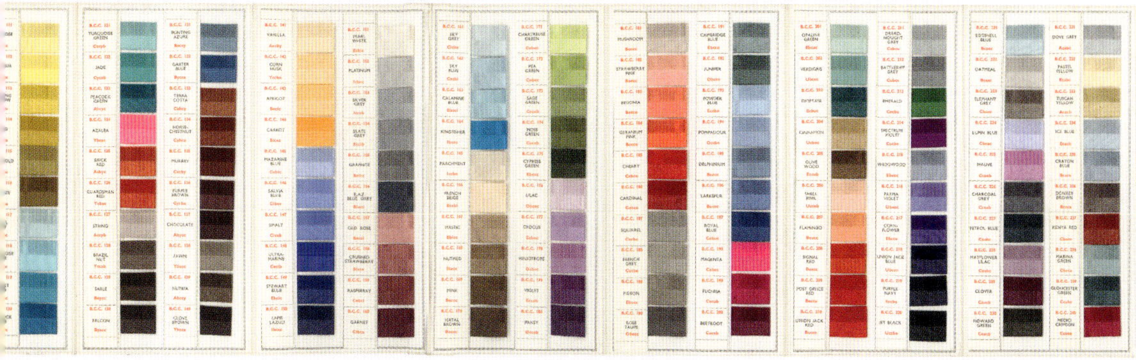

being such fanciful names as 'Zulu', 'Crushed Strawberry', 'Baby Blue', 'Woodbine Berry', 'Night Green', etc., besides such nonsensical names as 'Ashes of Rose' and 'Elephant's Breath'."

While the average consumer might have thought such names were just good fun, they often reflected a national or cultural bias that would become increasingly conspicuous. *Repertoire de couleurs*, a 1905 French color directory produced for horticulturalists (see p.110), had a peculiar definition of the commonly named "flesh" color, for example. Invariably a form of pale pink that recurred in multiple Eurocentric color dictionaries, the *Repertoire* glossed it as "the usual color of human skin, excluding the face, hands, and the female sex." It took until 1930 and the publication of a similar work, *Dictionary of Color*, before any lexicographer bothered to ask "For who shall say what type of complexion Flesh is to represent?"

In 1922 a certain E. Fellowes of the United Kingdom created *Colour: Charted and Catalogued*, a ringbound set of 400 colors with simple, recognizable names. Fellowes made a persuasive case for the need for standard nomenclature, and believed it was essential to find a common language to allow "a business man and an artistic craftsman" to speak on equal terms. Most of his labels were drawn from nature and had to be "known to the ordinary person," resulting in Apricot, Asparagus Tip, Black Cherry, Broad Bean (boiled), Golden Syrup, Lemon Peel, and Terracotta. Where he felt the need to add in more obscure terms (the presence of which rather defeated the point), these were glossed: Babbler Green referenced an Australian bird; Funkia Mauve alluded to a Japanese plant. Fellowes also acknowledged that he had been obliged to include some arbitrary yet popular color names, such as magenta. Artificially created in 1859, it was named, seemingly at random, after a recent battle that took place in an Italian town of that name.

A more capatious and authoritative attempt at identifying and naming all colors appeared in 1930 when Aloys Maerz (director of the American Color Research Laboratory) and Morris Rea Paul published the self-explanatory *A Dictionary of Color*. This was another valiant attempt to pin specific names to specific hues, to identify the platonic Prussian blue and the perfect pea green so all users spoke of particular colors with one tongue. For anyone wanting to know exactly which colors Ashes of Rose,

Fandango, or Confetti Sunrise referred to, the *Dictionary* had a sample. The authors' aim sounded simple enough: "to relate colors with the name by which they are commonly identified," but this was an enormous task, especially since the finished work reached over 7,000 tints and shades. The plan was to standardize the standards: to unite existing versions of named colors in the English-speaking industries. To do so, the authors gathered thousands of color samples from multiple sources for comparison and contrast. Like Fellowes, they hoped to democratize color terms and bridge the three cultures of art, science, and industry. Unlike the fashion business, Maerz and Paul were emphatically not trying to coin new color names—only to chart and measure the impact of long-established epithets. They too noted the "meaningless" terminology in vogue, citing the ever-maligned Elephant's Breath, but overall the pair were less censorious about linguistic frippery, and noted that even ridiculous terms had value when they "reflect the thought and conditions of the time." To put it all in perspective, Maerz and Paul cited the popularity of commercial color terms from nineteenth-century France, including Widow's Joy and the unimprovable Envenomed Monkey.

A Dictionary of Color contained fifty-six gridded plates of color variants in spectral order. A key on the verso page identified those with a common name. The plates were followed by a summary of the authors' research and included a polyglot table matching English color names to their equivalents in French, Italian, Spanish, and German. Reading across the columns revealed some cosmopolitan differences of expression (Cornflower Blue: B Centaurée, Az. fiordaliso, As. Centaurea, and Kornblumenblau), and some universality (Magenta: Magenta, Magenta, Magenta, Magenta). The work closed with an encyclopedic guide to the history of color names, with potted biographies of each and a bit of the authors' record-straightening and score-settling. They cleared up the misconception that Berlin blue was an inferior version of Prussian blue (in fact, the two were synonymous), and disentangled the various confused maritime blues: navy, marine, sailor, and seaman. Their exasperation occasionally surfaced, as in their frustration over the imprecision of the term nut brown ("Completely generic ... what kind of a nut?"). They also addressed an enduring controversy over whether "gray" and "grey" were two different colors, explaining that the former often referred to neutral color composed purely of black and white while the latter denoted "gray" with a tinge of another color. Frustratingly, the entry for Elephant's Breath noted that, although older generations remembered the name, the authors had never managed to identify a commercial sample; the precise shade that infuriated so many color compilers was to remain a mystery. Ultimately the authors expected their

OPPOSITE
The ISCC-NBS (USA) *Centroid Color Charts* (1955) excluded descriptive terms from its national standard of color nomenclature. Anything that could be open to interpretation was dispensed with and replaced with prosaic qualifiers resulting in color names such as v. deep red, blackish-red, and brilliant orange-yellow.

OVERLEAF
In 1955, the National Bureau of Standards (USA) issued *A Method of Designating Colors*, accompanied by a *Dictionary of Color Names* that functioned more like a thesaurus. The dictionary found synonyms for poetic color terms and related them to their closest match in different systems. In this example, multiple terms for Brilliant Green in use include Parakeet, Scarab Green, and Promised Land.

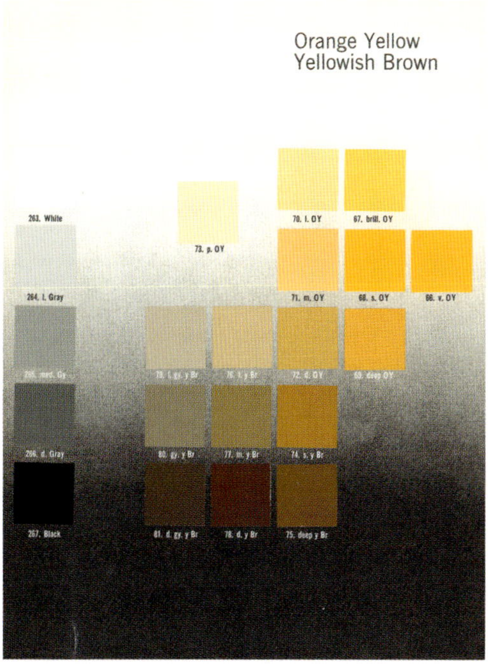
Orange Yellow
Yellowish Brown
263. White
73. p. OY
70. l. OY
67. brill. OY
71. m. OY
68. s. OY
66. v. OY
264. l. Gray
265. med. Gy
79. l. gy. y Br
76. l. y Br
72. d. OY
69. deep OY
266. d. Gray
80. gy. y Br
77. m. y Br
74. s. y Br
267. Black
81. d. gy. y Br
78. d. y Br
75. deep y Br

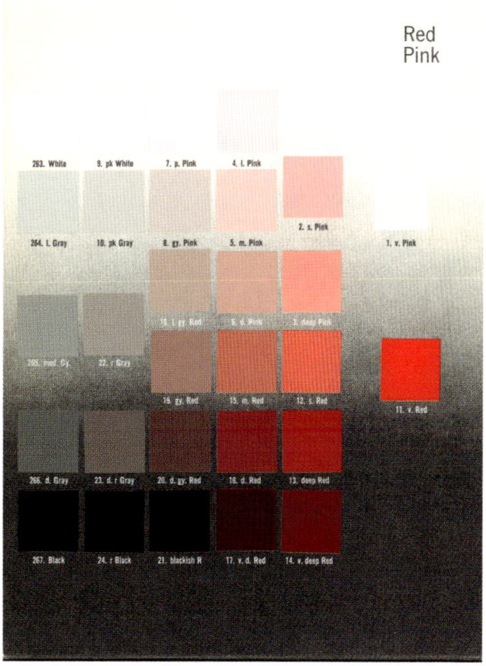
Red
Pink
263. White
9. pk White
7. p. Pink
4. l. Pink
2. s. Pink
264. l. Gray
10. pk Gray
8. gy. Pink
5. m. Pink
1. v. Pink
18. l. gy. Red
6. d. Pink
3. deep Pink
265. med. Gy.
22. r Gray
19. gy. Red
15. m. Red
12. s. Red
11. v. Red
266. d. Gray
23. d. r Gray
20. d. gy. Red
16. d. Red
13. deep Red
267. Black
24. r Black
21. blackish R
17. v. d. Red
14. v. deep Red

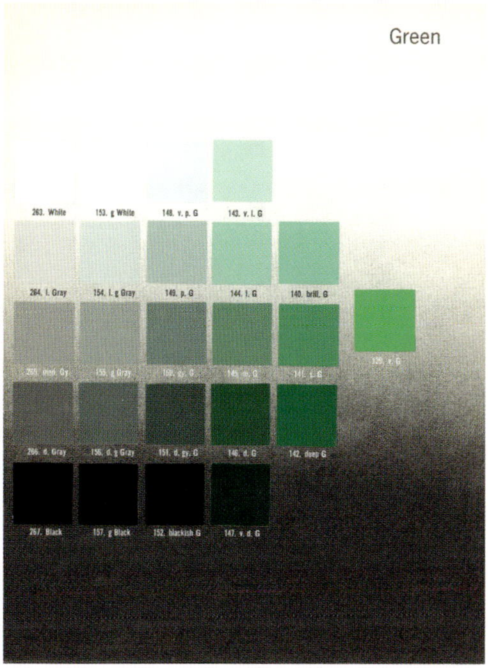
Green
263. White
153. g White
148. v. p. G
143. v. l. G
264. l. Gray
154. l. g Gray
149. p. G
144. l. G
140. brill. G
139. v. G
265. med. Gy
155. g Gray
150. gy. G
145. m. G
141. s. G
266. d. Gray
156. d. g Gray
151. d. gy. G
146. d. G
142. deep G
267. Black
157. g Black
152. blackish G
147. v. d. G

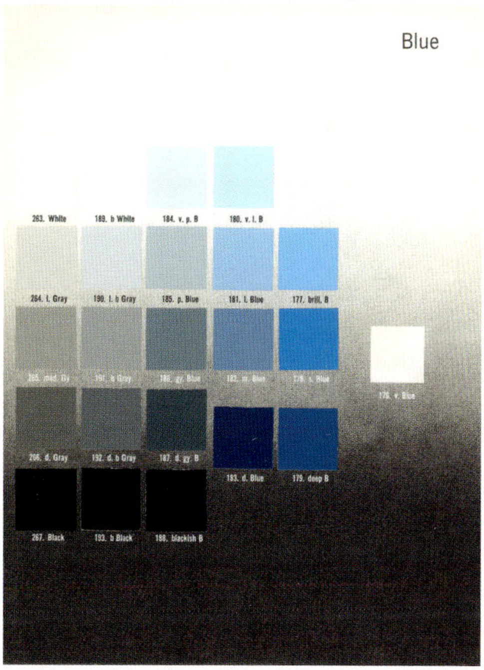
Blue
263. White
189. b White
184. v. p. B
180. v. l. B
264. l. Gray
190. l. b Gray
185. p. Blue
181. l. Blue
177. brill. B
265. med. Gy
191. b Gray
186. gy. Blue
182. m. Blue
178. s. Blue
176. v. Blue
266. d. Gray
192. d. b Gray
187. d. gy. B
183. d. Blue
179. deep B
267. Black
193. b Black
188. blackish B

Textile Color Card Association

Evergreen 70036
Green (USA) 65007
Hunter 70064

Other sources

Atroherbaceus .... B
Atroviridis .... B
Dark Green (USA) .... F 1440
Dark Green .... S
Dark Yellowish Green .... RC
Dull Green .... S
Dusky Yellowish Green .... RC
Forest Green (Y&D) .... F 1440
Green (Agr) .... F 1440
Green (BuOrd) .... F 2405
Green (MA) .... F 1440
Green Striping (N) .... F 1440
Green Boottopping (PC) .... F 1440
Herbaceus .... B
Spinach Green .... H 0960
Yellow Green .... S
Yellowish Green .... A

138. VERY DARK YELLOWISH GREEN

Maerz and Paul

Chasseur 24C11
Elephant Green 24C11
Fir [Green] 24E7
Hunter [Green] 24C11
Hunter's Green 24C11

Taylor, Knoche, Granville

Bottle Green g .... 22 pl
Cypress Green g .... 23 pn
Dark Bottle Green g .... 22 pn
Dark Green g .... 22 pl
Dark Hunter Green g .... 22 pl
Forest Green g .... 22 pl
Wintergreen g .... 22 pl

Textile Color Card Association

Evergreen 70036

Other sources

Chrome Green (PC) .... F 1430
Yellowish Green .... A

139. VIVID GREEN

Maerz and Paul

Spearmint 25L12

Plochere

Blarney .... 1009 Gyy 1–a
Emerald Isle .... 1010 Gyy 1–b
Killarney Green .... 1057 GY 1–a
Merry Green .... 1011 Gyy 1–c

Other sources

Bright Blue-Green .... S
Bright Green .... A
Bright Green .... S
Emerald .... S
Green .... S
Yellow Green .... S

140. BRILLIANT GREEN

Maerz and Paul

Chrysoprase [Green] 17A10
Emerald Green (pigment) 26C11
Emperor Green 26C11
Imperial Green 26C11
Kirchberger Green 26C11
Mitis Green 26C11
Parrakeet 25J10
Paris Green 26C11
Paul Veronese Green 26C11
Schweinfurt Green 26C11
Seafoam 17A9
Vienna Green 26C11

Plochere

Festival .... 964 Gy 1–d
Festoon .... 1012 Gyy 1–d
Lush Green .... 1013 Gyy 1–e
Meadow Green .... 1020 Gyy 2–d
Parrakeet .... 1019 Gyy 2–c
Promised Land .... 963 Gy 1–c
Salome Green .... 1021 Gyy 2–e
Summer Green .... 1014 Gyy 1–f

Ridgway

Light Blue-Green .... VII 39d
Viridian Green .... VII 37i
Vivid Green .... VII 37

Taylor, Knoche, Granville

Bright Emerald Green g .... 21 ia
Bright Green gm .... 22 la
Bright Kelly Green m .... 22 na
Bright Mint Green gm .... 22 ia
Light Emerald Green g .... 21 ia
Mint Leaf m .... 22 lc

Textile Color Card Association

Scarab Green 70214

Other sources

Atroviridis .... B
Blue-Green .... S
Bright Blue-Green .... S
Chrysocolla Green .... H 56
Emerald .... S
Green .... A
Green .... S
Light Green .... S
Nickel Green .... H 57
Viridian Green .... H 55
Viridi-Caeruleus .... B
Viridis .... B
Yellow Green .... S

141. STRONG GREEN

Maerz and Paul

Arsenate 25K11
Cadmium Green 20B12
Chrome Green 28K11
Emeraude 28K11
Empire 20B12
[French] Veronese Green 28K11
Ming Green 28J11
Transparent Chromium Oxide 28K11
Viridian 28K11

Plochere

Blarney .... 1009 Gyy 1–a
Ming .... 1018 Gyy 2–b
Promised Land .... 963 Gy 1–c

Ridgway

Viridian Green .... VII 37i

Taylor, Knoche, Granville

Bright Emerald Green g .... 21 na
Bright Green m .... 22 nc
Bright Jade Green gm .... 21 nc
Bright Kelly Green g .... 22 na
Emerald Green gm .... 21 pc
Kelly Green m .... 22 nc
Mint Leaf g .... 22 lc
Pepper Green g .... 22 ne

Textile Color Card Association

Primitive Green 70167

Other sources

Atroviridis .... B
Blue-Green .... S
Bright Blue-Green .... S
Bright Green .... S
Chrysocolla Green .... H 56
Dark Blue-Green .... S
Dark Green .... S
Deep Green .... S
Green .... A
Green .... S
Viridian Green .... H 55
Yellow Green .... S

142. DEEP GREEN

Maerz and Paul

Amarna 30K11
Service Corps 30K12

Taylor, Knoche, Granville

Dark Emerald Green g .... 21 pg
Dark Green g .... 21 pg
Deep Emerald Green g .... 21 pe
Deep Green g .... 21 pe

Textile Color Card Association

Irish Green 70168

Other sources

Bright Green .... S
Dark Green .... S
Deep Green .... S
Green .... A
Green .... S

143. VERY LIGHT GREEN

Maerz and Paul

Opaline Green 17A6

Plochere

Icy Morn .... 1031 Gyy 3–g
Island Green .... 1023 Gyy 2–g
Jealousy .... 1022 Gyy 2–f
La Mer .... 1015 Gyy 1–g
Pale Water .... 1038 Gyy 4–f
Pine Frost .... 1030 Gyy 3–f
Salome Green .... 1021 Gyy 2–e
Summer Green .... 1014 Gyy 1–f

Ridgway

Deep Greenish Glaucous .... XLI 33'''d
Variscite Green .... XIX 37'd

Taylor, Knoche, Granville

Ice Green g .... 21 ea
Light Green gm .... 22 ea
Light Mint Green gm .... 22 ga
Pale Emerald Green g .... 21 ea
Pale Green g .... 22 ca
Pale Mint Green g .... 22 ca

Other sources

Blue-Green .... S
Green .... A
Green .... S
Light Blue (Eng) .... F 2525
Pale Green .... S
Prasinus .... B
Viridi-Glaucus .... B
Yellow Green .... S

144. LIGHT GREEN

Maerz and Paul

Aden 27I8
Bouquet Green 27H7
Cabaret 27I6
Cameo Green 27B6
Chantilly 26F7
Chinese Green 18A8
Chrysoprase [Green] 17A10
Corsage Green 28G6
Elf 27E6
Elfin Green 27F7
Feldspar 27I9
Lo-kao 18A8
Mist Blue 27B6
Misty Blue 27B6
Motmot Green 27B10
Naiad 27B7
Neptune [Green] 27J8
Neuvider Green 17B8
Neuwieder Green 17B8
Seafoam 17A9
Serpentine 26I9
Source 28B6
Variscite Green 25B7
Veridine Green 26C9
Victoria Green 27G5

Plochere

Aden .... 1028 Gyy 3–d
Chantilly .... 1029 Gyy 3–e
Lovely .... 1037 Gyy 4–e
Meadow Green .... 1020 Gyy 2–d
Porcelain Green .... 1036 Gyy 4–d

Ridgway

Cobalt Green .... XIX 37'b
Dark Bluish Glaucous .... XLII 37'''b
Deep Glaucous-Green .... XXXIII 39''b
Light Blue-Green .... VII 39 d
Montpellier Green .... XXXIII 37''
Verdigris Green .... XIX 37'

Taylor, Knoche, Granville

Light Emerald Green g .... 21 ga
Light Mint Green g .... 22 ga
Mint Green gm .... 22 ic
Surf Green m .... 22 ie

Other sources

Aerugineus .... B
Blue-Green .... S
Brilliant Green .... RC
Dull Green .... S
Emerald .... S
Gray Green .... S
Green .... A
Green .... MUP 12
Green .... S
Griseo-Viridis .... B
Light Green .... RC
Pistaceus .... B
Verdigris .... H 655
Viridi-Caeruleus .... B
Yellow Green .... S

145. MODERATE GREEN

Maerz and Paul

Amazon 29J10
Blue Spruce 30H7
Chrome Green 28K11
Egyptian Green 28I10
Emeraude 28K11
Erin 29F12
French Green 29D8
[French] Veronese Green 28K11
Gobelin Green 30H9
Gretna Green 29E8
Hazy Blue 27B6
Hooker's Green No. 2 .... 29J11
Jasper Green 29H7
Kashmir 30E8
Killarney [Green] 20A9
Lizard [Green] 28F7
Locarno Green 20A11
Neptune [Green] 27J8
Pigeon's Throat 30J7
Pi Yu 29K10
Runnymede 29K9
Scarab 28K9
Ski 29D12
Transparent Chromium Oxide 29K11
Viridian 28K11

Plochere

Blue Spruce .... 1035 Gyy 4–c
Bottle Green .... 1034 Gyy 4–b
Colonial Exterior Green .... 1026 Gyy 3–b
Primeval .... 1027 Gyy 3–c

Ridgway

Ackermann's Green .... XVIII 35'k
Danube Green .... XXXII 35''m
Dark Viridian Green .... VII 37k
Dark Zinc Green .... XIX 37'k
Diamine Green .... VII 37m
French Green .... XXXII 35''i

dictionary to be used alongside Munsell's popular system of notation and their effort humanized and complemented the latter's colors by describing them in natural language rather than code.

A Dictionary of Color elegantly threaded words to visuals and wore its extensive research lightly. It drew high praise from leading American color consultant Faber Birren but failed to stand the test of time because too many of the terms, lifted from fashion and textiles, fell out of favor. The authors even predicted their own demise in the text, noting how quickly their antecedents became obsolete.

With industry in control of color, it staked a claim to new ranges and new hues, and unique names were a way to assert ownership of particular variants and to regulate sectors as a whole. The Textile Color Card Association of the United States and the British Colour Council (BCC) established definitive named ranges of color for the textiles industry (see p.47). The BCC's first edition of 220 colors arrived in 1934 in a slipcase: a set of color silks on a concertina board, and an accompanying booklike dictionary of color, clarifying the links between the specified BCC colors and the general language of color. The popular Quaker Grey, for example, matched the BCC's number 71 Gault Grey (although, the author noted, "all Quaker colors are inventions, as no definite color has ever been specified for this set"). The dictionary attempted to disambiguate, clarifying, for example, that there was no material difference between ecru, beige, and grège. Many colors were woven into the fabric of British life and named accordingly: RAF Blue Grey matched the official color of the Royal Air Force, while Union Jack Blue and Union Jack Red were the designated colors for the national flag.

In 1955, one other notable color dictionary appeared and, like *Dictionary of Color*, tried to provide the language to describe the many color variants in the coded Munsell system. A collaboration between the Inter-Society Color Council (USA) and the National Bureau of Standards, the *ISCC-NBS Method of Designating Colors* aimed to create a system of color terms that would be "used by science, art, and industry, and ... understood, at least in a general way, by the whole public." The ISCC-NBS system, as it was inelegantly called, abandoned all poetic and historical terms entirely, allowing only "meaningful" words. Most colors were categorized by basic hue names—red, green, blue, and so on—but with the many variants prefaced by modifiers, including, pale, brilliant, weak, and strong. For the grayest colors, the hue family name itself became the modifier, resulting in terms such as bluish-white or reddish-gray. Diagrams mapped the rectangular color spaces of particular hues, in Munsell code and ISCC-NBS words. A variant of red with the notation 5R 4/14 would be interpreted as "strong red", for example. The work also contained an extraordinary list of cross-referenced commercial color names with line after line of them filling page after page and including several hundred terms for red alone. Albers and his students could take note.

Trying to put color into words is both important and impossible. From the nineteenth century onward, language has swelled to accommodate the colors available, but often put more distance between the signifier and the signified. Color has even been at the heart of debates about so-called linguistic relativism: whether the extent of the vocabulary we possess for things (including colors) actually alters our perception of the world. The numerous lexicographers and chromatographers have always aspired to a definitive nomenclature but color keeps evolving outside of the terminology. Indeed, as Kandinsky concluded in trying to write about the subject himself, "Words are, and will remain, only hints, mere suggestions of colors."

1705

1835

EVERY

OBJECT

IN THE

CREATION

Newton's extraordinary revelations, exposing a kaleidoscopic world hidden in plain sight, cast a long shadow. For the next century and beyond, no one could investigate color, and publish their findings, without acknowledging a heavy debt to the author of *Opticks*. But the fact that such investigations persisted, that numerous modifications and variations of the color circle continued to appear as scholars refined the models for organizing the spectrum, was evidence of his theory's limits. The prism experiment appeared to explain where color came from and how it operated, but this outstanding articulation of the geometry and physics of light was also full of holes. What about the colors that were visible in the world but not in the spectrum, for example? There was no brown in Newton's circle, after all; no pink. How did we even see color anyway? And what could the experiment tell artists about how to mix colors with paint or dye? They could no more rely on a display of colored light to understand how to master color than they could draw on the surface of a lake.

Even obtaining the colors themselves was a tricky business in the eighteenth century, involving expense, effort, and risk. The hugely popular lead white, for example, was created by sealing up sheets of lead with vinegar and manure, resulting in a highly toxic pigment. Any progress in the synthesis of "artificial" color was grindingly slow, with only occasional successes. One of the earliest occurred shortly after the publication of *Opticks*, when Heinrich Jacob Diesbach of Berlin accidentally invented the first modern, synthesized pigment through a chance experiment with some waste potash. The deep and beautiful blue that surprised him was rich enough to rival the prohibitively expensive and remote ultramarine, sourced from Afghanistan, far from European markets. Named after its birthplace, Diesbach's Prussian blue was much closer to home, and far more affordable. Such occasional advances in the synthesis of artificial pigments enlivened the palette but came at a high price in other ways: Carl Wilhelm Scheele's invention of a rich, artificial green in 1775 contained potentially poisonous levels of arsenic. Even when refined by a paint company into a color marketed as "emerald green", it remained so toxic it doubled as an insecticide. Nevertheless, as color started to come under the control of chemists, these occasional chromatic revolutions released it from its status as an inherent property of things and began its transformation into a concept or object in and of itself. Our relationship with color was now subject to change.

Amid the struggle to make color, Newton's conclusions provoked further investigation. *Opticks* inspired an army of acolytes, and the odd antagonist, who would finesse, patch, and counter its theories, and this process continued for over a century. Newton's successors were an eclectic bunch, amateur scholars and "men of science' alike, drawn from all walks of life: interior designers,

The earliest known printed color wheels appeared as a pair in the small volume Traite de la peinture *(1708 edition) by an author known only as C.B. The first of the wheels divides colors into seven, probably inspired by Newton. This expands to twelve in the second, including the compounds made by mixing two adjacent colors and finding their midpoint.*

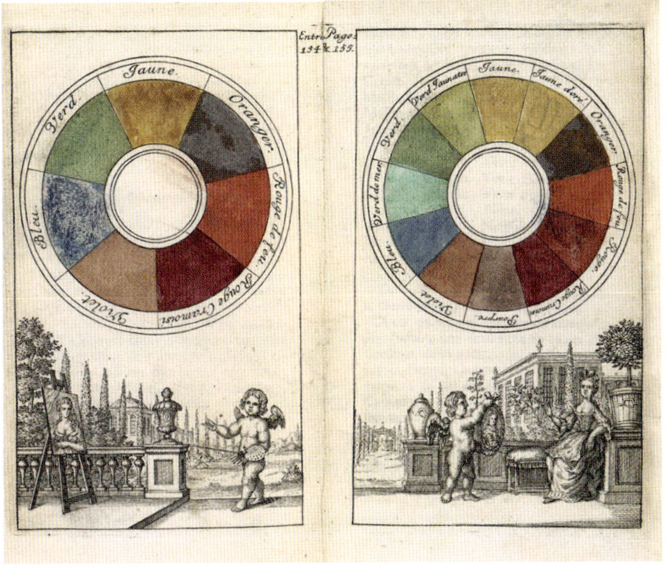

artists, chemists, poets. Entomologists and botanists were particularly visible in the quest, keen to master color to help describe the natural world, striving to capture all the colors of specimens they encountered and trap them in a grid. Once those outside the world of natural philosophy entered the realm of color studies, discoveries in science and art locked on to a similar trajectory to understand the extent and variety of color, its behavior and harmonic structures or rules. The aim was to gain sufficient knowledge to wield the palette successfully as a tool. Most were humbled by Newton, only apologetically modifying his conclusions, but this period culminated in a spectacular intergenerational disagreement, with German poet and playwright Johann Wolfgang von Goethe entering the fray to launch a polemic against the foundations of *Opticks*. In doing so, he re-asserted a schism between those who viewed color as an objectively measurable phenomenon and those who shared his belief that it could only be understood by centering the subjective, human experiences of perception and feelings.

Cultural and societal forces also performed a role in the way the understanding of color played out. In Europe, the momentum of Enlightenment thought advocated a model of the world in which things could and should be organized, named, and quantified. It was also the age of exploration. James Cook's voyages to Australia in the 1760s and 1770s, and the HMS *Beagle*'s travels to the Galapagos islands in the 1830s, the latter with Charles Darwin on board, consulting color charts to help describe his observations of the natural world, drove a need to render and convey the color of hitherto unseen marvels to audiences at home.

The landslide of data flowing in about the natural world demanded new ways to manage this accumulation of knowledge. Color was a tool that could impose boundaries, but where were the boundaries of color itself? It could bring clarity to taxonomies but could it be subjected to classification in its own right? In the eighteenth century, scientists and practitioners alike aspired to create an ultimate color system that could define every color in the world (once that elusive number had been established, of course). The resulting scheme would ideally be visualized through grids and geometric shapes; it would internationalize color and make it communicable across oceans, cultures, and disciplines, a chromatic key to all mythologies. But first, Newton's theories needed more work.

Why did *Opticks* require so much revision when it uncovered so much of the fundamentals of light and changed understanding of how color works for ever? Newton had done so by focusing on intangible colored light, emitted from a direct light source, such as the sun. Beams of light, however, behave entirely differently from the tangible color that we might apply to our walls, our fingernails, or our canvases. Newton had been concerned with additive color: different-colored wavelengths of light that add up to white. Physical color, in pigment and dye, the kind we register in fruit, hair color, or clothing, the kind that rubs off or stains, is a different manifestation in which perceived colors are the reflection (not the emission) of light. This is known as subtractive color. We see a green leaf not because it emanates an inherent greenness from within but because, when white light strikes it, its molecular surface absorbs (or subtracts) all the colors in the spectrum bar the combination needed to create that particular green—which bounces back to us for interpretation. The color of things is in the quality of external light and how the surfaces reflect it: all cats are gray in the dark, and no color exists if no one is there to see it. Chemist George Field described the distinction between the two types simply as "inherent, as in pigments, or transient, as in the sun-beam ... the first arising from reflection, the latter from refraction". Whether we call the two different modes of color subtractive and additive, inherent and transient, or tangible and intangible, the distinction is essential. Newton's focus on immaterial color held little to help painters master their paints.

Not long after the publication of *Opticks*, another of the earliest known color circles, devised to aid painters in composition, appeared in the 1708 edition of a work first published nearly three decades earlier, *Traite de la peinture et mignature* (*Treatise on miniature painting*). Attributed to "C.B.", often presumed to be a certain Claude Boutet, this work contained two color wheels: one in seven divisions like Newton's but this time based on the behavior of pigments and paints rather than light. Another fundamental difference was that the wheel itself appeared in color, with hand-painted segments. Crucially, C.B. identified red, yellow, and blue as the primary colors, or "primitives": these were the irreducible pigments, which could not be created through a combination of other colors, but could be mixed with each other to create many more discrete hues. C.B. included two types of red in his primary group: an orangey version close to vermilion and a bluish-red resembling carmine, amounting to a total of four primaries. Four became seven in the first wheel as C.B. added the compound (secondary) colors created by a mixture of any two of these adjacent primaries. For the second wheel, this was further expanded to a twelve-part version, including five further mixtures created in the spaces between the seven of the first wheel. These were the first known illustrated and

OVERLEAF LEFT
Moses Harris's brace of color circles adapted Newton's prismatic colors of light for painters by translating them into pigments. In his Natural System of Colours *(c.1766), Harris demonstrated that the primary colors of red, yellow, and blue can be mixed to make secondaries ("compounds") and then combined further to create tertiary colors.*

OVERLEAF RIGHT
The outlines of Moses Harris's circles themselves are engravings that have been individually hand-painted. These are from the second edition of 1811.

colored circles, revealing progressive mixing and relationships, clarifying how increasing numbers of colors could be created from the smallest core set. C.B. did not attempt to extrapolate rules for how colors should or should not be combined based on their position on the wheel, and he did not develop the model further to show darker or lighter versions of individual hues. Nevertheless, the circles were simple but powerful, and established a representation that endures.

Several decades later, entomologist and engraver Moses Harris (1730–c.1787) had a more sophisticated system in mind. Harris had plenty of incentives to build on Newton's findings. It is likely his fascination with the natural world, and need to represent it accurately, drove his quest to master color and translate the conclusions of *Opticks* into something tangible, with practical application. Harris's *Natural System of Colours* appeared around 1766 and in this he aimed to show how the colors we see reflected back at us in natural objects—the huge range of hues and shades of the beetle's exoskeleton or the butterfly's wings—could be matched in pigment. Running to just eight pages, with four plates, it was a sliver of *Opticks* but boasted an extraordinary enhancement: full-color illustrations, including two spectacular, detailed color wheels, among the best known and most significant in the history of color visualization. Across this brace of hand-colored engravings, Harris detailed a meticulous system, demonstrating how just three pure colors could be combined in numerous ways, then darkened and lightened to create 660 variants.

Harris's identification of three primary colors, or "primitives", which he named as variants of red, yellow, and blue, was fundamental to his work, as was his demonstration of their subsequent combination into three secondaries, or "mediates", and, eventually, tertiaries (mixtures of the secondaries). The basic color theory instilled in early-years education of many people's experience—that red and yellow make orange, and blue and yellow make green—was perfectly visualized by Harris. But the six-part segmentation was just the start. His color wheels were not uniform blocks but gradations of increasing darkness to show how primitive colors could be mixed, tinted, or shaded (lightened and darkened). His first wheel separated hues into eighteen segments rather than six because of the need to accommodate hybrids at the fringes: hyphenates such as "purple-red" or "yellow-green" described these transitional spaces and the proportion of color each contained ("red-orange" contained more orange than red, but the ratio was inverted for "orange-red").

The full title of his work promised a "regular and beautiful Order and Arrangement" of the primaries to show "the dependence they have on each other". It did not disappoint. This was a grand system, demonstrating how the relationships between colors and their harmonious connections, could render "every Object in the Creation". It was also concise and easily understood. Nature

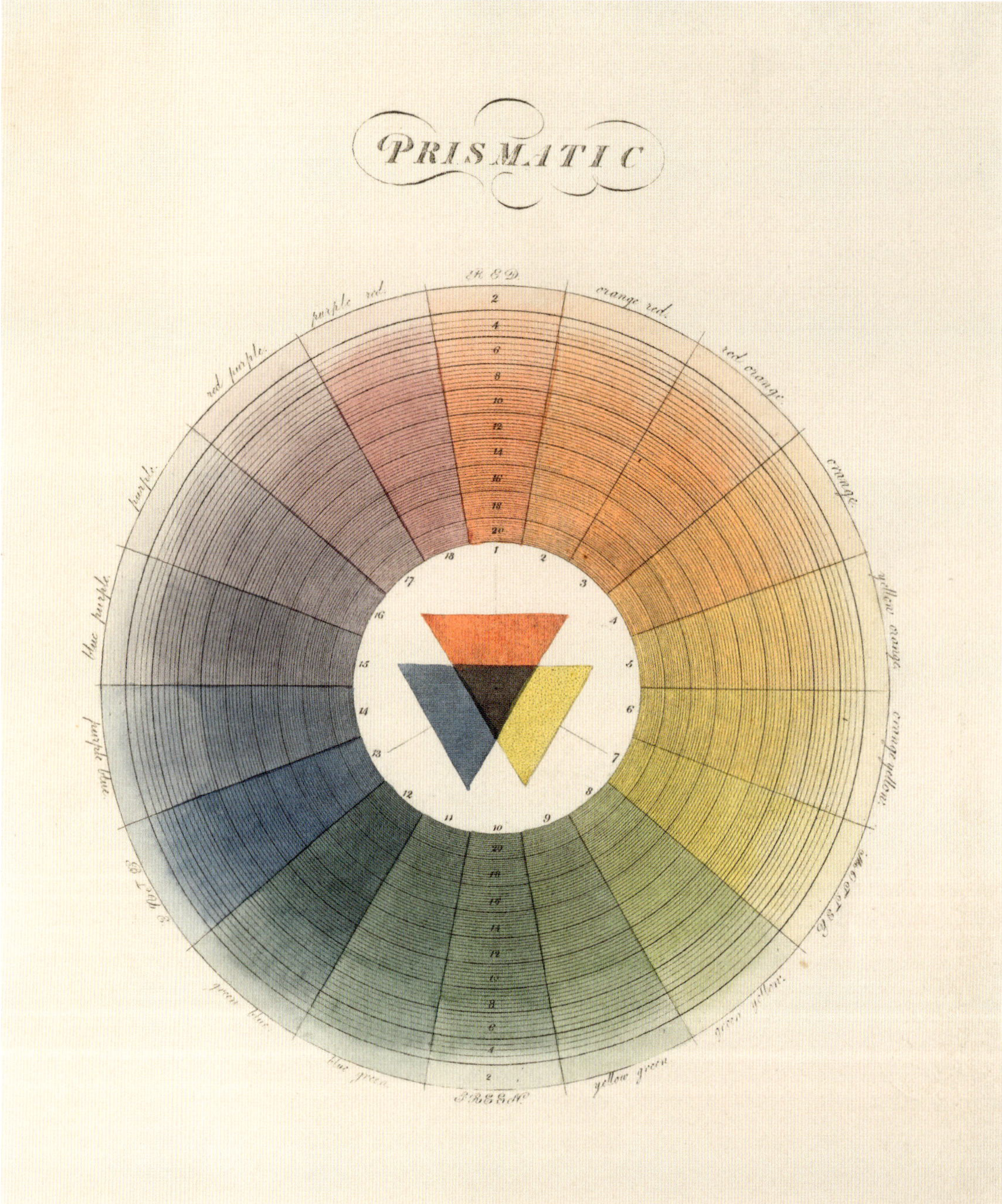
PRISMATIC
RED
orange red.
red orange.
orange.
yellow orange.
orange yellow.
green yellow.
yellow green
GREEN
blue green
green blue.
purple blue.
blue purple.
purple.
red purple.
purple red.

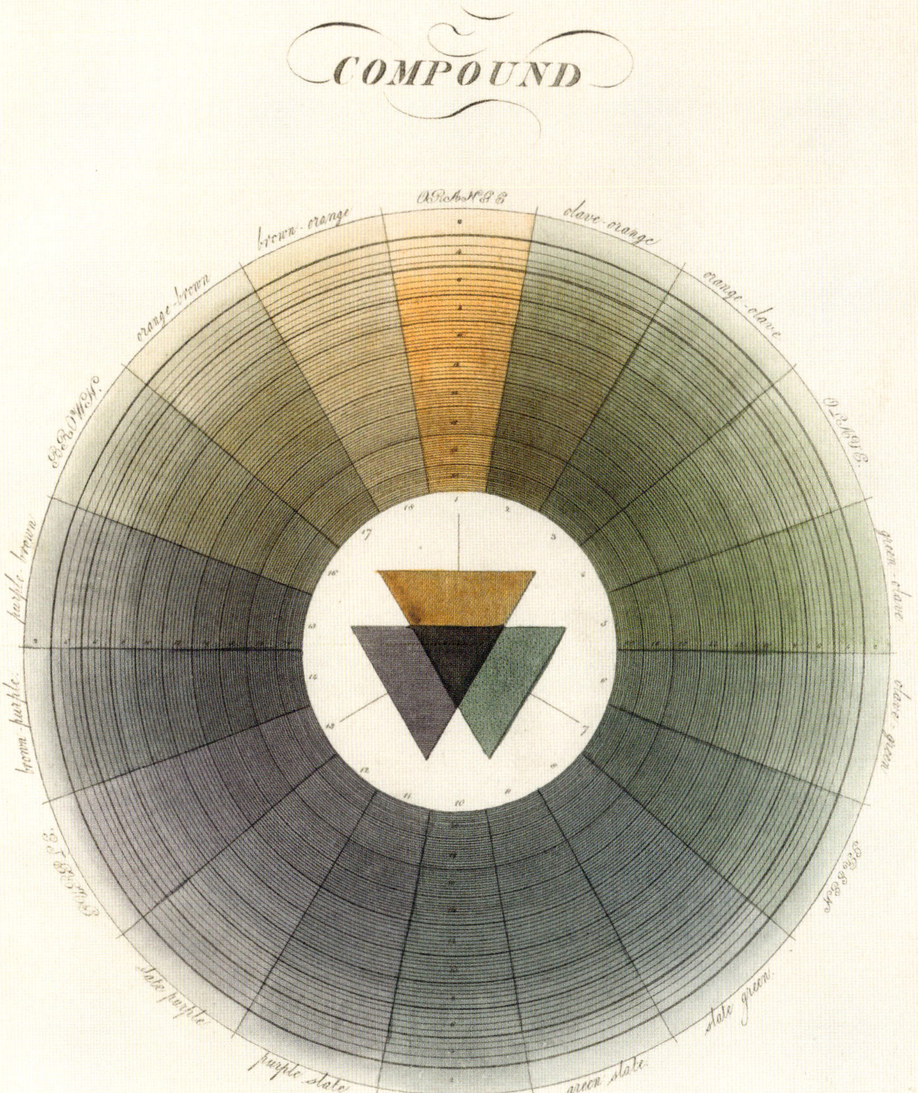
COMPOUND
ORANGE
olave-orange
orange-olave
OLAVE
green-olave
olave-green
GREEN
slate green
green slate
SLATE
purple slate
slate purple
PURPLE
brown purple
purple brown
BROWN
orange-brown
brown-orange

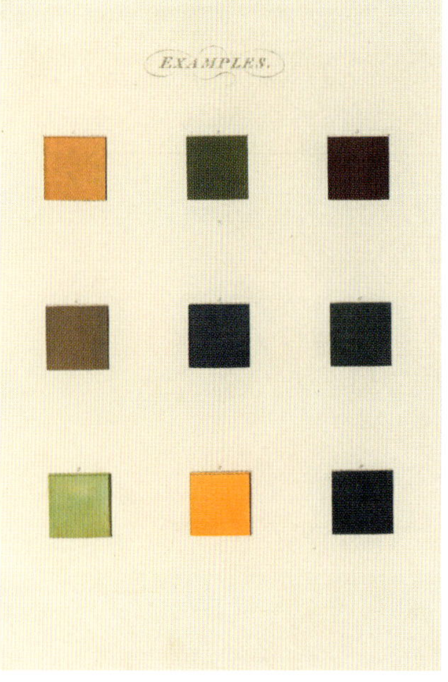

itself is simple and plain, Harris argued, so it was only right that his system should emulate its subject.

With the basic division into eighteen hues, each further divided into twenty concentric steps to visualize lighter and darker variants, skill was required to translate tints and shades into discernible transitions on the page for the reader. Color was lightened with diluted watercolor and darkened by black lines across the engraved sections, an optical trick like cross-hatched shadows in pen-and-ink drawings. Harris's first circle, the "prismatic" diagram spun out of the primary colors, displayed 360 different variants, including the secondary colors that then became the starting point of a second circle in their own right. This second "compound" wheel advanced deep into the tertiary colors, where two secondaries were mixed. He called the tertiaries brown, olive, and slate. As painters know, the more colors in the mix, the more the result inclines to mud, and Harris's system of initially differentiated and vibrant hues eventually succumbed to a kind of chromatic and aesthetic entropy. Indeed, the sludgy, earth colors were partly the point as the system moved to the palette of the natural world. Harris believed that a deep mixture of the primaries would eventually lead to something resembling black, and the slate and olive colors created on the way were perhaps more useful to the entomologist than the interior decorator.

It was Harris's treatment of black and white that most inverted Newton. In Harris's subtractive model, white occurred in complete absence of color, while black arose when all colors combined. But Harris could not escape Newton's influence, or the public recognition factor of the prism, even as he wrote about a model of color that operated on entirely different principles. Almost out of obligation, he called his first circle "prismatic" in reference to the phenomenon Newton had disclosed, although he reduced those seven identified spectral colors to six, abandoning the awkward indigo, like C.B. before him. Harris's even-numbered arrangement, where colors could be paired and opposed, was more elegant than either of his predecessors', and more coherent.

The accompanying text contained important practical advice for the painter, too: the color wheels were a harmonization tool as well as an aesthetic representation of a hierarchy. To find a complementary color, Harris explained, one must simply locate its opposite on one of his wheels: for red, connect to green; for blue, trace across to orange. In Harris's explanation, these complementaries were ideal because their opposite mediate contained no trace of its primitive: orange, facing blue, is a mixture of red and yellow, allowing all three primaries to co-exist in the form of two colors. Harris felt this was powerful information for the painter, enabling the artist to experiment within a scheme that operated on sound principles. Prior to his tint-mixing system, he lamented, the "systematic knowledge of colors in general hath been so dark and occult".

ABOVE

At the back of his Natural System of Colours, *Moses Harris provided nine painted examples of compound colors. The results were sharply outlined by a mask of cut-out squares but this could be lifted to show the colors' two individual components, overlapping and leaking beyond the borders of the regular shapes (opposite).*

OPPOSITE

Overlapping horizontal and vertical bands of color reveal the colors that were combined to create the compound. Moses Harris showed that some do not blend successfully at all. Numbers 4, 5 and 6, for example, which mix colors on opposite sides of the color wheel such as red and green, produce "unmeaning negative or neutral colour", a sign that they were precise opposites on the wheel.

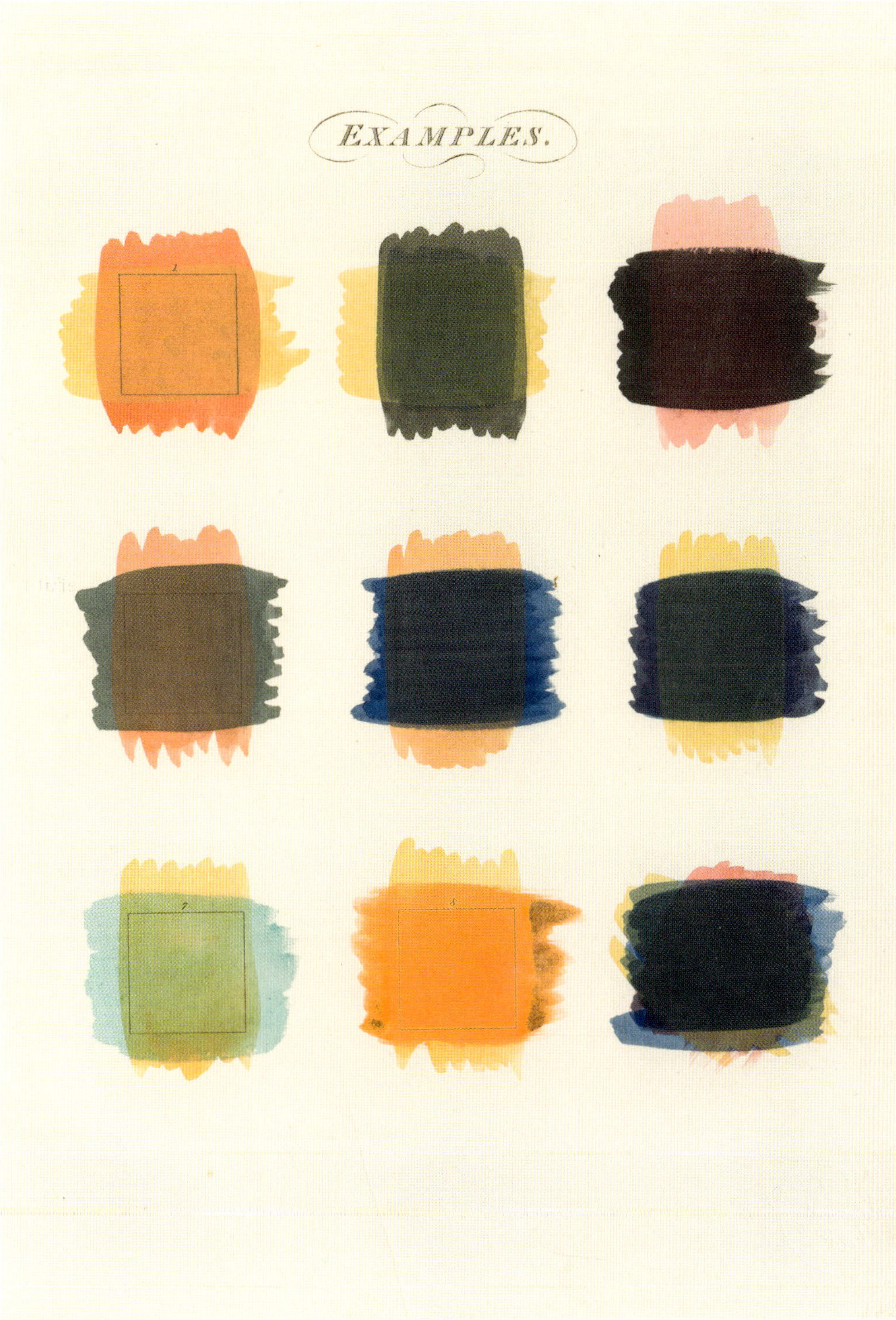
EXAMPLES.

Harris's book is one of the rarest in color history. Only four copies of the first edition have been identified, most of which are missing one of the colored plates. The work was dedicated to Joshua Reynolds, then President of the Royal Academy, suggesting Harris had close links to the artistic community. A second, posthumous, edition appeared in 1811. There were marked disparities in color between the two, suggesting the colorist of the later edition did not have a copy of the first for comparison, although Harris himself was quite specific regarding the pigments he felt came closest to his optimal red, yellow, and blue, favoring cinnabar or vermilion, royal yellow, and ultramarine.

Shortly after the appearance of the *Natural System*, another entomologist, Austria's Ignaz Schiffermüller (1727–c.1806), worked on a system to organize and name the colors of invertebrates (like Harris, he had a particular enthusiasm for butterflies). In 1772, he published *Versuch eines Farben-systems*; literally "attempt toward a color system". Schiffermüller created a genus of colors and identified twelve in his circle. Unlike the sharply delineated segments of Newton and Harris, where color was bounded by lines, Schiffermüller attempted a seamless blend from one to the next, the individual hues clearly distinguished but then dissolving to a blend before re-forming into another discrete hue. The full-strength colors of his circle were named *die blühenden Farben*—"the florid colors"—but he also explored tints and shades in an accompanying series of plates, demonstrating how a single color can become multitudes with the addition of progressive amounts of black or white. Each of the twelve colors on his circle was intended to refer to a separate table where their tints and shades were identified in rows labeled A to M (the full range was never completed). Users could pick a principal color from his circle first and then progress to its nuanced representation in the individual columns to specify it with precision.

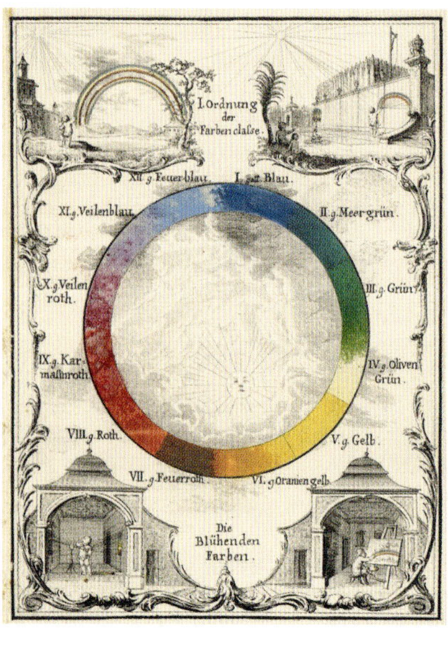

For anyone trying to create a visual representation of hues and their relationships, the eighteenth century was the golden age of the color circle. While there was a degree of artifice in Newton's looping of the spectrum, connecting its end to its beginning, there was also something satisfyingly whole about a circular representation. The user could start at any point and still travel through all the varieties. But color has been squeezed into many different shapes, its geometry never truly fixed. An intriguing color triangle, devised by German astronomer Tobias Mayer (1723–62), for example, was first presented in 1758 in a lecture but did not appear in print until 1775, by which time its creator had been dead for over a decade and Harris and Schiffermüller had published their circles. Mayer agreed all colors could be created by a combination of the three primaries of red, blue, and yellow, but unlike others he felt it important to emphasize that human perception limited the total that could be formed. He was convinced, wrongly, that humans could not differentiate more than twelve gradations

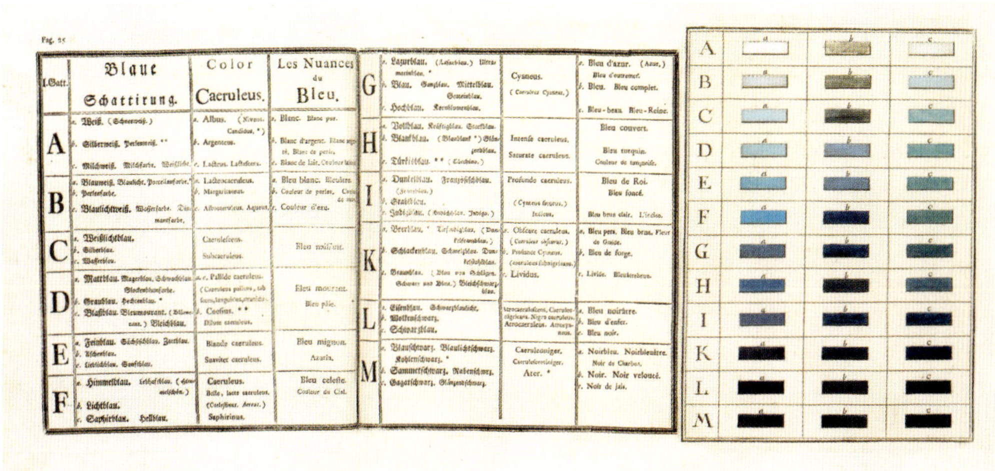

OPPOSITE
Austrian naturalist Ignaz Schiffermüller created a color circle of twelve seamlessly blending "florid" colors in his work of 1772.

ABOVE
Schiffermüller's table of blues modifies the full-strength color found in his circle and presents it as a series of tints and shades.

OVERLEAF
A wide range of optical phenomena as explained by Thomas Young in his Course of Lectures on Natural Philosophy and the Mechanical Arts *(1807). Images represented include a cross section of the human eye, solar halos, and the refraction of light. Fig. 427 is Young's color triangle, with its three primaries of light at each point and all other colors theoretically arising within the surface area of the shape.*

in the blend from one color to another, which made the task of mapping them all rather more manageable and finite. He placed the three primaries at each point of the triangle and introduced his twelve stages between each, then used notation to represent the proportions of each color in twelfths. This made red r12, while a perfect orange was r6y6. Taking all the possible combinations into account, Mayer hit upon a total of ninety-one colors. He also noted these could be modified in ten stages through the addition of black or white, amounting to 910 variants in total. The concept was subsequently expanded by the Alsatian mathematician Johann Heinrich Lambert (1728–77), who transformed Mayer's triangles into a pyramid, creating the first three-dimensional model of color, apparently demonstrating all the achievable colors, tints, and shades in the world. Lambert imagined this would be invaluable to textile merchants: by providing them with a handy reference to individual colors, they could accurately record what they had in stock. His system was based on readily available pigments of the time, so it also had practical application for artists, illustrating how common paints could be effectively mixed. In conceptualizing the arrangement of color, Lambert's model was a breakthrough. It acknowledged fully that color could not be expressed in all its varieties through lines on a page or two-dimensional shapes—there were just too many variables involved for them to survive a flattening.

PLATE XXX

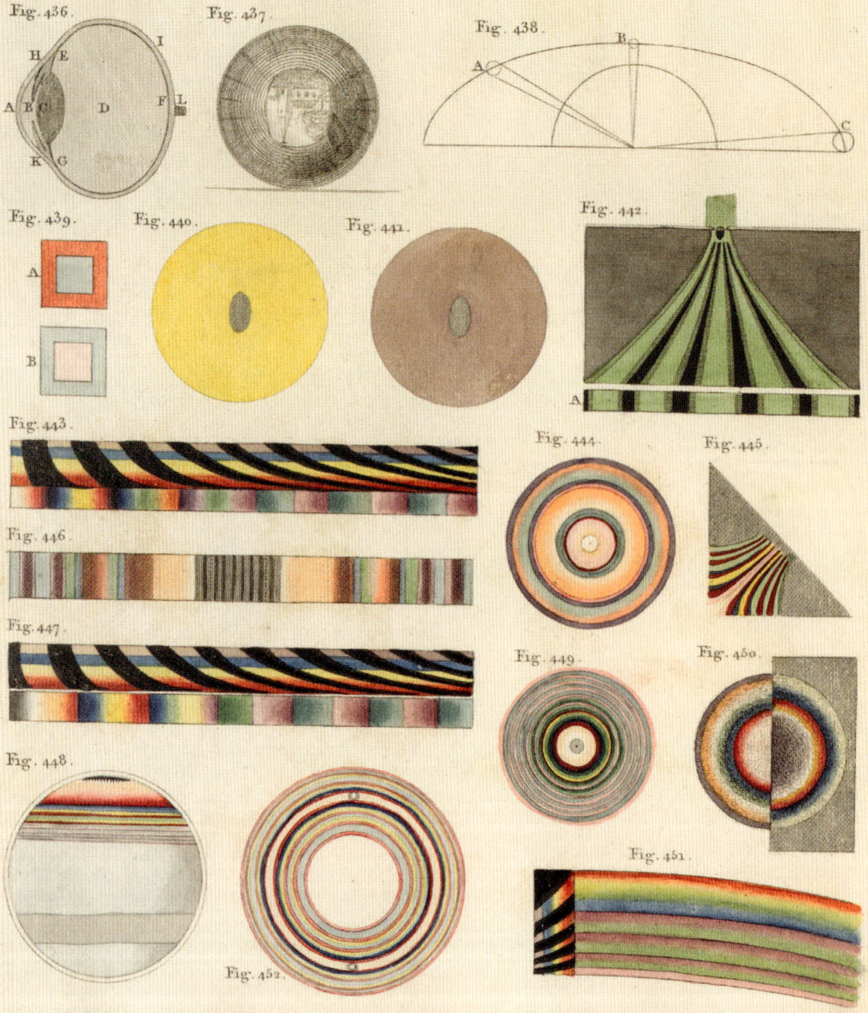

Pub. by J. Johnson, London 1 July 1806.

Joseph Skelton sc.

PLATE XXIX.

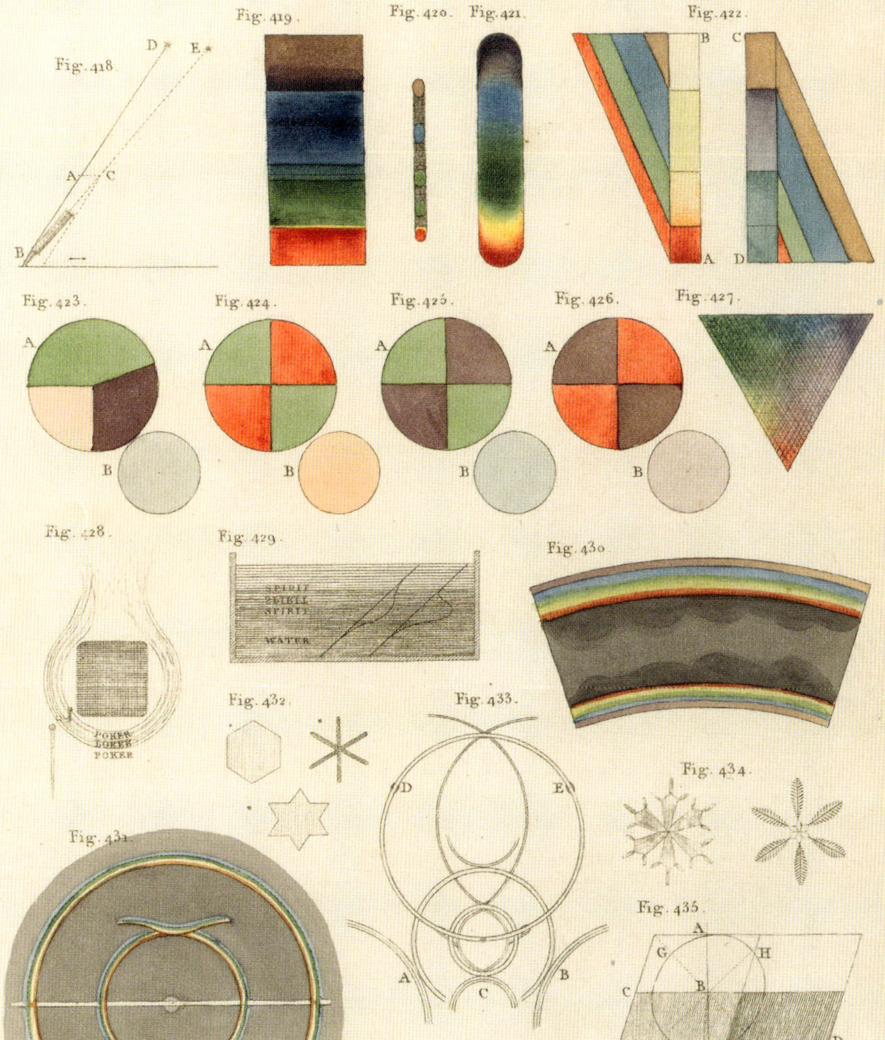

Pub. by J. Johnson London 1 July 1806.

Joseph Skelton sc.

Harris, Schiffermüller, Mayer, and Lambert might all have been able to depict numerous variants of a given color, but offered little to explain how we tell them apart. Physician and physicist Thomas Young (1773–1829) took up the challenge. Great strides in the understanding of color have often been made by polymaths and Young fitted the profile; his wide-ranging activities included consulting on the introduction of gaslight to London's streets, developing tuning methods for musical instruments, and deciphering Egyptian hieroglyphs. He was born a year after Schiffermüller's work appeared, and read Newton's *Opticks* by the age of seventeen, quickly cataloging its shortcomings. He felt light could be shown to exhibit more wavelike qualities than Newton had observed and set about proving this by demonstrating how it created interference patterns where two sources crossed, just as separate sound waves created "beats" where they met. The perfected version of his hypothesis is the famous "double-slit" experiment, but Young's early version echoed Newton's prism display: both involved blocking out the light but letting in a beam through a hole. Young placed a single piece of card in the ray and split it, noting evidence of interference where it fell on the wall.

Like many who studied light, Young's enquiries extended to color by default. Not only was he also able to calculate the individual spectral wavelengths but he set his mind to understanding how we are able to perceive so many different colors in the world at all. Appointed professor of natural philosophy at the Royal Society in 1801, Young delivered ninety-one lectures over two years, including "On the theory of light and colours", given as recipient of the Bakerian medal for his exceptional contribution to science. In this, he explored the hypothesis that humans require three separate types of nerve fiber in the retina to create color in the brain, each responding to different wavelengths of light. Young argued it was impossible that a single type of receptor could "undulate" in every possible way to embody the entire spectrum, convinced that the work must be shared somehow and recombined in the process of perception, just as multiple colors are created from three primaries on the palette. He surmised, for example, that someone seeing the color green was probably experiencing combined undulations from both blue and yellow receptors in tandem. Young first imagined these receptors tuned to red, yellow, and blue, like the primary palette, but he revisited this in a subsequent lecture and concluded that red, green, and violet were more likely candidates: one type for long waves, another for medium and a third for short. This revised theory was an early and largely accurate model of the workings of additive color and human perception. The understanding that red, green, and blue light could be combined to make other colors eventually formed the basis of the "RGB" model of immaterial color, the physics of which underpinned the pictures on color television screens in the twentieth century, and on smartphones in the twenty-first.

OPPOSITE
Johann Lambert's color pyramid, probably the first three-dimensional model of color, was published in 1772. The top of the pyramid represents white and the lightest colors, as if illuminated from above, with darkness increasing on the lower levels.

OVERLEAF
Mary Gartside's colored "blots" in her Essay on Light and Shade *(1805) explored harmonizing colors that arose in shadows and light. Each of the eight abstract shapes was individually hand-painted and each represented a principal color in all its complexity.*

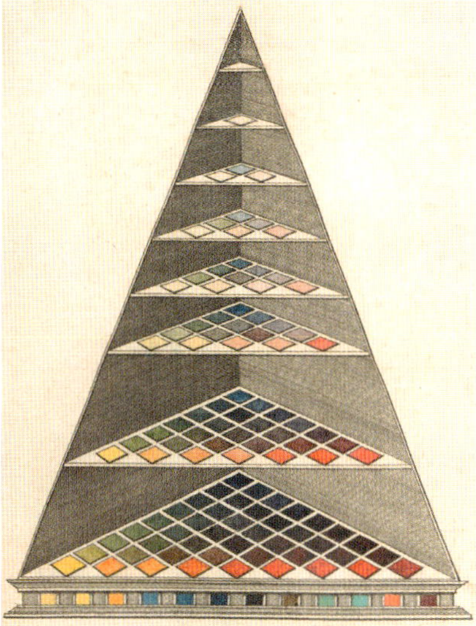

Artists of this era were a natural audience for, and driver of, developments in color theory, and their numbers swelled with the growth of painting as a leisure activity for amateurs. This in turn led to an increase in the publication of painters' manuals but, while color science was still in the early stages of development, such instruction was often a strange meld of the arts and sciences. Those claiming to offer authoritative guidance needed to refer to sound principles that underpinned their instruction. The writings of the obscure Mary Gartside (c.1755–1819), the first woman known to have published a theory of color, were a hybrid of practical tips for painters and rigorous analysis. Gartside contributed a rounded understanding of the nuances of dark and light within color, its three-dimensionality that the painter needed to master to render nature with accuracy and sensitivity. She likened those who would plunge in and try to paint intuitively without a grounding in color theory to mariners who set sail "without helm and compass". Her terminology was modern and accessible, identifying three classes of colors: "light, warm, and cold". In a later work, she similarly described "advancing" and "retiring" color.

Details of Gartside's life are themselves shadowy. She appears to have been an art teacher and published three books, including *An Essay on Light and Shade* (1805), a revised and expanded edition entitled *An Essay on a New Theory of Colours* (1808), and *Ornamental Groups* (1808). The absence of women from color theory, and scientific discourse in general, of this period made her work all the more remarkable. Gartside managed to secrete scientific analysis (of the proportions of colors in the spectrum, for example) and highly schematic models of color into what superficially appeared to be an instruction manual for watercolorists. The key lesson of *Light and Shade* was to master the colors within colors, to understand how those hidden tones in shadow related to the highlights, and to control these relationships through use of "harmonising tints" in order that the wrong colors did not dominate. This was a balancing act and required concentration. "If one colour is out of place,' she warned, "it destroys that harmony of colour."

Gartside illustrated her theory with a remarkable sequence of full-page, hand-colored "blots". Each of these eight different amorphous shapes of pure color embodied the range of others within it that would be glimpsed wherever it caught the light or fell in the shade. Her variants of green, crimson, yellow, and blue illustrated the limits to which single colors could be stretched and the blots embodied how their shadows needed to be expressed in almost counter-intuitive color combinations. The hand-coloring and impressionistic technique (no two copies were exactly alike) lent a sense of something fluid and imprecise to color. Divorced from figurative representation, Gartside's blots seemed to undulate on the page, spreading to its edges like billowing smoke or rolling clouds. Their shapelessness was at odds with the striated diagrams of her contemporaries, where

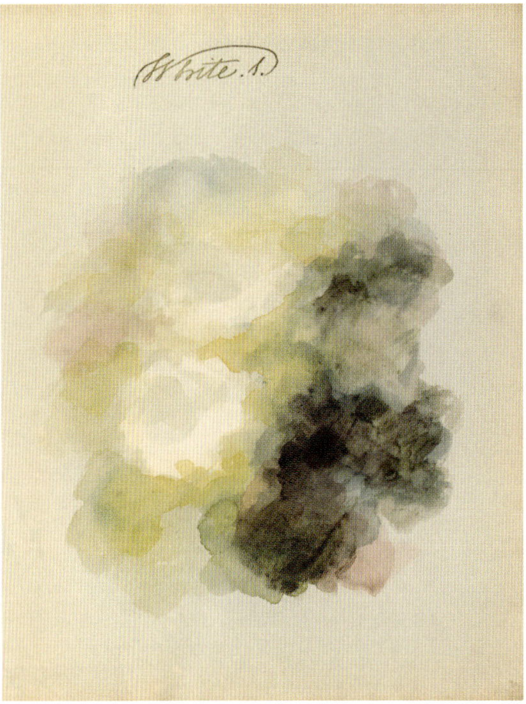
White. 1.

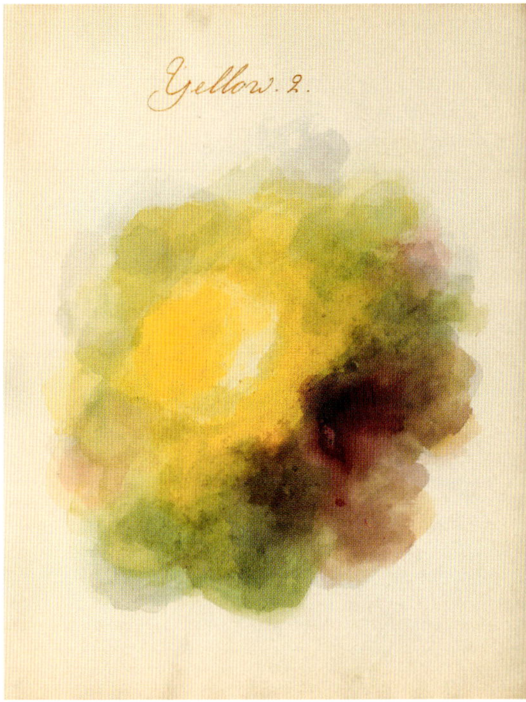
Yellow. 2.

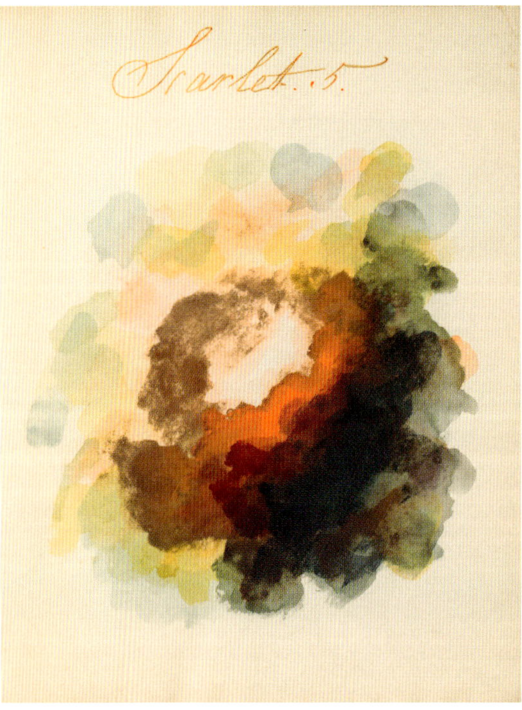
Scarlet. 5.

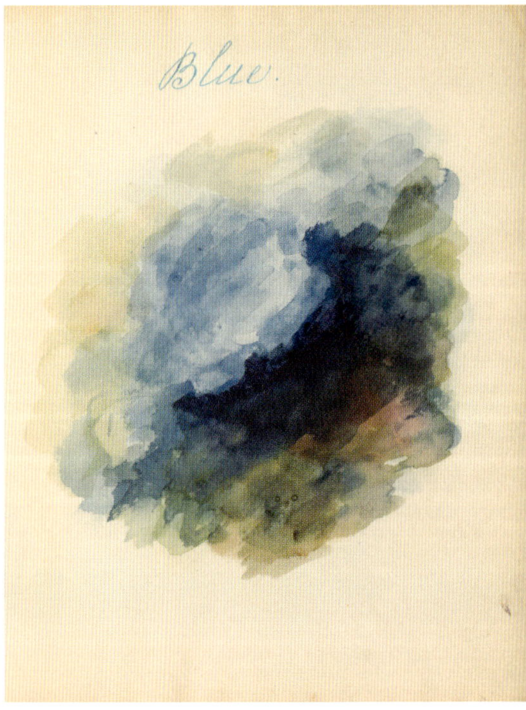
Blue.

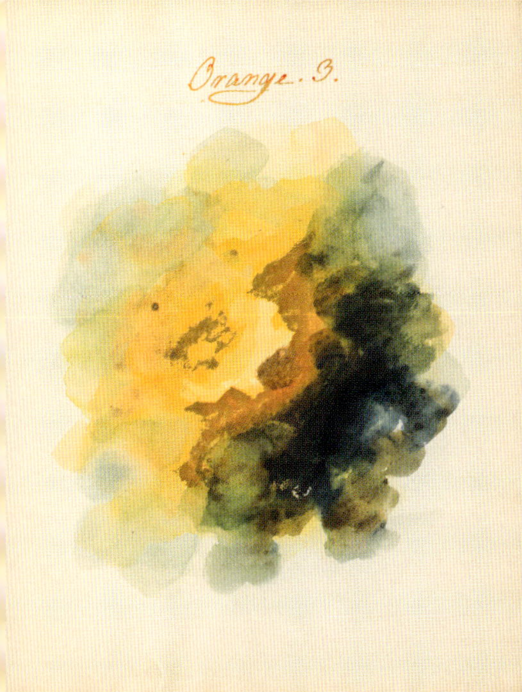
Orange. 3.

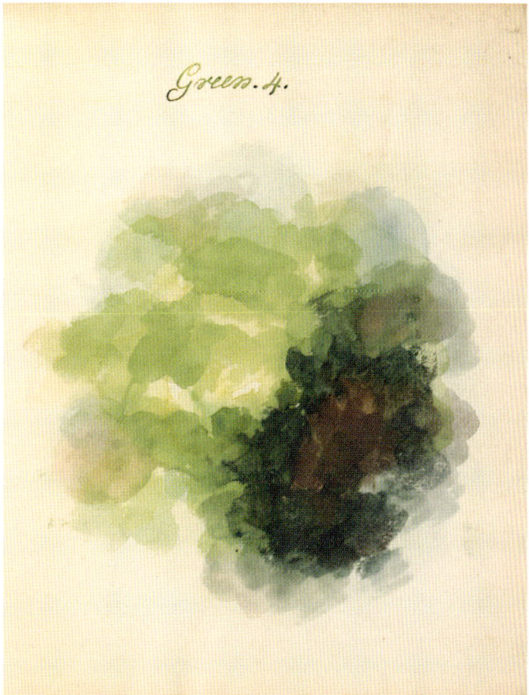
Green. 4.

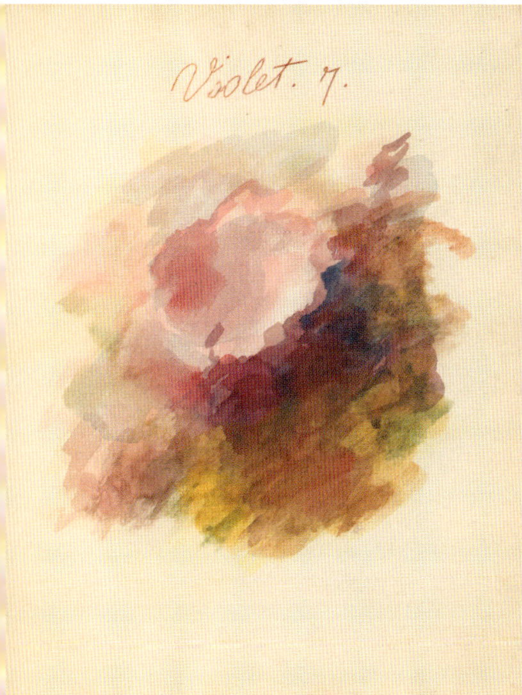
Violet. 7.

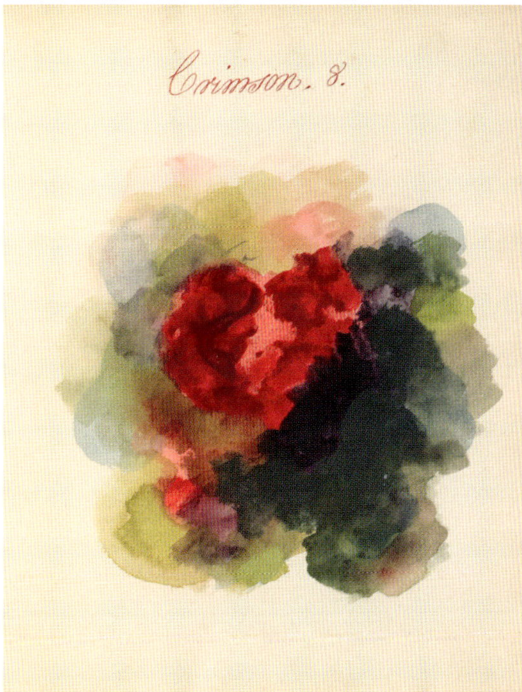
Crimson. 8.

BELOW
Gartside included a table of vibrant "prismatic" colors, but added an intriguing second table of more complex hues. In this, she demonstrated how to make "second order" colors out of secondary colors combining, for example, orange and green to make an unusual, off-key yellow.

OPPOSITE
Mary Gartside's "color ball" in An Essay on Light and Shade *(1805), intended to show the relative brilliancy of the spectrum in an order different from the sequence revealed by Newton. Gartside's colors in this spectrum run G-B-I-V-R-O-Y.*

OVERLEAF
James Sowerby's elaborate multishaped diagram to represent color relationships in his A New Elucidation of Colours *(1809).*

differences in tint and shade were locked into lozenges, triangles, or squares, carved out by the engraver's tools then bounded by line. Gartside's color, by contrast, was a force of nature.

Again, despite focusing on material color, Mary Gartside's work was structured by the order of the spectrum revealed by Newton; no one, it seemed, could tackle the subject without acknowledging his famous prism demonstration and Gartside even summarized it in a footnote (apologetically prefaced "it is scarcely necessary to explain the well-known spectacle alluded to"). *An Essay on Light and Shade* had the sense of a quest to reach an ideal model of harmony that had not yet been achieved. Yet the qualifications and uncertainties frequently admitted in Gartside's text ("others may succeed better than I have done"), were quite at odds with the radicalism and ingenuity of her approach.

One of Gartside's near contemporaries was mineralogist and painter James Sowerby (1757–1822), a well-known specialist in natural history and botany. He was a contributor to *Flora Londinensis,* an eighteenth-century guide to plant life in London, and wrote and illustrated scores of works in the realm of natural science. As a botanical illustrator, he had an innate interest in color and a desire to show how it could be mixed and controlled to aid communication to the public. Sowerby strove to convey nature's marvels with accuracy and consistency and developed his color theories in response to growing frustration at the fugitive nature of the pigments used in his illustrations. He also wanted to contribute to the perfection of a color system that could be standardized across fields of study and he looked forward to a future in which "the mineralogist, the botanist and the zoologist may ... agree in their descriptions ... so as to identify them to all parts of the world."

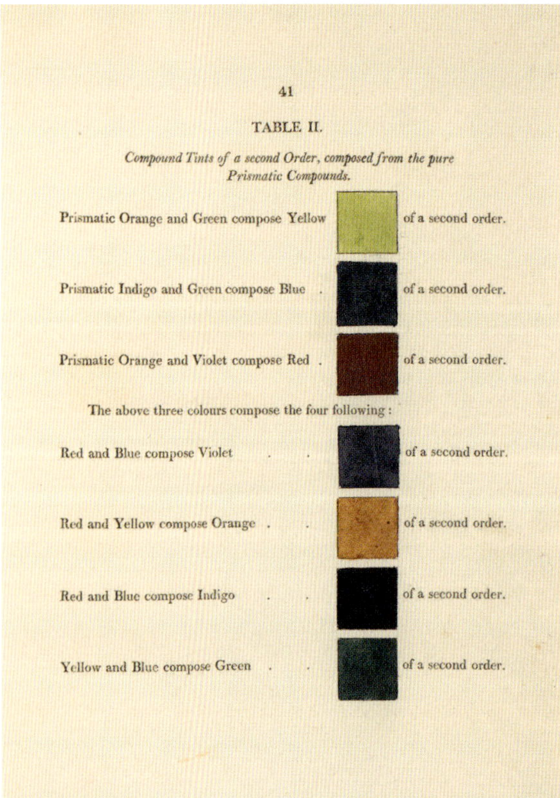
41

TABLE II.

Compound Tints of a second Order, composed from the pure Prismatic Compounds.

Prismatic Orange and Green compose Yellow — of a second order.
Prismatic Indigo and Green compose Blue . — of a second order.
Prismatic Orange and Violet compose Red . — of a second order.

The above three colours compose the four following:

Red and Blue compose Violet . . — of a second order.
Red and Yellow compose Orange . . — of a second order.
Red and Blue compose Indigo . . — of a second order.
Yellow and Blue compose Green . . — of a second order.

Sowerby's book, *A New Elucidation of Colours* (1809), was another attempt to show how all colors grew out of red, yellow, and blue. Once more it was written in the shadow of Newton and even dedicated to his memory. Sowerby also explored "optical mixtures" that resulted when multiple stripes of primary color were applied to paper, and was interested in the effects of contrast. His "chromatometer" system was an early attempt to measure samples of colors that could be created through light. One plate consisted of blocks of black on a white background and the user was expected to refract light through a prism onto this surface, using controlled lighting, and to view the fringes that appeared around the blocks through the prism. This allowed them to measure the amount of

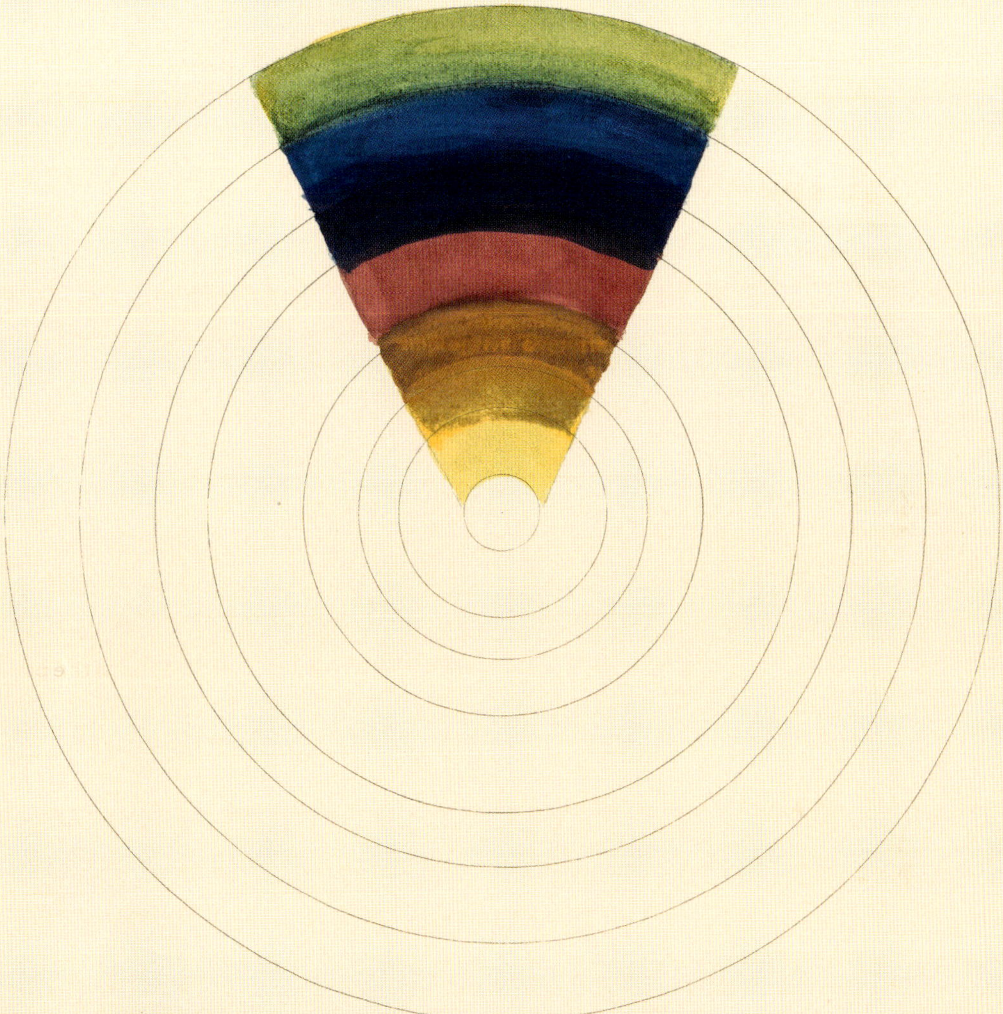

It has already been said that it is not meant to arrange the colours in circles in a Picture; for besides the absurdity of that, the proper quantity of each could not be observed as may be seen here, if each circle was filled with its own colour. Therefore nothing more must be looked for in this than the proper situation for each colour in respect to the others, which is shewn by the small portion that is coloured, and if the effect of Light & Shade on a Ball and concave object is considered, it may be known directly what degree of brilliancy or shade should be given to each colour in every different part of it. This Idea will be of use if kept in mind when Painting Objects from nature.

Published as the Act directs Nov.r 1 1804, by T. Gardiner, Princes Street, Cavendish Square

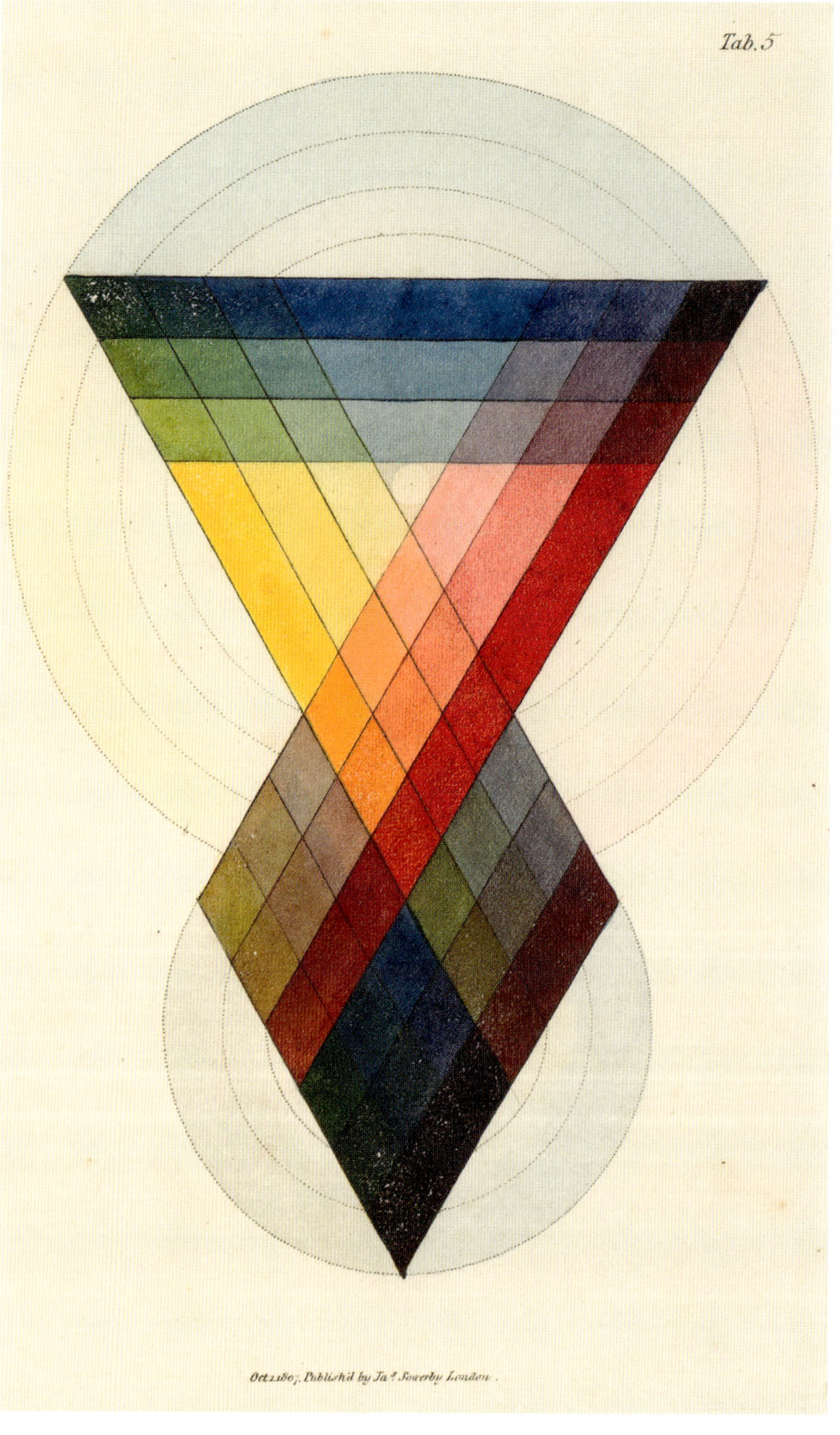
Tab. 5
Oct 2 1807, Publish'd by Ja.s Sowerby London.

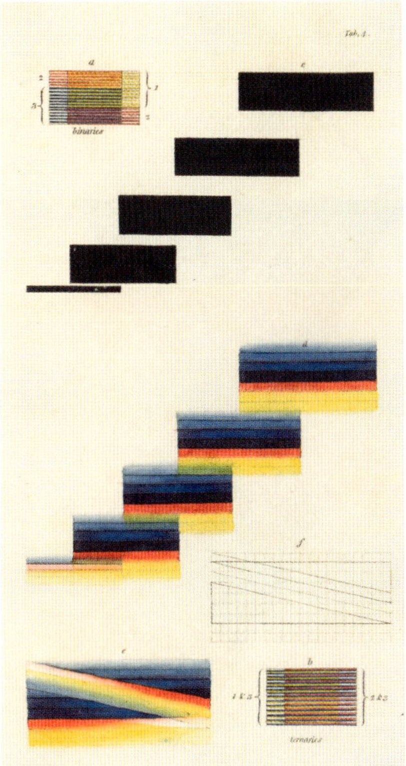

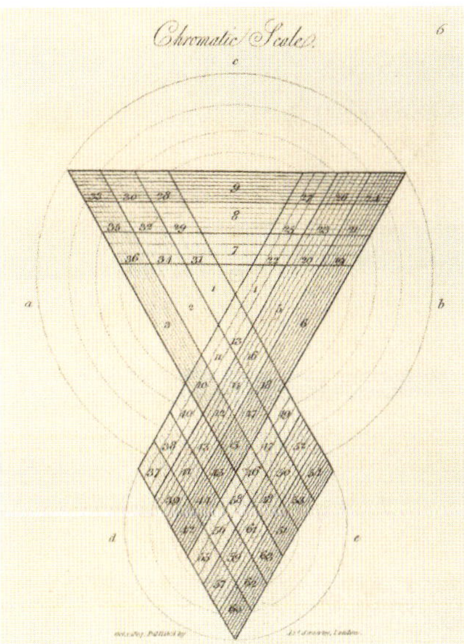

light and darkness within a given hue and Sowerby believed this data could establish harmonious color relationships in an almost mathematical way. In practice, his method was far too fiddly to catch on, especially since ambient light was out of the user's control for any fellow botanists working in the field. Sowerby's illustrations were hand-colored in watercolor and the rather Byzantine but striking geometric design embodying his main color diagram, which incorporated interlocking triangles, diamonds and circles, required some de-coding (helpfully, he included a key).

All these meticulous, and sometimes ravishing, color diagrams, snaking and circling, segmented and blurring, each attempting to capture color in its natural yet ever-changing state, were somewhat hampered by their appearance in books, held flat between hard covers. But almost simultaneously, in continental Europe, Philipp Otto Runge (1777–1810) was laboring with similar concepts of primary colors, darkness and light, while ushering the concepts off the page and trying to mold them into a three-dimensional form. A painter himself, and a player in the German Romantic movement, Runge included artist Caspar David Friedrich and poet Johann Wolfgang von Goethe among his confrères. He first met Goethe in Weimar in 1803 and their rapport was sparked in part by their mutual fascination with color. Both agreed that artists, whose entire practice required mastery of the palette, had been abandoned by scientists who only understood color when it could be explained through the soulless manipulation of light rays. In contrast to the sobriety and rigor of Harris or Gartside, Runge inclined to the mystical and labored to find symbolic relationships between colors. He mapped blue, yellow, and red to the Holy Trinity of Christian belief, for example.

Runge's fascination with color stemmed from his practice as a painter. He held to the principle that "only three colors exist, and these are red, yellow, and blue", as he explained in a letter to Goethe of 3 July 1806. All others were spawned from a blend of these primaries. Others had already made the same uncontentious point, but in attempting to represent precisely

LEFT ABOVE
Sowerby experimented by directing light through a prism onto black surfaces, usually blocks of different widths on a white piece of paper. By aligning the resulting spectrum with the bands of black, he believed it was easier to establish the relative proportions of different colors and their composition.

LEFT BELOW
A numbered, engraved representation of Sowerby's complicated color diagram with coded sections to denote "primaries, binaries, and terneries". Sowerby used lower case, capital, and italicised letters to denote colors in three different strengths. For example, y, y, and Y represented light, middle, and full yellows, respectively.

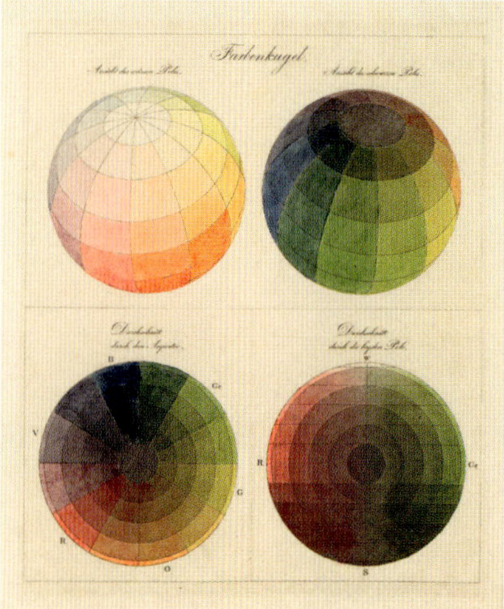

Philipp Otto Runge devised a complex "color sphere" in 1810 to try to reconcile the multiple attributes of different colors and represent them in all their varieties of light and shade. The top two illustrations are the light and dark hemispheres, while the bottom two are horizontal and vertical cross-sections of the sphere. Full-strength colors wrapped around the sphere's "equator".

how colors were created and accommodated within a universal system, Runge developed the unusual notion of a color sphere. Several before had settled for circles, sometimes concentric ones, but Runge believed an extra dimension was required to better express gradations. Three years later, his model was published as *Farben-Kugel* (*Color Sphere*, 1810). In his sphere, black and white formed the top and bottom poles to reflect gradations of darkness, with gray at the core. From this axis, different hues could wrap around the globe, all spaced at equal distances from pure white or black, expressed in different degrees of darkness and light, with the purest colors around the "equator". His illustrated chart contained twelve colors, each inching toward the central gray. While aesthetically satisfying, the even spread of color and tone was hard to replicate in practice and assumed a uniformity of behavior and range that different colors did not possess. Runge was one of the first of many to discover that, however elegant the scheme, color does not always play ball and resists being shaped to fit geometrical forms. He died, aged thirty-three, in the year of his work's publication, never able to refine his promising thinking further.

Most of Newton's successors worked independently to secure the foundations of his theory and extend it. The German poet Johann Wolfgang von Goethe (1749–1832), however, just wanted to blow the whole thing up. Goethe's ideas and observations were summarized in his totemic yet controversial *Zur Farbenlehre* (*Theory of Colors*, 1810), which included a prolonged assault on Newton, a conflagration sparked by the clash where art met science and found its explanations wanting. The book originally appeared in three volumes: an account of Goethe's observations, including his own experiments with prisms; a polemical section against Newton; and a historical section. The first English edition of 1840 omitted the entire anti-Newton section, with translator Charles Eastlake mindful of the problems of publishing a work so hostile toward a national treasure, and troubled by the vehemence of Goethe's language. "There can be no doubt," Eastlake wrote in his preface, "that much of the opposition Goethe met with was to be attributed to the manner as well as to the substance of his statements."

Goethe's agenda was that of a German Romantic whose interest in color was piqued when he found the artists in his milieu had no way of articulating its rules. Though lacking a scientific background, he set about exhaustively experimenting over decades, writing 2,000 pages on the subject between 1790 and 1823. He believed his dedication and subjective experience endowed him with special insight, pronouncing: "I am the only person who knows the truth in the difficult science of colors"—a bold claim in a crowded field.

What was it in Newton's observations that so incensed the poet, and how could the prism experiment be disputed when its physical evidence of the spectrum could be so easily conjured for all to see? Where Newton demonstrated that all color is drawn from within pure white light, Goethe's controversial thesis held that colors arose through a combination of light and dark, their interplay moderated through a medium. When he looked through a prism at a white wall, he argued, the wall stayed white, but when he moved the prism across shadowed areas, glimmers of color emerged from the dark corners. Goethe also experimented with the effects of prisms of different lengths, believing Newton's findings seemed convincing simply because his prism was placed in a sweet spot to create a perfect spectrum (as indeed it was), a lucky break that demonstrated nothing universal. He also fervently believed that exploring light as Newton did, in artificial and controlled conditions, missed the point entirely and that it must be investigated through field work in normal light, without the need to draw blinds and poke holes in them. As he wrote: "It didn't take long before I knew here was something significant about color to be brought forth, and I spoke as through an instinct out loud, that the Newtonian teachings were false." The prism was not a neutral tool, as Newton had it, but played an active role in the creation of color. Color, Goethe argued, was produced by light, "as well as by what stands against it," modified by a "turbid medium", whatever light passed through on its travels, be that air, dust, water droplets—or a prism. Darkness and shadows were component parts of color, not an absence of it. Look, he argued, how a dimmer white light becomes yellow, or a lightening black color inches toward dark blue.

While some of the behaviors he described seemed reasonable and replicable, Goethe was not formulating a scientific theory and nor did he aspire to. "Search nothing beyond the phenomena," he counseled, "they themselves are the theory." Positioning himself against Newton in both approach and conclusions, he aimed to rescue color from "atomic abstraction" and return it to the "dynamic flow of life and action". Goethe wanted to foreground the human observer and believed the most accurate and trustworthy form of color measurement was the human eye. In some respects, his views were advanced, in his description of the physiological effects of color on the viewer, for example, and the behavior of color contrast. His understanding of color perception, which assumed the interaction of opponent pairs of colors, was decades ahead of the science, and inspired the arrangement of his color wheel, in which colors that naturally evoked one another appeared on opposing sides. In Goethe's system, specific pairings were key and likened to poles of a magnet, or equivalent to a warm and cold contrast: blue-yellow, red-green; orange-violet. His circle could be used to create harmonies or contrasts, depending on whether the viewer approached it from the left or right side. He also assigned numbers to individual colors to denote their relative luminosity: yellow scored a nine, for example, with blue just a four.

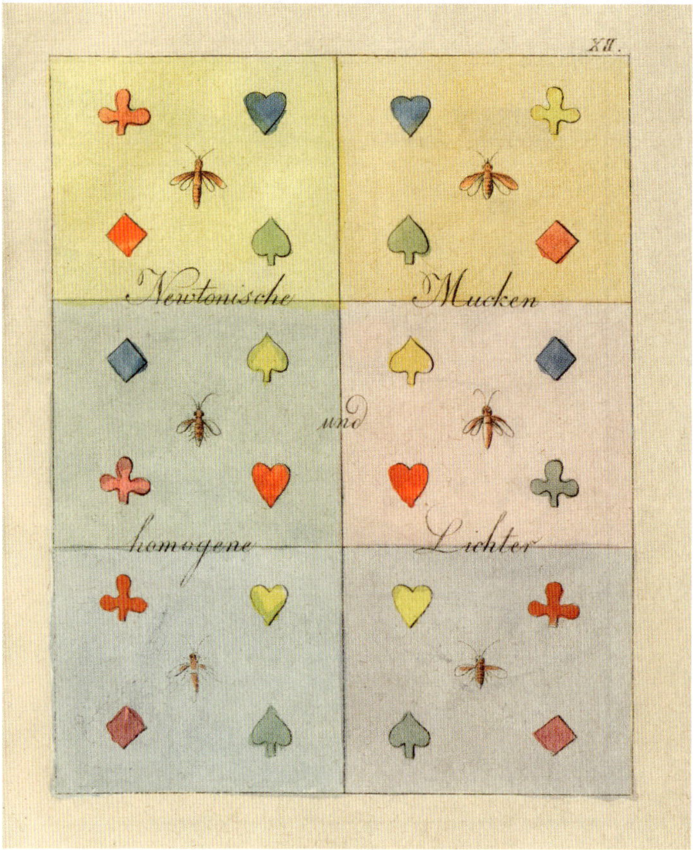

ABOVE

Plate XII of Goethe's Theory of Colors *(1810) includes six squares of main colors on which the suits of playing cards and illustrations of insects have been superimposed. Goethe instructed readers to view these through a prism when the ambient light matched the background color. Newton claimed the shapes would all appear dark, but Goethe disputed this and observed more prismatic colors arising at the edges.*

OPPOSITE

Several of the elements of Plate I in Goethe's Theory of Colors *(1810) explore the effects of acyanopsia, a type of color blindness. The color wheel in the top right contains an inner ring to represent how the six main colors are experienced by someone with the condition. The bottom landscape represents how such a scene might appear to the same person.*

Though controversial, Goethe's work on color found a huge and receptive readership. It was read by Beethoven, Schopenhauer, Caspar David Friedrich, and J.M.W. Turner. Later admirers included the Pre-Raphaelites, Wassily Kandinsky, and Werner Heisenberg. Its emphasis on day-to-day experiments and observations may have helped it find an audience of practitioners more readily than Newton. However, while evidently opposed to Newton's analytical approach and conclusions, Goethe's emphasis on the personal experience of color was not wholly antithetical to them. Color studies in the main struggle to reconcile the tension between objectivity and subjectivity in the discipline, when its very subject exists both out in the world awaiting measurement and deep inside the mind, triggering feelings. The two stances invite us to examine the nature of color from opposite ends of the telescope: Newton determined color in the world, Goethe divined color in the psyche. In the great battle of ideas between the two, sitting on the fence may be as valid as picking a side.

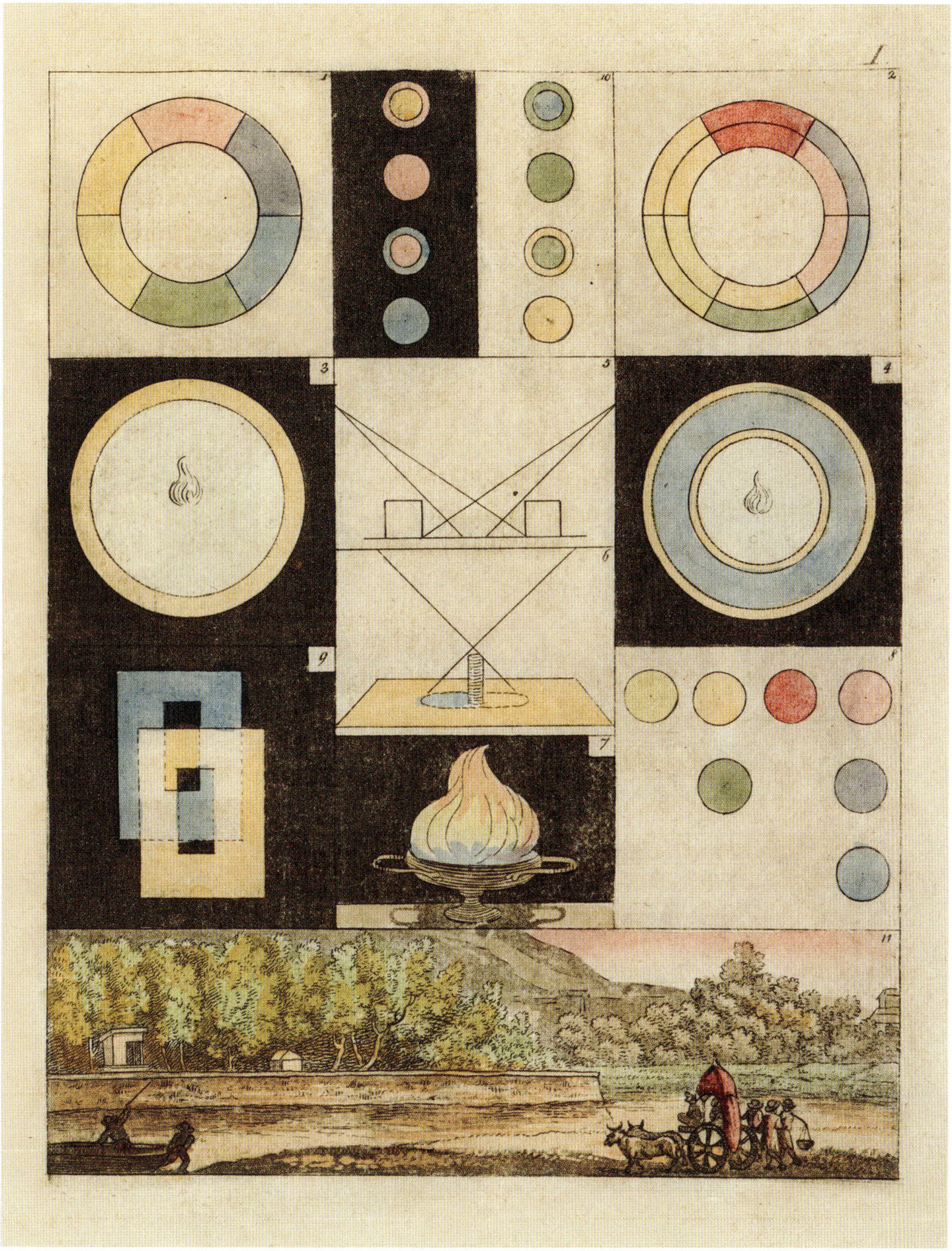

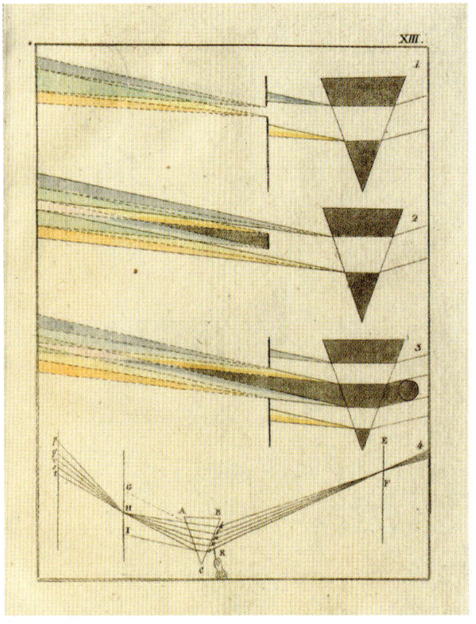

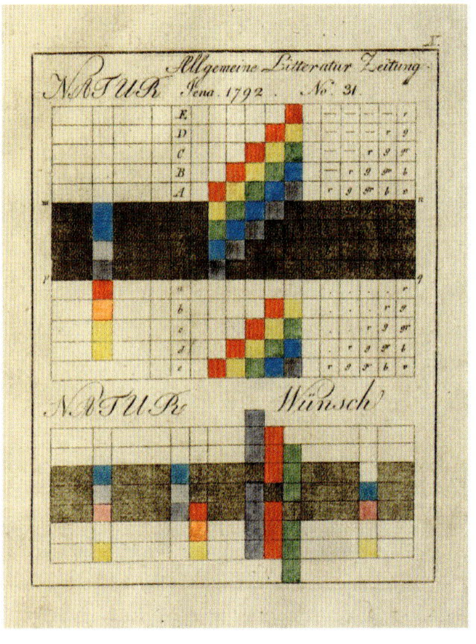

TOP
In Plate XIII, Goethe explored his contention that spectra arose in colored boundaries between darkness and light, which he thought prisms helped reveal rather than create.

ABOVE
Plate X is one of a pair in which Goethe attacked Newton and his followers. In this example, he ridiculed what he saw as an overly schematic and reductive attempt by Wunsch, a student of Newton, to arrange the spectral colors in table order.

By the 1810s, artists' paints and pigments were improving, bolstered by French pharmacist Louis-Nicolas Vauquelin's discovery of chromium. This mineral, derived from an unusual form of lead chromate, was the basis of several new synthetic colors, including rich and warming additions to the palette, such as chrome yellow and chrome orange. As color became more attainable, and pliable, a glut of instructional painting manuals appeared on the market. And the color kept coming. In 1828, ultramarine was finally successfully synthesized by another French chemist, Jean-Baptiste Guimet, from a formula that included quartz and sulphur. The French Society for Encouragement of National Industry had offered a cash prize to incentivize discovery of an artificial alternative to this most precious of pigments, and Guimet duly claimed his reward.

Two other figures rounded out this period of quantification and refinement of color systems. Charles Hayter (1761–1835) and George Field (1777–1854) represented the involvement of more commercial trades in the realm of color scholarship, and each attempted to stake a claim to color systems in their fields. Hayter was an architect-turned-miniaturist. A talented painter, he taught perspective to Princess Charlotte of the United Kingdom, George IV's daughter, who also acted as his patron. The model in his *New Practical Treatise on the Three Primitive Colours Assumed as a Perfect System of Rudimental Information* (1826) was not dissimilar to that of Moses Harris, but he did not acknowledge the debt, believing instead that he was building on the legacy of the great natural philosophers Newton and Young. He did, however, grapple with the fundamental differences between material and immaterial color, and explored more deeply the addition of white and black to expand the possible variants of a given color. Hayter called his three color wheels "compasses" and they all represented blends of red lake, gamboge, and Prussian blue. He also explored how primary, secondary, and tertiary colors in different degrees of saturation behaved as they darkened.

George Field was an English chemist who produced two influential works on color theory, *Chromatics* (1817) and *Chromatography* (1835). His professional role, in which he confected and perfected pigments for artists' use, grew out of frustration at his inability to obtain madder from Holland. In response, he attempted to cultivate the plant in England, something no one had successfully done before. His work preparing commercial pigments, particularly the ravishing madder lakes he eventually achieved, won him a gold medal from the Society of Arts.

To further his practice, he built and ran a number of factories, which he called "elaboratories", as places to experiment with pigments and improve the processes for their synthesis or extraction. Unlike the many chemists who discovered colors as a by-product or a sideline of other activities, color for Field was always the end goal. His allegiance was to the quality and purity of hues

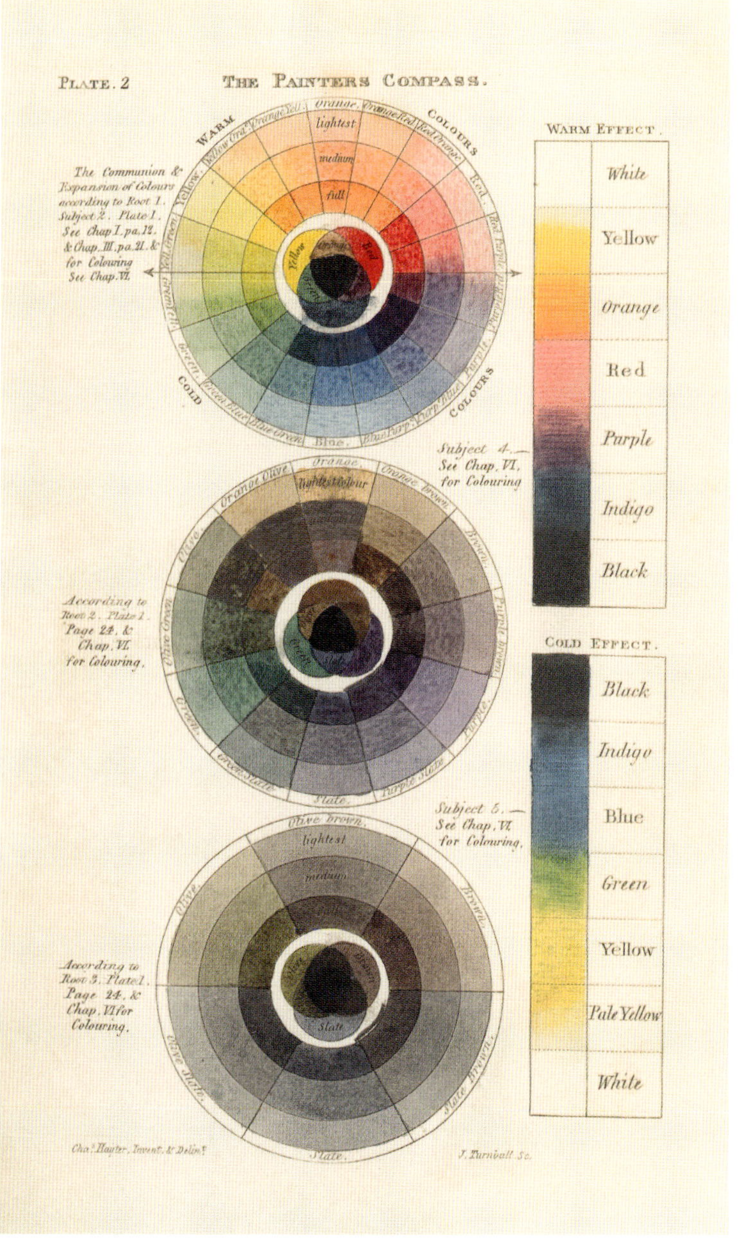

LEFT

Charles Hayter's scheme in his New Practical Treatise on the Three Primitive Colours *(1826) included discrete diagrams for primary, secondary, and tertiary colors. On the right are two paths from black to white, one made up of warm colors and the other of cold.*

OVERLEAF LEFT

The colors from Hayter's three circles are expressed as tints and shades and in stronger and weaker variants. The circle at the bottom is an illustration of a disc composed of the primaries. If colored according to the proportions, it should, in theory at least, appear white if spun at sufficiently high speed.

OVERLEAF RIGHT

The frontispiece of chemist George Field's Chromatography *(1835). Field's color wheel contains six principal hues and the circle includes descriptive labels for opposing pairs of colors such as "hot/cold" and "advancing/retiring".*

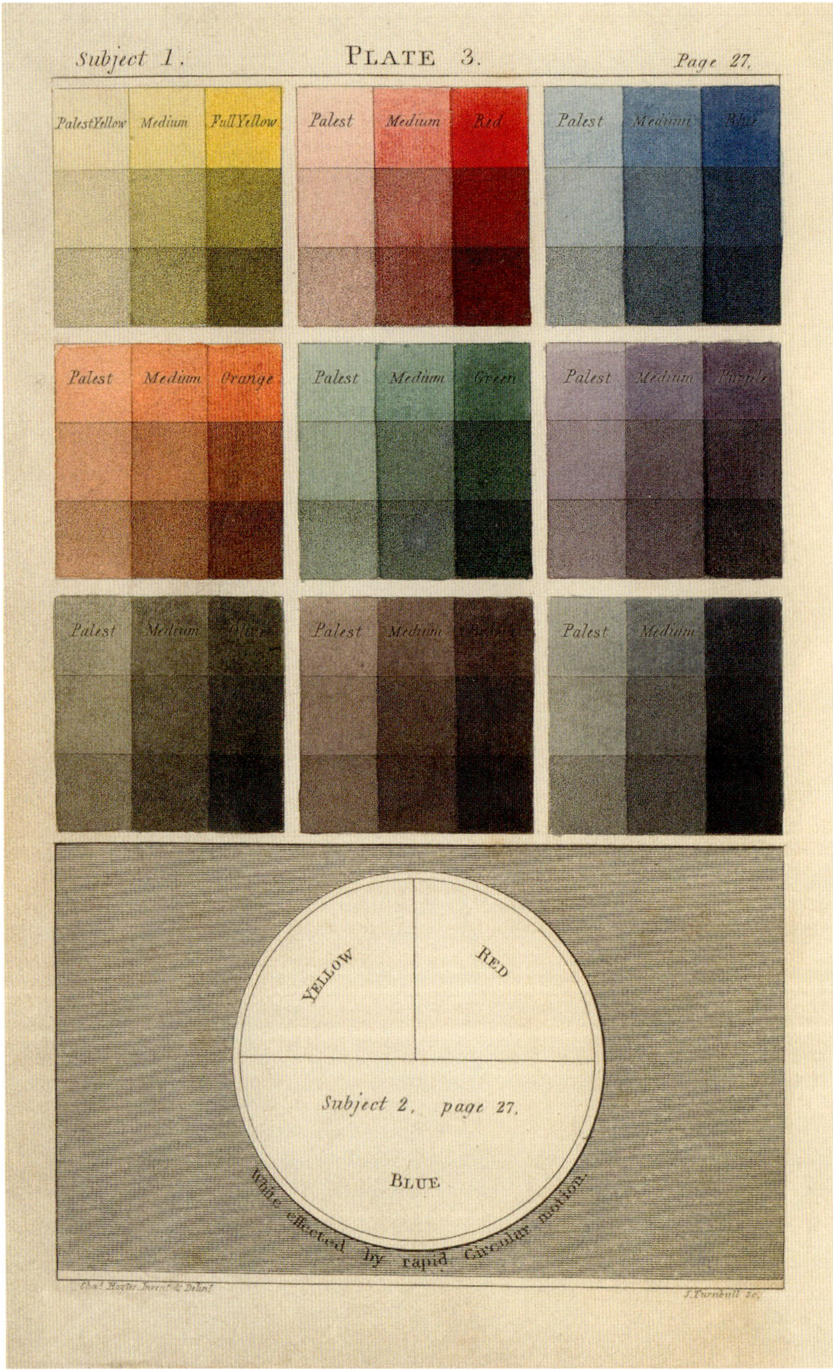
Subject 1.
PLATE 3.
Page 27.
Palest Yellow
Medium
Full Yellow
Palest
Medium
Red
Palest
Medium
Palest
Medium
Orange
Palest
Medium
Green
Palest
Medium
Palest
Medium
Palest
Medium
Palest
Medium
YELLOW
RED
Subject 2, page 27.
BLUE
White effected by rapid Circular motion.

Fig. 1
Experiment I.

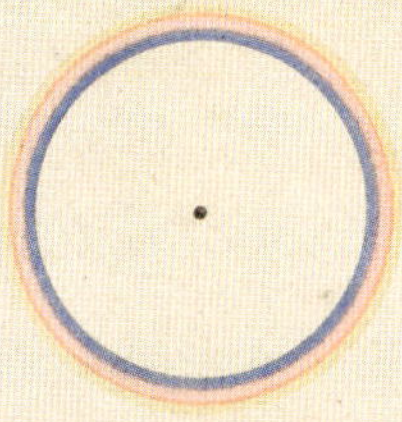

Chromatic Equivalents.

Fig. 2. Exp. XXVIII.

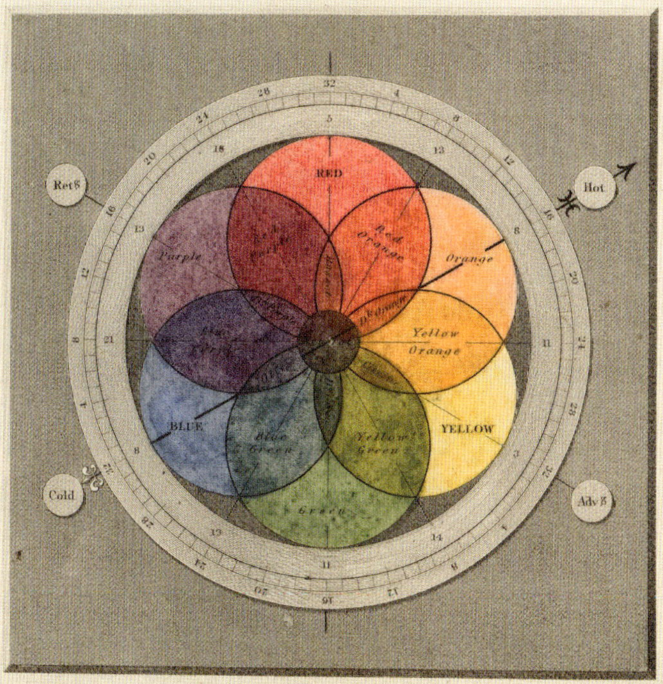

Definitive or Fundamental Scale of Colours

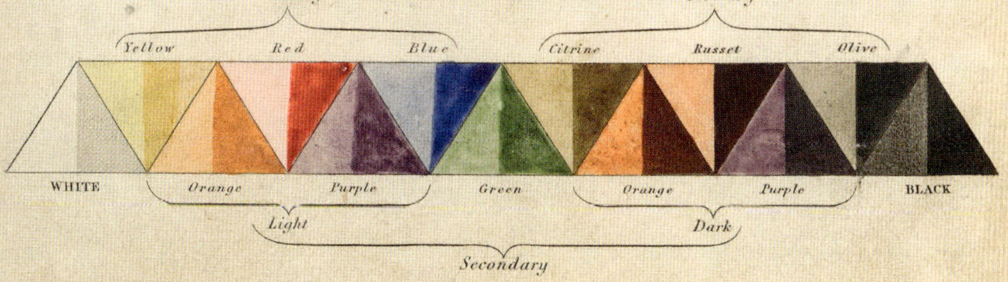

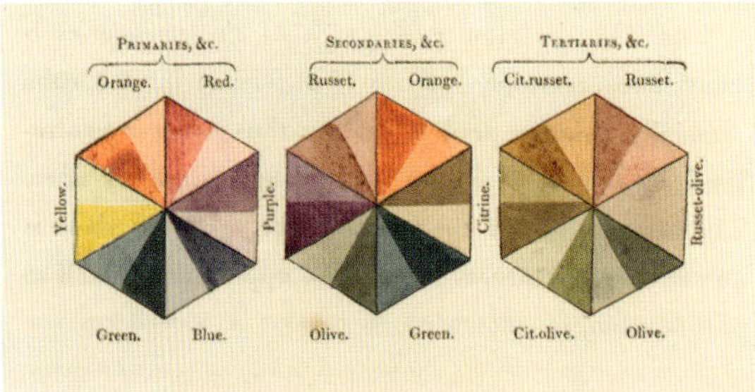

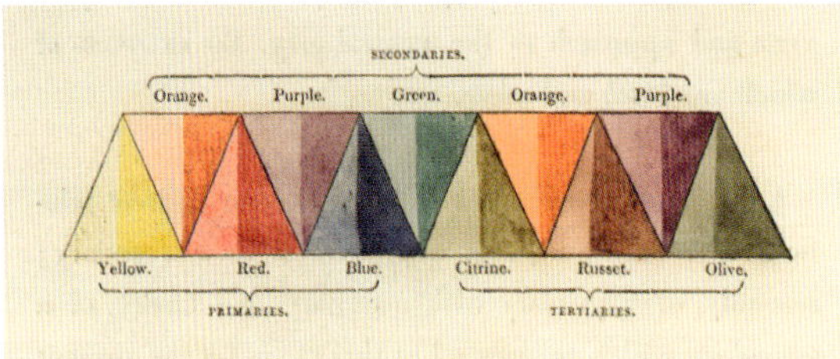

TOP
Example X from Field's Chromatics *(1817) demonstrated how compounds could create perfect neutrals but the author stressed the need to pay attention to how some colors predominate, with blue strongest among the primaries, and red more dominant than yellow.*

ABOVE
In this example from Chromatics, *Field illustrated how primary colors are "neutralized" by the secondary color composed of the other two primaries: "thus blue is neutralized or extinguished by orange, red by green, and yellow by purple".*

he produced, regardless of the methods by which they were obtained. He valued natural sources, preferring traditional ultramarine over Guimet's synthetic rival, but he also moved on from convention wherever he could. After dabbling with classical methods of manufacturing Indian yellow (notoriously believed to be derived from the urine of cows fed on mango leaves), for example, he turned instead to platinum to create his own lemon yellow. His influence on the artistic community was deep, and he supplied a number of artists and trades with the latest pigments, including J.M.W. Turner and the founders of Winsor & Newton, manufacturer of art materials.

Field's first published work, *Chromatics* (1817), put forward a theory of harmony that fused different concepts in circulation at the time. He was particularly driven by a desire to relate the colors of the spectrum to the musical scale (see p.208) and reasserted a link between the primary colors and the Holy Trinity of Christian belief, echoing Runge's recently published work. Field's organization of color was also predicated on an anti-Newtonian physics that argued, as Goethe had, that blue emerged from shadow and yellow grew out of the light. For Field, red fell in the middle: it weakened when in light and deepened when in shade; it warmed up when it moved toward yellow and cooled down toward blue. Field's echoes of German thought may have just been coincidence, however, as neither work had been translated into English at the time *Chromatics* was published.

The later *Chromatography* (1835) was a long-gestating work, the product of years of experimentation and note-taking. Less theoretical and more practical than its predecessor, the book was essentially a guide to different pigments, their composition, and qualities. Its solitary color illustration represented Field's circle of six principal colors: red, yellow, blue, orange, green, and purple. He believed in the power of each to create "total harmony" but only the right proportions of the correct colors could do this and his design contained numbers to denote the required arrangement. The proportions were worked out with the aid of Field's "metrochrome", a device of his own invention composed of red, yellow, and blue vessels, through which colored light could be projected to establish the proportions of each primary within it. In practice, the device was difficult to master and almost impossible to calibrate. Field's color diagram in *Chromatography* was a little more accessible. His symmetrical design of overlapping circles allowed anyone to find the perfect contrast to a given color by locating its equivalent opposite. He also included terminology to describe the qualities of the colors, including "hot" and "cold," and "retiring" and "advancing." Each pair of terms was placed at polar opposites on the wheel.

Field's work as a chemist continued to inform much of his approach, and he included practical advice on the fastness or fugacity of certain pigments and their overall handling. He cautioned against enthusiasm for newly invented pigments and processes, noting, for example, that reds derived from iodine were "chameleon colors" compared with the dependable vermilion, while the blues derived from cobalt, "beautiful and abundant as they are", could never outshine ultramarine. In his analysis of individual colors, Field also scattered numerous literary extracts across the pages, lyrical references to the spectrum from Shakespeare, Spenser, and Milton. In parts, *Chromatography* resembled little more than a dictionary of color quotations, but Field's intent was to provide a body of evidence for the psychological and symbolic dimensions of individual colors.

The rest of his book was essentially an encyclopedia of pigments, one color family per chapter. A section on yellow, for example, carefully surveyed sixteen varieties, including chrome, Naples, orpiment, gamboge, and Indian. Some entries were further subdivided and he included five types of ochre alone. Subscribers to the first edition of *Chromatography* included John Constable, William Etty, and J.M.W. Turner. The work underwent several reprints and remained popular for decades, but quite how useful his readers found a book that tried to do several different things at once was another matter. John Ruskin summed up the ambivalence: "If you wish to take up coloring seriously, you had better get Field's *Chromatography* at once; only do not attend to anything it says about principles or harmonies of color, but only to its statements of practical serviceableness to pigments, and of their operations on each other when mixed." The review in the *Athenaeum* was more scathing, judging the whole exercise "a most unwise pandering to the public taste for that gay lady—Colour."

Field was a transitional figure, anticipating the full industrialization of color. While the natural philosophers, writers, and artists of the age had lofty aims of modeling perfect color systems to mirror nature, the industrial and scientific revolutions ground away in the background. Despite the aesthetic charms of many of the color diagrams devised throughout this period, they all encountered, and were qualified by, the limitation of available pigments and the shortcomings of color printing. As advances in chemistry progressed, however, with improvements to the creation of synthetic dyes and pigments, from Prussian blue to Scheele's green, the forces of commerce inexorably came into play. These ushered the branching applications of theory into a world where color had a price, and a more perfect or unusual color had a higher one. Some of the most extraordinary discoveries, about both our perception of color, and the colors waiting to be unleashed through chemistry, were bubbling away, just around the corner.

4

THE COLOR OF

NATURE

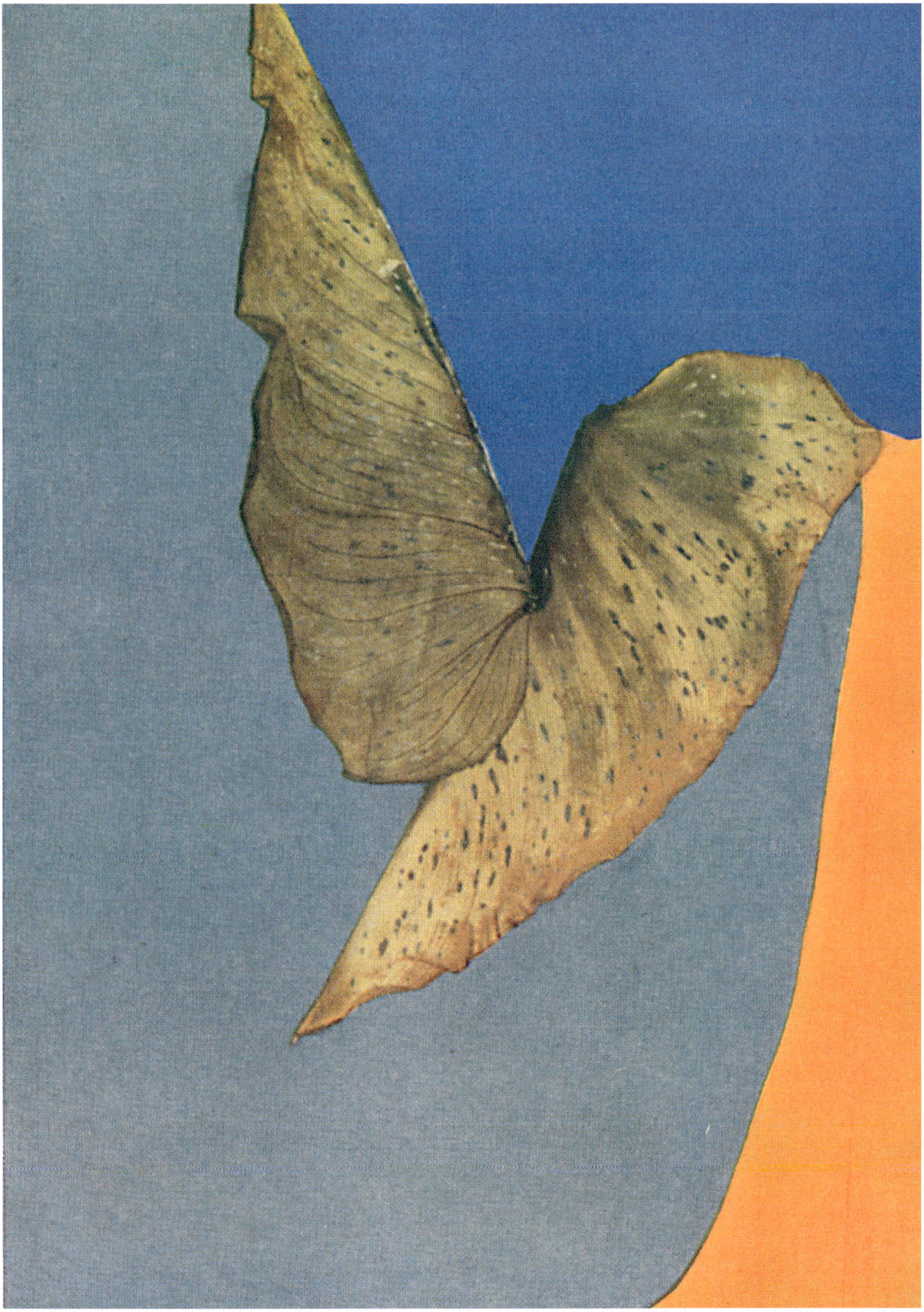

In the modern world of limitless color choices, of hot pinks and fluorescent yellows, it is too easy to forget what an artificial state of affairs this is. For most of human existence, the polychromy we experienced was limited to the peacocking displays of nature. When attempts to catalog all known colors gathered pace in the eighteenth century, some scholars even believed that the natural world already contained all the colors it was possible for a human to see, and that these just needed to be cataloged.

Even with its preponderance of muted greens and slates, nature has a way with dramatic contrast: historically, a splash of red berries against green foliage was a warning, or a temptation. Early pigments and dyes syphoned color from animals, plants, and minerals. Ochre, extracted from clay, was a founding pigment for cultures around the world, used in the cave drawings of Lascaux from around 40,000 BCE, and in the rituals of the ancient Egyptians and the indigenous peoples of Australia and North America. With each new discovery over many thousands of years, the palette broadened. By the seventeenth century, for example, many reds were available, whether drawn from cinnabar (vermilion) or beetles (cochineal). Nature supplied a continuous flow of color for human hands to repurpose.

In the eighteenth and nineteenth centuries, botanists' increasing knowledge of the natural world was accompanied by a parallel revolution in the description of the colors of flora and fauna; practitioners of the former were often adventurers in the latter by necessity. Richard Waller (*c.*1660-1715) was an early pioneer who created a

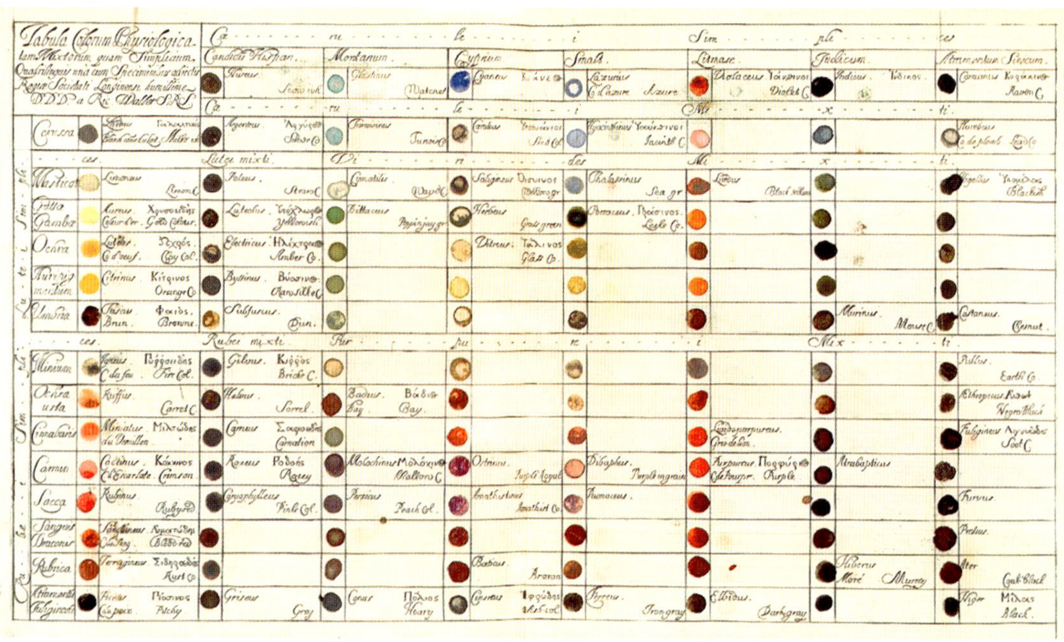

reference point for specimens from nature in his *Catalogue of Simple and Mixt Colours* (1686), published by the Royal Society. Displaying 119 hand-colored, tabulated hues, Waller's chart allowed for cross-referencing with samples encountered in the wild. Yet in practice, the chart was ahead of its time and failed to find a large enough community to propel it to the status of a standard. More successful was entomologist Moses Harris (1730–c.1787, see p.75). As well as creating a revolutionary pair of color wheels in his *Natural System of Colours* (c.1766), Harris included another in his later *Exposition of English Insects* (1776) specifically to allow readers to visualize the colors of the insects he described. In four concentric circles, the palette moved outwards from pure hues (more butterfly than beetle) to progressively muddier, more "natural"-looking colors such as cream and nut brown. In practice, many readers razored out the page containing the color wheel to provide a portable reference tool.

Rendering color in the wild was tricky and the elements were often against the plucky botanical illustrators. A palette of brilliant petals and verdant foliage was difficult to get down in the open air, and samples from distant lands often decayed on the way home once uprooted from their natural ecosystem. Perhaps the greatest botanical illustrator of all time, Ferdinand Bauer (1760–1826), had a simple solution: remove color from working sketches entirely and reassemble it when safely back home. Bauer first joined Oxford's professor of botany John Sibthorp on expeditions to Greece and the Levant to gather samples of flowers and later produced the sumptuous

PREVIOUS PAGE
Plate XXV-5 from Josef Albers's *Interaction of Color* (1963) and one of his students' "Fall leaf studies". In this exercise, Albers instructed the class to collect autumn leaves and combine them with colored paper to make collages with unusual juxtapositions of color.

OPPOSITE
The "Tabula Colorum" of 119 colors from Richard Waller's *Catalogue of Simple and Mixt Colours* in *Philosophical Transactions of the Royal Society of London*, vol. 6 (1688). Waller was attempting to provide a universal reference for colors in nature.

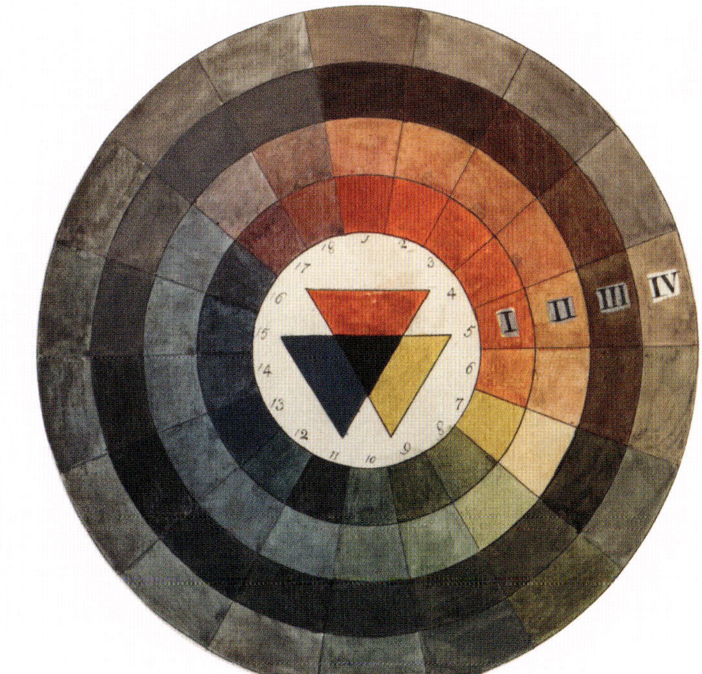

RIGHT
Entomologist Moses Harris's four-ring color wheel for identifying specimens, as included in his *Exposition of English Insects* (1776).

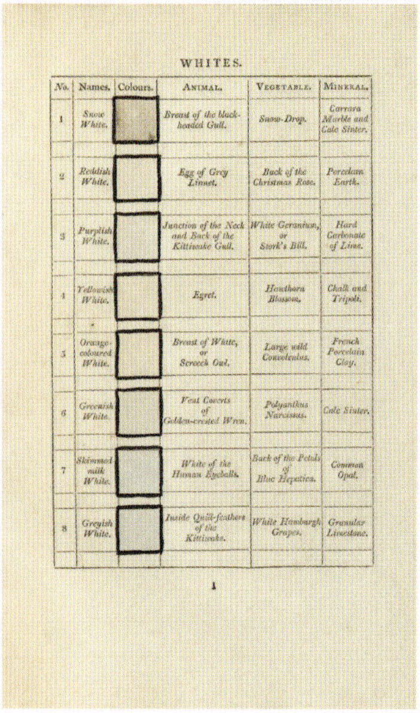

WHITES.

No.	Names.	Colours.	Animal.	Vegetable.	Mineral.
1	Snow White.		Breast of the black-headed Gull.	Snow-Drop.	Carrara Marble and Calc Sinter.
2	Reddish White.		Egg of Grey Linnet.	Back of the Christmas Rose.	Porcelain Earth.
3	Purplish White.		Junction of the Neck and Back of the Kittiwake Gull.	White Geranium, or Stork's Bill.	Hard Carbonate of Lime.
4	Yellowish White.		Egret.	Hawthorn Blossom.	Chalk and Tripoli.
5	Orange-coloured White.		Breast of White, or Screech Owl.	Large wild Convolvulus.	French Porcelain Clay.
6	Greenish White.		Vent Coverts of Golden-crested Wren.	Polyanthus Narcissus.	Calc Sinter.
7	Skimmed-milk White.		White of the Human Eyeballs.	Back of the Petals of Blue Hepatica.	Common Opal.
8	Greyish White.		Inside Quill-feathers of the Kittiwake.	White Hamburgh Grapes.	Granular Limestone.

1

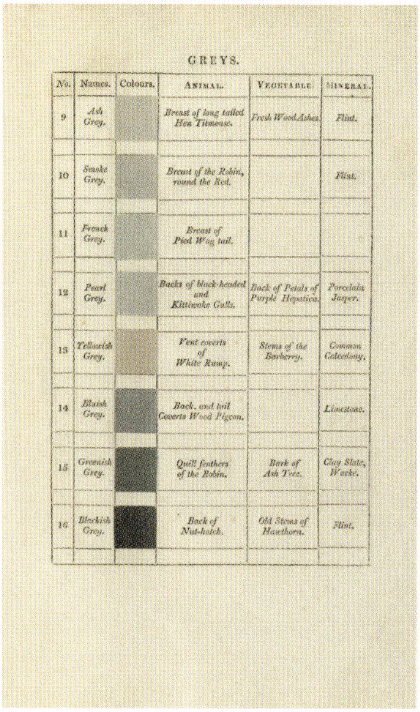

GREYS.

No.	Names.	Colours.	Animal.	Vegetable.	Mineral.
9	Ash Grey.		Breast of long tailed Hen Titmouse.	Fresh Wood Ashes.	Flint.
10	Smoke Grey.		Breast of the Robin, round the Red.		Flint.
11	French Grey.		Breast of Pied Wag tail.		
12	Pearl Grey.		Backs of black-headed and Kittiwake Gulls.	Back of Petals of Purple Hepatica.	Porcelain Jasper.
13	Yellowish Grey.		Vent coverts of White Rump.	Stems of the Barberry.	Common Calcedony.
14	Bluish Grey.		Back, and tail Coverts Wood Pigeon.		Limestone.
15	Greenish Grey.		Quill feathers of the Robin.	Bark of Ash Tree.	Clay Slate, Wacke.
16	Blackish Grey.		Back of Nut-hatch.	Old Stems of Hawthorn.	Flint.

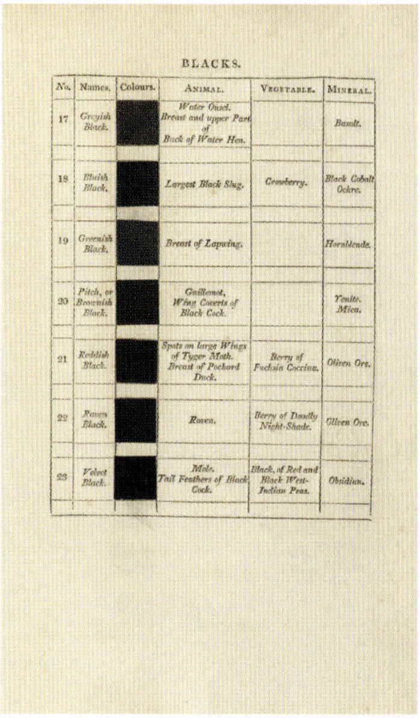

BLACKS.

No.	Names.	Colours.	Animal.	Vegetable.	Mineral.
17	Greyish Black.		Water Ousel. Breast and upper Part of Back of Water Hen.		Basalt.
18	Bluish Black.		Largest Black Slug.	Crowberry.	Black Cobalt Ochre.
19	Greenish Black.		Breast of Lapwing.		Hornblende.
20	Pitch, or Brownish Black.		Guillemot, Wing Coverts of Black Cock.		Yenite. Mica.
21	Reddish Black.		Spots on large Wings of Tyger Moth. Breast of Pochard Duck.	Berry of Fuchsia Coccinea.	Oliven Ore.
22	Raven Black.		Raven.	Berry of Deadly Night-Shade.	Oliven Ore.
23	Velvet Black.		Mole. Tail Feathers of Black Cock.	Black, of Red and Black West-Indian Peas.	Obsidian.

Some of the color families in Patrick Syme's *Werner's Nomenclature of Colours* (1814). Each of the 108 colors in the book (which included seven types of black and eight varieties of white) was mapped to the animal, vegetable, and mineral kingdoms.

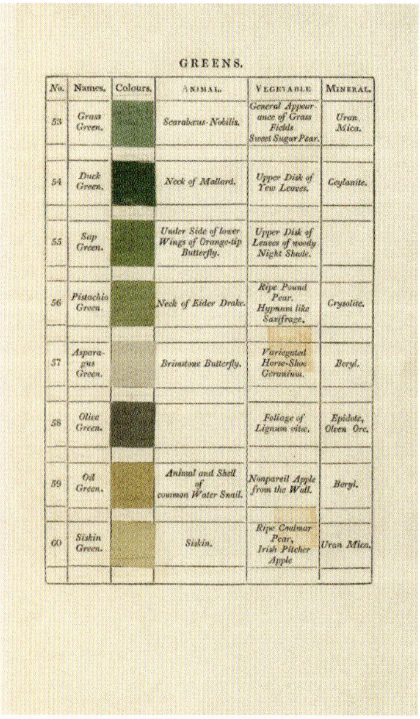

GREENS.

No.	Names.	Colours.	Animal.	Vegetable.	Mineral.
53	Grass Green.		Scarabæus Nobilis.	General Appearance of Grass Fields Sweet Sugar Pear.	Uran Mica.
54	Duck Green.		Neck of Mallard.	Upper Disk of Yew Leaves.	Ceylanite.
55	Sap Green.		Under Side of lower Wings of Orange-tip Butterfly.	Upper Disk of Leaves of woody Night Shade.	
56	Pistachio Green.		Neck of Eider Drake.	Ripe Pound Pear. Hypnum like Saxifrage.	Crysolite.
57	Asparagus Green.		Brimstone Butterfly.	Variegated Horse-Shoe Geranium.	Beryl.
58	Olive Green.			Foliage of Lignum vitæ.	Epidote, Olven Ore.
59	Oil Green.		Animal and Shell of common Water Snail.	Nonpareil Apple from the Wall.	Beryl.
60	Siskin Green.		Siskin.	Ripe Coalmar Pear, Irish Pitcher Apple	Uran Mica.

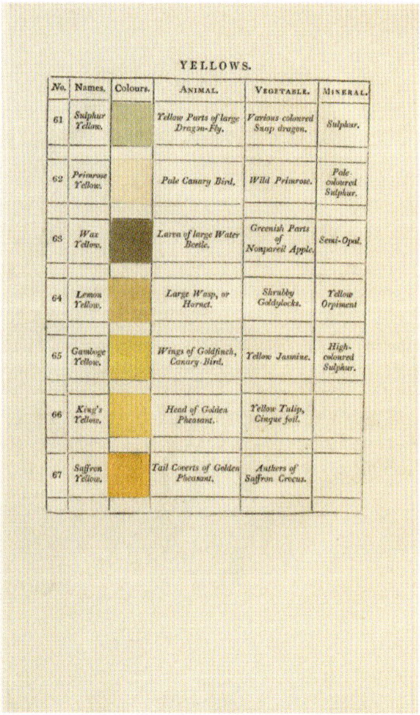

YELLOWS.

No.	Names.	Colours.	Animal.	Vegetable.	Mineral.
61	Sulphur Yellow.		Yellow Parts of large Dragon-Fly.	Various coloured Snap dragon.	Sulphur.
62	Primrose Yellow.		Pale Canary Bird.	Wild Primrose.	Pale coloured Sulphur.
63	Wax Yellow.		Larva of large Water Beetle.	Greenish Parts of Nonpareil Apple.	Semi-Opal.
64	Lemon Yellow.		Large Wasp, or Hornet.	Shrubby Goldylocks.	Yellow Orpiment
65	Gamboge Yellow.		Wings of Goldfinch, Canary Bird.	Yellow Jasmine.	High-coloured Sulphur.
66	King's Yellow.		Head of Golden Pheasant.	Yellow Tulip, Cinque foil.	
67	Saffron Yellow.		Tail Coverts of Golden Pheasant.	Anthers of Saffron Crocus.	

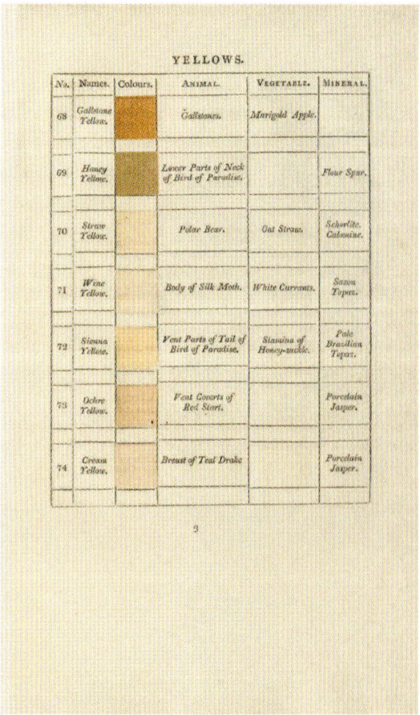

YELLOWS.

No.	Names.	Colours.	Animal.	Vegetable.	Mineral.
68	Gallstone Yellow.		Gallstones.	Marigold Apple.	
69	Honey Yellow.		Lower Parts of Neck of Bird of Paradise.		Flour Spar.
70	Straw Yellow.		Polar Bear.	Oat Straw.	Schorlite. Calamine.
71	Wine Yellow.		Body of Silk Moth.	White Currants.	Saxon Topaz.
72	Sienna Yellow.		Vent Parts of Tail of Bird of Paradise.	Stamina of Honey-suckle.	Pale Brazilian Topaz.
73	Ochre Yellow.		Vent Coverts of Red Start.		Porcelain Jasper.
74	Cream Yellow.		Breast of Teal Drake		Porcelain Jasper.

3

PURPLES.

No.	Names.	Colours.	ANIMAL.	VEGETABLE.	MINERAL.
34	*Bluish Lilac Purple.*		*Male of the Lebellula Depressa.*	*Blue Lilac.*	*Lepidolite.*
35	*Bluish Purple.*		*Papilio Argeolus. Azure Blue Butterfly.*	*Parts of White and Purple Crocus.*	
36	*Violet Purple.*			*Purple Aster.*	*Amethyst.*
37	*Pansy Purple.*		*Chrysomela Goettingensis.*	*Sweet-scented Violet.*	*Derbyshire Spar.*
38	*Campanula Purple.*			*Canterbury Bell, Campanula, Persicifolia.*	*Fluor Spar.*
39	*Imperial Purple.*			*Deep Parts of Flower of Saffron Crocus.*	*Fluor Spar.*
40	*Auricula Purple.*		*Egg of largest Blue-bottle, or Flesh-Fly.*	*Largest Purple Auricula.*	*Fluor Spar.*
41	*Plum Purple.*			*Plum.*	*Fluor Spar.*
42	*Red Lilac Purple.*		*Light Spots of the upper Wings of Peacock Butterfly.*	*Red Lilac. Pale Purple Primrose.*	*Lepidolite.*
43	*Lavender Purple.*		*Light Parts of Spots on the under Wings of Peacock Butterfly.*	*Dried Lavender Flowers.*	*Porcelain Jasper.*
44	*Pale Blackish Purple.*				*Porcelain Jasper.*

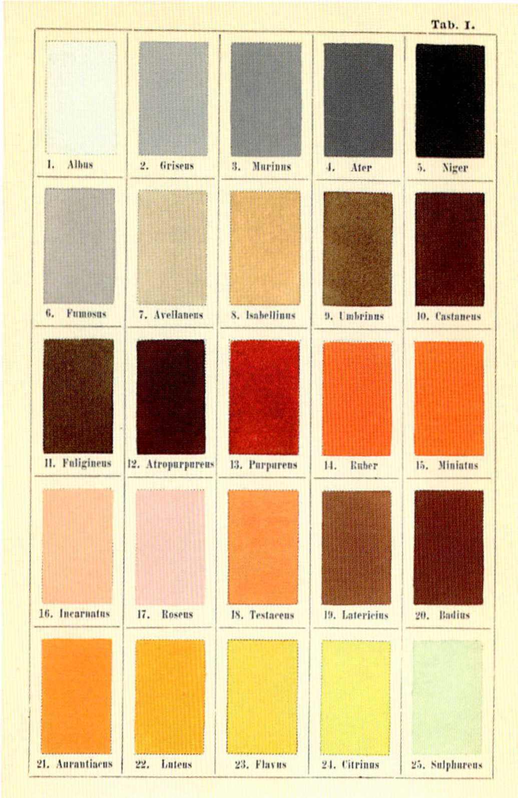

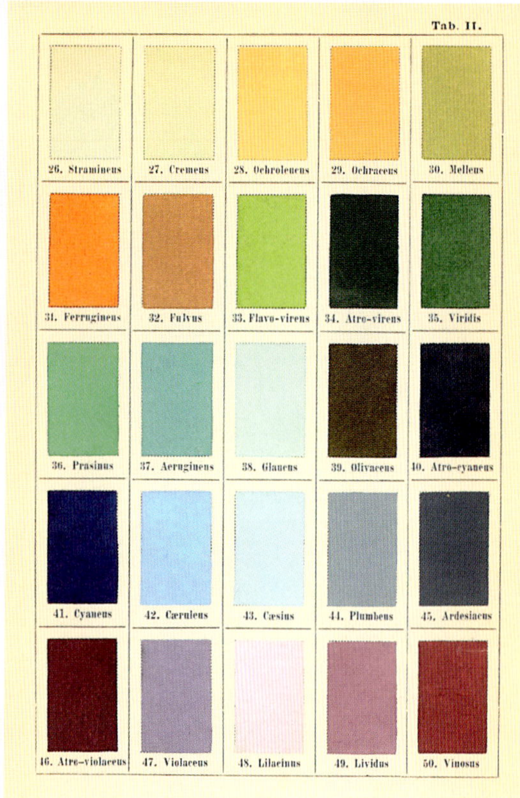

Plates I and II of Pier Andrea Saccardo's 1894 chromotaxy scale appeared in his work *Chromotaxia* (1894) and were inspired by his work as a mycologist.

ten-volume *Flora Graeca* (1806–40) from his drawings and notes. He devised a detailed numerical system to record individual colors of samples he sketched in the wild in order to relate them to a series of charts of pre-painted samples back in the studio. Crudely put, it was a paint-by-numbers system and, like Waller's table, it failed to catch on with others.

A more influential attempt at a taxonomy of color was made by self-described flower painter Patrick Syme (1774–1845) of Edinburgh. In 1814, Syme published a work entitled *Werner's Nomenclature of Colours* that tried to encapsulate the natural world in 108 colors. As its title suggested, *Werner's Nomenclature* was not all Syme's own work. Instead, he adapted and transformed mineralogist Abraham Gottlob Werner's eighteenth-century classification scheme for the identification of minerals by appearance and color. Initially containing fifty-four samples in eight "Hauptfarben" (color families), Werner's *On the External Characteristics of Fossils* (1774) did not include any color, although the author assembled a special collection of physical specimens for comparison by students. Unusually, he devoted one of his color families to shades of gray, treating it as a color in its own right because of its prevalence in rocks. While a moderately useful work, this original nomenclature was wholly reconceptualized when Syme picked up the baton several decades later. He increased the Hauptfarben to include purple and orange and expanded the work along another axis as well, finding not just equivalent colors in rocks but matches in up to three of the "kingdoms" of nature classified as animal, vegetable, and mineral by taxonomist Carl Linnaeus in his *Systema Naturae* (1735).

Laid out in a table, colors with accompanying names could be matched to up to three different samples. The animal, vegetable, and mineral columns provided countless striking examples of encounters between abstract colors and their living embodiments, and much of the terminology now appears accidentally poetic. Sample number 7, or Skimmed milk White, was made manifest in "the white of the human eyeballs", the "back of the petals of Blue Hepatica", and the "common opal". Elsewhere, Syme found equivalents of the largest black slug, the leaves of leeks in winter, gallstones, and polar bears. Each had its own formula: "Skimmed milk White is snow white mixed with a little Berlin blue, and ash grey." The largest sections belonged to blue and red, but there were also sixteen greens, including sap, pistachio, and olive, reflecting the verdant richness of the natural world. Syme also identified both arterial and veinous [*sic*] shades of red, in reference to the circulatory system, and the different appearance of bright red oxygenated blood and its darker deoxygenated variety.

The physical manifestation of the colors themselves on the page was a fastidious effort. Individually hand-painted sections were cut into strips and tiny squares pasted into place, distilling nature's plenty into thirteen plates. But despite his wide net, Syme could not catch everything. Once he expanded the range of colors from Werner's original set, the scheme broke free from its roots in mineralogy as some colors simply had no equivalent in that kingdom. Many cells in his tables were left blank. The animal kingdom apparently held no Ink Black or Plum Purple creatures, for example, but the empty spaces lent an anticipatory sense to the project, as if with further exploration the gaps could be filled, not unlike the missing elements that would later be predicted by Mendeleev's periodic table.

The book was so useful it was rapidly accepted in a number of disciplines. Professor Robert Jameson, who had been both a pupil of Werner and an admirer of Syme, pressed for it to be adopted by pathologists and hydrographers and suggested it could be used to describe everything from gangrene to meteors. Most famously in retrospect, a copy was owned by Charles Darwin who carried it with him on his voyages on HMS *Beagle* (1831–6). In terms apparently lifted from Syme, Darwin described glaciers as "beryl blue" and noted the "French grey" and "hyacinth red" of the cuttlefish he encountered. Syme's terminology and samples promised fixity and permanence in a natural world of flourishment and decay.

Any attempt to encapsulate the entirety of the natural world was like trying to bottle lightning, but Syme always knew his hundred-odd colors would not be enough, that the beryl blue of Darwin's glacier was the tip of the iceberg. Instead, he hoped his selection would raise the standards of general knowledge of colors and allow readers to recognize and name them in the wild.

Later nature-inspired color palettes differed in scope and function. Some remained rooted in their field, a realm such as horticulture, ornithology, or mycology, while others hoped to become universally accepted. Some started as the former and mushroomed into the latter. The small volume *Chromotaxia* (1894) by mycologist Pier Andrea Saccardo (1845–1920) contained only fifty color samples, along with a record of their names in different languages, but the author hoped they could be extended beyond the fungi and plants of his specialization. Saccardo's contemporary, ornithologist Robert Ridgway (1850–1929, see p.234), held twin lifelong passions for birds and color that overlapped in his published work. Two of his books were principally about color, intended to map its range and terminology for naturalists. Both stemmed from a place of wanting to provide universal references for ornithologists: to not only identify a particular bird by the color of its plumage but to know what to call those colors in its display.

Ridgway claimed his first effort, *A Nomenclature of Colors for Naturalists* (1886) with its nearly 200 different samples, was the first book of its kind since Syme's *Werner's Nomenclature*. Although the number of color samples he included was still small, he argued that all colors in nature could be matched with a surprisingly limited palette of thirty-six varieties. Unlike Saccardo and his modest range, Ridgway's ambition grew, as evidenced by the increase in the number of color samples between his two directories, from 186 to 1,115 in his later *Color Standards and Color Nomenclature* (1912). Yet he actively resisted overtures from industry to make his color ranges more useful to commerce, and never wanted to lose sight of the relationship of his work to nature, however expansive it became.

Ridgway's parallel writing on birds, in his exhaustive multivolume *Birds of North and Middle America* (1901–19) used color differently, moving from the general to the specific, from lexical to visual identification. By the time he reached the 1905 volume, the numerous line drawings were becoming colorized, adding vital information to help the reader quickly differentiate between fast-moving species.

As printing technology improved, many compendia of flora and fauna like these were published, taking in the chromatic variety of numerous subjects from the iris of the human eye to the petals of the iris in the field. In fact flowers, and the need to define their full range of colors, spurred a number of developments in color standards. In late nineteenth-century France, for example, a new standard was demanded to address the national craze for cultivated chrysanthemums that were being grown in many "new" colors. Sponsored by the Chrysanthemum Society of France, authors Henri Dauthenay and René Oberthür produced *Repertoire de couleurs* (1905), a two-volume loose-leaf multicolored directory intended for "the determination of colors of flowers, foliage, and fruit". The 365 color samples (each of which was further broken into four tints, apparently inspired by the color ladders of Chevreul, see p.148) were accompanied by a brief history of each color, its synonyms, and examples of

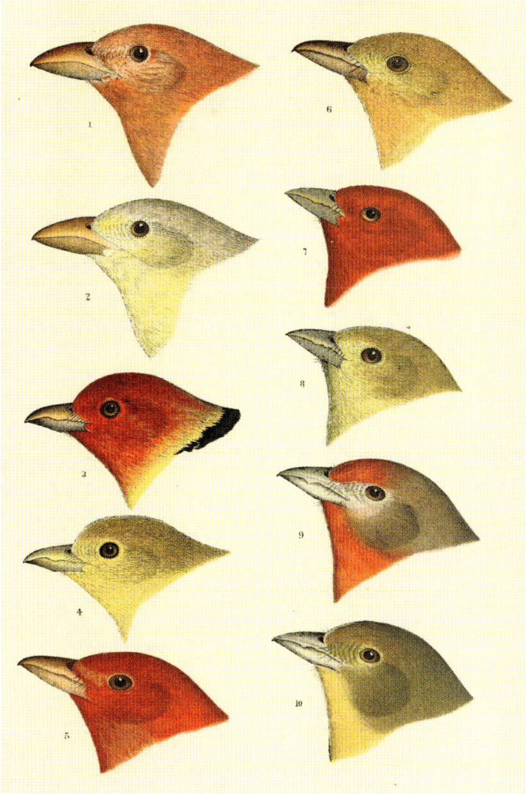

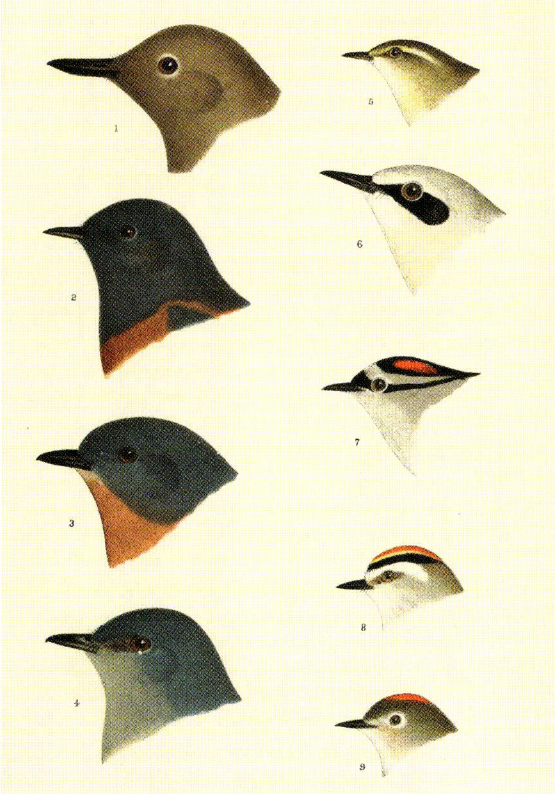

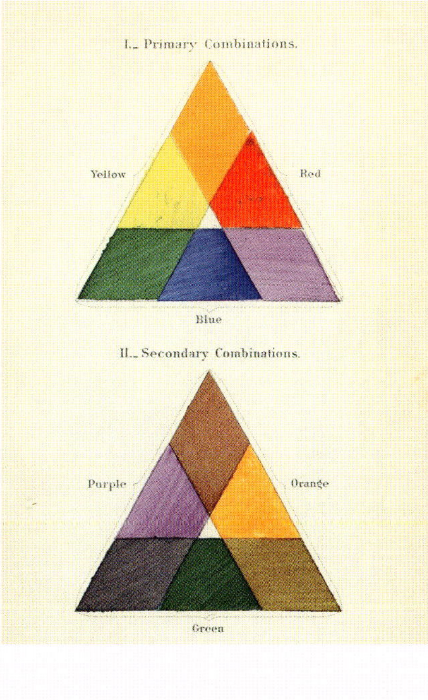

ABOVE
Colored illustrations helped identify the often subtly different varieties of birds in Robert Ridgway's *A History of North American Birds* (1905). Ridgway's twin passions were birds and color and he published widely on both.

RIGHT
Color triangles of primary and secondary color combinations in Robert Ridgway's *A Nomenclature of Colors for Naturalists* (1886).

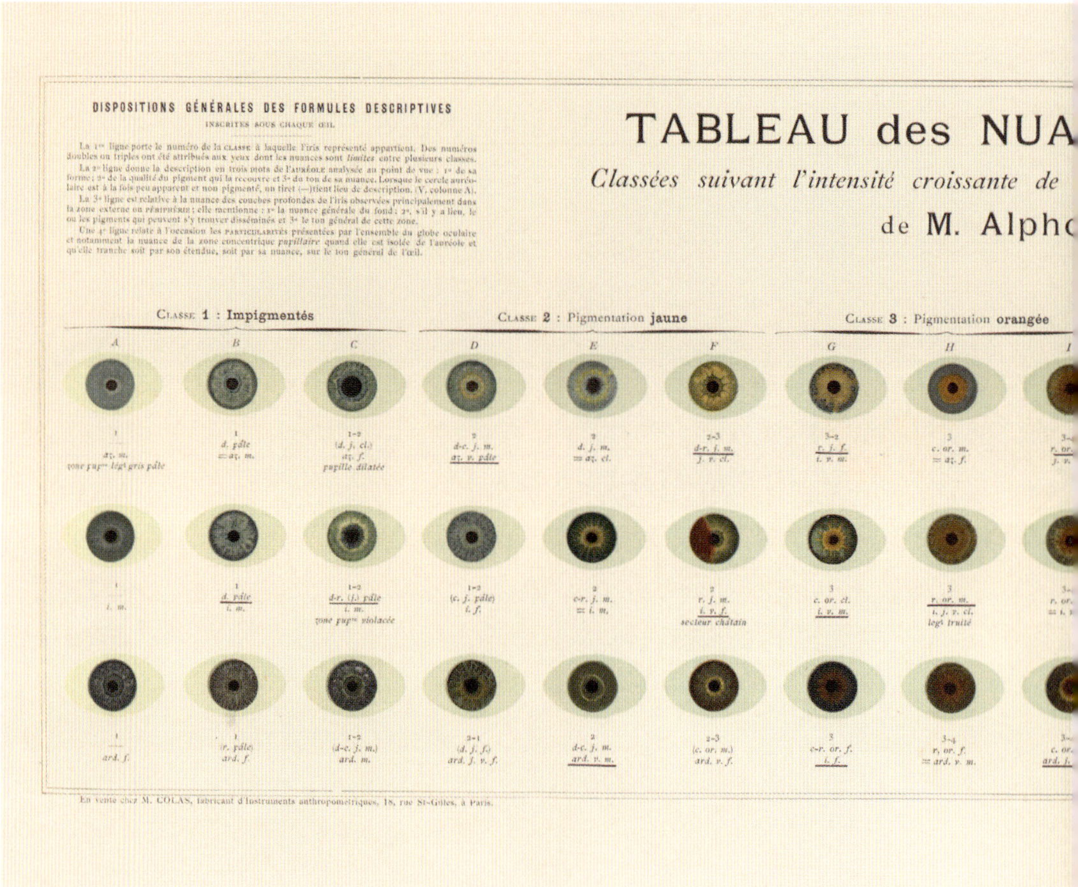

where it could be found in nature. The tone was often effusive and breezily unscientific, celebrating the everyday experience of color: oxblood was cheerfully described as "the ordinary color of the blood coming from the slaughter of oxen and flowing in the streams of the abattoir"; sky blue was "reminiscent of pure sky, in Paris, in the summer". Given the samples' potential for fading in sunlight, it was unfortunate that the authors had to advise users not to take them out into the garden with them.

Repertoire de couleurs struck a balance between dictionary and thesaurus by including equivalent terms for named colors, along with synonyms in several languages. Many guides tried to show all colors to all people. The *Wilson Colour Chart*, for example, appeared in two volumes in 1938 and 1942, under the aegis of the British Colour Council (see p.50) and its director Robert Wilson. Described as a "Horticultural Colour Chart" and obviously influenced by *Repertoire de couleurs*, right down to its page layout, it nevertheless took the colors of nature as a starting point that could be applied to the world of industry in the twentieth century, with "a use and value far outside its horticultural scope". Like so many other attempts to monopolize color

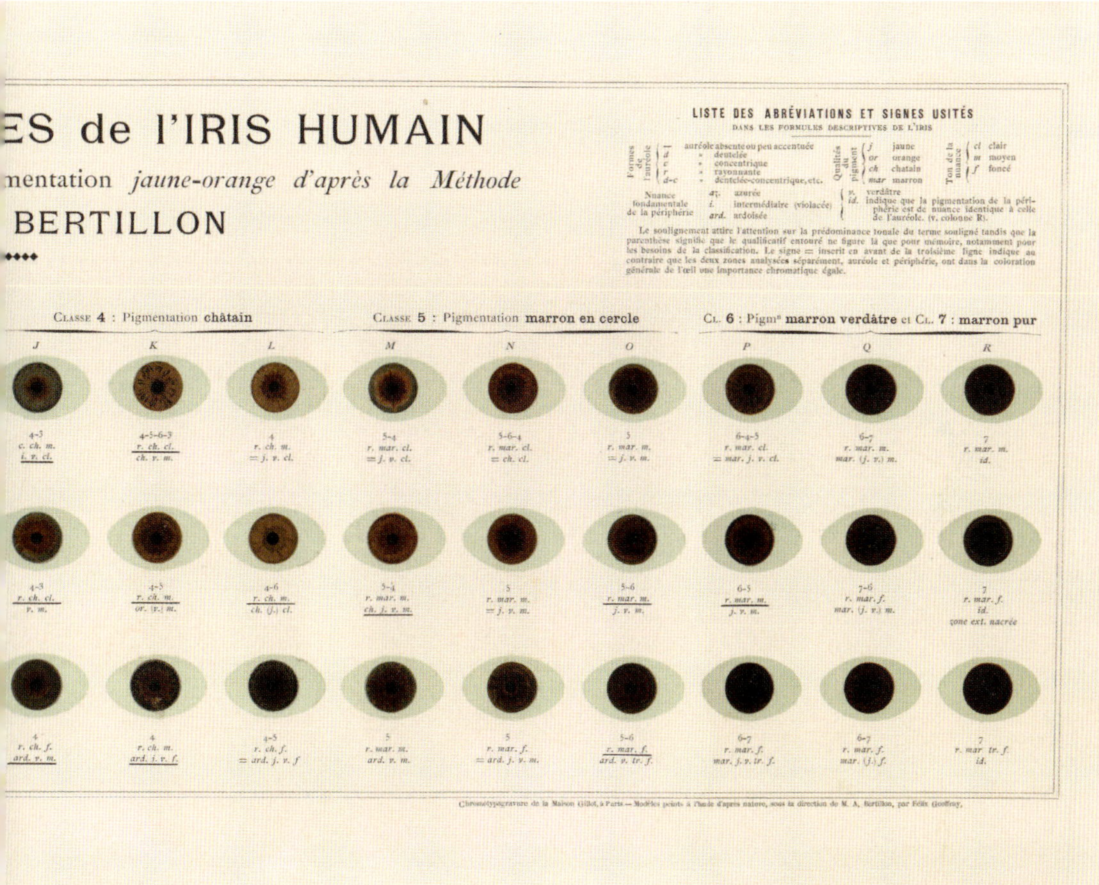

ABOVE
A table of human eye colors in Alphonse Bertillon's *Identification anthropometrique* (1893). Bertillon was a French police officer who used the techniques of anthropometry, a series of measurements of the human body, to identify criminals. His work contained a chart to pinpoint the color of an individual's eyes by providing a universal reference to the variety of human irises.

OVERLEAF
Entries from the two-volume, loose-leaf *Repertoire de couleurs* (1905), a publication of France's Chrysanthemum Society.

in a competitive world, Wilson assumed he had cracked it, making bold claims for the rigor of his solution, insisting "there will thus be but one colour name recognized for each hue in the textile and all colour-using industries as well as by artists' colourmen."

Most of these florally inspired color reference publications were not directly linked to proprietary color standards in industry but an exception was Ernst Biesalski's *Pflanzenfarben-Atlas* (1957), a highly specialized horticultural identification system. Not only did Biesalski's color samples remain firmly planted in the world of flora (featuring conifer frosty-blue and

Jaune Soleil

Origine : Couleur de la fleur du Soleil commun (*Helianthus annuus*) en capitules à complet développement. Le Jaune Soleil industriel est de l'acide paranitrotoluène sulfoné avec de la lessive de soude.

Synonymes français : Jaune de Chrome brillant (Lorilleux). Jaune de Cadmium clair (Bourgeois).

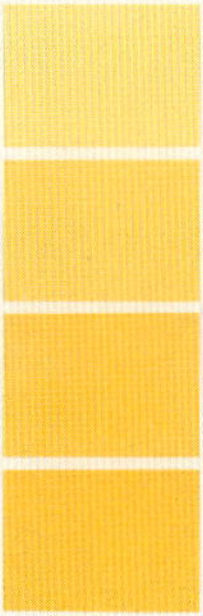

1
2
3
4

Synonymes étrangers :

All. : Reinesgelb, auch Goldgelb.
Angl. : Sunflower yellow. Cadmium yellow, light.
Esp. : Amarillo de Girasol. A. de Tornasol. A. de Elianto.
Ital. : Giallo di Girasole.

Remarques :

Ton 1 : Calcéolaire rugueuse *Triomphe de Versailles*. — *Sternbergia lutea*.

Ton 2 : *Helianthus multiflorus Soleil d'Or*.

Ton 3 : Ligules du *Silgugina trilobata*.

Tons 2 à 4 : Couleur d'ensemble du Chrysanthème *Amiral Avellane*; ton 1 : revers des ligules; ton 2 : dessus des ligules âgées; ton 3 : dessus des ligules du cœur; ton 4 : reflets du cœur. (Dans les capitules près d'atteindre leur complet développement, le cœur, vu par transparence, donne du Jaune de Cadmium moyen.

Rouge écarlate

Origine : Le véritable Écarlate provient de la Cochenille traitée par la crème de tartre et le chlorure d'étain. On compte aujourd'hui une vingtaine d'Écarlates fabriqués avec des dérivés de la Houille (1).

Synonymes français : Écarlate de Cochenille : E. des Gobelins. E. de France. E. de Venise. — Écarlates de substitution : E. Palatin. E. de Cumidine. Rouge d'Alger. Cinabre de Géranium (Lefranc). Rouge Vermillon (Lorilleux).

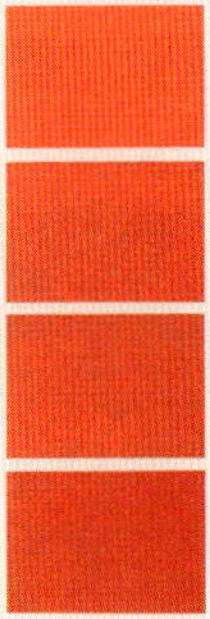

1
2
3
4

Synonymes étrangers :

All. : Scarlachrot. Scarlach.
Angl. : Scarlet.
Esp. : Escarlata.
Ital. : Scarlatto.

Remarques :

Ton 1 : Pélargonium zoné *Ville de Bruxelles*, dans ses parties les plus rouges.

Tons 1 et 2 : Pélargoniums zonés *La Destinée* et *Monsieur Cordeau*.

Ton 3 : Pélargonium zoné *Étincelle*.

Ton 4 : Tonalité générale des inflorescences du *Salvia splendens Edouard Le Couteulx*.

(1) L'Écarlate Palatin et l'É. de Cumidine teignent la laine et le coton dans les tons montrés ici.

Rouge Sang-de-bœuf

Origine : Couleur ordinaire du sang provenant de l'abattage des bœufs et coulant dans les ruisseaux des abattoirs. — *Atrosanguineus*.

Synonymes français : néant.

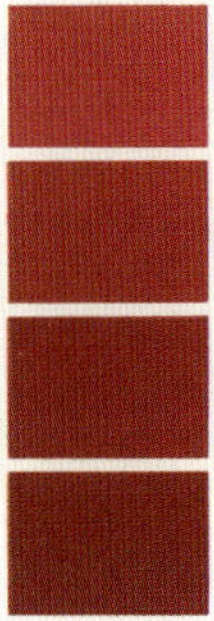

1
2
3
4

Synonymes étrangers :

All. : Ochsenblutrot.
Angl. : Ox's blood red.
Esp. : Sangre de buey.
Ital. : Rosso sangue di bue.

Remarques :

Tons 1 et 2 : Nuance foncée résultant des panachures, dans l'Œillet *Princesse de Radziwill*.

Tons 3 et 4 : Couleur d'ensemble des fleurs du Cyclamen *Prince Albert Victor*, à complet épanouissement.

Bleu Paon

Origine : Couleur rappelant certaines nuances observées sur le plumage du Paon.

Synonymes français : Bleu verdâtre.

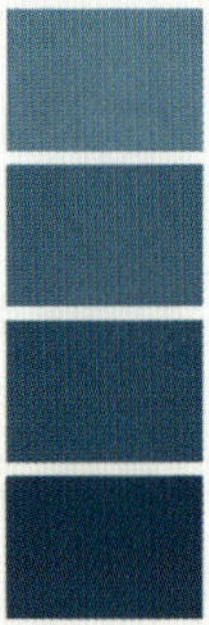

1
2
3
4

Synonymes étrangers :

All. : Pfaublau.
Angl. : Peacock blue.
Esp. : Azul de Pavon.
Ital. : Azzuro o Bleu di Pavone.

Remarques :

L'une des couleurs par lesquelles passent, en automne, les fruits du *Clerodendron trichotomum* et de l'Herbe aux Turquoises (*Ophiopogon japonicus*). — Ces nuances s'observent aussi sur l'étendard de la corolle du *Lathyrus pisiformis*.

Vert de Prusse

Origine : Dénomination de cette couleur dans le commerce des couleurs.(1)

Synonymes français : Vert Myrte (impropre).

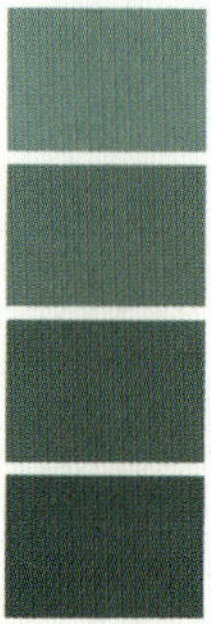

1
2
3
4

Synonymes étrangers :

All. : Preussichgrün.
Angl. : Prussian green. Myrtle green (impropre) (2).
Esp. : Verde de Prusia.
Ital. : Verde di Prusia.

Remarques :

Pas d'exemples.

(1) Le Vert de Prusse industriel est une solution chaude de ferrocyanure traitée par du chlore. Siccatif, mais ne résiste pas à la lumière.

(2) W. B. Warhurst, *A Col. Dict.*

Vert de Chypre

Origine : Dénomination commerciale de cette couleur (Bourgeois). Laque d'Aniline.

Synonymes français : néant.

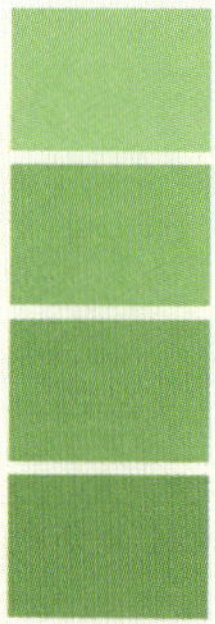

1
2
3
4

Synonymes étrangers :

All. : Cyprischgrün.
Angl. : Cyprus green.
Esp. : Verde Cipré.
Ital. : Verde Cipro.

Remarques :

Pas d'exemples.

Fraise écrasée

Origine : Couleur rappelant celle du jus de la Fraise (ton 4) plus ou moins mélangé avec sa chair (tons 1 à 3).

Synonymes français : Laque écarlate, tons clairs (Bourg.).

1
2
3
4

Synonymes étrangers :

All. : Erdbeerfleisch-rot.
Angl. : Crushed Strawberry.
Esp. : Fresa aplastada.
Ital. : Fragola stiacciata.

Remarques :

Tons 1 à 3 : Macules et lavis sur le centre des fleurs du Pélargonium zoné *Jean Pâquét*. — Nuances sur la partie centrale du limbe des fleurs de la Jacinthe de Hollande *Solfatare* après complet épanouissement.

Ton 4 : Nuance observée sur une variété du Cognassier du Japon (*Cydonia japonica*).

— 109 —

Magenta rougeâtre

Origine : Combinaison du Magenta et du Solférino.

Synonymes français : Solférino de Lorilleux (impropre). Solférino violacé.

1
2
3
4

Synonymes étrangers :

All. : Rotmagenta.
Angl. : Rosy Magenta. Magenta[1] (impropre).
Esp. : Magenta rojizo.
Ital. : Magenta rossastro.

Remarques :

Tons 1 à 4 : Tonalité générale de la Rose *Reine des Violettes* (fleurs jeunes).

Ton 3 : Salicaire effilée (*Lithrum virgatum*.

Ton 4 : Macule du labelle de nombreux *Cattleya labiata*. — Dolique Lablab (*Dolichos Lablab*). — *Cuphea Jorullensis*.

Les différents tons de cette couleur s'observent fréquemment sur le labelle d'un grand nombre d'Orchidées, notamment des *Lelia*, *Lelio-Cattleya* et *Cattleya*.

(1) Amer. Flor. : *A Chart of Col.*

— 169 —

Violet pourpré

Origine : Reproduction du Pourpre des Anglais et des Américains, mais qui, à notre avis, doit être plutôt appelé Violet pourpré.

Synonymes français : Violet Cobæa. Violet Cobée.

1
2
3
4

Synonymes étrangers :

All. : Purpurviolett.
Angl. : Deep Purple[1]. Purple[2].
Esp. : Viola púrpura.
Ital. : Viola porpora.

Remarques :

Tons 1 à 4 : Couleur d'ensemble des fleurs du *Cobæa scandens*; ton 1 : parties foncées de l'extérieur du tube de la corolle; ton 4 : pourtour du retroussis du limbe, autour de la gorge.

Ton 3 : Tube de la corolle (extérieur) du *Lobelia Gerardi*.

Ton 4 : Limbe de la corolle du *Lobelia Gerardi*. — Labelle de certains *Lelia Anceps* fortement nuancés, et dont les autres pièces périanthales sont de couleur Mauve.

(1) Amer. Flor. : *A Chart of Col.*
(2) W. B. Warburne, *A Col. Dict.*

— 185 —

Terre d'Ombrie brûlée

Origine : Dénomination de cette couleur dans le commerce des couleurs; par corruption on dit aussi : « Terre d'Ombre brûlée ».

Synonymes français : Bois, Vieux-Chêne. — Analogue : Brun de Mars (Bourg.).

1
2
3
4

Synonymes étrangers :

All. : Umbra gebrannt.
Angl. : Burnt Umber.
Esp. : Tierra de Umbria tostada.
Ital. : Terra d'Umbra bruciata.

Remarques :

Ton 1 : Couleur ordinaire du grain du Haricot de *Saint-Fiacre*, bien mûr.

Tons 1 à 4 : Tons de l'une des colorations que prennent les fructifications des Fougères au cours de leur développement. — Revers des feuilles du *Magnolia grandiflora*.

Tons 2 et 3 : Calice (persistant) desséché de l'*Hypericum calycinum*.

Ton 4 : Fruit (sec) de l'*Hypericum calycinum*.

— 304 —

Ocre de Mars

Origine : Dénomination commerciale de cette couleur (Bourgeois). — *Voir* Ocre vraie.

Synonymes français : Manille. Jaune de Manille. Paille de Manille.

1
2
3
4

Synonymes étrangers :

All. : Mars-Ocker.
Angl. : Mars yellow.
Esp. : Paja de Manille.
Ital. : Paglia di Manilla.

Remarques :

Tons 1 et 2 : Couleur ordinaire d'ensemble de l'Agaric en conque (*Agaricus conchatus*), et du chapeau de l'*Agaricus catinus*.

Tons 2 et 3 : Nuance ordinaire du grain du Haricot *jaune hatif de Chalandray*.

— 316 —

Gris de Payne

Origine : Dénomination commerciale de cette couleur (Bourgeois)[1].

Synonymes français : Gris d'Acier.

1
2
3
4

Synonymes étrangers :

All. : Payne's Grau.
Angl. : Payne's grey.
Esp. : Gris de Acero.
Ital. : Grigio acciaio. G. di Payne.

Remarques :

Pas d'exemples.

(1) Couleurs à l'aquarelle : mélange d'Indigo et de Laque carminée. *Voir note*, pl. 359.

— 356 —

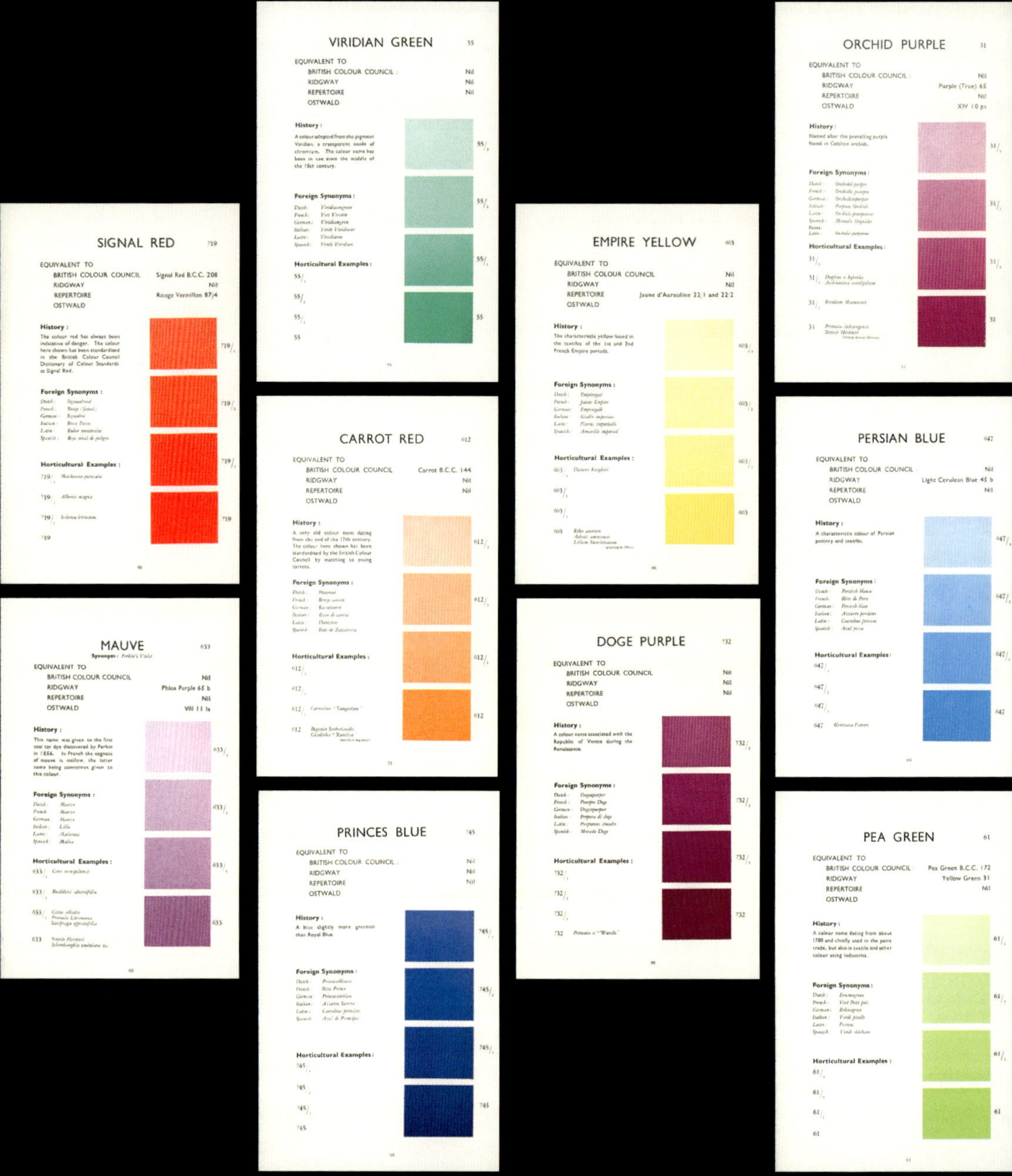

SIGNAL RED 719

EQUIVALENT TO

BRITISH COLOUR COUNCIL	Signal Red B.C.C. 208
RIDGWAY	Nil
REPERTOIRE	Rouge Vermillon 87/4
OSTWALD	

History:
The colour red has always been indicative of danger. The colour here shown has been standardised in the British Colour Council Dictionary of Colour Standards as Signal Red.

Foreign Synonyms:

Horticultural Examples:

MAUVE 633

Synonym: *Perkin's Violet*

EQUIVALENT TO

BRITISH COLOUR COUNCIL	Nil
RIDGWAY	Phlox Purple 65 b
REPERTOIRE	Nil
OSTWALD	VIII 11 la

History:
This name was given to the first coal tar dye discovered by Perkin in 1856. Its French the cognate of mauve is mallow, the latter name being sometimes given to this colour.

Foreign Synonyms:

Horticultural Examples:

VIRIDIAN GREEN 55

EQUIVALENT TO

BRITISH COLOUR COUNCIL:	Nil
RIDGWAY	Nil
REPERTOIRE	Nil
OSTWALD	

History:
A colour adopted from the pigment Viridian, a transparent oxide of chromium. The colour name has been in use since the middle of the 19th century.

Foreign Synonyms:

Horticultural Examples:

CARROT RED 612

EQUIVALENT TO

BRITISH COLOUR COUNCIL	Carrot B.C.C. 144
RIDGWAY	Nil
REPERTOIRE	Nil
OSTWALD	

History:
A very old colour term dating from the end of the 17th century. The colour here shown has been standardised by the British Colour Council by matching to young carrots.

Foreign Synonyms:

Horticultural Examples:

PRINCES BLUE 745

EQUIVALENT TO

BRITISH COLOUR COUNCIL:	Nil
RIDGWAY	Nil
REPERTOIRE	Nil
OSTWALD	

History:
A blue slightly more greenish than Royal Blue.

Foreign Synonyms:

Horticultural Examples:

EMPIRE YELLOW 603

EQUIVALENT TO

BRITISH COLOUR COUNCIL	Nil
RIDGWAY	Nil
REPERTOIRE	Jaune d'Aureoline 22/1 and 22/2
OSTWALD	

History:
The characteristic yellow found in the textiles of the 1st and 2nd French Empire periods.

Foreign Synonyms:

Horticultural Examples:

DOGE PURPLE 732

EQUIVALENT TO

BRITISH COLOUR COUNCIL	Nil
RIDGWAY	Nil
REPERTOIRE	Nil
OSTWALD	

History:
A colour associated with the Republic of Venice during the Renaissance.

Foreign Synonyms:

Horticultural Examples:

ORCHID PURPLE 31

EQUIVALENT TO

BRITISH COLOUR COUNCIL:	Nil
RIDGWAY	Purple (True) 65
REPERTOIRE	Nil
OSTWALD	XIV 10 pa

History:
Named after the prevailing purple found in Cattleya orchids.

Foreign Synonyms:

Horticultural Examples:

PERSIAN BLUE 647

EQUIVALENT TO

BRITISH COLOUR COUNCIL	Nil
RIDGWAY	Light Cerulean Blue 45 b
REPERTOIRE	Nil
OSTWALD	

History:
A characteristic colour of Persian pottery and textiles.

Foreign Synonyms:

Horticultural Examples:

PEA GREEN 61

EQUIVALENT TO

BRITISH COLOUR COUNCIL:	Pea Green B.C.C. 172
RIDGWAY	Yellow Green 31
REPERTOIRE	Nil
OSTWALD	

History:
A colour name dating from about 1780 and chiefly used in the paint trade, but also in textile and other colour using industries.

Foreign Synonyms:

Horticultural Examples:

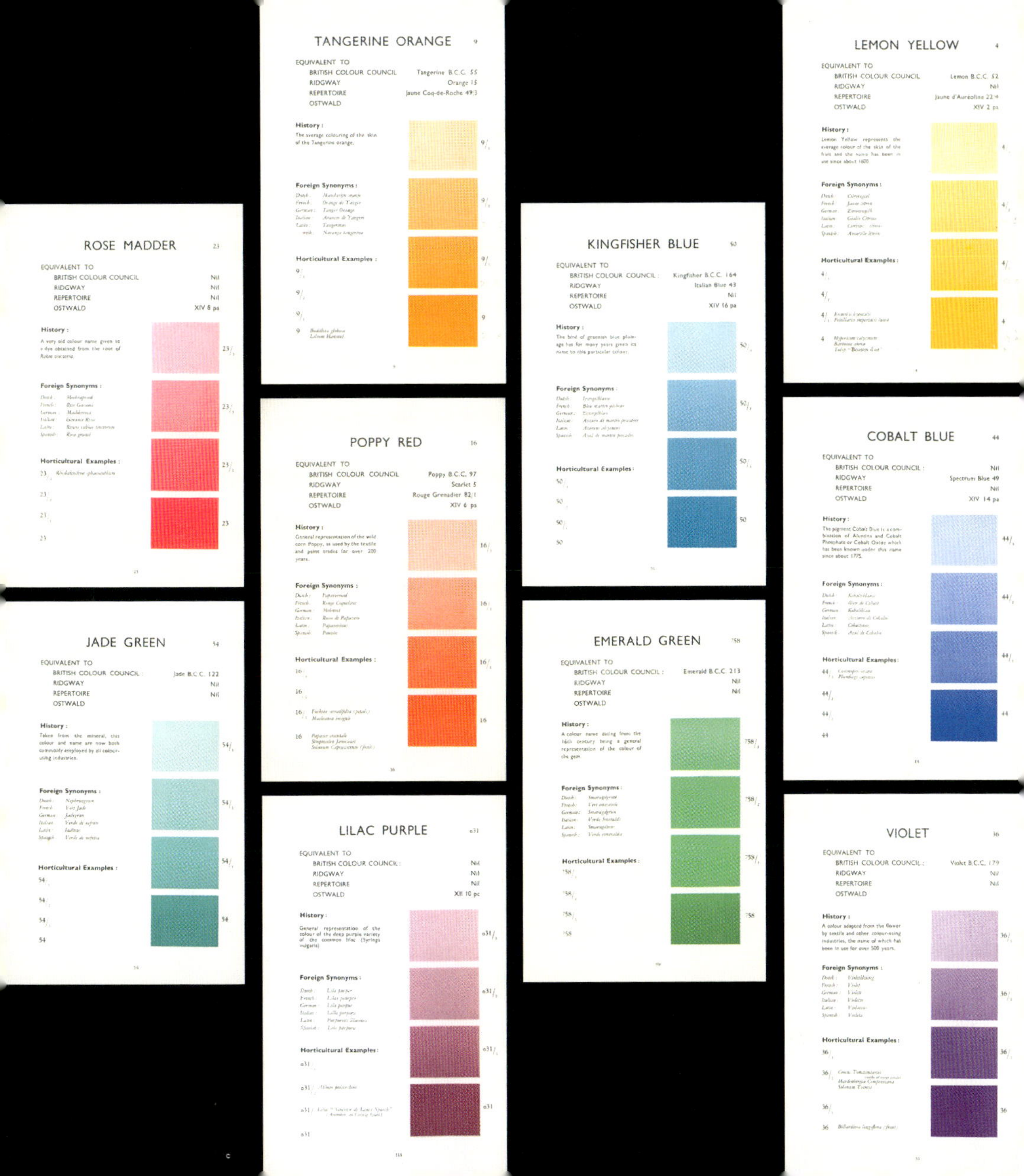

TANGERINE ORANGE 9
EQUIVALENT TO
BRITISH COLOUR COUNCIL Tangerine B.C.C. 55
RIDGWAY Orange 15
REPERTOIRE Jaune Coq-de-Roche 49/3
OSTWALD
History :
The average colouring of the skin of the Tangerine orange.
Foreign Synonyms :
Horticultural Examples :
LEMON YELLOW 4
EQUIVALENT TO
BRITISH COLOUR COUNCIL Lemon B.C.C. 52
RIDGWAY Nil
REPERTOIRE Jaune d'Auréoline 22/4
OSTWALD XIV 2 pa
History :
Lemon Yellow represents the average colour of the skin of the fruit and the name has been in use since about 1600.
Foreign Synonyms :
Horticultural Examples :
ROSE MADDER 23
EQUIVALENT TO
BRITISH COLOUR COUNCIL Nil
RIDGWAY Nil
REPERTOIRE Nil
OSTWALD XIV 8 pa
History :
A very old colour name given to a dye obtained from the root of Rubia tinctoria.
Foreign Synonyms :
Horticultural Examples :
KINGFISHER BLUE 50
EQUIVALENT TO
BRITISH COLOUR COUNCIL Kingfisher B.C.C. 164
RIDGWAY Italian Blue 43
REPERTOIRE Nil
OSTWALD XIV 16 pa
History :
The bird of greenish blue plumage has for many years given its name to this particular colour.
Foreign Synonyms :
Horticultural Examples :
POPPY RED 16
EQUIVALENT TO
BRITISH COLOUR COUNCIL Poppy B.C.C. 97
RIDGWAY Scarlet 5
REPERTOIRE Rouge Grenadier 82/1
OSTWALD XIV 6 pa
History :
General representation of the wild corn Poppy, as used by the textile and paint trades for over 200 years.
Foreign Synonyms :
Horticultural Examples :
COBALT BLUE 44
EQUIVALENT TO
BRITISH COLOUR COUNCIL Nil
RIDGWAY Spectrum Blue 49
REPERTOIRE Nil
OSTWALD XIV 14 pa
History :
The pigment Cobalt Blue is a combination of Alumina and Cobalt Phosphate or Cobalt Oxide which has been known under this name since about 1775.
Foreign Synonyms :
Horticultural Examples :
JADE GREEN 54
EQUIVALENT TO
BRITISH COLOUR COUNCIL Jade B.C.C. 122
RIDGWAY Nil
REPERTOIRE Nil
OSTWALD
History :
Taken from the mineral, this colour and name are now both commonly employed by all colour-using industries.
Foreign Synonyms :
Horticultural Examples :
EMERALD GREEN 758
EQUIVALENT TO
BRITISH COLOUR COUNCIL Emerald B.C.C. 213
RIDGWAY Nil
REPERTOIRE Nil
OSTWALD
History :
A colour name dating from the 16th century being a general representation of the colour of the gem.
Foreign Synonyms :
Horticultural Examples :
LILAC PURPLE 031
EQUIVALENT TO
BRITISH COLOUR COUNCIL Nil
RIDGWAY Nil
REPERTOIRE Nil
OSTWALD XII 10 pc
History :
General representation of the colour of the deep purple variety of the common lilac (Syringa vulgaris).
Foreign Synonyms :
Horticultural Examples :
VIOLET 36
EQUIVALENT TO
BRITISH COLOUR COUNCIL Violet B.C.C. 179
RIDGWAY Nil
REPERTOIRE Nil
OSTWALD
History :
A colour adapted from the flower by textile and other colour-using industries, the name of which has been in use for over 500 years.
Foreign Synonyms :
Horticultural Examples :

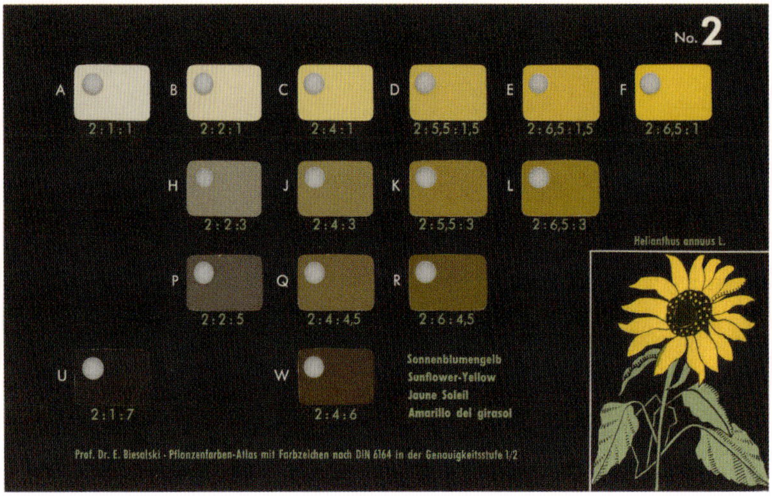

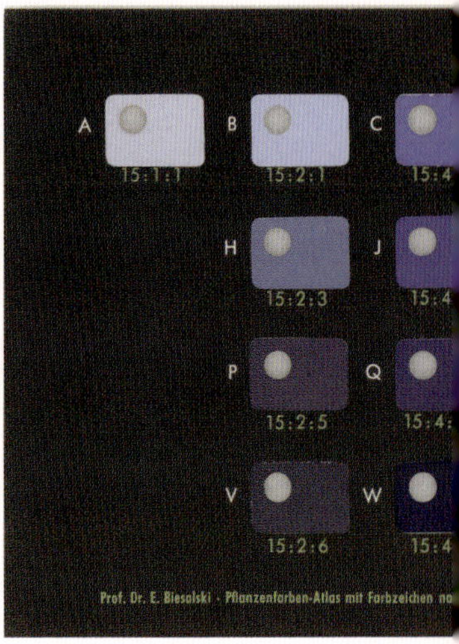

PREVIOUS PAGES
Samples from the *Wilson Colour Chart*, Volumes I and II (1938 and 1942), a publication clearly modeled on *Repertoire de couleurs* for British readers.

THIS PAGE
Ernst Biesalski's *Pflanzenfarben-Atlas* (1957) attempted to relate the colors of flower petals to Germany's national standard of color specification, DIN 6164.

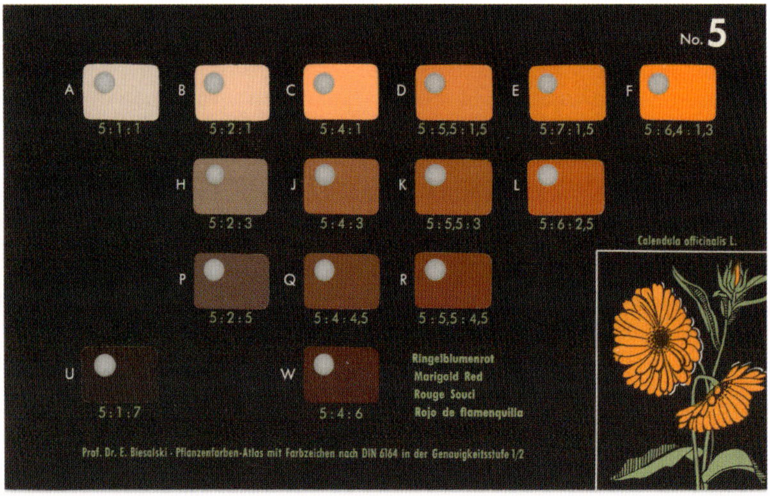

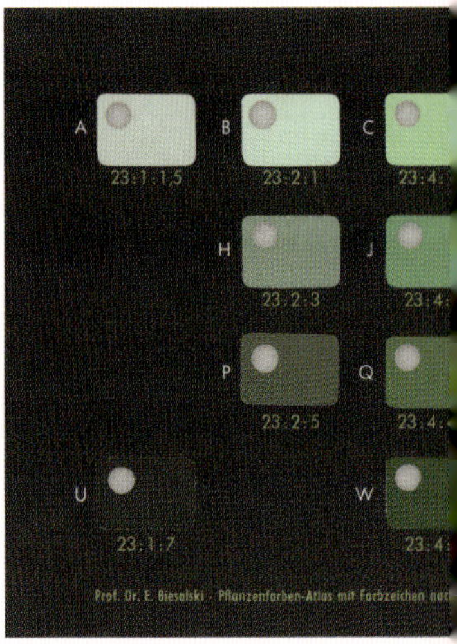

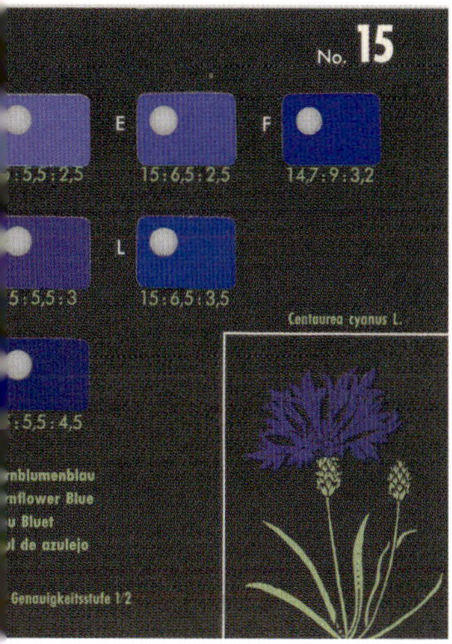
No. 15
E
F
15:6,5:2,5
14,7:9:3,2
L
15:6,5:3,5
Centaurea cyanus L.

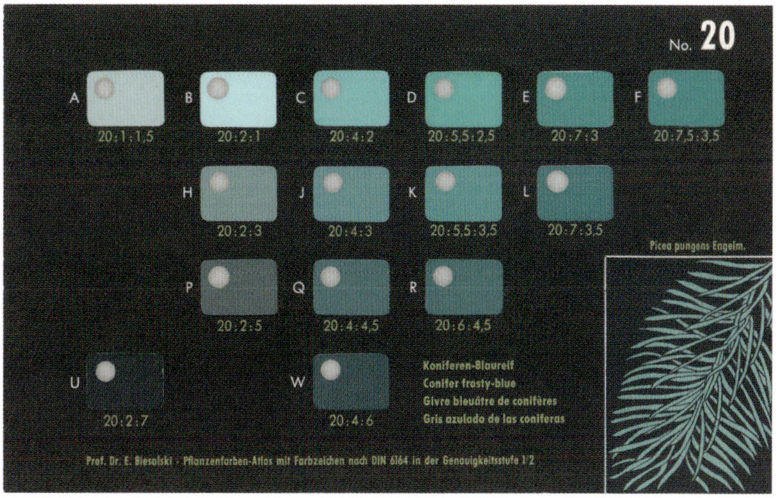
No. 20
A
B
C
D
E
F
20:1:1,5
20:2:1
20:4:2
20:5,5:2,5
20:7:3
20:7,5:3,5
H
J
K
L
20:2:3
20:4:3
20:5,5:3,5
20:7:3,5
Picea pungens Engelm.
P
Q
R
20:2:5
20:4:4,5
20:6:4,5
U
W
20:2:7
20:4:6
Koniferen-Blaureif
Conifer frosty-blue
Givre bleuâtre de conifères
Gris azulado de las coniferas
Prof. Dr. E. Biesalski · Pflanzenfarben-Atlas mit Farbzeichen nach DIN 6164 in der Genauigkeitsstufe 1/2

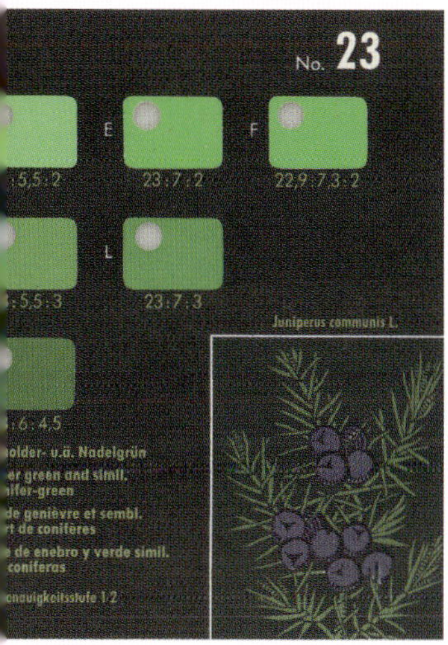
No. 23
E
F
23:7:2
22,9:7,3:2
L
23:7:3
Juniperus communis L.

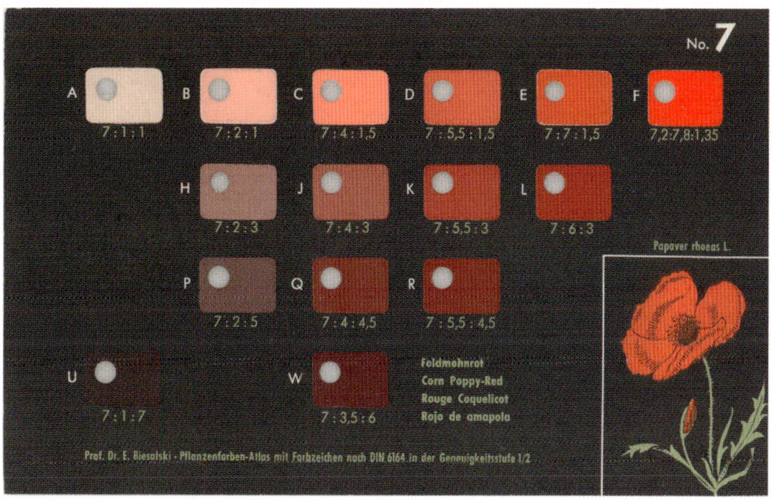
No. 7
A
B
C
D
E
F
7:1:1
7:2:1
7:4:1,5
7:5,5:1,5
7:7:1,5
7,2:7,8:1,35
H
J
K
L
7:2:3
7:4:3
7:5,5:3
7:6:3
Papaver rhoeas L.
P
Q
R
7:2:5
7:4:4,5
7:5,5:4,5
U
W
7:1:7
7:3,5:6
Feldmohnrot
Corn Poppy-Red
Rouge Coquelicot
Rojo de amapola
Prof. Dr. E. Biesalski · Pflanzenfarben-Atlas mit Farbzeichen nach DIN 6164 in der Genauigkeitsstufe 1/2

juniper green), the colors he specified were examples of Germany's DIN 6164, a national color standard that aimed to simplify the Ostwald system (see p.222). This slimline work included thirty ringbound cards displaying a total of 450 color chips linked to flower colors and named species, from marigold red to cornflower blue. Each tint and shade had a hole punched through its top corner to allow the user to pass a physical sample of a petal below and align it with its perfect match.

Love of nature and love of color are so often symbiotic that the relationship has frequently been explored in teaching manuals, with the creative process of the artist likened to the intricacies of the natural world, itself a universal sourcebook of color combinations. The subject recurred throughout classic texts on the use of color, including the writings of Ogden Rood (see p.168), Emily Noyes Vanderpoel (see p.231) and Albert Munsell (see p.225). It was also present in *The Grammar of Ornament* (1856), Owen Jones's sourcebook of global design principles (see p.195) in which he repeatedly praised cultures that drew inspiration from nature and observed its compositional laws. Chapter 20 of this handsome volume was dedicated to leaf shapes in outline, and one full-color plate (No. 8) was the work of the exceptional young designer Christopher Dresser, a "geometrical arrangement of natural flowers" expressed as plans and elevations. In a neat echo, the carpets of leaves in *Grammar* recurred a century later in Josef Albers's immersive, inspirational workbook *Interaction of Color* (1963, see p.242), complete with its many luminous screenprints of visual color exercises. Albers, a Yale professor by way of the Bauhaus school in Germany, included a leaf-based series of color plates designed by his students in a section entitled "Fall leaf studies—an American discovery". These presented juxtapositions of the natural colors of Connecticut autumn leaves with samples of brightly and artificially colored paper, resulting in bold contrasts and disrupted palettes, a collision of organic and inorganic hues. For Albers, "they [the leaves] add innumerable tints and shades with modulations and shapes that color papers do not have". Arguably reflecting the enthusiasm of the émigré professor for the colors of a New England fall, the "discovery" of the title may have been as much the teacher's as his pupils'.

Naturalists who anatomized color just as they dissected specimens attempted the impossible: to cram the colors of the natural world between the hard covers of small publications, like petals in a Victorian flower press. These bibliographic specimen cases both divorce color from its natural habitats and amplify it. Color catalogers and artists alike have always used the colors of nature to spur creativity: dragging the palette out of the woods and into the home, whether in the form of earth-toned household paint or vibrant soft furnishings. Nature's colors could be tamed, even while they remained nonpareil. After all, as nineteenth-century painter F.W. Moody observed, and Emily Noyes Vanderpoel repeated: "There is hardly anything in nature that is not perfect in color."

Plate No. 8 from the section "Leaves and Flowers from Nature" in Owen Jones's repository of the decorative arts *The Grammar of Ornament* (1856). This plate, illustrated by the accomplished designer Christopher Dresser, charted leaf and petal formations.

PLATE XCVIII

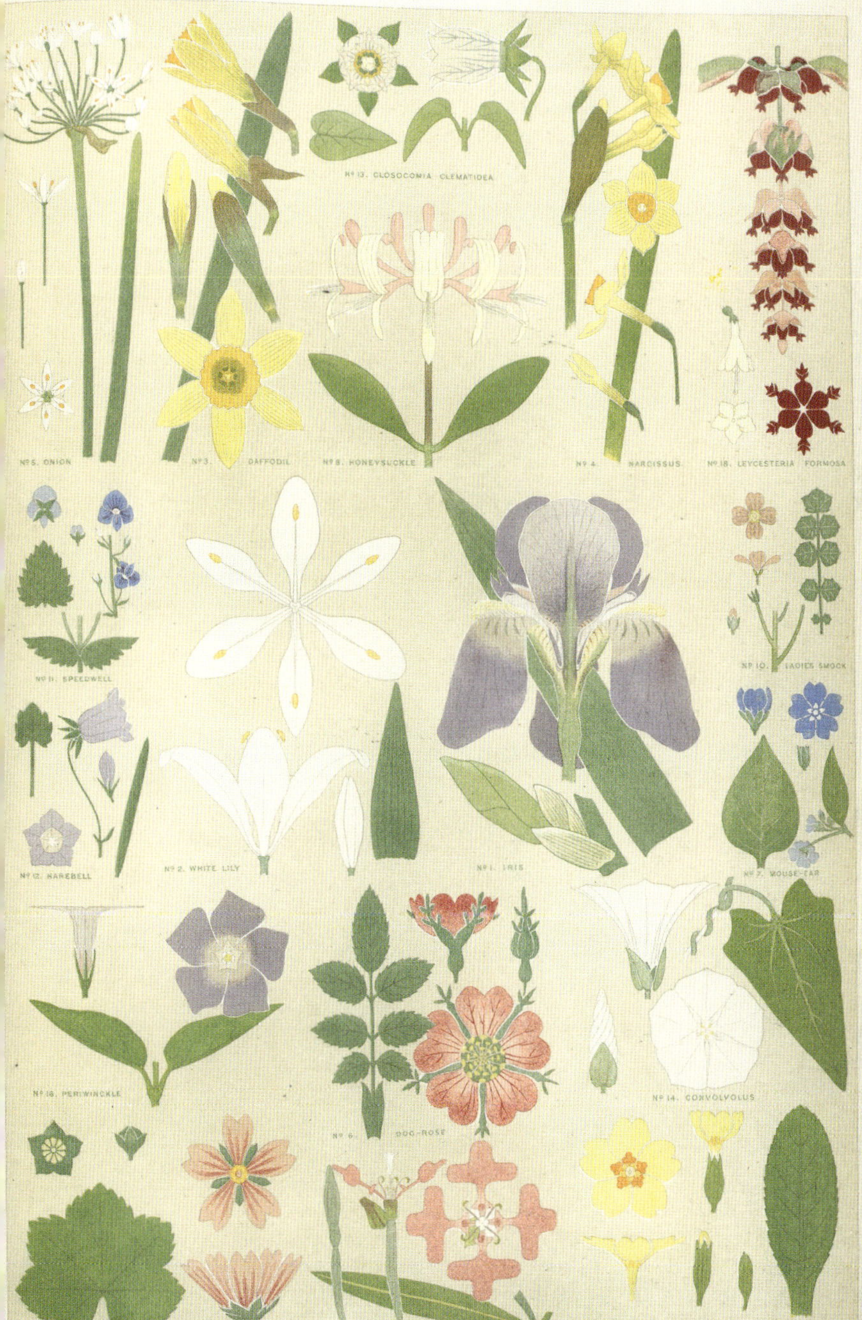

LEAVES AND FLOWERS FROM NATURE No 8

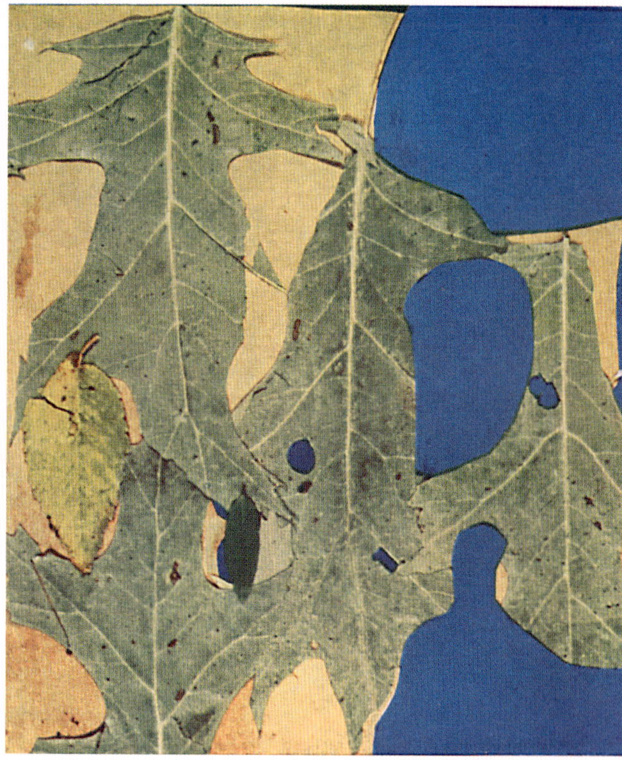

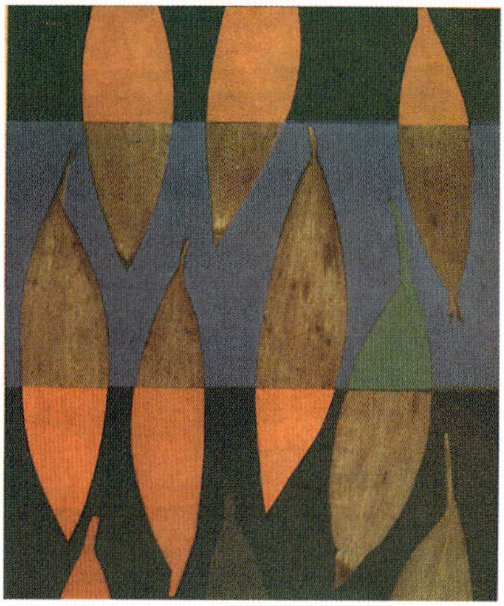

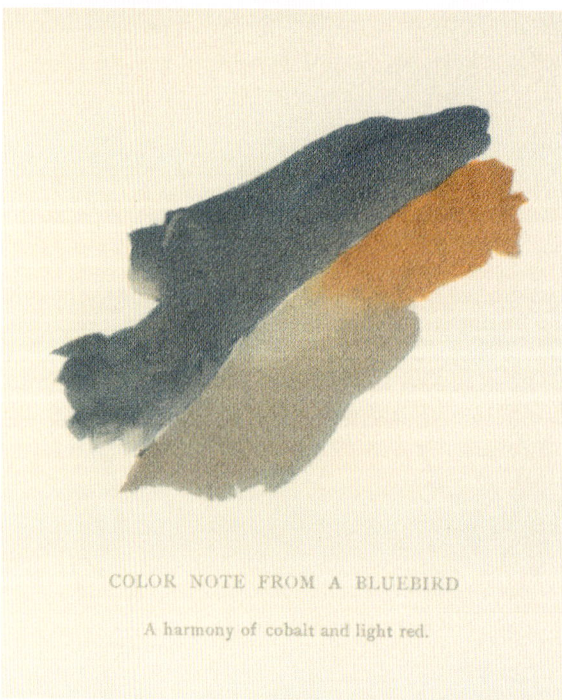

ABOVE AND OPPOSITE

Fall leaf studies from Josef Albers's *Interaction of Color* (1963).

LEFT

One of Emily Noyes Vanderpoel's color abstractions in her work *Color Problems* (1901) recording the color palette of a bluebird.

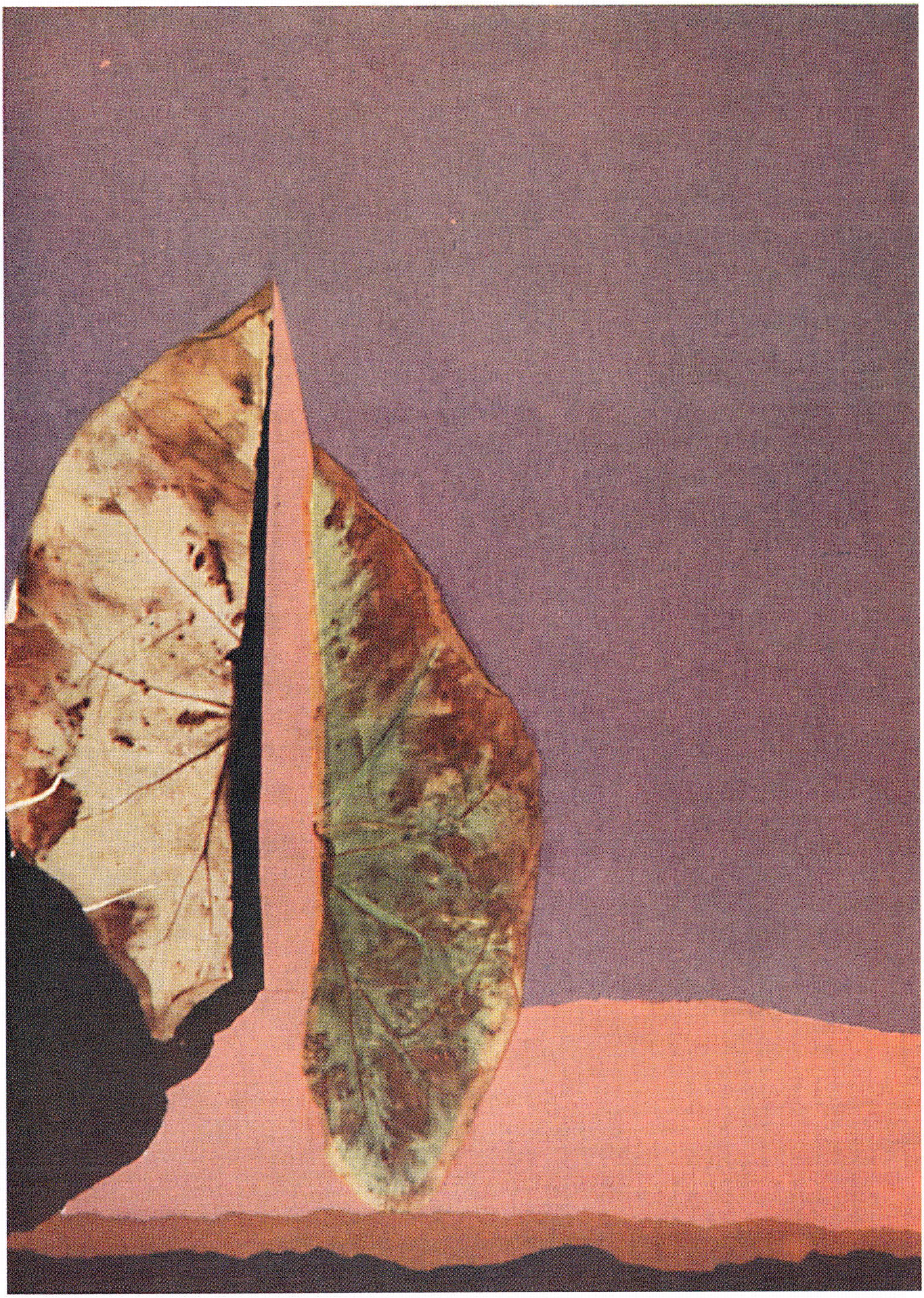

5

THE COLOR OF

FOOD

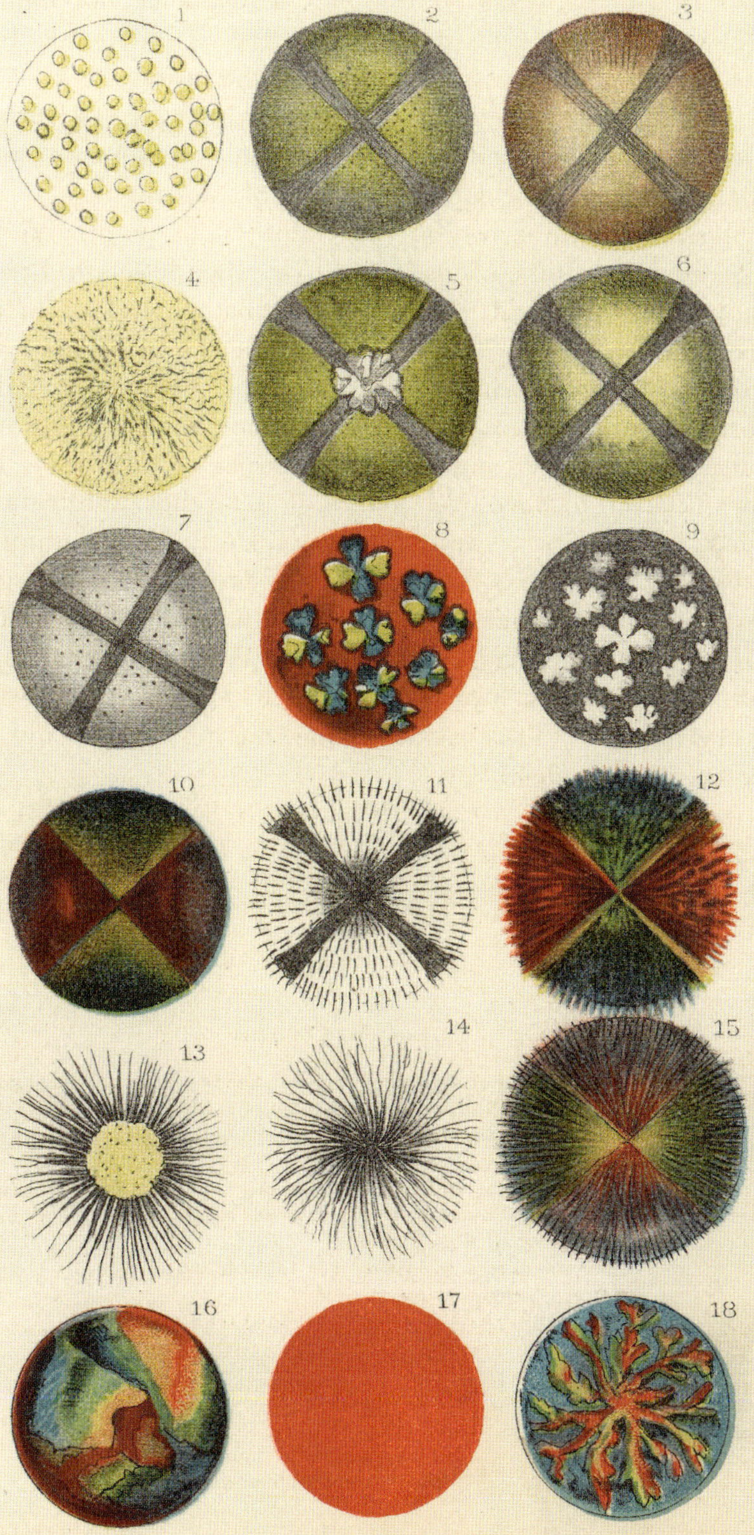
1
2
3
4
5
6
7
8
9
10
11
12
13
14
15
16
17
18

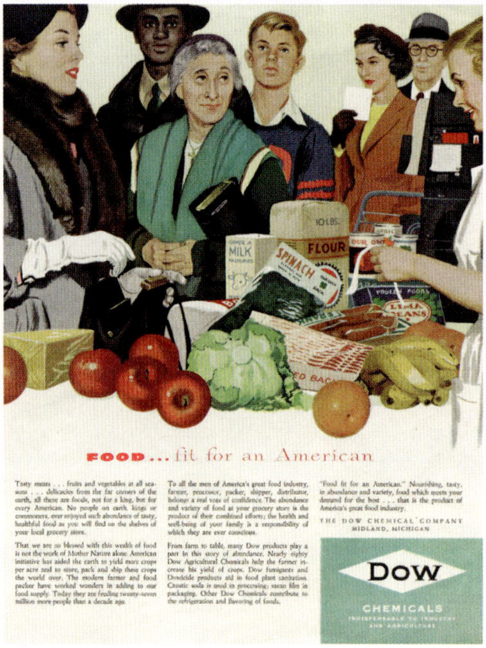

Historically, the relationship between color and food was a matter of life and death. Evolutionary psychology helps explain our enduring reactions to certain colors: how our ancestors learned to avoid the poisonous reds and purples of berries, for example, or to recoil from blue-green mold on spoiled food. In *The Art of Color* (1961) painter and color educator Johannes Itten shared a story about an odd-sounding businessman who, while hosting an extravagant dinner, sprang a trick on his guests by adjusting the lighting to change the dishes' appearance midcourse. As the ambient light switched from white to blue, the roast meat everyone had been enjoying transformed on the fork to appear rotten, while the side of potatoes seemed to become riddled with mold. Some left the room in disgust and "no one could think of eating". Implausibly, we are told everyone cheered up again as soon as the white lights came back on but, Itten concluded, "who can doubt that colors exert profound influences upon us?"

There have been numerous experiments in which the conventional color of food and drink has been manipulated, with no impact on flavor, to see what effect this dissonance has on our enjoyment and our perceived taste. The results broadly conclude that color adjustments can make food either more or less flavorsome, or sweeter. In one study, the number of people believing a cherry-flavored drink tasted of lime shot up when it was colored green rather than red. Even wine connoisseurs have been deceived into believing a white wine was red when it was artificially colored to match. The color of crockery on which food is served also has an effect. An experiment conducted with the test kitchen of chef Ferran Adrià of the El Bulli restaurant found that a strawberry dessert was significantly preferred, and judged to be sweeter, when served on a white plate rather than a black one. Other studies concluded that hot chocolate tasted better from an orange-colored cup, while the flavor

PREVIOUS PAGE
"Crystals of fats, butter, beef, and lard, representing butter, oleomargarine and butterine", in Dr Thomas Taylor's pamphlet *Reply to Science, Relating to the Crystals of Butter, Animal Fats and Oleomargarine* (1886).

ABOVE
"Food Fit for an American", a color advertisement for the Dow Chemical Company (1952). The company's message promoted its use of chemicals to increase crop yields, and its development of cling film. The rich colors of the produce in the illustration denote their quality and freshness.

of red wine improved when sipped from a blue glass.

The color of drinks was itself the subject of scientific investigation and standardization in the late nineteenth century when a British brewer, Joseph Williams Lovibond (1833–1918), invented a device, the Tintometer, to define the quality of malts and beers by measuring their precise color. A small sample was held in a glass receptacle that adjoined a series of red, blue, and yellow filters, twenty of each. These could be slotted alongside and rearranged, incrementally, adjusted through trial and error, until a visible color match was achieved. In his book *Light and Colour Theories and Their Relation to Colour Standardisation* (1915), Lovibond described how all his efforts began with a quest for something he called "golden amber", convinced that the color of beer was a marker of its quality. The Tintometer was a successful, effective device for visual color measurement that found wide application beyond its original role in the brewing industry (see p.180).

While there have been a few significant publications on the psychology of food color and the chemical composition of natural and artificial colors, food as a subject of study in relation to color theory was rarely considered in the many practical manuals of color use. An exception was found in Emily Noyes Vanderpoel's *Color Problems* (1901, see p.231). Vanderpoel uniquely analyzed successful color combinations in life and art by breaking them down into grids to represent the composition and color proportions of her subjects. One of her examples was a prize-winning display of a dinner service at a flower show in Madison Square Garden. Vanderpoel praised the effective and harmonious juxtaposition of purple grapes, yellow candies, and yellow-brown almonds.

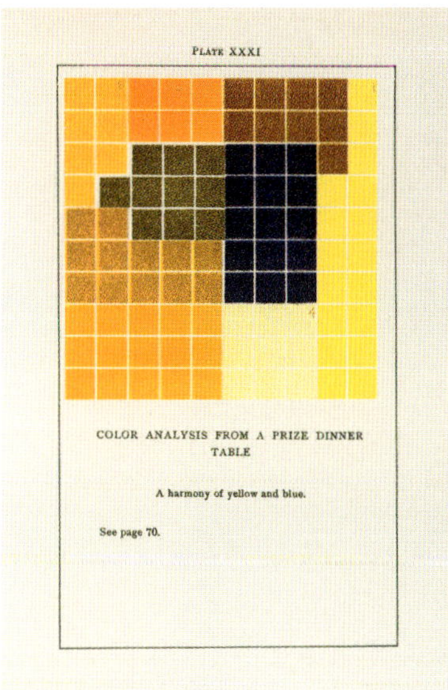

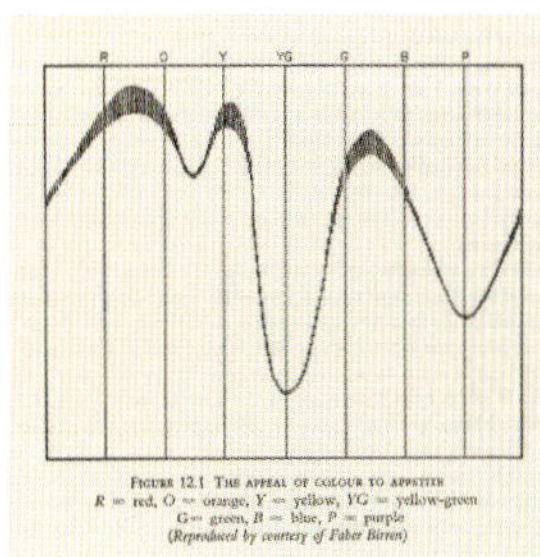

RIGHT
The color composition of a prize-winning table display of nuts and grapes as recorded and analyzed by Emily Noyes Vanderpoel in her work *Color Problems* (1901).

FAR RIGHT
A graph in color consultant Eric P. Danger's study *Using Colour to Sell* (1968). Borrowed from his associate Faber Birren, it charted the effect of food colors on appetite. A clear peak among red-orange foods sharply contrasts with those that are yellow-green, which, Danger suggested, are too redolent of sickness.

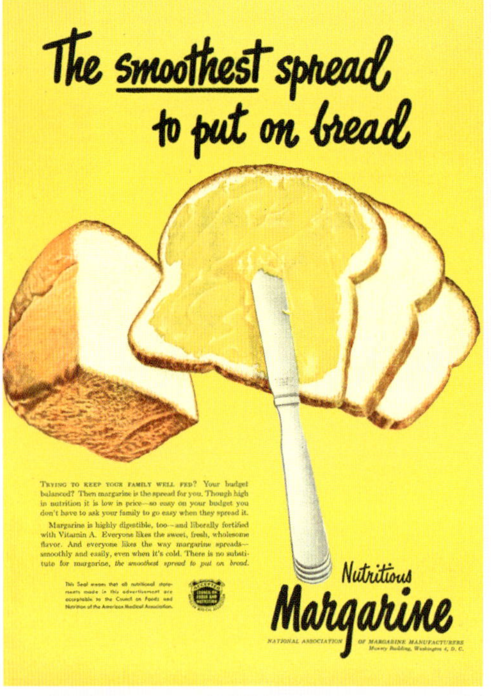

In the West, few consumer goods, including food, were untouched in the so-called color revolution of the early twentieth century, as the home came alive with brightly colored products that exploited the recent advances in synthetic dyes. A more colorful future meant a brighter future, and one that could be glimpsed even at mealtimes. As the range of synthetic food colors expanded, a balance had to be struck between making food appetizing through enhancement of natural hues, and rendering it uncanny and off-putting. The American food industry began to color foods artificially as early as the 1870s, when dye producers started to supply the dairy industry with colorants to boost their products' visual appeal. By the 1930s, the palette and menu of artificially colored food had expanded to include sausages, tinned foods, and ice cream. In 1930, the National Aniline & Chemical Company, one of a small number of US manufacturers with government approval to produce food coloring, issued a guide to colors "officially authorized for use in food products after proper certification" that was part product card and part instruction manual. Claiming that these colors were the ones used by the "most particular" products, including confectionery, ice cream, and drinks, the guide was structured into primary and secondary series of colors, with the primaries, including the alarmingly yellow Tartrazine and the electric Brilliant Blue, resembling the pure unmixed hues of an artist's palette. Once blended into a wider range of secondaries, however, the colors were softened and received names that reflected idealized colors for familiar foods, including Peach, Egg, Wine, Strawberry, Pistachio, and Coffee. The publication instructed manufacturers to use rich and brilliant colors for (child-friendly) candy but subtle and natural ones for ice cream. Sometimes the garish primaries were used unadulterated. Brilliant Blue was used to colorize cake frosting and to intensify the color of tinned peas. National Yellow was soluble in fat and recommended for dyeing butter and margarine, but much of North America was caught up at the time in regulations that prohibited margarine manufacturers from the use of yellow food coloring in their product after the dairy industry lobbied vociferously against it, rightly fearing competition. Instead, in a bizarre case of industry regulation, many manufacturers were compelled to dye margarine other colors to make clear it was emphatically not butter, resulting in the unappetizing spectacle of pink- or gray-colored spreads at the breakfast table.

The problem with artificial food coloring was that it set impossibly high standards for "natural" produce, and the proliferation of bright, gaudy color in the advertising of fruit and vegetables established a link between the intensity and brightness of colors and the goodness and quality of the food. If produce was an off-putting color, consumers would vote with their feet, but how to decide on

OPPOSITE
Advertisement of the National Association of Margarine Manufacturers (US) promoting margarine in its overwhelmingly yellow variety (1948).

RIGHT
In 1930, the National Aniline & Chemical Company (US) produced a guide to colors authorized for use in food. It included recommended palettes for ice cream, confectionery, and drinks.

BELOW
Plate 17 in Maerz and Paul's *A Dictionary of Color* (1930) was used by the US Department of Agriculture to identify the type of green acceptable for Grade A frozen peas.

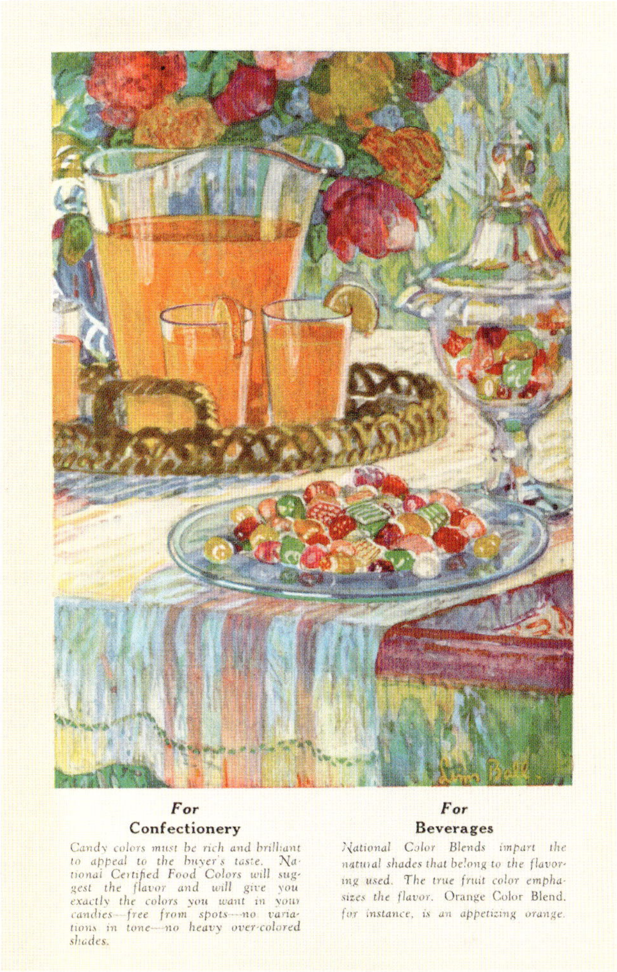

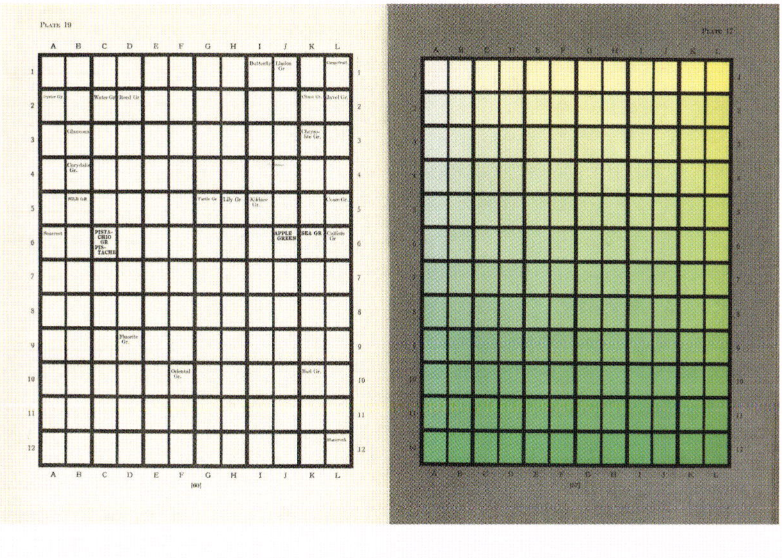

the acceptable quality for sale? The food industry turned to established general color standards, most notably the Munsell system of the early twentieth century (see p.222) to specify particular optimal hues, but other systems were put to use as the years unfolded. In 1930, the same year that the National Aniline & Chemical Company issued its guide to artificial colors, an exhaustive compendium, *A Dictionary of Color* by Aloys Maerz and Morris Rea Paul, was published (see p.65). Bursting with over 7,000 individual tints and shades, complete with standardized references to individual color names, this was an enormous, authoritative gridded swatch book of possible terminology, intended for wide reference and use. It was quickly applied to unexpected industries, and taken up by the US Department of Agriculture not only for specification purposes but to establish minimum standards of color saturation and value for fruit and vegetables for grading purposes. If, for example, frozen peas were lighter than the green sample with coordinates L9 (see p.129, below), they could not be graded higher than a B. Plainly the best peas were the greenest peas, even if they were not, ironically, the same color that Maerz and Paul defined as "Pea Green" elsewhere in their book.

Much has been written about both the psychology and chemistry of food coloring, but with few efforts to apply color theory to actual meal-planning and the art of cookery. One scholar who gamely attempted to formalize a link was Annikki Avotie of Finland, author of *Gastronomic Colour Theory and Composition* (1994). Avotie, a painter, rightly noted the paucity of references to food in the color canon, and tried to bring classic theories of composition to the kitchen and dining table. Influenced in particular by Goethe and Itten, along with Finnish architect Seppo Rihlama, she aimed to create menus where the food's aesthetic visual harmony took precedence over its nutritional value. Avotie explained that her interest in the color theory of food was piqued when she started to explore how Japanese cooks played with light and dark by making tiny cuts in fruit and vegetables. She made frequent reference to Rihlama's own color wheel, the so-called RA system, based on a circle of twenty-four numbered bright colors. Inspired by Itten's *Art of Color*, Rihlama identified many different types of contrast, and Avotie provided examples of food combinations for each. A cold-warm contrast, for example, could be created with shredded red cabbage piled alongside grated carrot. Other food combinations reflected dyads and triads uncovered by Itten's theories; quite a challenge when blue is almost entirely absent from food sources, and vegetable colors cannot be easily blended like paint from a tube. Avotie suggested different cooking techniques, such as boiling vegetables to create tints, and using sprinklings of herbs, spices, and edible flowers to create impactful, contrasting garnishes. If this all sounded complicated and restrictive, exasperated dinner-party hosts might be relieved by the section "When to ignore the rules". Ultimately, *Gastronomic Colour Theory and Composition* was a high-concept and high-effort approach to the simple pleasures of cooking.

Although there may be good reasons why color theory cannot fruitfully be applied to food, the relationship between the two is a long and close one, not least in the naming of colors themselves. Common terms for secondary and tertiary colors—orange and olive—refer directly to their edible namesakes and the name of the orange fruit long preceded its use as a color category. In the twentieth-century revolution of mass-marketed paint and dyes, when color looked good enough to eat, marketers frequently reached for evocative associations in their terminology. The resulting inventories, stuffed with aubergine, mushroom, walnut, plum, turmeric, and cinnamon, often read less like a catalog of dye samples and more like a grocery list.

RIGHT

The National Aniline & Chemical Company's guide to food coloring (1930) included sets of primary and secondary colors for use in food. The primaries were shockingly bright but were blended into more natural tones, approximating cherry, pistachio, and chocolate, among others.

BELOW

Finnish artist Annikki Avotie produced a book on "gastronomic color theory" in 1994, demonstrating how Johannes Itten's laws of contrast in composition could be applied to food on the plate.

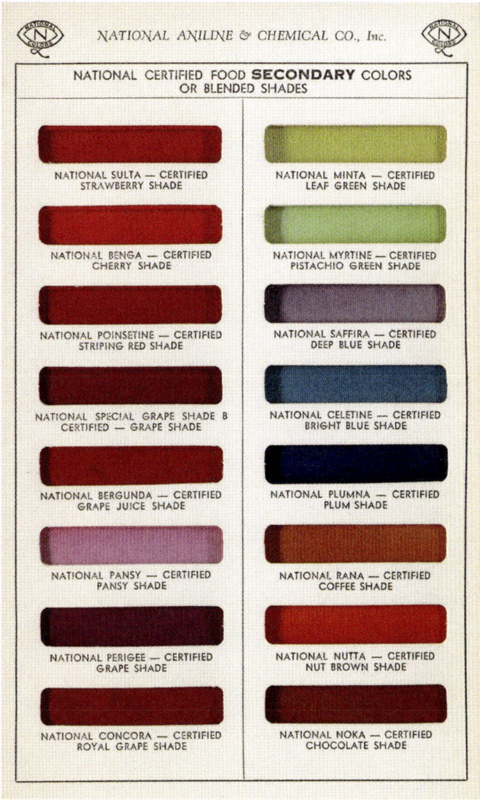

NATIONAL ANILINE & CHEMICAL CO., Inc.

NATIONAL CERTIFIED FOOD **SECONDARY** COLORS OR BLENDED SHADES

NATIONAL SULTA — CERTIFIED STRAWBERRY SHADE	NATIONAL MINTA — CERTIFIED LEAF GREEN SHADE
NATIONAL BENGA — CERTIFIED CHERRY SHADE	NATIONAL MYRTINE — CERTIFIED PISTACHIO GREEN SHADE
NATIONAL POINSETINE — CERTIFIED STRIPING RED SHADE	NATIONAL SAFFIRA — CERTIFIED DEEP BLUE SHADE
NATIONAL SPECIAL GRAPE SHADE B CERTIFIED — GRAPE SHADE	NATIONAL CELETINE — CERTIFIED BRIGHT BLUE SHADE
NATIONAL BERGUNDA — CERTIFIED GRAPE JUICE SHADE	NATIONAL PLUMNA — CERTIFIED PLUM SHADE
NATIONAL PANSY — CERTIFIED PANSY SHADE	NATIONAL RANA — CERTIFIED COFFEE SHADE
NATIONAL PERIGEE — CERTIFIED GRAPE SHADE	NATIONAL NUTTA — CERTIFIED NUT BROWN SHADE
NATIONAL CONCORA — CERTIFIED ROYAL GRAPE SHADE	NATIONAL NOKA — CERTIFIED CHOCOLATE SHADE

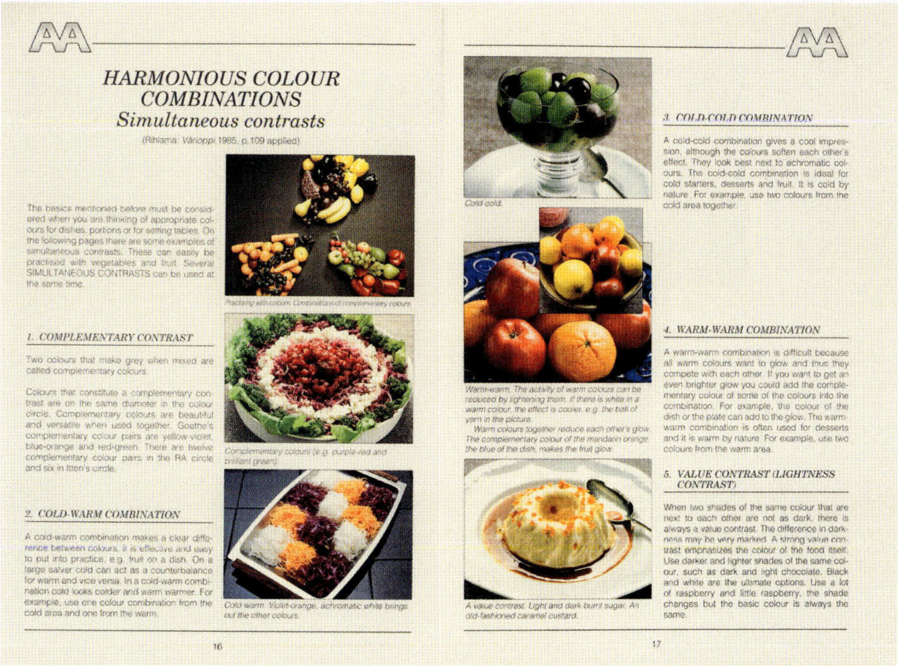

HARMONIOUS COLOUR COMBINATIONS

Simultaneous contrasts

(Rihlama: *Värioppi* 1985, p.109 applied)

The basics mentioned before must be considered when you are thinking of appropriate colours for dishes, portions or for setting tables. On the following pages there are some examples of simultaneous contrasts. These can easily be practised with vegetables and fruit. Several SIMULTANEOUS CONTRASTS can be used at the same time.

Practising with colours. Combinations of complementary colours.

1. COMPLEMENTARY CONTRAST

Two colours that make grey when mixed are called complementary colours.

Colours that constitute a complementary contrast are on the same diameter in the colour circle. Complementary colours are beautiful and versatile when used together. Goethe's complementary colour pairs are yellow-violet, blue-orange and red-green. There are twelve complementary colour pairs in the RA circle and six in Itten's circle.

Complementary colours (e.g. purple-red and brilliant green).

2. COLD-WARM COMBINATION

A cold-warm combination makes a clear difference between colours. It is effective and easy to put into practice, e.g. fruit on a dish. On a large salver cold can act as a counterbalance for warm and vice versa. In a cold-warm combination cold looks colder and warm warmer. For example, use one colour combination from the cold area and one from the warm.

Cold-warm. Violet-orange, achromatic white brings out the other colours.

16

Cold-cold.

3. COLD-COLD COMBINATION

A cold-cold combination gives a cool impression, although the colours soften each other's effect. They look best next to achromatic colours. The cold-cold combination is ideal for cold starters, desserts and fruit. It is cold by nature. For example, use two colours from the cold area together.

Warm-warm. The activity of warm colours can be reduced by lightening them. If there is white in a warm colour, the effect is cooler, e.g. the ball of yarn in the picture.

Warm colours together reduce each other's glow. The complementary colour of the mandarin orange the blue of the dish, makes the fruit glow.

4. WARM-WARM COMBINATION

A warm-warm combination is difficult because all warm colours want to glow and thus they compete with each other. If you want to get an even brighter glow you could add the complementary colour of some of the colours into the combination. For example, the colour of the dish or the plate can add to the glow. The warm-warm combination is often used for desserts and it is warm by nature. For example, use two colours from the warm area.

5. VALUE CONTRAST (LIGHTNESS CONTRAST)

When two shades of the same colour that are next to each other are not as dark, there is always a value contrast. The difference in darkness may be very marked. A strong value contrast emphasizes the colour of the food itself. Use darker and lighter shades of the same colour, such as dark and light chocolate. Black and white are the ultimate options. Use a lot of raspberry and little raspberry, the shade changes but the basic colour is always the same.

A value contrast. Light and dark burnt sugar. An old-fashioned caramel custard.

17

1836

1900

MAGICAL

DRAPERY

In the early decades of the nineteenth century, publications on the subject of color began to move from the "how" to the "how-to". Physicists had explained what color was made of; naturalists had structured and named it. There was a broad understanding of where color had come from, but it was time to think about where it was going. Against the background noise of the Industrial Revolution, the commodification of color gathered pace in the business of pigments and dyes. Scientists, scholars, artists, and makers began to examine how the colors of the earth, and the ever-increasing range created through chemistry, could be most satisfactorily applied to works of art and decorative schemes. Commercial forces encroached upon Enlightenment values and development was rapid.

The middle of the century was pivotal. The Great Exhibition of the Works of Industry of All Nations, which took place in London in 1851, celebrated new technology and global design, a cavernous showcase of international color palettes and preferences. Just a few years later, the enormous and lucrative textile industry was aglow, aesthetically and commercially, with a new synthetic purplish color brought to market under the name mauve (from the French word for mallow). It was discovered accidentally by the young chemist William Perkin, who had been experimenting with aniline, a colorless liquid extracted from coal tar, the unpleasant black waste product of gas lighting. Perkin's innovation transformed the market, spurring a short-lived but intense fashion for the color, and was a gateway to creating a wide range of resplendent dyes. While "new" colors were becoming possible, traditional hues could be aped through chemical concoctions with none of the grinding, onerous extraction and processing that natural sources required. By the century's end, this had devastating implications for the livelihoods of suppliers of traditional color: the cultivators of the insects that produced cochineal in Mexico, or the many artisans who grew and processed indigo in British-controlled India.

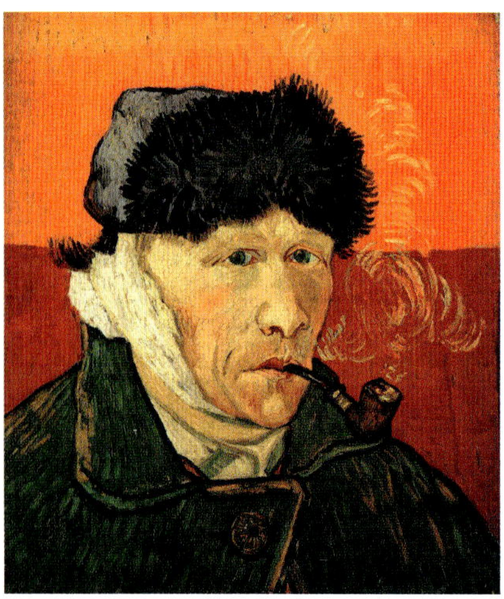

Convenient accidents abounded, unintentionally pushing the science into new areas. Ongoing research into improved manufacturing processes in different disciplines, including ceramics and cosmetics, stumbled across synthetic colorants as by-products that could be redeployed by artists and makers as color jumped from one discipline to another. Once it became cheaper to create and control, color also began to spread from the traditional industries of paints, pigments, and glazes to the printed page, as innovations such as chromolithography (see p.194) increased their reach. All the while, as human exposure to color bloomed, physiologists peered deeper into the eye itself, to understand the processes that turned light waves into the polychromatic pictures of human experience.

The market for instruction manuals for artists, decorators, and makers was booming but the great explainers of color were often still men of science, and one chemist in particular

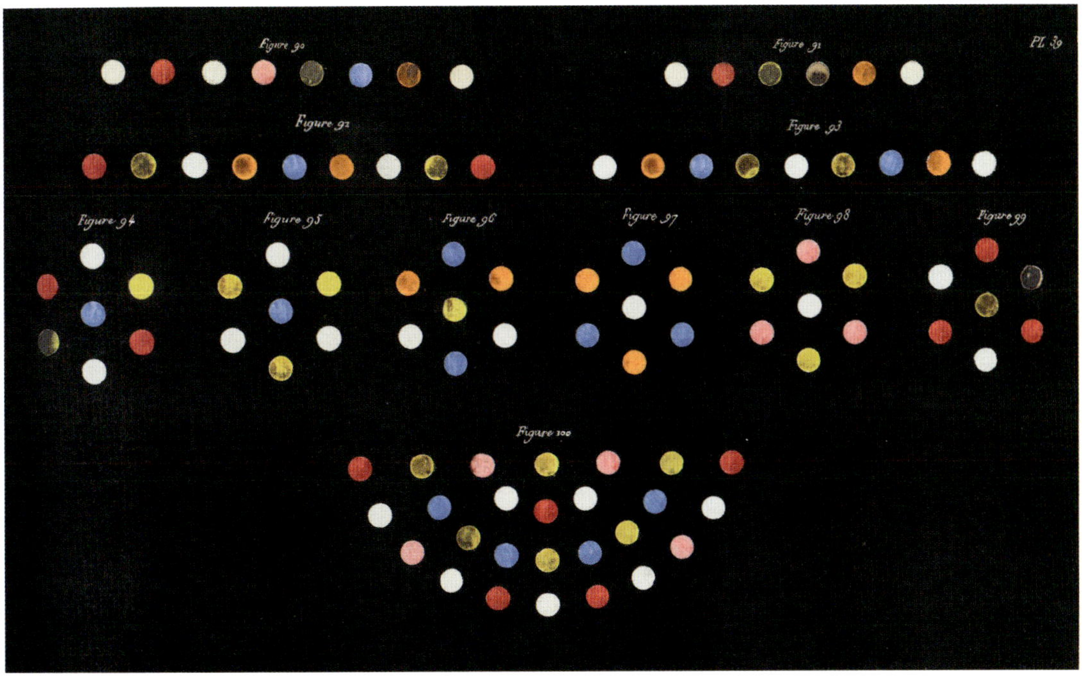

OPPOSITE
Vincent van Gogh, Self-Portrait With Bandaged Ear and Pipe *(1889). The color pairings of orange and blue-gray in the upper section and the green against red in the lower adhere to some of the principles of contrast explored by Chevreul earlier in the century.*

ABOVE
Recommendations for arrangements of flowers in beds and baskets from M.E. Chevreul's color atlas to accompany his work on contrast (1839). Chevreul recommended these juxtapositions for chrysanthemums and asters in order to maximize the contrast between their colors. His prescriptions deeply influenced the garden designer Gertrude Jekyll in later years.

dominated the work of all who followed for decades thereafter. By the century's close, scientists and artists alike were aware of the work of Michel Eugène Chevreul (1786–1889). Although renowned in his field, Chevreul's principal contribution to our better understanding of color had nothing to do with the synthesis of pigments and dyes. Instead, he plunged deep into the world of color perception and optical illusions, exploring how color could be volatile and powerful when applied correctly, exposing its secret rules of behavior and its multiple weird effects on the brain.

Many of the great color books of the era were a deft blend of science and art, communicating the findings of the former to the practitioners of the latter. Chevreul was a master of the genre, exemplified by his panoramic, perception-enhancing work *De la loi du contraste simultané des couleurs* (*On the law of the simultaneous contrast of colors*, 1839). Like many whose contribution to the canon is incalculable, his work on color was initially a tangent, an alluring distraction from other, supposedly more respectable, research. In fact, his original focus was the study of soap and fats: he discovered and named cholesterol, and his work on the analysis of fatty acids directly improved production processes in industry. In 1824, his career took a different turn when he was appointed director of dyeing at the prestigious Gobelins Manufacture, a tapestry factory in Paris. Gobelins was synonymous with quality, supplying

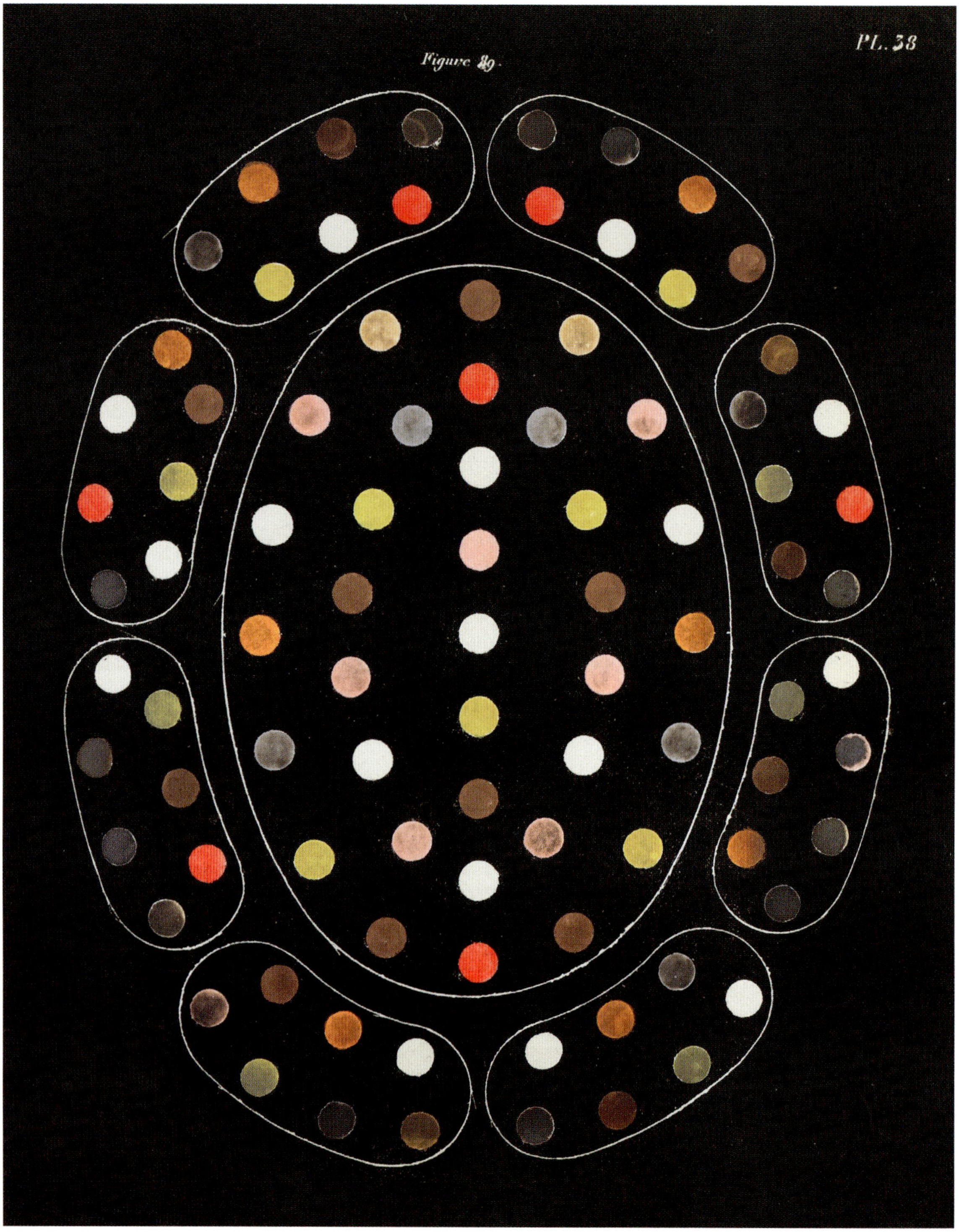
Figure 89.
PL. 38

royalty and government with magnificent wall hangings, but Chevreul soon found himself unexpectedly having to defend the caliber of the company's dyes, especially from in-house critics, where the separate camps of dyers and weavers were engaged in an ongoing feud. The weavers felt the black and violet wool samples supplied to them were below par and complained that a particularly intense black appeared weak and reddish when the completed tapestries were installed. Naturally Chevreul carried out the obvious tests to establish the color fastness but concluded the dye was not at fault. Something stranger was going on, neither on the wall nor in the fibers, but in the eye of the beholder. After careful observation and experimentation, he concluded that any two colors placed side by side in any context, including adjacent sections or threads in the tapestries, changed their appearance from how they looked in isolation. It was as if each color was modifying its neighbor, reacting against it, and shifting it into something else. Sometimes the changes visible in the base colors were so pronounced, one could hardly believe one's eyes.

Chevreul had identified something astonishing. In his own summary, he demonstrated that "where the eye sees at the same time two contiguous colors, they will appear as dissimilar as possible" and named this phenomenon the law of simultaneous contrast. More specifically, Chevreul demonstrated that a color tended to appear to take on the quality of the complementary of its neighbor: a solid black next to a deep blue appeared slightly orangey red, for example, the very complaint of the weavers.

None of these unsteady colors, of course, was changing at the molecular level, but the human observer could not help but interpret them differently. So hard-wired was this tendency of the brain to push apart adjacent colors that the phenomenon worked even in grayscale, as demonstrated when a light gray appeared even lighter when set against a dark gray than in isolation. The effect reached its zenith when two purely complementary colors, those on opposite sides of the color wheel, were juxtaposed. Placing pure orange and blue side by side, for example, resulted in a more orangey orange and an even bluer blue.

While all this suggested color's appearance could be unsteady and unpredictable, making its use in trusted product lines such as tapestries potentially risky, Chevreul saw the bigger picture. He concluded that its behavior, while counterintuitive, was nevertheless consistent among humans and thus entirely predictable. Those who studied his law would be apprised of a powerful tool: the ability to control and heighten contrast for effect in multiple fields, adding luminosity and intensity to a composition through careful pairings of colors. Chevreul worked his observations into a massive volume extending to well over 700 pages and *De la loi* ... was finally published in 1839 after years of work.

Chevreul's recommended arrangement of dahlias in a basket. The "pell-mell" jumble of colors was intended to work more effectively than an overly symmetrical design.

Much of the book described the practical application of these visual effects and provided advice to the artist or maker to help

The color atlas that accompanied Chevreul's work on contrast (1839) included a range of fold-out color schemes set against gray and black backgrounds. These were intended for use by milliners, painters, wallpaper designers, and gardeners, among others. Each dot was hand-painted as Chevreul's vision was beyond the possibilities of color printing at the time.

ramp up or tone down any optical surprises. This dense slab of a publication ambled across the disciplines, describing the effective use of color in contexts including tapestry, furniture, carpets, cartography, interiors, clothing, and horticulture. Practical, evidence-based tips abounded. Chevreul advised women on the optimal colors for their attire depending on their skin tone, and instructed cartographers on colorizing landmasses to ensure placenames remained legible. Museum curators, meanwhile, were told to paint the walls of their institutions white so no background color could distort the beauty of any polychrome specimens on display. (An exception would be made for white marble statuary, which should, of course, be set off against a colored backdrop.)

Chevreul's recommendations were not so much suggestions as statements: advice so grounded in empirical research as to appear incontestable. Many important figures followed his advice for the rest of the century. When painter Gertrude Jekyll reinvented herself as a successful garden designer, it was her memory of studying Chevreul's theories at the National Art Training School in London in the 1860s that led her to experiment with contrasting juxtapositions of blooms, punctuated by neutral colors. In the 1880s, Vincent van Gogh encountered Chevreul's ideas through the mediated writings of Charles Blanc (see p.161), and key principles surfaced in the artist's later paintings. In response to Chevreul's study of contrast, van Gogh juxtaposed blues and oranges in landscapes and experimental self-portraits (reddish hair lent itself readily to this), and wrote that the effect on two complementary colors would "raise both the one and the other to an intensity so violent that human eyes will scarcely be able to bear to look at it". Chevreul would have endorsed the gist, if perhaps not succumbed to the hyperbole.

Chevreul may have even indirectly inspired the very brushstrokes of some artists. While there is little evidence that he influenced the Impressionists, the dot formations in the colorful sample plates in his books resemble the method of the Neo-Impressionist and Divisionist movements of the late nineteenth century, which favored sharp strokes or spots of isolated color. Several decades after the first publication of his law, Chevreul's work shaped the methods of Paul Signac and Georges Seurat, both of whom were animated by the science of color theory where the Impressionists had been left cold. Few tackled Chevreul's work in the raw, however, and he was normally encountered through later mediators, including Blanc, who presented the ideas in a more digestible format.

De la loi... appeared in 1839, but had been ready for publication some years earlier. Its production was delayed by Chevreul's need to create elaborate colored plates to demonstrate the effects described, and his struggle to find a publisher with pockets deep enough to solve its technical challenges. The main 735-page volume was divided into three sections of text: theoretical, practical, and experimental. It was accompanied by a forty-page "atlas"—a

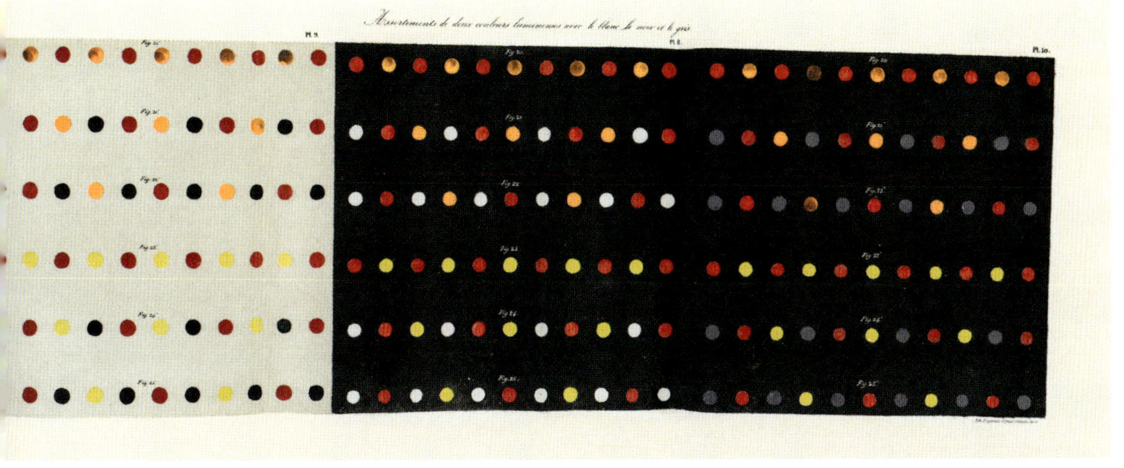

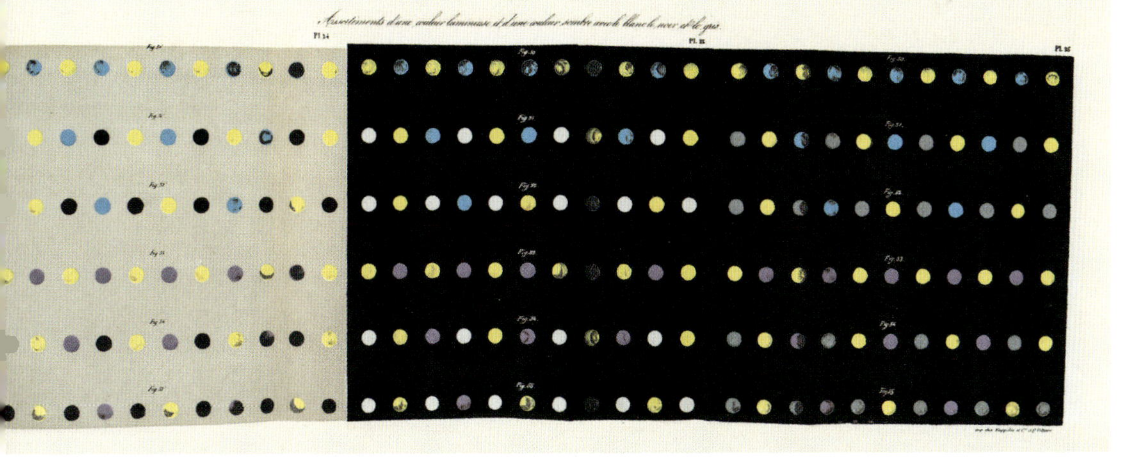

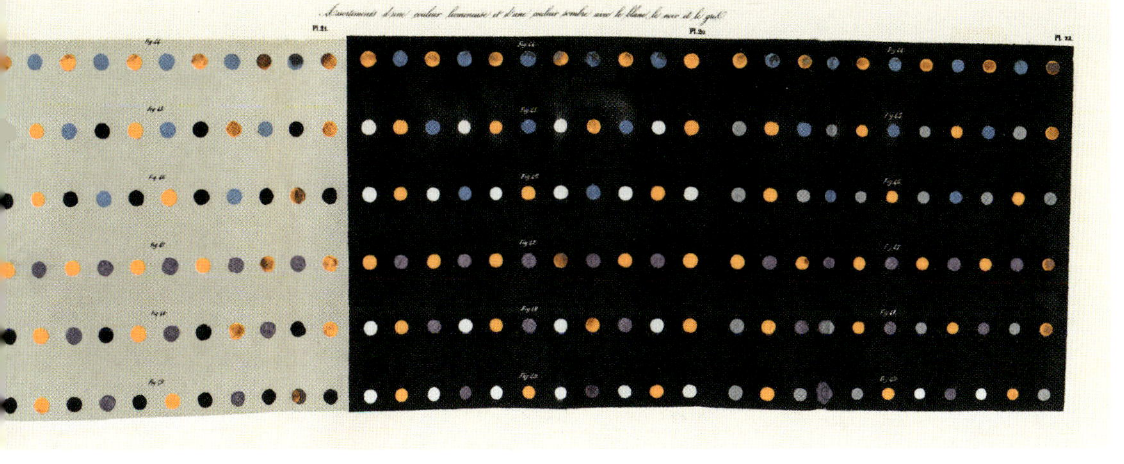

separate but related volume that contained demonstrations of some of the phenomena outlined in its companion piece, resulting in a compendium of tipped-in pages, fold-out plates, colored grounds, and paper engineering. In combination, these pushed printing technology to its limits. Punchy, fold-out sheets of colored dots on white, black and gray backgrounds, each spot hand painted, brilliantly demonstrated the inconsistency of bright color in different contexts. A vivid mint-green glowed against a black background, but visibly dulled when the eye wandered across to its equivalent on gray or white. A piece of placeholder text printed in black ink on different-colored paper stocks illustrated the relationship between contrast and legibility. This volume also included Chevreul's clever representation of a three-dimensional color hemisphere, in which he used a simple paper flap that could be lifted to stand at ninety degrees from the page surface to demonstrate how this model could embody all colors in their different manifestations.

An English translation of the main text by Charles Martel appeared in 1854, without the accompanying atlas or even any color plates at all. Martel explained that use of color would have raised the price "at least threefold, and probably have placed it out of the reach of those most likely to benefit by its use". Instead, he encouraged the reader to recreate the effects using colored paper. *De la loi* ... was reissued in France fifty years after its first publication to celebrate Chevreul's hundredth birthday, and that edition employed specially formulated inks to create 15,000 different tones. In the twentieth century Chevreul's work fell into obscurity, although Bauhaus teachers kept his memory and theories alive, until the book was finally re-issued in 1967.

Among the later publications to which Chevreul's name was attached, the most exquisite was arguably his "*cercles chromatiques*", published in 1861 as *Des couleurs et de leurs applications aux arts industriels à l'aide des cercles chromatiques* (*Colors and their application to industry, using colored circles*) and revised in 1864. Created in close collaboration with master engraver René-Henri Digeon, this was a triumph of color printing, using chromochalcography, a four-color aquatint process that involved separate plates for red, blue, yellow, and black. The book included a series of color "ladders" showing twenty-one-step iterations of hues, rather like Schiffermüller's work of 1772 (see p.80). More notably, this book included ten full-page color wheels, divided into seventy-two hues. As the reader turned the pages and progressed through the book, the colors became increasingly darker as the shades took ever firmer hold, and the distinctionbetween each, so clearly demarcated in the first circle, became barely perceptible by the final iteration. The effect was rather like watching a bowl of fresh fruit progressively spoil.

The long and remarkable career of the indefatigable Chevreul ended with his retirement at the age of ninety-seven. The chemist who had grown up during the French Revolution died aged 103, shortly after his son predeceased him. Chevreul defined a

OPPOSITE

An extract of placeholder text by the Marquis de Condorcet was printed in black ink on a wide range of colored papers in Chevreul's atlas (1839) to demonstrate the effect of different color contrasts on legibility. Crisp text on yellow is easy to read, while the red makes the process a struggle.

OVERLEAF

*Chevreul's twelve "*cercles chromatiques*" (1861) charted the progression of the color wheel into ever-darker variants. In total, Chevreul identified 14,400 shades, tints and tones in his system. The circles were printed using the advanced technique of "*chromochalcographie*", a four-color aquatint process.*

Chevreul had a large physical model of his color circle, woven in wool, on display in his studio, where it was admired by visitors including Owen Jones and Albert Munsell.

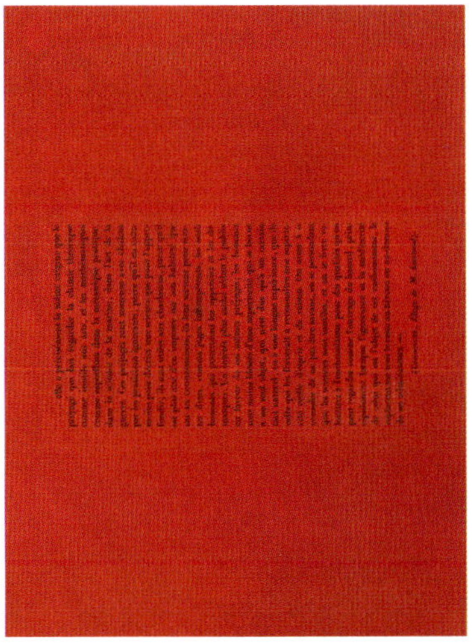

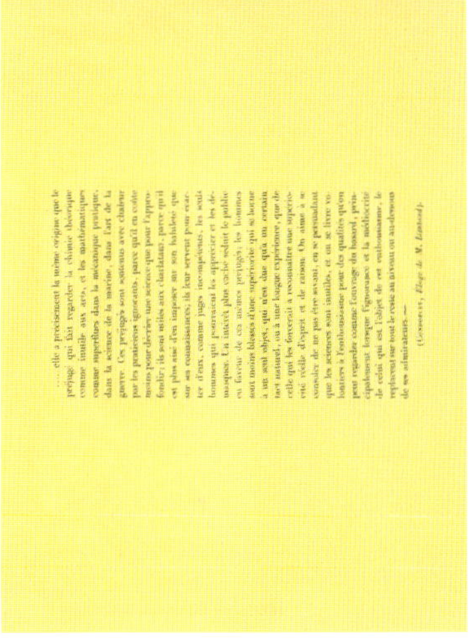

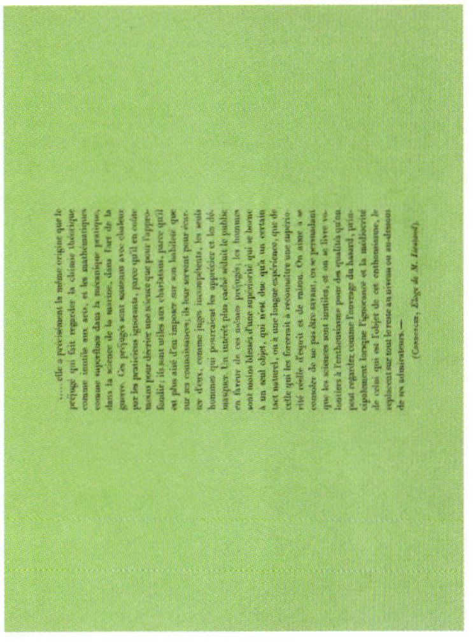

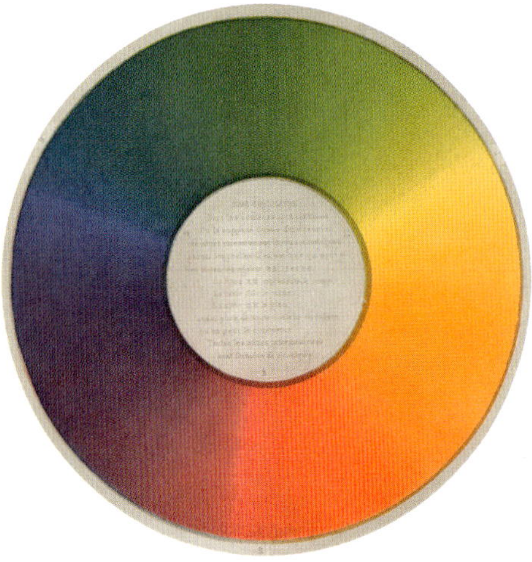

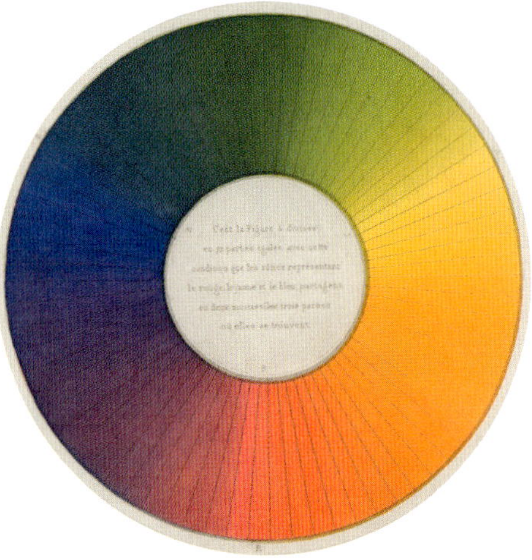

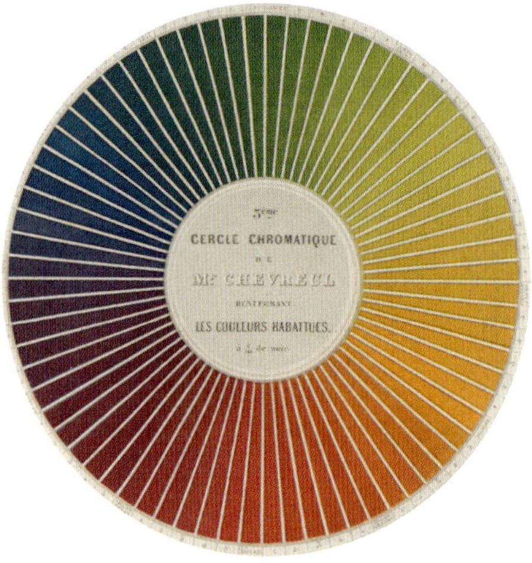
CERCLE CHROMATIQUE
DE
Mr CHEVREUL
LES COULEURS RABATTUES.

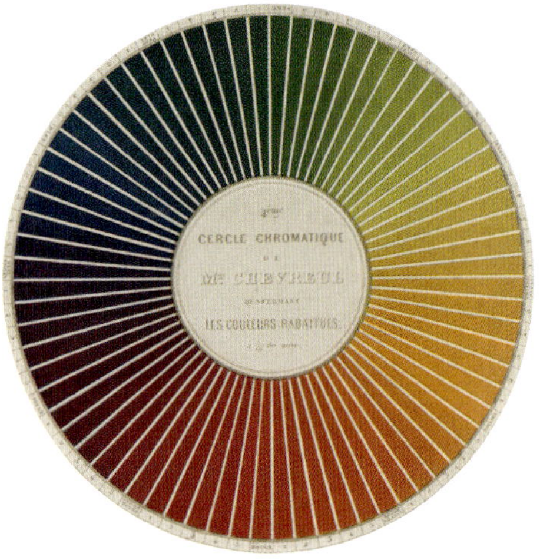
CERCLE CHROMATIQUE
Mr CHEVREUL
LES COULEURS RABATTUES.

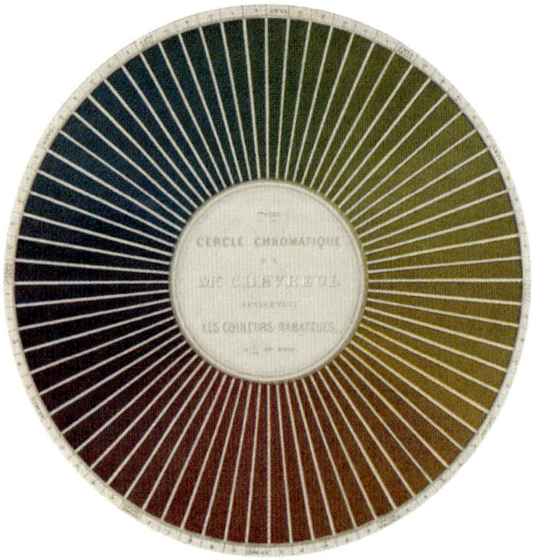
CERCLE CHROMATIQUE
Mr CHEVREUL
LES COULEURS RABATTUES.

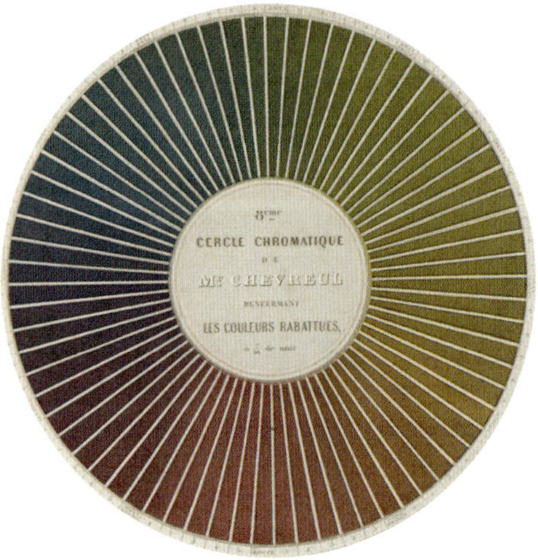
CERCLE CHROMATIQUE
Mr CHEVREUL
LES COULEURS RABATTUES.

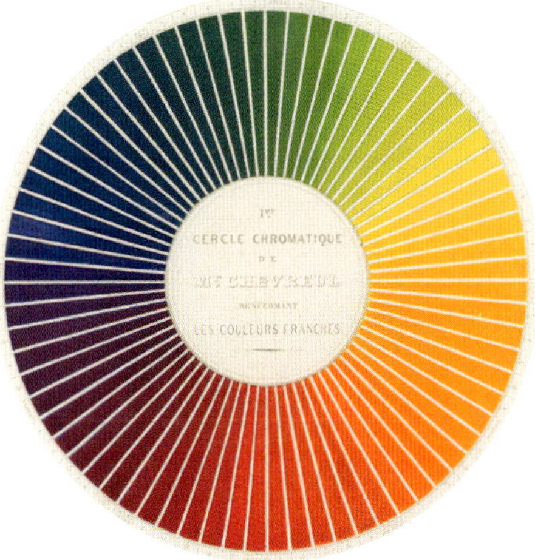
1er
CERCLE CHROMATIQUE
DE
Mr CHEVREUL
RENFERMANT
LES COULEURS FRANCHES.

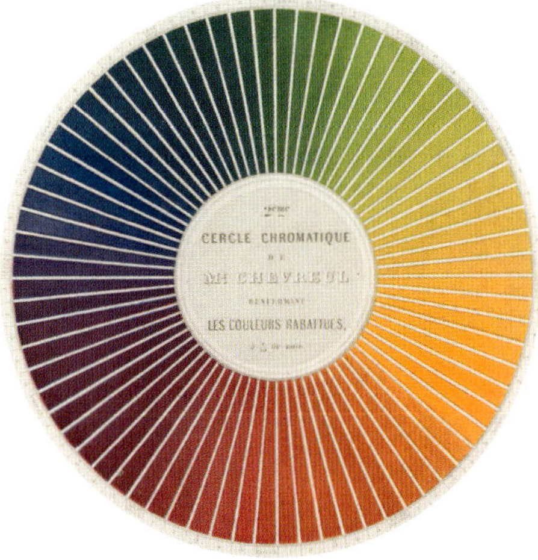
2me
CERCLE CHROMATIQUE
DE
Mr CHEVREUL
RENFERMANT
LES COULEURS RABATTUES,

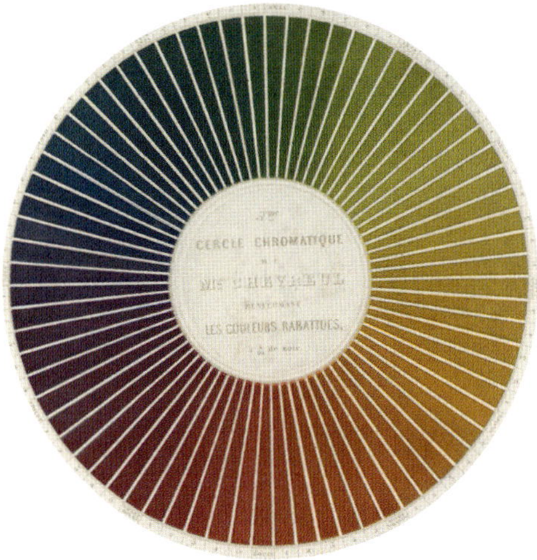
CERCLE CHROMATIQUE
DE
Mr CHEVREUL
RENFERMANT
LES COULEURS RABATTUES,

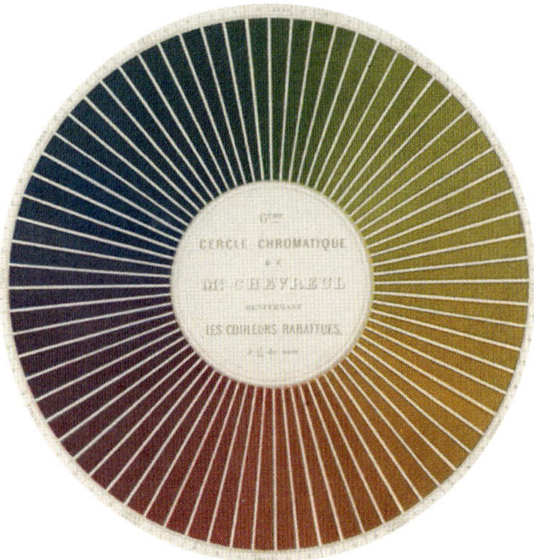
6me
CERCLE CHROMATIQUE
DE
Mr CHEVREUL
RENFERMANT
LES COULEURS RABATTUES,

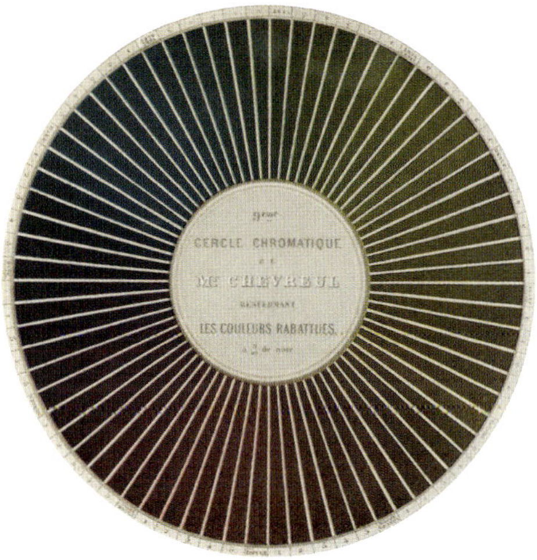
9me
CERCLE CHROMATIQUE
DE
Mr CHEVREUL
RENFERMANT
LES COULEURS RABATTUES,

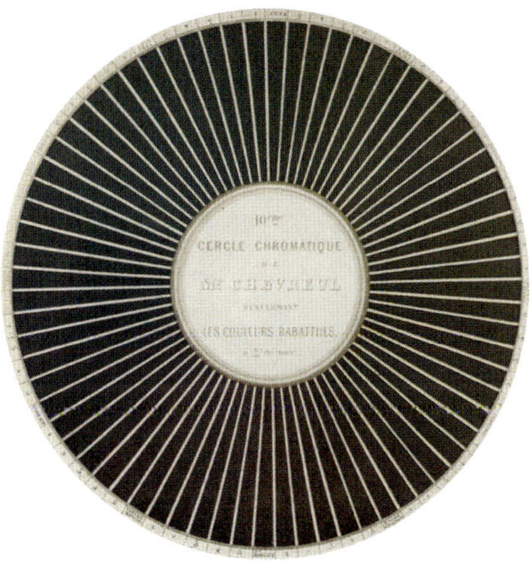
10me
CERCLE CHROMATIQUE
DE
Mr CHEVREUL
RENFERMANT
LES COULEURS RABATTUES,

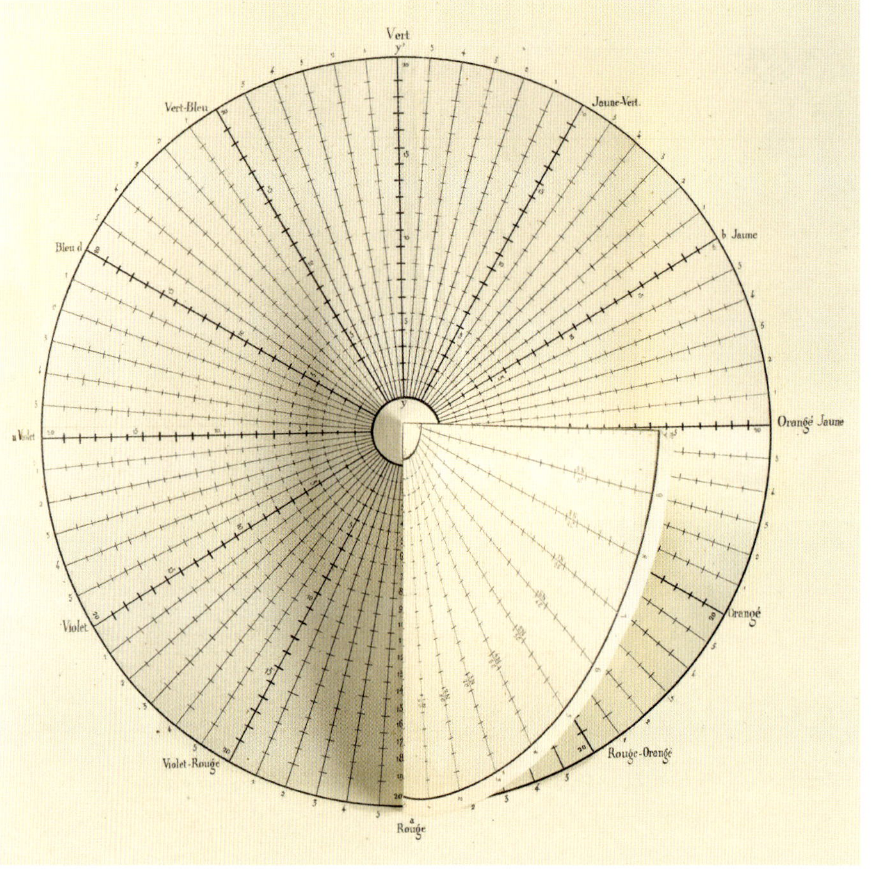
Vert
Jaune-Vert.
b Jaune
Orangé Jaune
Orangé
Rouge-Orangé
Rouge
Violet-Rouge
Violet
a Violet
Bleu d
Vert-Bleu

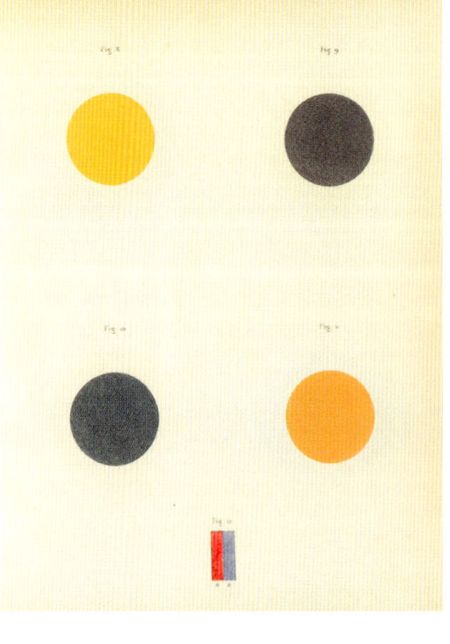

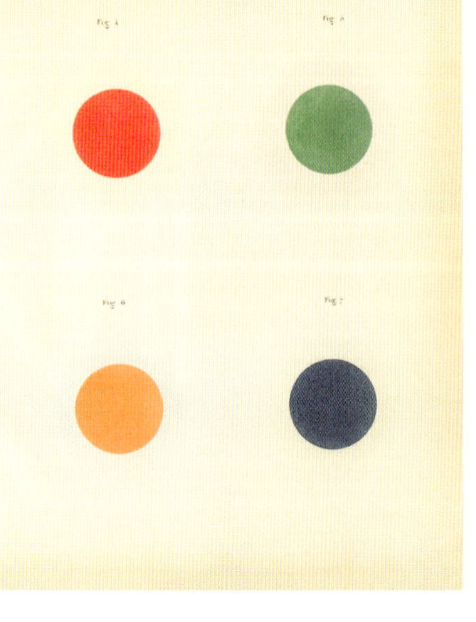

phenomenon and his findings touched everything. His law was as wide as it was deep, demonstrating the totalizing effect of color in all walks of life and craft, while cracking some of its secrets and exposing its capacity to deceive.

Chevreul dominated the discourse on color after the publication of *De la loi* ..., but others were not deterred from weighing in with their own models and explanations. After all, Chevreul had focused exclusively on how color behaved, not what it conveyed. Ample space remained to explore its subjective qualities from a philosophical standpoint. In contrast to Chevreul's physically imposing tome on simultaneous contrast, his compatriot J.C.M. Sol (*fl.* mid-nineteenth century) said all he wanted to say in under sixty pages. Sol was a French poet who felt color could be organized into a system governed by human logic rather than the rules of physics. His work *La palette théorique ou classification des couleurs* (1849) was notable for its detailed lithographed plate. Nestled at the back of the book, awaiting a keen reader to unfold it like a celestial chart, or a treasure map, it opened up to nine times the size of one of the book's standard pages.

Sol grouped color into three categories of uneven quantities. In the first, he placed white in isolation, believing it to be peerless. In the second lay all the primary colors, along with their secondary and tertiary compounds. The third category belonged to those colors softened with white, resulting in pastels and grays. In his model, color only went meaningfully in one direction: toward the light. In Sol's view, just adding a little black to color, to create shades, was a dead end that narrowed the palette down to interchangeable muddy color (Chevreul's "*cercles chromatiques*" rather proved his point). Sol charted the transitions, or "nuances", of the primary colors to white, locating pink at the halfway point between red and white, and a light blue equivalent between blue and white that he called azure.

Color books often support a mixed approach of registers, veering from the rarefied to the convivial, the abstract to the practical, and Sol's book was no exception. He supplemented his charts with a discursive section he called "A few insights", in which he discussed the qualities of different colors and tried to ascribe a moral dimension to them. Where others had written of warm and cool colors, Sol introduced the humanizing terms "attractive" and "sad", emphasizing the reception of color over its innate qualities, more Goethe than Chevreul.

With a growing range of colors available for household paints, wallpaper, and wall hangings, the domestic interior became a fundamental and universal site for color expression and a place to explore and manipulate its effects. Chevreul may have apportioned some of his hefty volume to considering color in interiors but others made it their specialization. Edinburgh-based David Ramsay Hay (1798–1866) was an apprentice interior decorator and house painter. He was consumed by the possibility and potential of applying universal principles and systems to

OPPOSITE ABOVE

Chevreul attempted to represent color in a three-dimensional form with some paper engineering in his 1839 atlas. He created a color hemisphere by adding a flap to his color circle that could stand up to suggest a third dimension and a third quality needed to define each color. Each color could then be defined according to its hue (color name), tone (intensity), and purity (grayness).

OPPOSITE BELOW

Chevreul began his color atlas with a series of different-colored circles on a white ground. The reader was expected to note how the surface around the colors could be influenced by the solid hues.

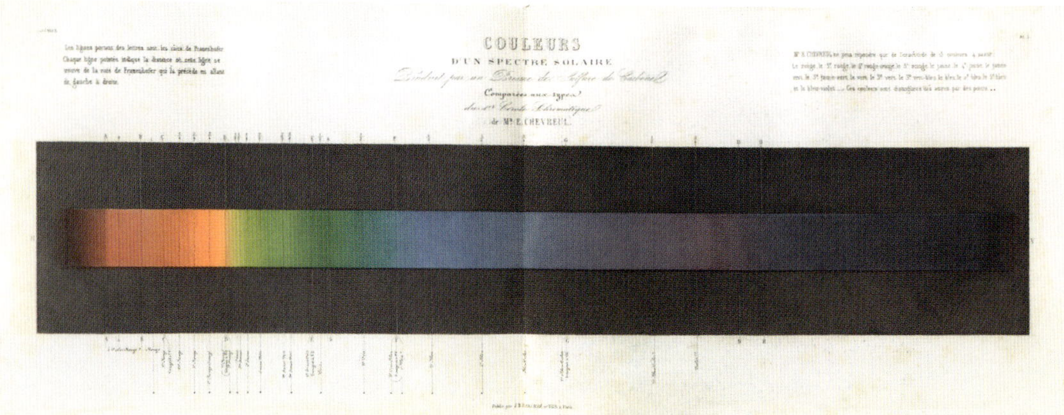

the art of design and decoration, and was particularly interested in finding ways to map musical conventions, such as chords and keys, to shapes and color (see p.208). Among other schemes, Hay devised a numerical system to specify and describe color relationships, a project that suited his pattern-forming brain. He believed the human mind was hard-wired to appreciate pleasing composition and relationships and that these could manifest in different forms, whether through color, music, or proportions, all of which were governed by the same harmonic laws. Hay held the post of Queen Victoria's official decorator (he styled himself as "Decorative Painter to Her Majesty, Edinburgh") and was a collaborator with renowned architect William Playfair. Yet despite his pedigree and seemingly rigorous methodology, there remained something speculative and unscientific about his approach, his drawing together of cosmic threads.

By the time he came to publish on the subject of color, Hay had concluded that the membership of the primary colors, about which there had been some debate, had finally been established beyond doubt as red, yellow, and blue. He did not consider black and white to be true colors in quite the same way (although he did refer to them as "the two most dangerous colors [...] they each require particular management"); rather, they were modifiers of the primary and compound colors, and could adjust them "almost to infinity" by creating tints and shades.

Hay's first major book on color was the 1828 work *On The Laws of Harmonious Colouring Adapted to House Painting*. This book attempted to find common ground between the structures of color and music, visual aesthetics and aural harmony, with particular reference to the practice of interior design. It was successful enough to be revised and re-published in a further five editions, its sixth and final incarnation appearing in 1847, by then re-drafted and expanded far beyond its origins.

Chevreul's fold-out visualization of the visible solar spectrum in his 1861 and 1864 "cercles chromatiques"*. Dotted lines denote the borders between colors while the diagram makes their relative proportions clear.*

Hay offered simple concepts and maxims for the decorator to consider. He drew a distinction between taste, which was mutable and capricious, and color, "founded on natural principles" and subject to fixed laws that could be learned. And if color could be taught, Hay was ready to instruct. The book contained detailed descriptions of the most harmonious and appropriate color combinations for bedrooms and parlours, even taking into account the likely play of sunlight on the walls and mixtures of floor coverings and furnishings. The triangular system he introduced in his book would show, he promised, "that all the colours, in their greatest intensity, may be brought together without crudity or harshness". And he warned against the "monotony" that would surely be induced by anyone so intimidated by color that he or she stuck to neutral tones throughout the home to play it safe.

Another of Hay's major works on color, *A Nomenclature of Colours, Applicable to the Arts and Natural Sciences,* was published in 1845 and was both more and less practical. More, because it contained a large range of color samples, arranged in harmonious combinations, for handy reference and inspiration outside of theory or systems. Less, because it was still an attempt toward a complex mathematisation of the arrangement of colors, with an inscrutable system of numerical annotations. The book appeared as two separate publications bound into one volume, one containing the text and another featuring forty plates, six related colored triangles pasted onto each. Like J.C.M. Sol, Hay paid more attention to tints than shades, believing there was greater scope for nuance in lighter tones than dark. In common with many color books of this era, Hay's reach exceeded his grasp. For budgetary reasons he was unable to include the full range of colors (he identified a further 144) that his scheme was designed to encompass.

Perhaps unintentionally, the physical separation of the book into two volumes (a likely necessity to solve the technical problems of its printing) emphasized the sensory experience of a wordless volume of pure color. Hay juxtaposed colors on the basis of aesthetic satisfaction rather than measurable relationships, no doubt influenced by his professional practice as a decorator, and not unlike an artist working intuitively on the palette. He started from an exploration of appealing color relationships and then proceeded to find a system into which they could be fitted. The result was not always coherent but his work was well received by the scientific community, including the Scottish physicist James Clerk Maxwell (see p.152), who appreciated Hay's efforts to define color relationships and adapted it to his own work on color. While the numerical basis of his recommendations might have seemed reassuring, it was the range and immediacy of the color samples, where the power and beauty of its subject glowed on the page, that gave the book its value as a reference tool.

Hay's *Nomenclature of Colours* was well received and influential. It was adopted by Richard Redgrave, Headmaster of the National Art Training School of South Kensington in London (later the Royal College of Art), who used it to inform the color theory component of his notoriously prescriptive and inflexible syllabus. Color as an object of study and vehicle for expression was by then gaining more respect within the art industries. Previously neglected, or even maligned, compared with the more established principles of composition, line and shade, the intelligent, intentional use of color finally began to be associated with rigorous design and treated as a subject that could be learned. Redgrave's curriculum involved slavish copying of design principles, an approach exported to the provincial art schools and parts of the British Empire. His answers to questions of color were expounded in his slender, standalone *An Elementary Manual of Colour* (1853), its prescriptive principles acknowledged by the author himself as a "catechism". The book was even accompanied by a wall chart, designed to be installed in classrooms to keep students from straying from the safe path of established harmonies. And Redgrave was far from alone in encouraging a new-found seriousness and reverence toward color in design. In 1856, Welsh architect Owen Jones published a lavish sourcebook of global patterns in design, *The Grammar of Ornament* (see p.195). The book was inspired by the treasures on display in the Great Exhibition of 1851 in London, a world's fair that dazzled the public with its displays reflecting the international aptitude and taste for color, from Canada to India, sculpture to steam engines.

While the abundance of guidebooks on successful color usage seemed to suggest the practical "problems" of color (selection, proportion, combination) were soluble, the mysteries of color perception endured, in particular the fundamental question of how tangled wavelengths of light became multicolored pictures in the brain after entering the eye. The work of three polymathic scientists in particular, James Clerk Maxwell (1831–79), Hermann von Helmholtz (1821–94), and Karl Ewald Hering (1834–1918), dug around the foundations of early understanding of color vision, approaching the question from different angles, sometimes dovetailing, occasionally colliding. Both Maxwell and Helmholtz tried to measure the precise relationship between the stimulation of color receptors in the retina and the range and intensity of color perceived as a result. Their research both confirmed and complicated the connection between the two. While those with typical color vision could be shown to exhibit similar effects in the perception of colors, anomalies started to appear in certain individuals, who experienced a type of color blindness, where some colors could not be perceived at all and instead were substituted with others from a more limited range. Maxwell and Helmholtz concluded those affected must possess a malfunctioning type of color receptor, or lacked a particular kind altogether. The existence of this condition was a clue to the mysteries of color vision in their entirety.

Chevreul's color "ladders" demonstrate how individual colors in his circle arise between the extremes of black and white. In twenty-one stages, different tints and shades of each are shown.

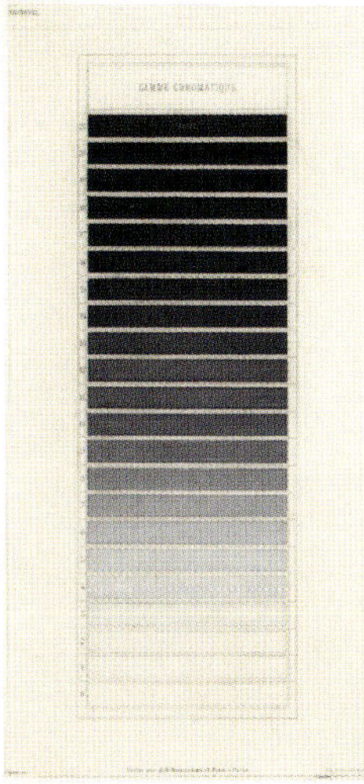
GAMME CHROMATIQUE
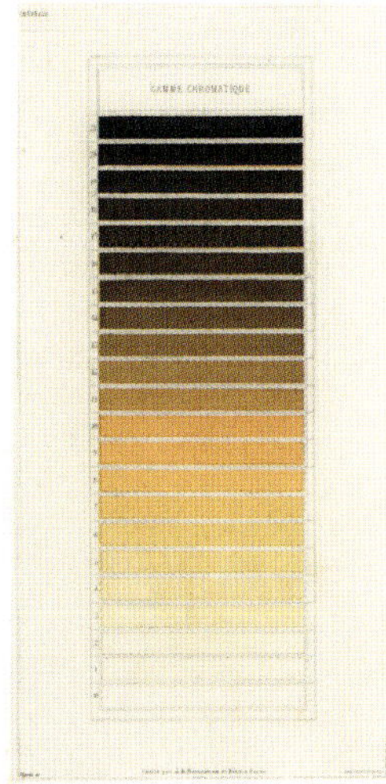
GAMME CHROMATIQUE
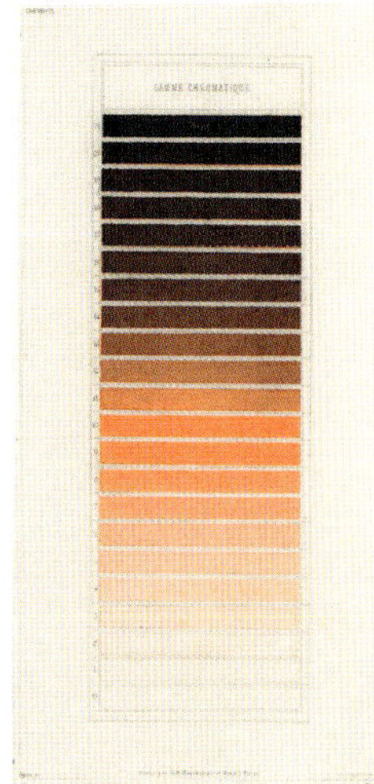
GAMME CHROMATIQUE
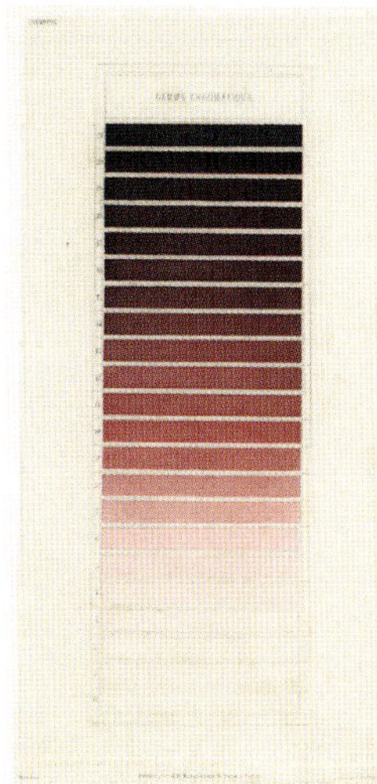
GAMME CHROMATIQUE
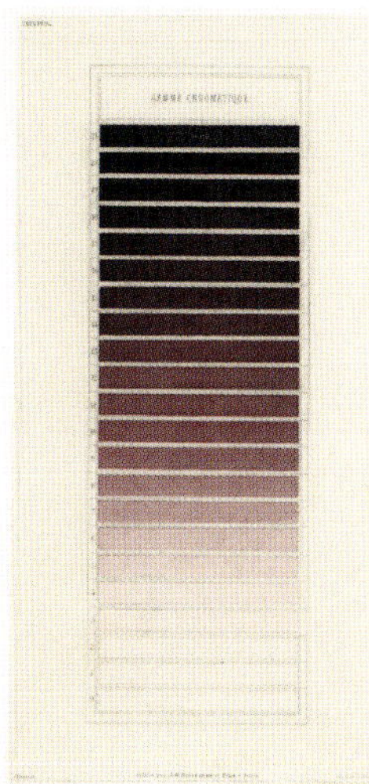
GAMME CHROMATIQUE
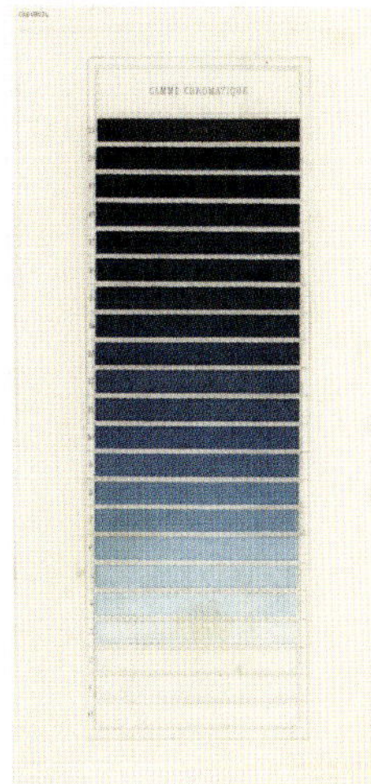
GAMME CHROMATIQUE
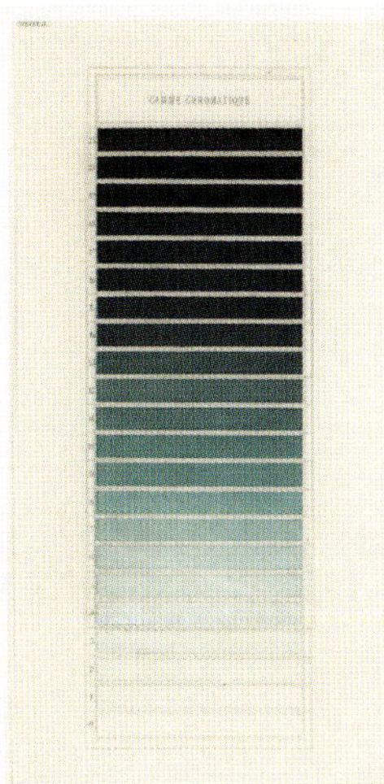
GAMME CHROMATIQUE
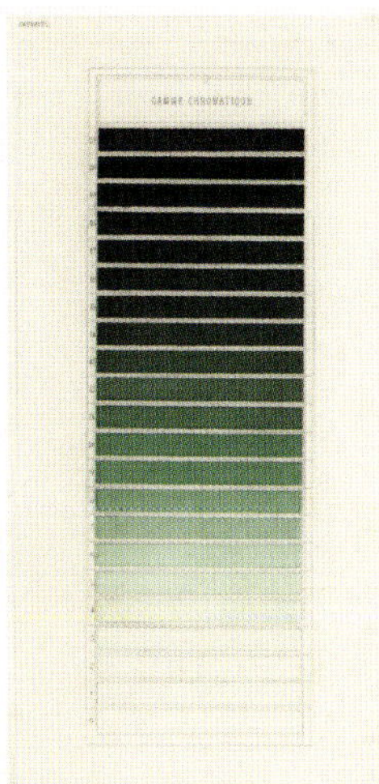
GAMME CHROMATIQUE
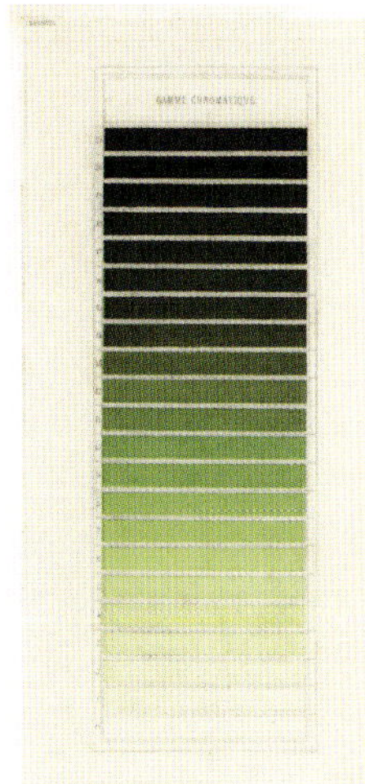
GAMME CHROMATIQUE

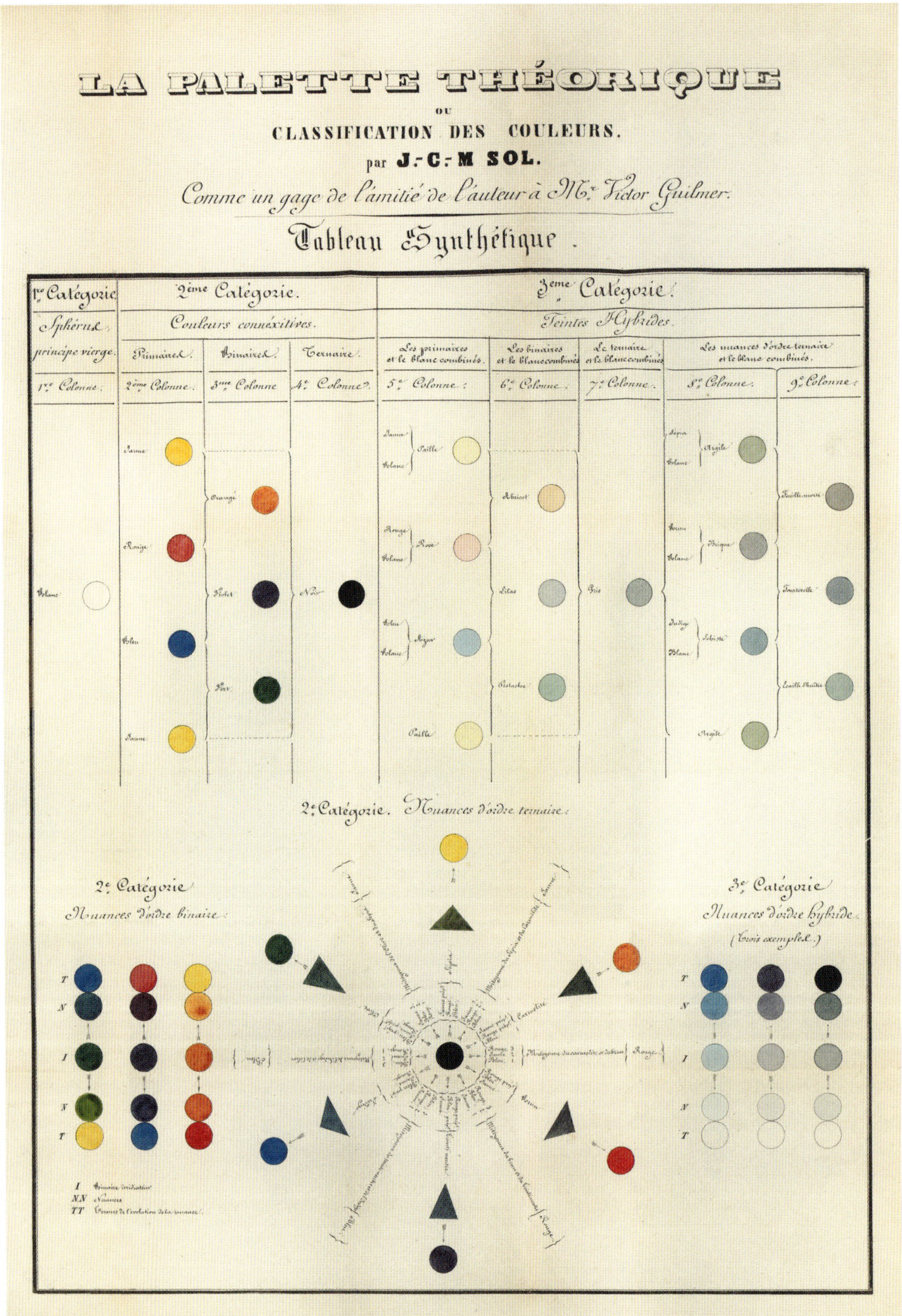

LA PALETTE THÉORIQUE
OU
CLASSIFICATION DES COULEURS.
par J.-C.-M SOL.
Comme un gage de l'amitié de l'auteur à Mr. Victor Guilmer.
Tableau Synthétique.
1re Catégorie
Sphérus principe vierge.
1re Colonne.
2ème Catégorie.
Couleurs connéxitives.
Primaires.
2ème Colonne
Binaires.
3me Colonne
Ternaire.
4e Colonne.
3ème Catégorie.
Teintes Hybrides.
Les primaires et le blanc combinés.
5e Colonne.
Les binaires et le blanc combinés
6e Colonne.
Le ternaire et le blanc combinés
7e Colonne.
Les nuances d'ordre ternaire et le blanc combinés.
8e Colonne.
9e Colonne.
Blanc
Jaune
Orangé
Rouge
Violet
Noir
Bleu
Vert
Jaune
Paille
Rose
Azur
Abricot
Lilas
Pistache
Gris
Argile
Brique
Feuille morte
Tourterelle
Écaille d'huître
2e Catégorie. Nuances d'ordre ternaire.
2e Catégorie
Nuances d'ordre binaire.
3e Catégorie
Nuances d'ordre hybride
(Trois exemples.)
T
N
I
N
T
Rouge
I Binaire irritative
NN Nuances
TT Termes de l'évolution de la nuance.

Albert Einstein would later claim "one scientific epoch ended and another began with James Clerk Maxwell". A child prodigy, Maxwell had already published a paper on geometry by the age of fourteen. He experimented with color and light at home and, like Ibn al-Haytham (see p.15) and Isaac Newton before him, he used geometry and mathematics to solve the riddles of seemingly inexplicable phenomena, such as why the rings of Saturn appeared and disappeared in the night sky. Maxwell had been impressed by the theories of Thomas Young (see p.84), and Young's conviction that there must be a physical or biological significance behind the existence of just three primary colors. While Young convincingly argued for the presence of three different types of receptors in the human eye, working together to create all colors by acting in combination, it was not something that could be easily proved. But Maxwell repurposed a tool invented by James Forbes, a professor of natural philosophy, to provide an evidential basis for the theory. It took the form of a spinning wheel, rather like a child's spinning top, on which paper discs of solid color could be screwed down. These overlapped in a way that allowed them to be adjusted, one sliding atop another, to display different proportions of two or more segmented colors in a circle. The hand-operated device (later versions would be motorized) could then spin the wheel at such speed that the eye could no longer differentiate between the individual colors. Instead, the brain combined them into a persistent hybrid color, based on the simultaneous responses firing from the retinal cones. Crucially, the visual phenomenon of colors mixing at high speed triggered the brain to process them as if they were colored lights, allowing the material color made from pigments (the painted discs) to mimic the quite different behavior of immaterial color. An inner ring was also used to hold the same colors in different combinations, for side-by-side comparison, or black and white discs that allowed users to establish the tonality of different colors once they appeared to match the particular gray of the inner ring.

Maxwell eventually uncovered a fundamental difference between material and immaterial color: their three primaries did not match. When spinning the artists' primaries of red, yellow, and blue on his disc, he found they failed to combine into white; rather the colors needed to be red, *green*, and blue to create something that looked more like pure white daylight, and to create many other colors when their proportions were adjusted. He had defined not the primary pigments of material color but the primary colors of light. Maxwell's discs could thereafter be used to determine the proportions of numerous color combinations and he worked out a way to express these mathematically. The device and its operations were described in his paper "Experiments on colour, as perceived by the eye" (1855).

The discs would spin for a long time. As the device could also be used as a tool to establish and measure all color combinations quantitatively, Maxwell influenced color

OPPOSITE
J.C.M. Sol's palette for color classification (1849), which measures 25 × 18½ in (66 × 47cm), organized color into categories. Sol was particularly interested in exploring "nuances", tints of increasingly lighter colors

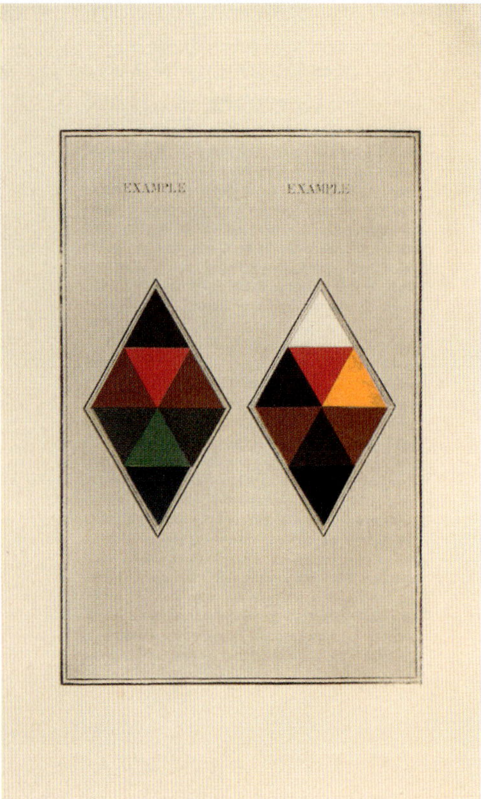

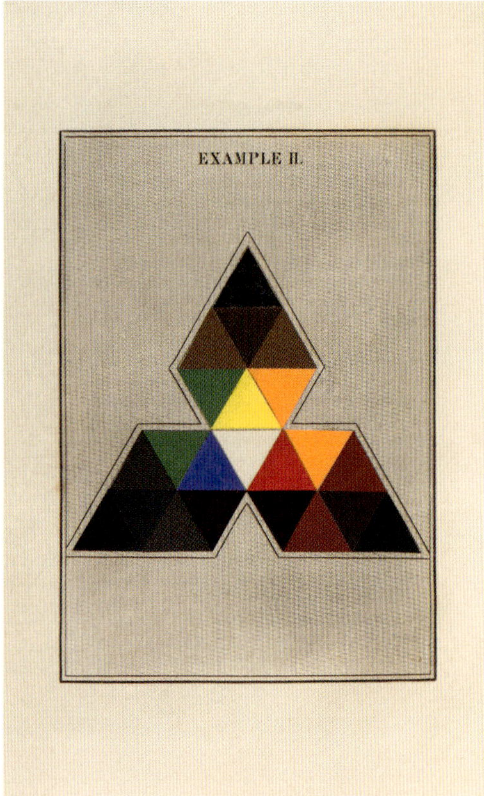

ABOVE LEFT
A demonstration of colors that harmonize with red included in David Ramsay Hay's Laws of Harmonious Colouring *(fifth edition, 1844).*

ABOVE RIGHT
Hay's three-limbed diagram (one per primary color) extended from white to black, through secondary and tertiary colors. This model appeared in the fifth edition of his Laws of Harmonious Colouring *(1844).*

OPPOSITE
The three-limbed diagram was revised for the sixth edition of Laws of Harmonious Colouring *(1847). In all Hay's color illustrations, the triangles were printed separately in solid color and then tessellated and pasted into place.*

researchers for the rest of the century and into the next, as evidenced by the large number of illustrations of the technique in subsequent publications. As a footnote, Maxwell noted in his paper that the first colors he used for the sections of the disc were made by "coloured papers procured from Mr D.R. Hay". For a subject so universal, color scholars often turned out to inhabit a small world.

Maxwell also devised a color triangle to represent the blending of the primaries, inspired by Young's earlier visual (see p.84). With white at its center and red, green, and blue at its points, all colors could in theory be found somewhere between them, just as they arose from a blend of three primary colored lights. Was this really a revelation? Artists had long grasped the importance of three irreducible colors as the building blocks of all others, so in some ways this discovery was nothing of the sort. But the world of science seemed caught off guard by the notion that an infinity of colors could be so dramatically reduced to essentials. Physicists had also felt oddly constrained by Newton's demonstration of *seven* apparently pure, unmixable colors (give or take the inclusion of the contested indigo), not

DIAGRAM
OF THE
PRIMARY, SECONDARY & TERTIARY COLOURS

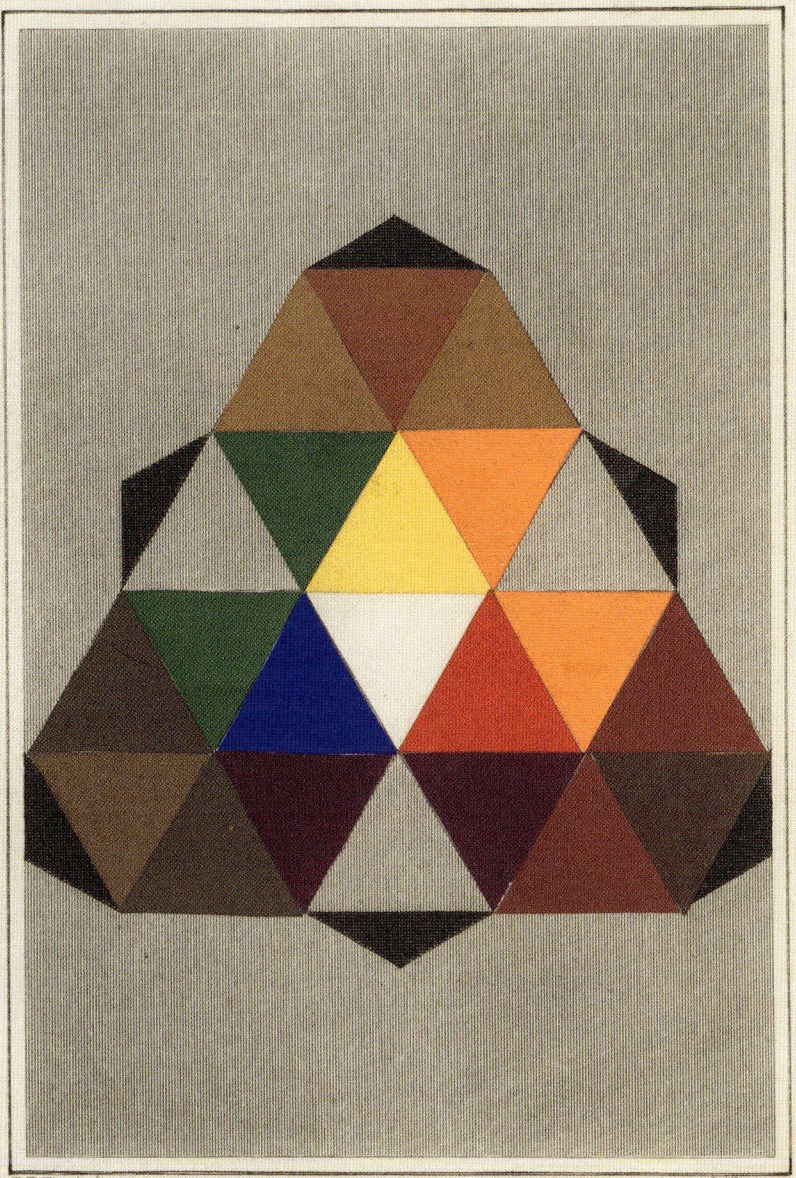

D.R.Hay, inv^t. G.Aikman sc.

EXAMPLE IV.

BINARY MODIFICATIONS
OF
THE SECONDARY COLOURS.

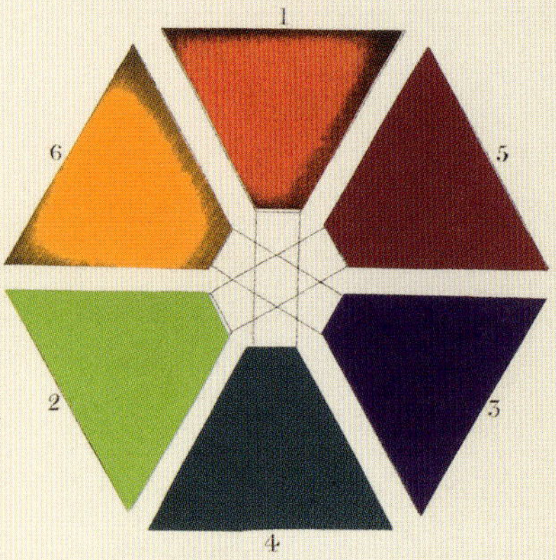

D.R. Hay Invt.   Lizars Sc.

EXAMPLE V.

THE PRIMARY AND SECONDARY COLOURS
TEMPERED.

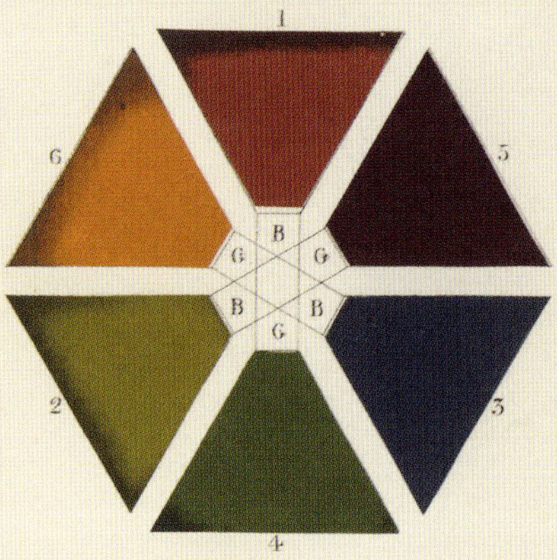

D.R. Hay Invt.   Lizars Sc.

EXAMPLE X.

HARMONY OF THE SECONDARY
GREEN.

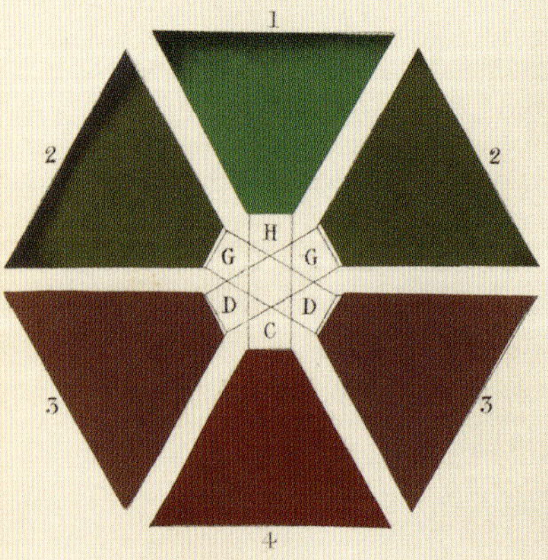

Lizars Sc.

EXAMPLE XI.

HARMONY OF THE PRIMARY
YELLOW.

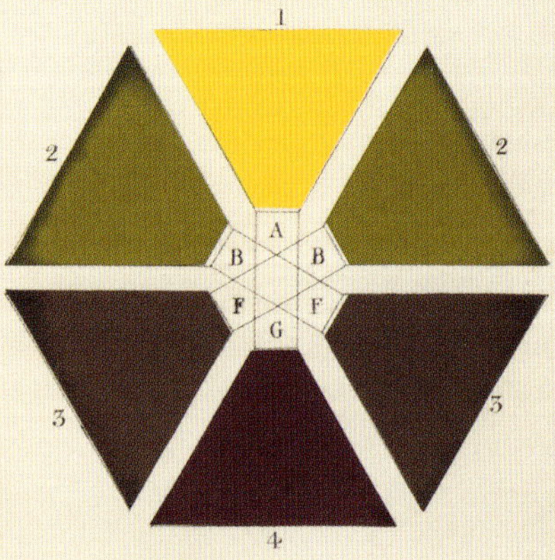

D.R. Hay Invt.   Lizars Sc.

EXAMPLE VII.

THE SECONDARY COLOURS CONTRASTED
WITH
THE TEMPERED PRIMARIES.

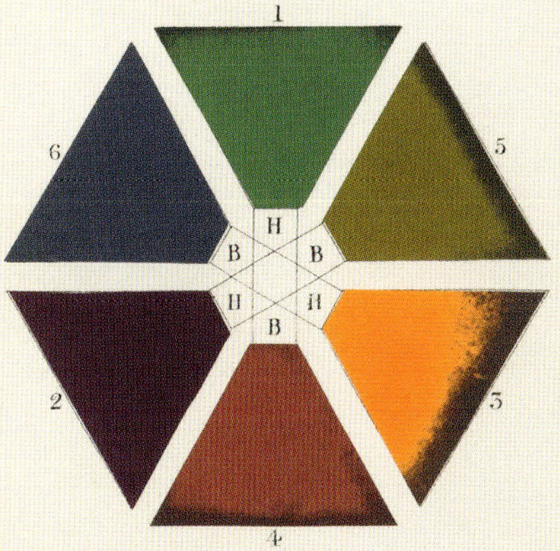

EXAMPLE IX.

HARMONY OF THE PRIMARY
RED.

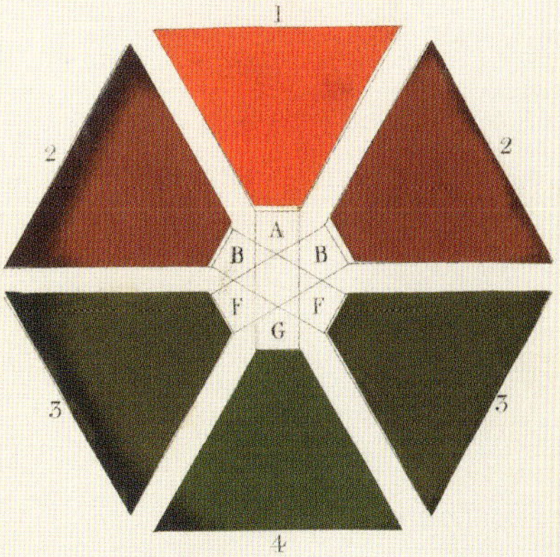

D.R. Hay Inv.t Lizars Sc.

EXAMPLE XIII.

HARMONY OF THE PRIMARY
BLUE.

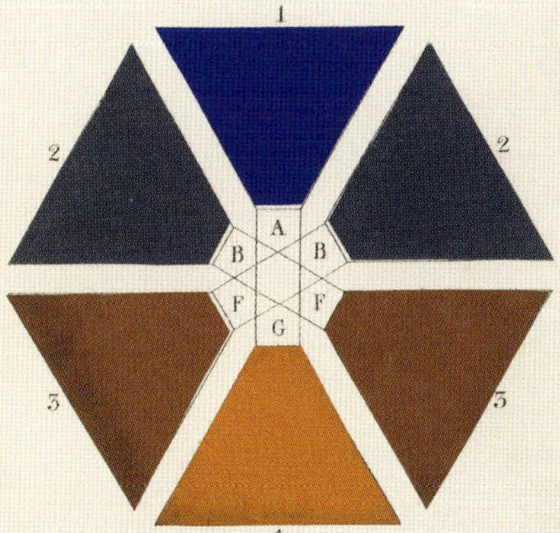

D.R. Hay Inv.t Lizars Sc.

EXAMPLE XIV.

HARMONY OF THE SECONDARY
ORANGE.

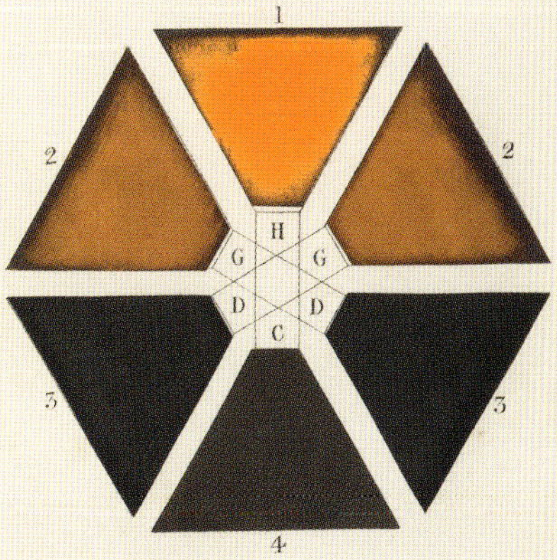

D.R. Hay Inv.t Lizars Sc.

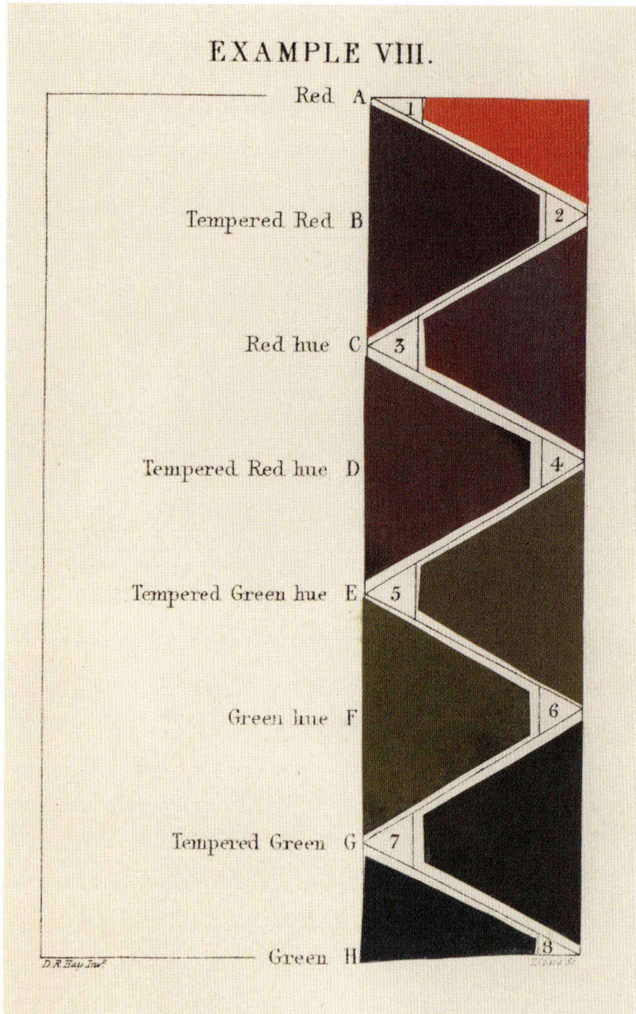

PREVIOUS PAGES
In his Principles of Beauty in Colouring Systematized *(1845), David Ramsay Hay deepened the quest for greater harmony of complementary and contrasting colors by adjusting and "tempering" particular varieties. These plates are from the second edition (1849).*

ABOVE
This diagram in Hay's Principles of Beauty in Colouring Systematized *(second edition, 1849), explored varying degrees of contrast between different types of red and green. Both were displayed in pure and "tempered" forms to ensure one could not overpower the other.*

wanting to overturn his model, and failing to appreciate fully that this number could be simplified further.

Although a pioneer, Maxwell was not entirely alone in his endeavors. In his 1855 paper he referred repeatedly to the parallel work of "M. Helmholtz". Hermann von Helmholtz was his opposite number in Germany and the two read and admired each other. Helmholtz himself was an acknowledged titan of the natural sciences, who formulated the mathematics required to express the principle of the conservation of energy and the first law of thermodynamics. Color, light, and vision were enticing subjects for Helmholtz, who was also excited by the discipline of psychophysics, the study of the relationship between measurable external stimuli and the sensation they created when experienced by humans. He invented an ophthalmoscope to look inside the eye and understood the perception of color as a process that involved not only the stimulation of receptors but the complex work of the brain to translate sensations into visual comprehension. Not coincidentally, Helmholtz was also a Renaissance man, and his deep love of art and music helped inform his investigations, reminding him always of the centrality and meaning of human response.

For years he pored over the workings of the optic nerve, the retina, and lens. His efforts resulted in a three-volume study, *Handbuch der physiologischen Optik* (later translated as *Treatise on Physiological Optics*), published in stages between 1856 and 1867. This exhaustive work attempted to resolve the contradictions in physiological optics but its author was plagued by self-doubt, fearing his work would be quickly superseded by others, and questioning whether it should even be published at all. Where the first volume concerned itself largely with the workings of the eye, the second focused on color vision, color mixing, and related phenomena. Helmholtz's essential topic was vision rather than color, but many insights into the latter arose en route to an understanding of the former.

Helmholtz identified three qualities needed to define a color fully and accurately: hue (color category), saturation (richness), and brightness. His work paved the way for a greater understanding of the difference between the retina's two distinct types of receptors, rods and cones, and the eventual confirmation by German anatomist Max Schultze that the role of the rods was to sense light and dark while cones were devoted to color. After the preceding century and a half of debates about material and immaterial color, Helmholtz conclusively established the fundamental difference between the two types. He showed that the spectrum Newton unveiled was essentially composed of brighter and more saturated colors than could possibly be achieved through pigments: "[T]he mixed pigment does not give at all a color that would be the resultant of mixing the two kinds of lights ... Most of the light reflected from a mix of colored powders is due, not to an addition of both colors, but a subtraction." In other words, with each successive color in the mix, more of the wavelengths were absorbed and removed (subtracted) from the white light, leaving an ever-smaller combination to reflect an object's apparent color. This, he explained, was why "mixtures of pigments are much darker than the separate ingredients". The more color you add, the more it drains away.

Helmholtz, like Maxwell, built on Thomas Young's trichromatic theory: that color vision arises through the stimulation of three types of sensors in the retina, tuned to three primary colors working in combination to create all other colors. He recapitulated Young's important ideas to such an extent that he essentially gained a co-authorship credit and the conclusions became known as the Young–Helmholtz theory. Time put to rest any doubts about the value of his own work. Later scholars worked to expand his conclusions rather than overturn them, with one notable exception.

Although a consensus between Maxwell and Helmholtz had grown, a schism was opening on another front. Helmholtz faced

OVERLEAF
Eight plates of the forty in Hay's Nomenclature of Colours *(1845), each containing complementary sets of colors. These were adjusted to include different tints and shades of the same hue.*

Plate 1.

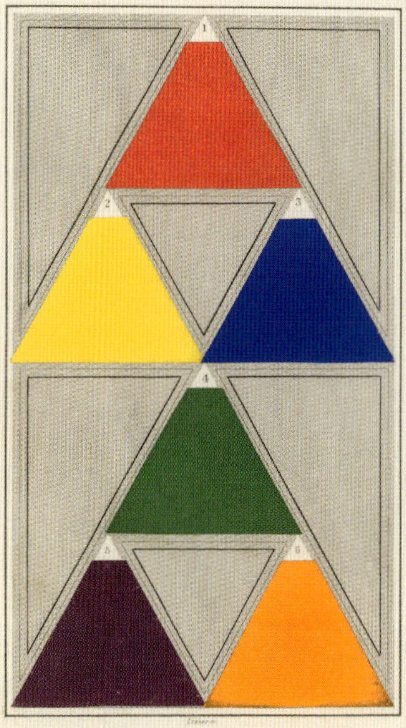

Plate 2.

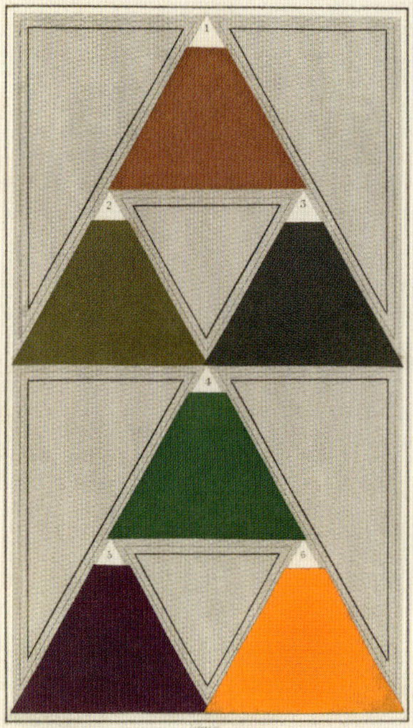

Plate 29.

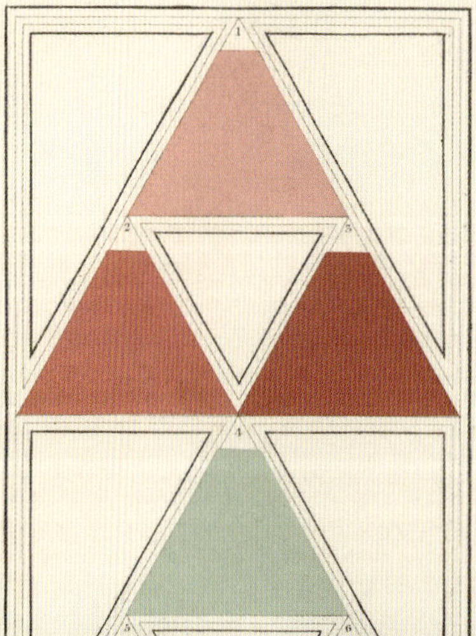

Plate 30.

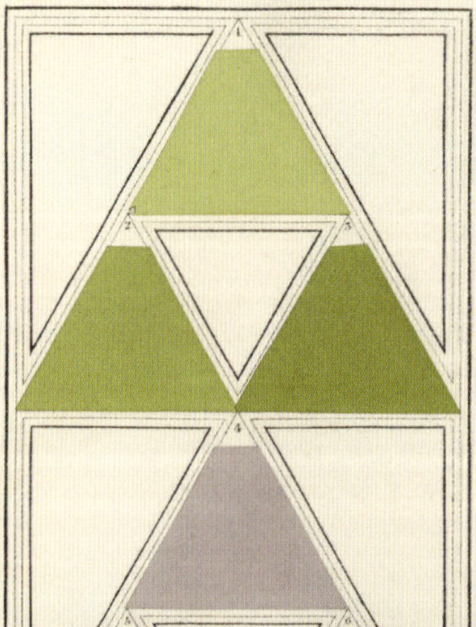

PLATE 5.

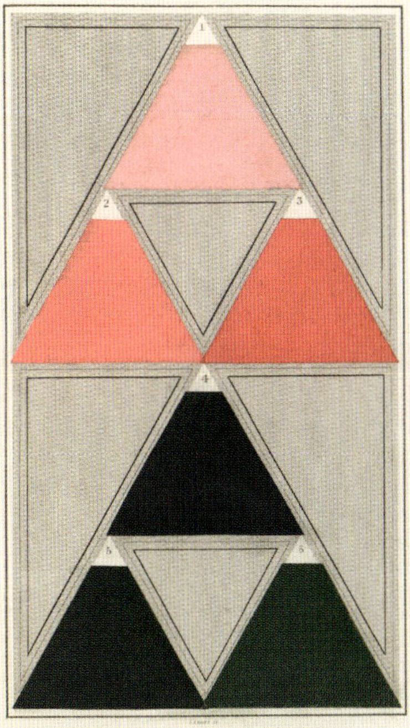

PLATE 6.

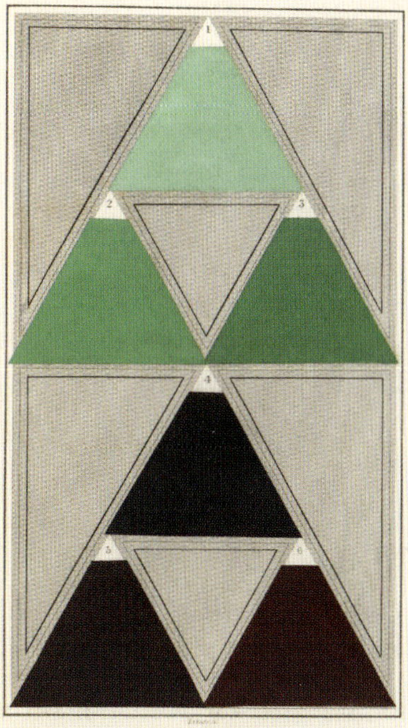

PLATE 38.

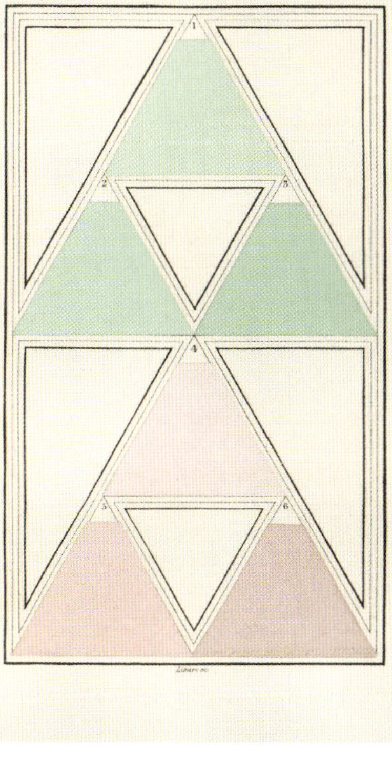

PLATE 39.

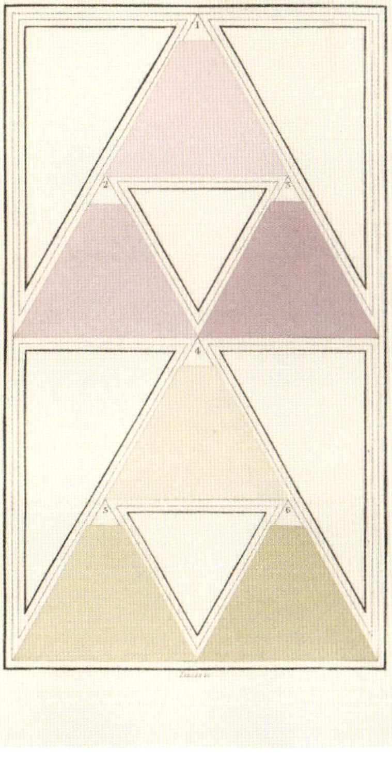

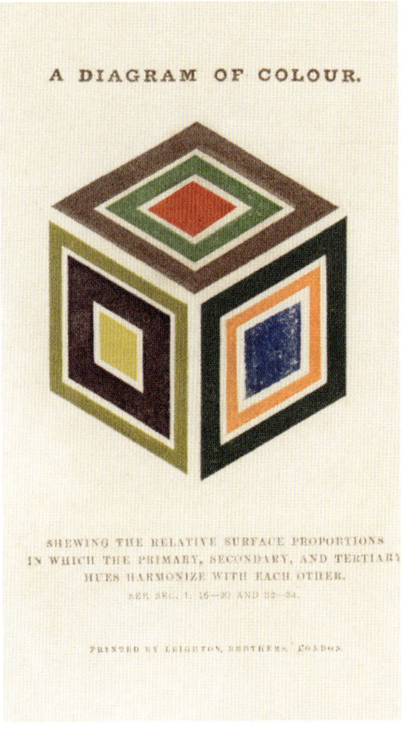

ABOVE
The printed color frontispiece to Richard Redgrave's Elementary Manual of Colour *(1853). The illustration demonstrated not just acceptable color combinations but the relative proportions of the different colors Redgrave expected his students to use.*

OPPOSITE, LEFT
Different types of colored paper discs could be overlapped and attached to a spinner to establish their composition and relative proportions. This illustration appeared in the explanatory pamphlet The Rotation of Coloured Discs Applied to Facilitate the Study of the Laws of Harmonious Colouring *(1859) by John Gorham.*

a vocal detractor in Karl Ewald Konstantin Hering (1834–1918), a physiologist and physician from Leipzig whose denunciation of his compatriot bordered on the venomous, rivaling Goethe's disdain for Newton. Hering diverged from emerging thinking around the trichromatic theory and instead advanced his so-called opponent-process theory. This held that human perception of color arose in response to an antagonistic stimulation of three different *pairs* of colors: red-green, yellow-blue, and white-black. We cannot see a reddish-green Hering argued, because cells switch off their response to green when red light is present, and correspondingly quell the response to red under green light. In other words, our brains can only properly perceive one half of a pair of opponent colors at once. This helped to explain the phenomenon of after-images in which someone staring at a particular color might experience a flash of its complement after shifting their gaze away to a white surface. In opponent theory, this could be understood by the explanation that the red-stimulated cells have become tired and, in need of rest, swap over to its oppositional color the moment the subject looks away.

Hering first began to attack Helmholtz's theories in his lectures at the Academy of Sciences in Vienna, later published as the multivolume *Principles of the Theory of Sensitivity to Light* (1878). Hering particularly took issue with Helmholtz over the role and perception of yellow. Helmholtz's theory held that red and green light combined to make yellow (as indeed they do), but Hering felt this ran counter to nature, to the human understanding of yellow as something fundamental and, indeed, primary: hardly something that could be conjured up only by combining two entirely different colors. Instead, he believed that Leonardo da Vinci must have been right centuries earlier when he had identified four "simple" colors as red, blue, yellow, and green, and that the operations of this quartet as equals must hold the key to perception.

Who was right? Several twentieth-century peacemakers, including Erwin Schrödinger, saw the merit in both and attempted to reconcile the theories. Greater understanding of the retina confirmed that the Young–Maxwell–Helmholtz camp had always been correct in identifying three receptors that responded to short, medium, and long wavelengths of light. But further research in the 1960s provided some support for the actions of an opponent process occurring in perception, if not quite along the lines Hering detailed. The disproportionate animosity Hering expressed publicly toward Helmholtz (his name-calling was a largely one-way campaign and the more temperate Helmholtz refused to take the bait) may seem bizarre, but the dialectical process ultimately led to a more rounded understanding.

Theories about vision and arguments over the function of cone cells, though fundamental to our understanding of color, could seem far removed from the ever-growing opportunities for delight in color in day-to-day life. Instruction manuals for makers and artists continued to appear during the latter half

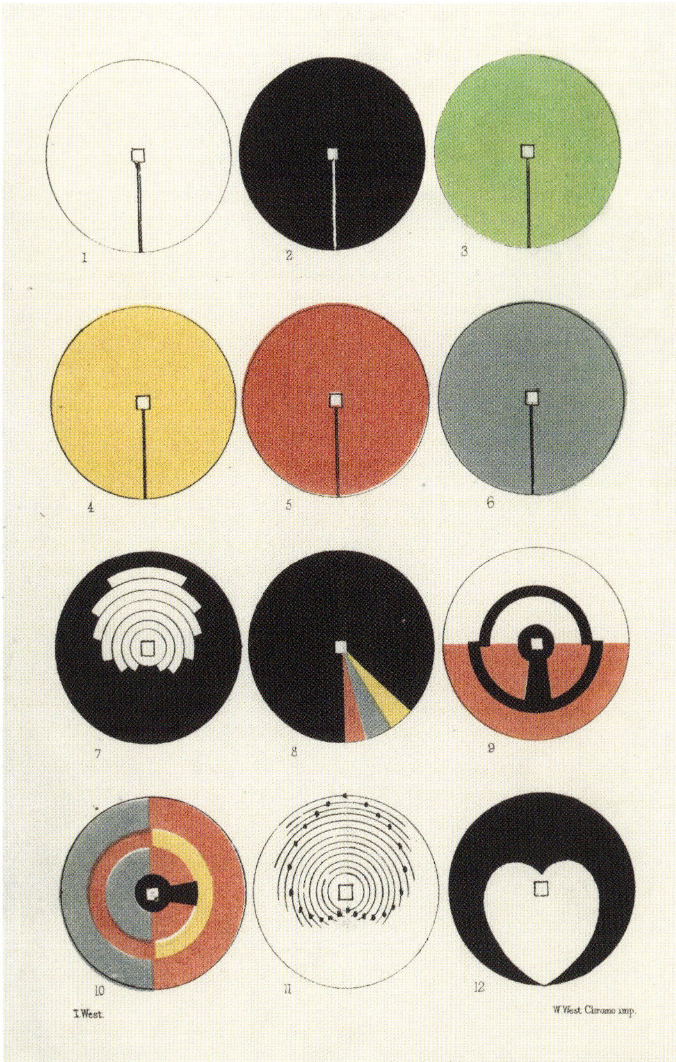

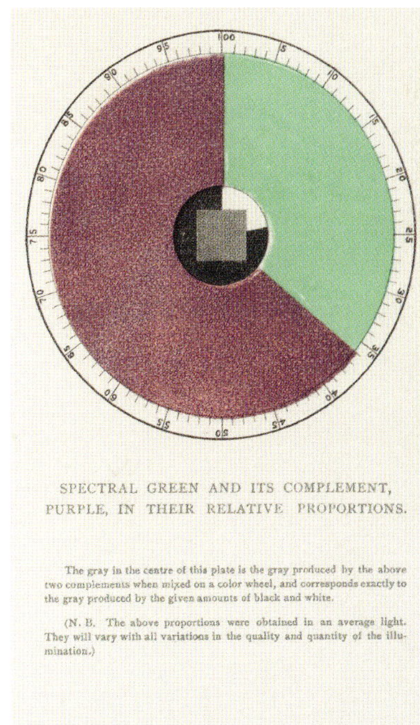

ABOVE
An example of the spinning discs refined by James Clerk Maxwell, although this illustration comes from a later work, Emily Noyes Vanderpoel's Color Problems *(1901). In this example, complementary purple and green discs are interlaced and spun. The ratios of the two colors are adjusted until their appearance resembles the same neutral gray formed by the spinning black and white disc on top of the colored ones. Through this means, the relative proportions of the complementary colors are established.*

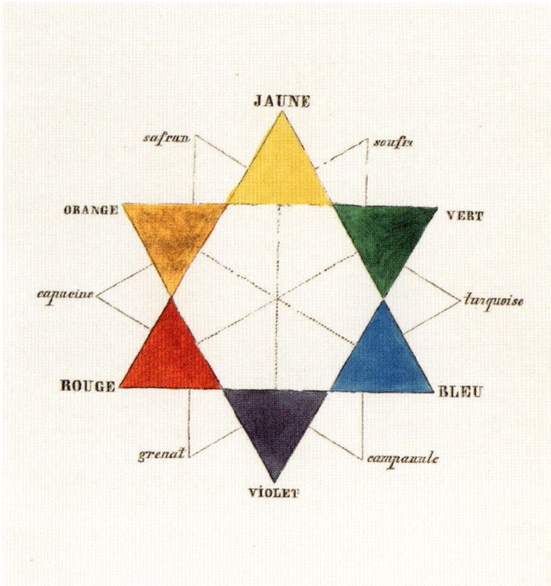

of the nineteenth century articulating the rules of color while taking advantage of the increasing availability of pigments and dyes, but to what end? Why study color at all? Architect William Benson (*fl.*1868–71) made a powerful case, writing in 1871: "The whole subject is full of interest and beauty [...] it teaches us in a very remarkable way to distinguish between sensations and their causes, and not to judge hastily according to the appearance of things." Benson had begun to make a name for himself with *Principles of the Science of Colour* (1868), a work that marked the first appearance of a color system based on the shape of a cube (it was only a matter of time before someone came up with that notion, after the parade of circles, spheres, triangles, and pyramids that preceded it). It was also remarkable for its fine color plates, representing edges and faces of his cube design and the color combinations that arose in its sections and planes. Falling into exquisite clusters, the plates offered cascading, ready-made palettes of layered color, full of surprising juxtapositions and with a satisfying visual punch. The 1868 edition of his work underwent different printings with the colors either lithographed or "hand-painted in the finest watercolors". Whichever version was consulted, the plates were always exciting and attractive. While Benson intended them as precise sections of a complex model in a careful sequence, superficially they possessed the energy of pure color in a jumbled, rich, and joyous display.

Benson wanted to bring his readers up to date with the more recent understanding of primary colors revealed by Maxwell and Helmholtz, which he thought wholly undermined chemist and colorman George Field's model (see p.96) of red, yellow, and blue, arranged in "chromatic equivalents", or optically harmonious proportions. Where Benson's work fell down was in his unfathomable system of color relationships—it was not easily used as a diagnostic, predictive, or analytical tool, something that might have helped artists and decorators resolve their own color choices effectively. It also suffered from the limits imposed by the cuboid form, lacking the capacity to include all the levels of brightness required. Benson's cube, designed to contain all perceptible colors, turned out to be more of a prison cell than a box of delights.

Around the same time that Benson was publishing his unusual arrangement, a color star appeared in the work of Charles Blanc (1813–82), who was perhaps the most successful and influential of Chevreul's popularizers. Blanc directly inspired Vincent van Gogh, having been influenced in turn by witnessing the practical experiences of his painter friend and former classmate Eugène

ABOVE
Charles Blanc developed a color model that dispensed with black and white entirely. This six-pointed star appeared in his work Grammaire des arts du dessin *(1867).*

OPPOSITE
Diagram from Ewald Hering's Principles of the Theory of Sensitivity to Light *(1878) representing his four-color opponent process. This theory held that color vision is based on two pairs of opponent colors: blue-yellow and red-green. Only one of these in each pair can be active at a time, so it is not possible to see a reddish-green or a bluish-yellow and those colors do not overlap in the top circle. The bottom circle demonstrated the colors that can be created by mixing any one of the four primaries with any one or other of its opponents.*

Delacroix. Delacroix liked to explore how midtones of individual colors could be more effectively mixed not by the addition of small amounts of black, but by blending a given hue with its complementary, neutralizing its vitality in a more rounded and sympathetic way. The deadening quality of black paint could therefore be dispensed with entirely and inspired Blanc to create a color system without any role for black or white. Forged of six triangles of primary and secondary colors, these clustered to form a six-pointed star.

In Blanc's view of color relationships, pairing and blending colors was a battle for successful harmony that could go either way. Complementary colors placed side by side were heroic allies but, once mixed, they became antagonistic enemies. This contrast between the very different effects of juxtaposition and fusion cut to the heart of the problems of color palettes and the volatility of color combinations. Ultimately, Blanc was more ambivalent about color than his scheme suggested and, in his *Grammaire des arts du dessin architecture, sculpture, peinture* ... (1867), in which his color star first appeared, he expressed scepticism of its role in the aesthetics of art and design. He did not deny its importance, but characterized it pejoratively as the feminine subordinate of line (which, by contrast, was assertive and, inevitably, masculine). Just as it was starting to gain respectability, color was pushed back down the pecking order of the principles and techniques of design, below composition and chiaroscuro.

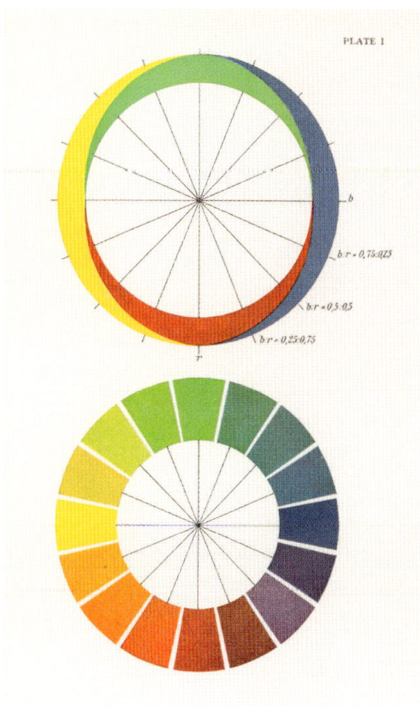

Grammaire des arts du dessin found a wide audience and appeared in many editions. It was a handbook that explained Chevreul's law of simultaneous contrast and instructed practitioners in applying it to different disciplines but in a more accessible manner than the original. To reconcile theory with practice, Blanc drew particularly on Delacroix's application of Chevreul's work to painting. Blanc paid attention to the effects of *mélange optique*—optical mixing—and how it too could be exploited by painters. In this technique, discrete dots of color, viewed at a distance, supposedly created a heightened color fusion, visually blending rather than being forced apart as in simultaneous contrast. The possibilities of this would be more fully explored by the Neo-Impressionists of the 1880s, Georges Seurat, Camille Pissarro, and Paul Signac among them.

As the science began to settle, two warmer and more accessible guides to color appeared in the closing decades of the nineteenth century. Superficially similar in tone and content, Wilhelm von Bezold's *Theory of Color* (1874; US edition, 1876) and Ogden Rood's *Modern Chromatics* (1879) rounded off the century neatly, summarizing and simplifying scientific advances while addressing their potential applications for a wide readership, including artists.

Like so many for whom color was an accidental obsession, German physicist and meteorologist Bezold (1837–1907) took the long way round to an interest in color, on diversion from

BELOW

Wilhelm von Bezold devised a color "cone" with black at its point and white on its base. The colors around the circumference were divided into ten types, including two types of blue. Harmonic triads could be identified by rotating a triangle within the circumference and noting which colors touched its points.

OPPOSITE

Cross-sections of Bezold's cone in his Theory of Color *(1876). The top illustration is the view from below and the lower is the view from above. Bezold noted that all the colors in his circle could be found in the spectrum with the exception of purple. He recorded its artificial creation by turning the curve of its section of the circle into a straight line, joining red and violet.*

other pursuits. By the time he had risen to become director of the Prussian Meteorological Institute, Bezold decided he wanted to streamline and simplify the overwhelming amount of color literature of the preceding decades, and to make it intelligible and useful to the average reader.

Bezold believed the subject of color had by then become so advanced it could support a theory as robust as any that underpinned anatomy or geometry. But, while framing his work in the terms of scientific discourse, his intended audience was artists, dyers, and designers. The result was published as *Die Farbenlehre im Hinblick auf Kunst und Kunstgewerbe* (1874). A rapid English translation ("enlarged and improved") appeared in the United States soon afterward, titled *The Theory of Color in its Relation to Art and Art-Industry* (1876). In the preface to the American edition, Bezold expressed a will to domesticate and democratise color: "To bring all experiments into a form which will admit of their being repeated even by the unprofessional reader, and with the most simple materials." As if to counter Blanc's demotion of the subject, Bezold also prefaced his work with a defence of color as worthy of study in its own right. He acknowledged the uphill struggle to convince artists, a breed generally full of self-belief in their own talents, of the need to study color at all, and indeed the challenge of persuading pretty much anyone to take a scientific approach to art seriously.

The rapid pace of technological advance made it timely to consider color principles and effects, especially in those industries such as printing, textile, and wallpaper design where color was becoming ever more consistent. Science was expanding the field, and aesthetics and industry had to keep up. Bezold positioned himself as just the man to make sense of it all, but he also acknowledged the extraordinary conclusions of Maxwell and Helmholtz, and their implications for artists, noting "the physical and physiological side of the theory of color had first

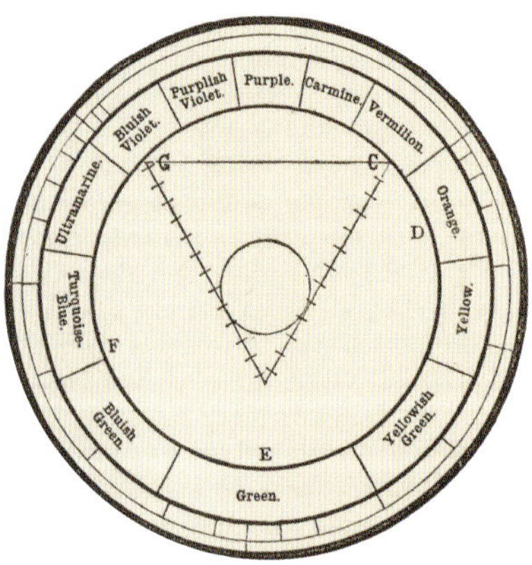

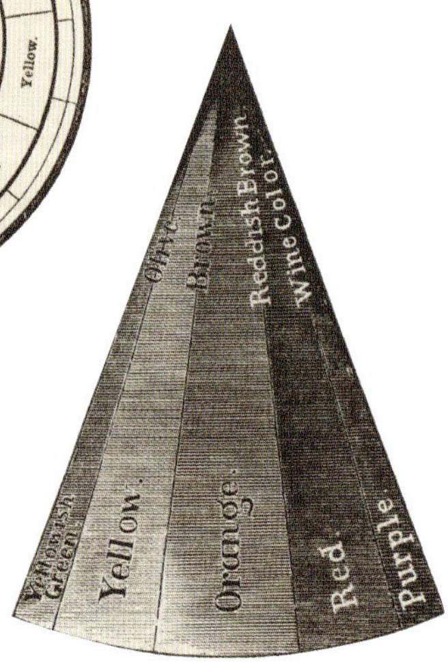

OVERLEAF

Bezold included examples of solid black text on colored paper to demonstrate different effects in a way similar to Chevreul in his atlas (see p.141). "Black ink", he noted, tends to "show a slight tinge of the color which is complementary to the ground". The effect was heightened when viewed through translucent tissue paper. Bezold also noted that cold colors heighten the contrast more than warm ones.

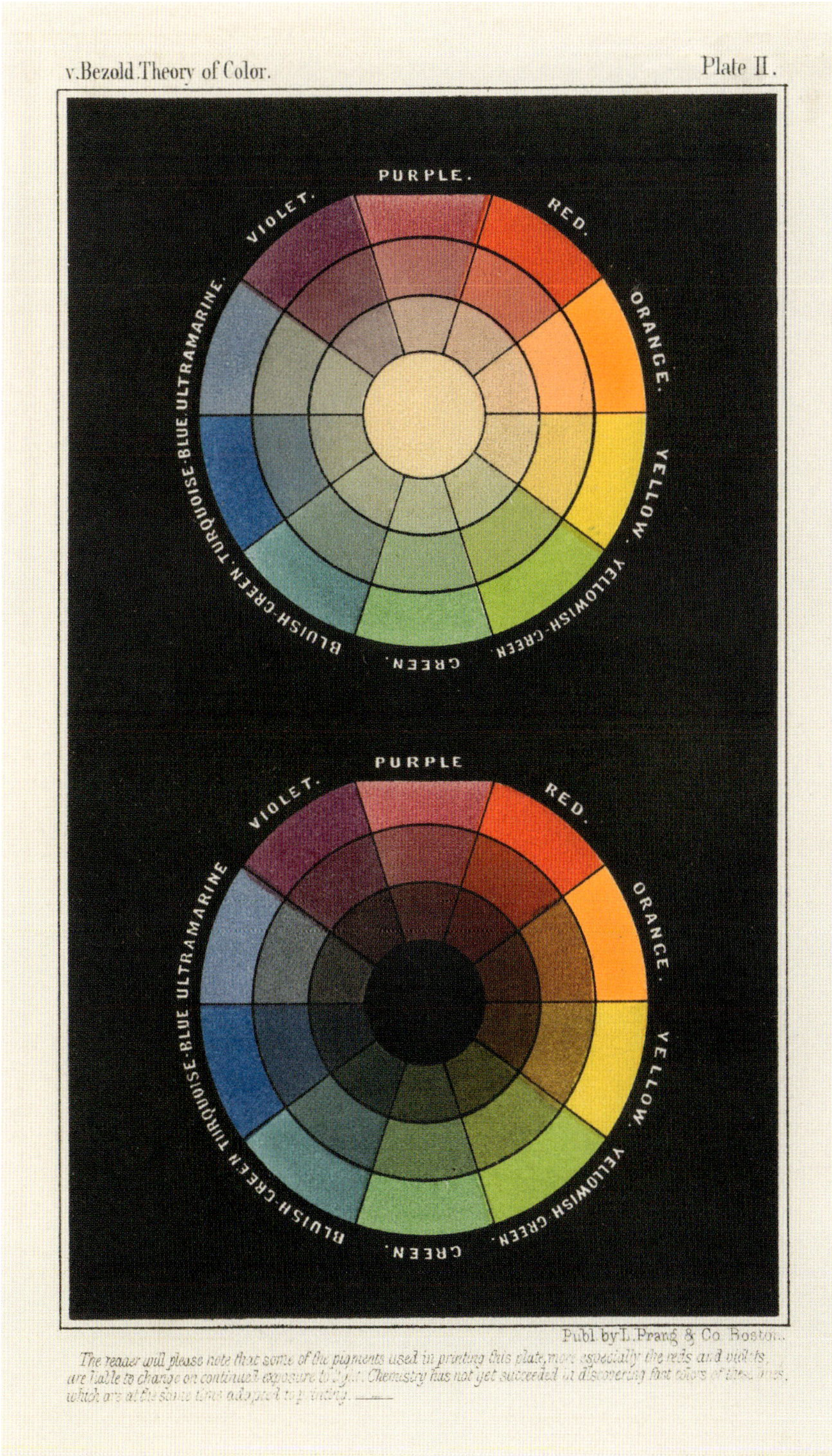
v.Bezold Theory of Color.
Plate II.
PURPLE.
RED.
ORANGE.
YELLOW.
YELLOWISH-GREEN.
GREEN.
BLUISH-GREEN.
TURQUOISE-BLUE.
ULTRAMARINE.
VIOLET.
PURPLE
RED.
ORANGE.
YELLOW.
YELLOWISH-GREEN.
GREEN.
BLUISH-GREEN.
TURQUOISE-BLUE.
ULTRAMARINE
VIOLET.
Publ. by L. Prang & Co. Boston.
The reader will please note that some of the pigments used in printing this plate, more especially the reds and violets,
are liable to change on continued exposure to light. Chemistry has not yet succeeded in discovering
which are at the same time adapted to printing.

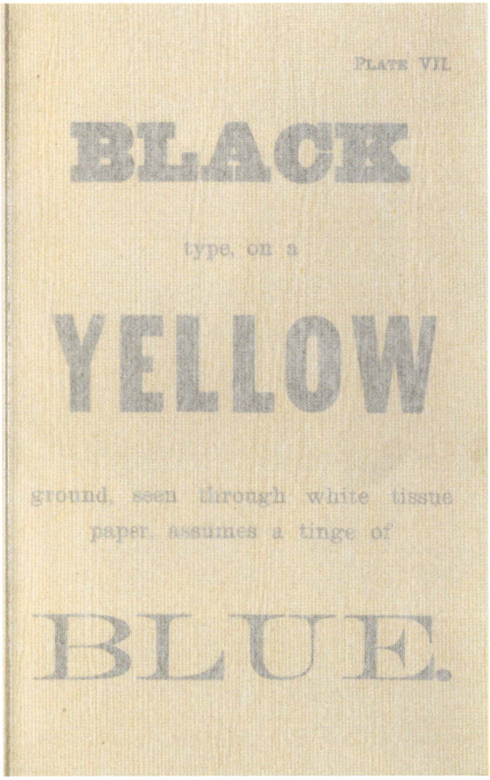

Plate VII.

BLACK

type, on a

YELLOW

ground, seen through white tissue paper, assumes a tinge of

BLUE.

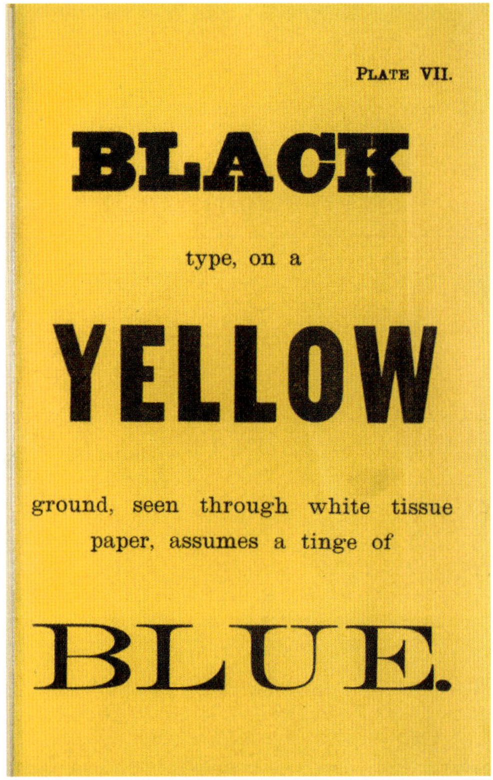

Plate VII.

BLACK

type, on a

YELLOW

ground, seen through white tissue paper, assumes a tinge of

BLUE.

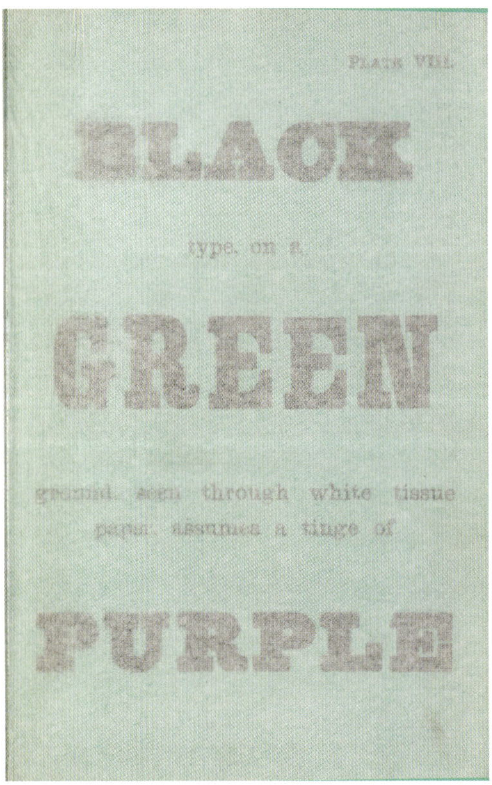

Plate VIII.

BLACK

type, on a

GREEN

ground, seen through white tissue paper, assumes a tinge of

PURPLE

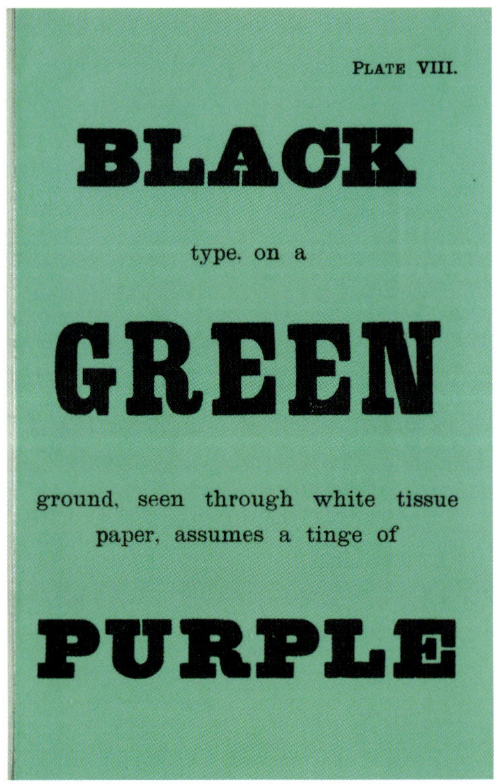

Plate VIII.

BLACK

type. on a

GREEN

ground, seen through white tissue paper, assumes a tinge of

PURPLE

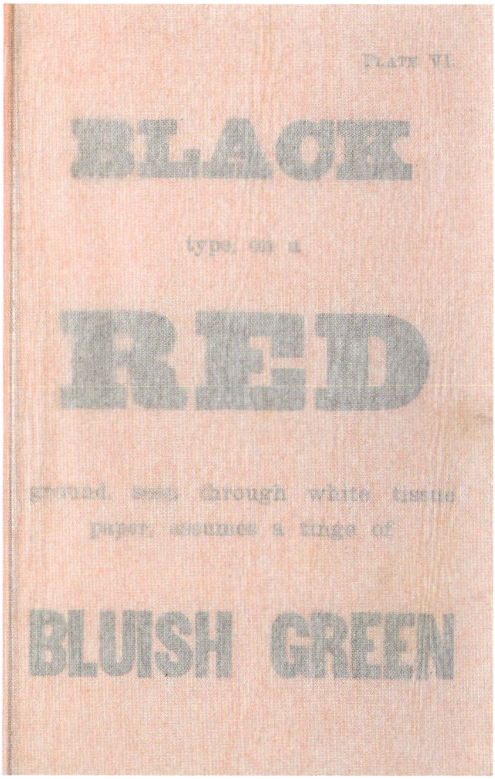

PLATE VI.

BLACK

type, on a

RED

ground, seen through white tissue paper, assumes a tinge of

BLUISH GREEN

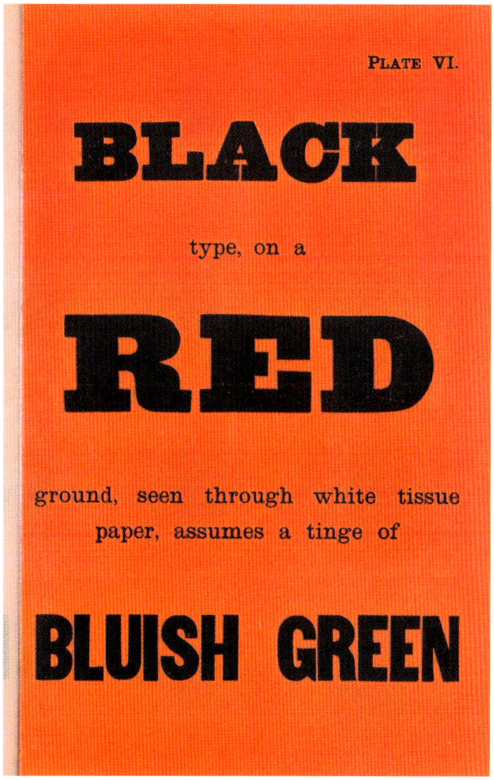

PLATE VI.

BLACK

type, on a

RED

ground, seen through white tissue paper, assumes a tinge of

BLUISH GREEN

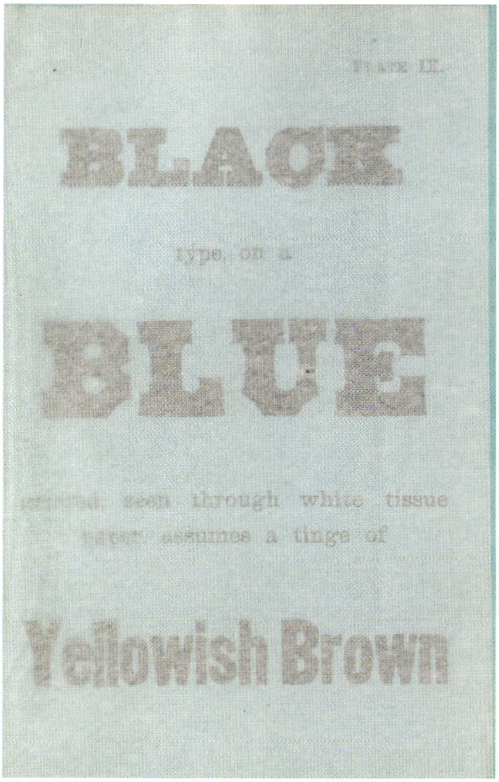

PLATE IX.

BLACK

type, on a

BLUE

ground, seen through white tissue paper, assumes a tinge of

Yellowish Brown

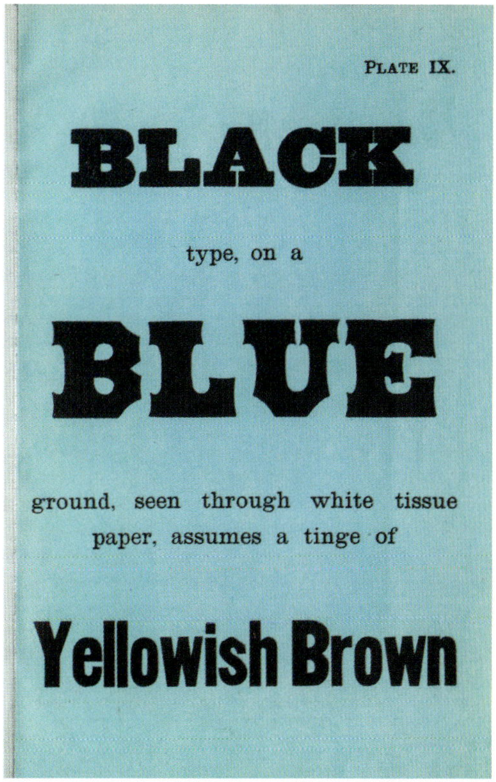

PLATE IX.

BLACK

type, on a

BLUE

ground, seen through white tissue paper, assumes a tinge of

Yellowish Brown

BELOW
In these three plates, Bezold provided an optical illusion in which two red circles of slightly different colors were made to look identical, or darker than they actually were, when juxtaposed against two different-colored grounds. The exercise recalled Chevreul's work of earlier decades and anticipated Josef Albers's exercises in Interaction of Color *(1963) nearly a century later.*

to be sufficiently developed [...] before it could be made available as a basis for practical aesthetic enquiries." Bezold's book, in other words, had come along at just the right time.

Illustrated by charming woodcuts of experiments and eleven plates of resplendent chromolithography to demonstrate physiological effects, Bezold's guide unfolded over five chapters. The first four provided a survey of scientific discoveries and experiments, conveyed to the layperson, analyzing everything from the greenness of leaves to the behavior of white light. In the third chapter, he introduced his notion of the color cone, yet another three-dimensional model of color relationships and qualities. The fifth and final chapter, however, spoke directly to the artistic community, to help its members put all that theory into practice. He even recommended that some readers start his book at the end. Reading the book out of sequence was certainly one way to navigate the tension between theory and practice that the subject always grappled with, and the different needs of the multiple audiences drawn to it.

The book's final section also stood as a defence of color and a philosophy of it. Our innate understanding of color and its power, Bezold believed, came from the experience of being alive in a natural world of overwhelming beauty. The universal delights of flowers, feathers, and rocks would always, he argued, inform and inspire the decorative arts; how could they not? But he also found much to love in the human-made elements of our colorful world by surveying exemplary color combinations from the past, including artefacts of ancient Egypt, Assyrian ornaments, Greek polychromy, and the mosaics of the Alhambra. He particularly praised Islamic ornamental art, which, through its avoidance of direct representation of nature, enabled color "to develop itself much more independently", making its designs and patterns an ideal realm in which to study color harmony.

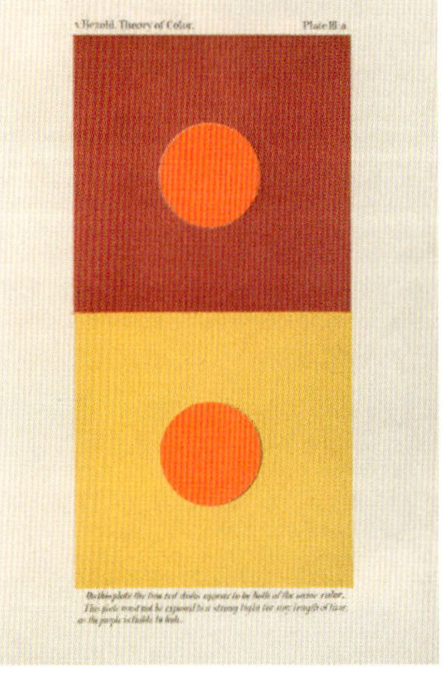
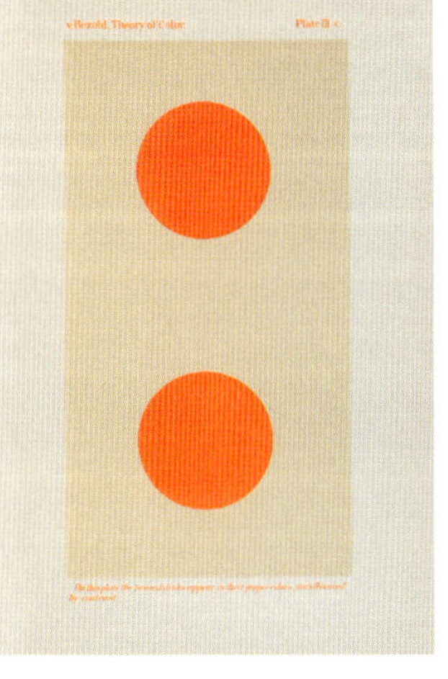
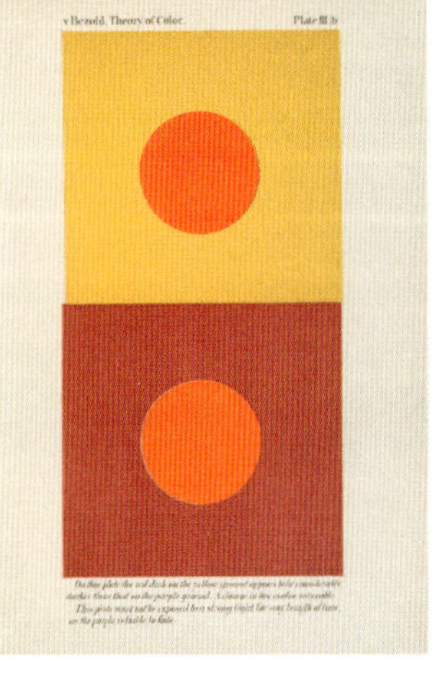

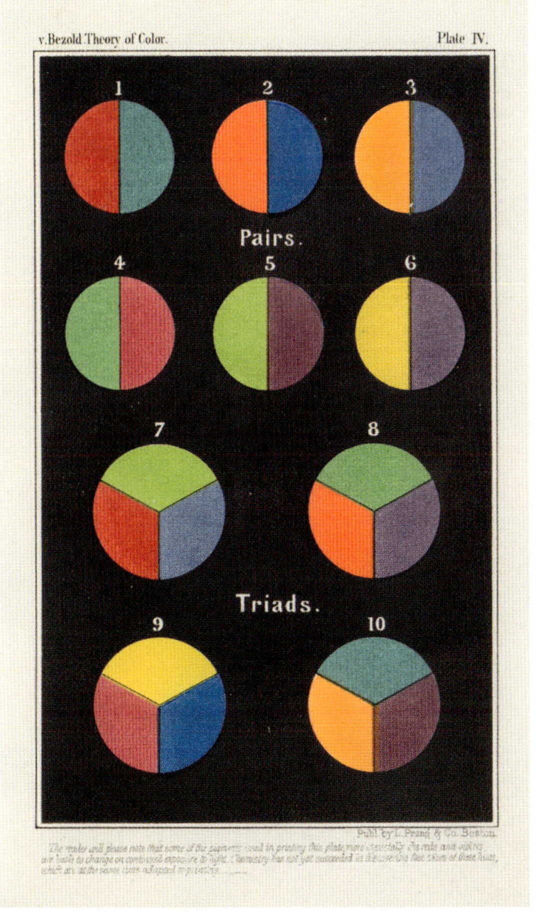

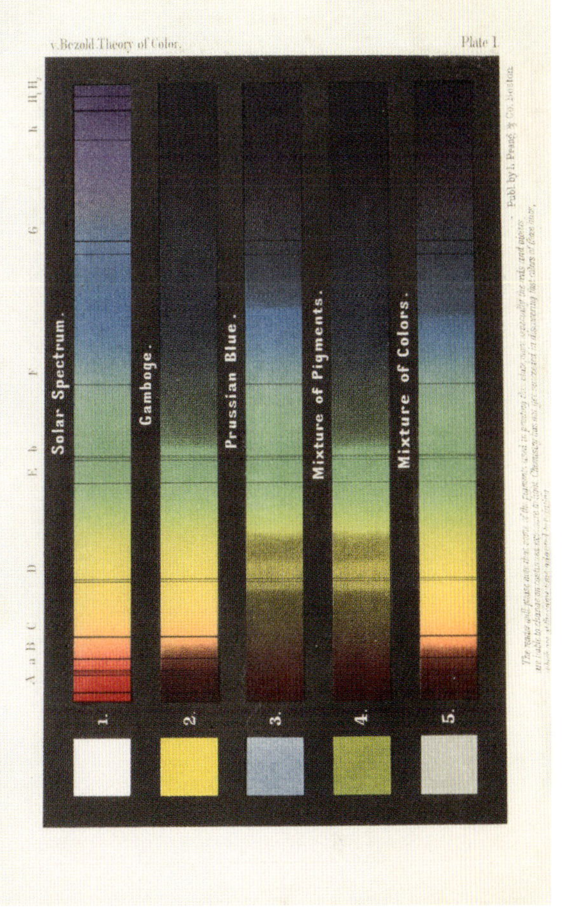

ABOVE LEFT

A range of Bezold's recommended pairs and triads of color included some that were not strictly complementary, yet, he wrote, "all these ... form good combinations".

ABOVE RIGHT

Plate I contains a representation of the spectral composition of the pigments gamboge and Prussian blue, alongside the full visible spectrum. Bezold demonstrated how a blend of these two pigments created green in their overlap by absorbing all the other colors in their respective spectra.

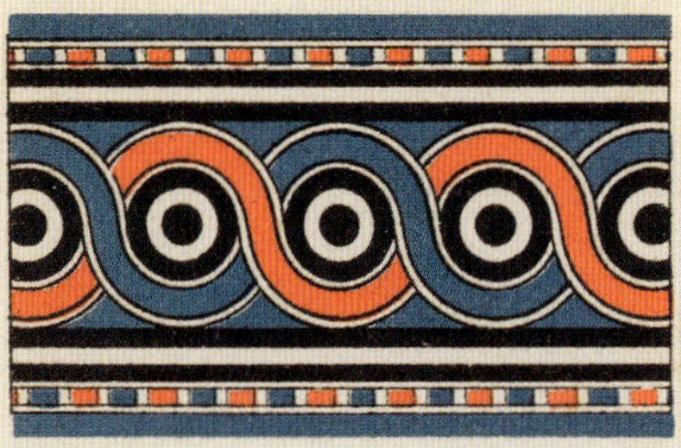

1

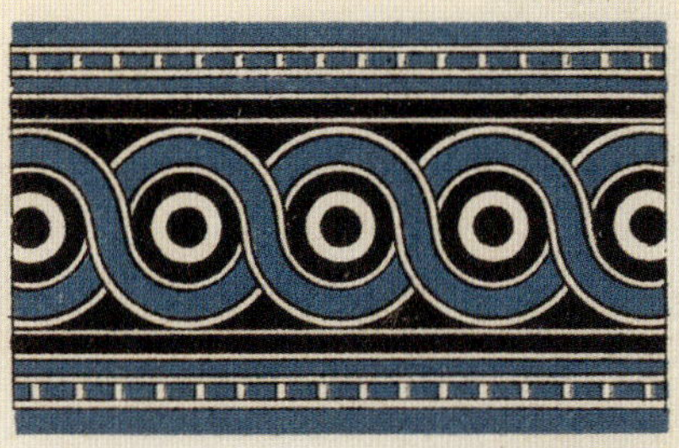

2

3

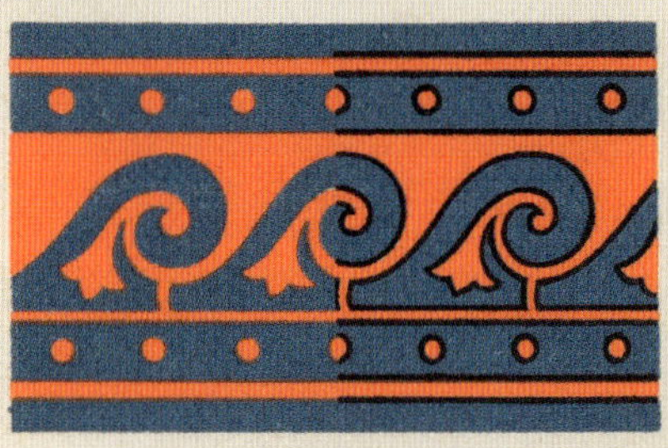

4

5

6

7

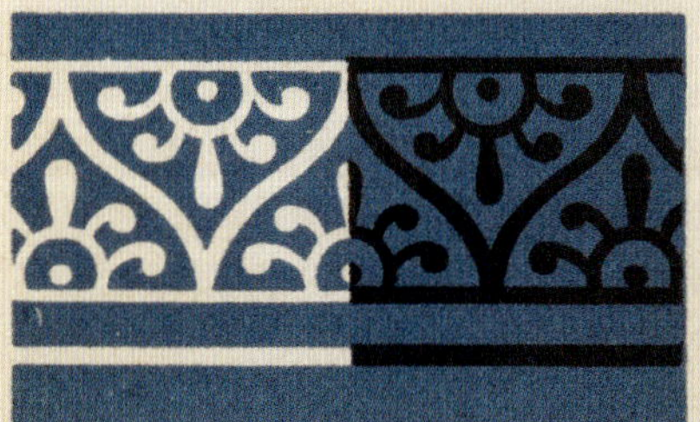

8

Publ. by L. Prang & Co. Boston.

Bezold's advice to artists and makers included guidance on a hierarchy of colors, which placed gold and silver in the first order, and a section on "bad combinations". This latter category typically involved any two colors close together on a color wheel, such as purple and vermilion, which would be too different to be perceived as a whole but too similar to create a pleasing pairing. Bezold's tone was often gently argumentative. He disputed the idea that complementary colors were inherently satisfying, judging the pairing of blue and yellow, for example, to be "far from elegant". Like others, he openly refuted many of the claims of George Field. Respect and loyalty, however, stopped him from fully destroying his compatriot Goethe in print, and he admitted to pulling his punches on the author of *Zur Farbenlehre* (see p.92) out of "a feeling of veneration for the great poet".

While he described and prescribed seemingly objective rules of harmony, Bezold did not shy away from the psychological dimension of color, in which he was influenced by the writings of psychologist Ernest von Brücke. The color Bezold wrote about was not an abstract phenomenon that could be dispassionately observed, but something that had a physiological effect on the onlooker and drew power from its physical and cultural placement in the world. Bezold's aims and style could be lofty to the point of evangelism but were also undeniably infectious, demystifying and encouraging.

A more enduring impact was made by Ogden Nicholas Rood (1831–1902), an American physicist but also an accomplished amateur painter. Rood's book *Modern Chromatics* (1879) made a big enough splash in Europe for him to be named as one of the key scholars who had directly influenced the artists of the time. Camille Pissarro, in a letter to his dealer, described his method as "a modern synthesis of methods based on science, that is, based on M. Chevreul's theory of color and on the experiments of Maxwell and the measurements of N.O. [*sic*] Rood." And while Rood's influence began with the French Neo-Impressionists, his legacy continued into the twentieth century through his enthusiastic adoption by the Italian Futurists. His longevity can be ascribed to the accessibility of *Modern Chromatics*, a sturdy and practical guide to color for students (its alternative title was *Students' Text-Book of Color*), another work that adroitly blended science and art.

Modern Chromatics was a highly technical book, but not at the expense of being practical and readable, with homely and well-integrated woodcuts to illustrate the experiments described. It offered a roving, explicatory perspective on the mechanics of color, and shared a kinship with Bezold's work in its overall appearance, its attempt to synthesize theory and practice, and its direct address to artists. Both works were peppered with illustrations of impressively moustachioed gentlemen scholars, poring over candles, prisms and lenses.

Plate V of Bezold's Theory of Colors *(1876) explored pairs and triads of colors and how the patterns in decorative schemes could disrupt their natural affinity. He noted how the lack of outlines in Fig. 3 and Fig. 4 resulted in "a sensation of disquietude in spite of the harmony ... between the two colors." In Fig. 5, the same red appears darker on the left-hand side than the right.*

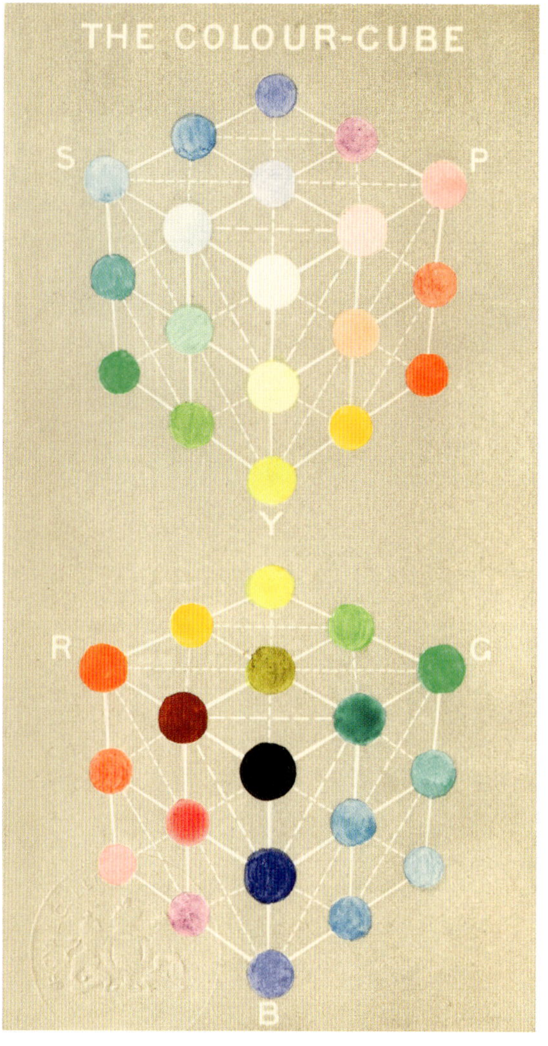

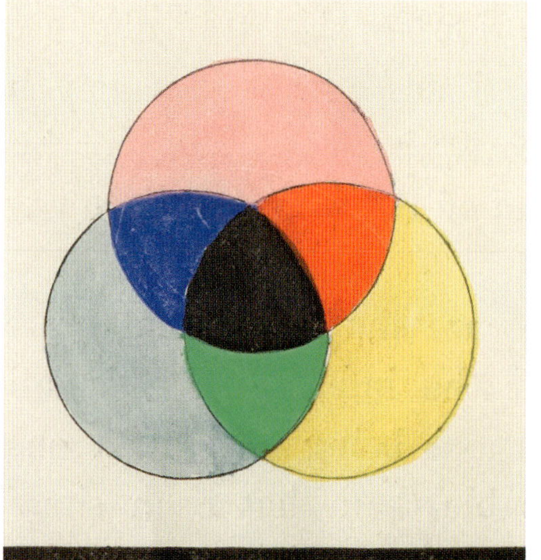

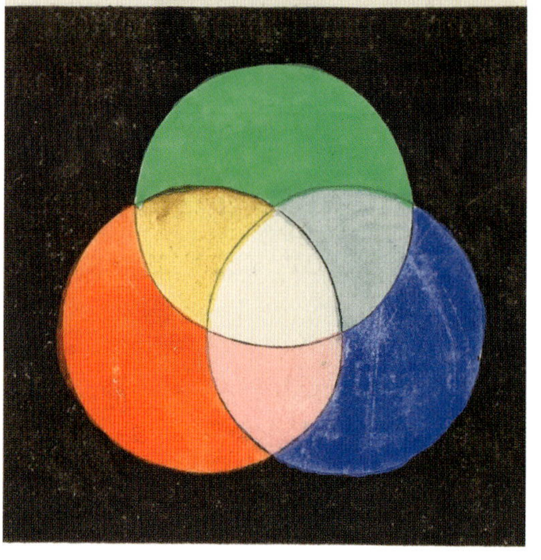

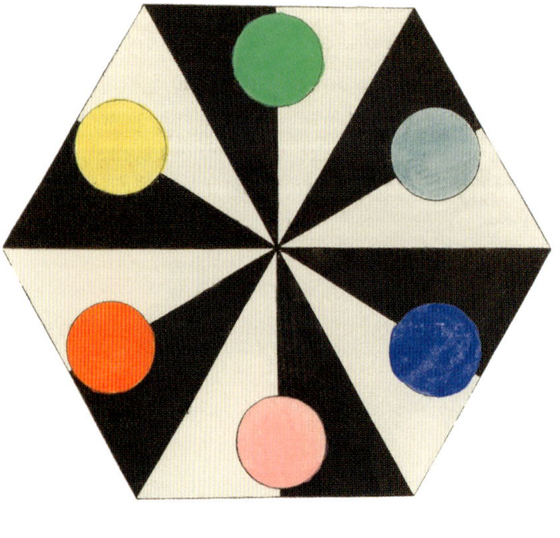

ABOVE LEFT
Simplified diagram of Benson's color cube as it appeared in his Manual of the Science of Colour *(1871).*

ABOVE RIGHT
William Benson's "diagram of the eight principal colors" of light, including black and white. The overlapping areas of the primary colors of light anticipate the technique of CMYK printing, which uses negatives of red, green, and blue.

BELOW LEFT
Benson's tool to identify the midpoint between two colors. An alternative to Maxwell's spinning discs, this method involved placing a polished piece of glass along the straight lines of the diagram and lining up the reflection of one coloured dot so it overlapped with another, creating a middle colour that combined both.

OPPOSITE
Sections of Benson's color cube demonstrating color groupings and potential combinations.

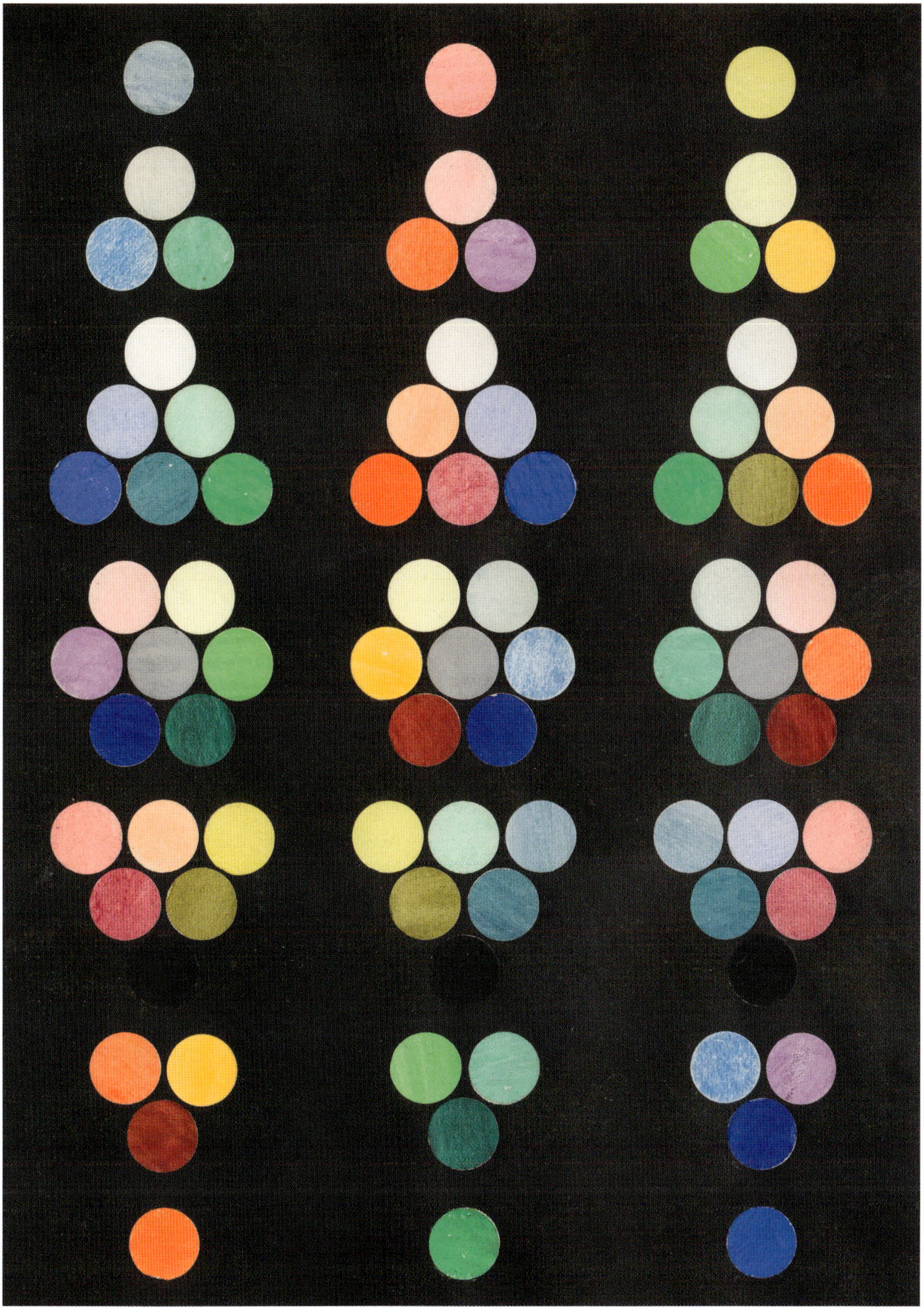

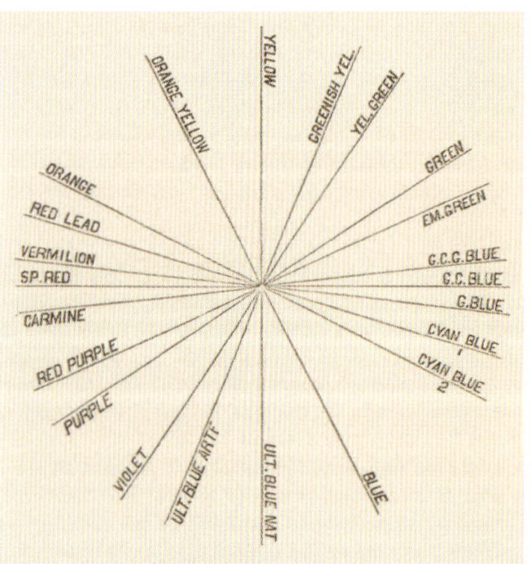

Ogden Rood's contrast diagram in Modern Chromatics *(1879) identifies the most effective pairs of contrasting colors. Georges Seurat translated it into French and retained a copy in his studio for reference.*

Rood paid considerable attention to the behavior and effects of light, and his work appeared in the same year Thomas Edison produced the first commercial incandescent light bulb. That transformative technology, which changed the appearance of the world and the colors it bathed, came just too late for Rood, who focused predominantly on the nature of daylight, gaslight, and candle light. His many bite-sized subjects included an analysis of opalescent color, an explanation of the workings of the retina, a survey of the colors of sunsets, and a section on color blindness.

Most of the book detailed the mechanics of color through replicable experiments. The practical application was not always specified and sometimes left to the reader to extrapolate, but the final chapter, "On the Use of Color in Painting and Decoration", offered useful hints to anyone wishing to master color in creative practice. Rood drew a distinction between a decorator's relationship with color and an artist's. The former should use color to instil joy, he argued, while the painter had a free hand and could legitimately use color to trigger sorrow. Where many color theorists of the late eighteenth and early nineteenth centuries bemoaned the fact that existing pigments failed to match the platonic models of perfect color they had devised, Rood's experiments recorded specific pigments and then accommodated them within his system by name.

Modern Chromatics included a synthesis and re-statement of some of the most useful observations of Chevreul, Helmholtz, and Maxwell, and even found time to acknowledge Bezold's comparatively recent work and his "interesting observations". Rood weighed up historical color systems in the chapter "Modes of Arranging Colors in Systems" and found many of them wanting, for all their superficial charms and persuasive claims. Indeed, he was pragmatic enough to admit the flaws inherent in any attempt: "In point of fact, our knowledge of color and our means of experimenting on it are not at present sufficiently advanced to enable us even to propose a plan for a truly philosophical classification, and between the proposal and its execution there would be many weary steps." But he wanted to find common ground between science and art, both sides united in the strength of their response to color in the world and its capacity to inspire. "Even the most profound mathematicians," he wrote, "are never weary of studying the colors of polarized light". Color had the capacity to move everyone, immeasurably enriching human experience, yet in his direct address to artists, Rood noted the paradox that color was largely inessential to human existence. Our species, he insisted, could function perfectly well if we only perceived the world in monochrome but that just made our sensory range of color more precious, a "magical drapery, which is thus cast over the visible world".

Rood's book received a muted reception in his homeland but was warmly taken up in France. Along with the work of Charles Blanc, Rood's description of the operations of perception inspired

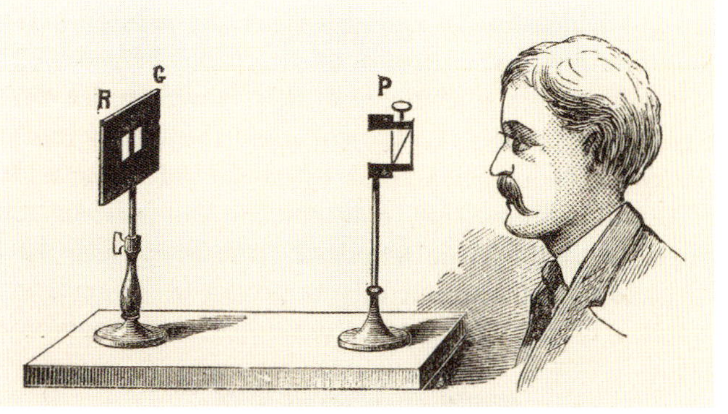

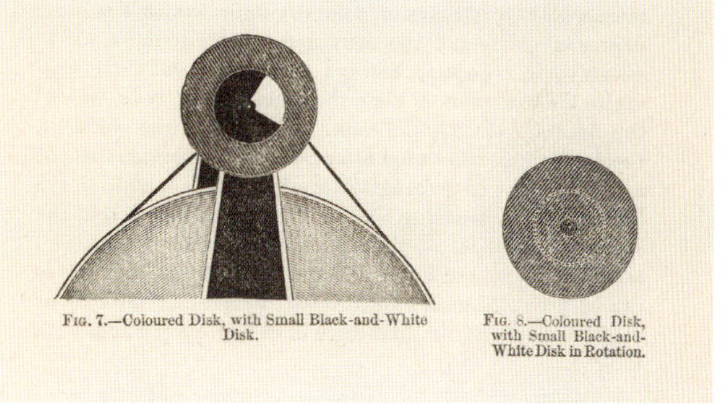

Georges Seurat to experiment with what would become known as Pointillism. The Neo-Impressionists found an invaluable crib sheet in a simple diagram of contrasting colors in *Modern Chromatics*; Seurat was known to have created a copy for quick reference, translating the color names into French. Where Chevreul had identified adjacent colors as heightening the contrast between them, Rood explored how tiny dots of different colors could seemingly meld into a new color when viewed at a distance. He summarized what would be understood as optical mixing as "the custom of placing small dots of two colors very near each other, and allowing them to be blended by the eye placed at the proper distance". Although Charles Blanc also referred to the technique, it was Rood's explanation that described it with the greatest clarity, thrilling artists with its potential. *Modern Chromatics* helped sate the Neo-Impressionists' desire for a clear scientific basis for the arrangement of color on canvas. The iridescence of Seurat's *A Sunday Afternoon on the Island of La Grande Jatte* (1884–6) and the spiralling kineticism of Signac's portrait of the art dealer Félix Fénéon (1890) were painted with meticulous placement of discrete colors intended to conjure the energetic light of a summer's day or Fénéon's anarchic personality. By reducing pigment-based color to self-contained dots, the artists thought they could make it behave more like

TOP

An illustration of "Dove's apparatus" included in Rood's Modern Chromatics *(1879). The device allowed the user to experience the difference between immaterial and material color and involved looking at light through panes of red and green glass and a prism. The colored glass could be removed and stacked on a flat surface to produce the effects of material (pigment-based) color.*

ABOVE

Illustration of a motorized device to spin colored Maxwell discs and determine the luminosity and value of different colors. In this example, a vermilion disc is attached and a smaller combination of black and white is superimposed upon it. The correct proportions of black and white are established once both values match when the discs are spinning.

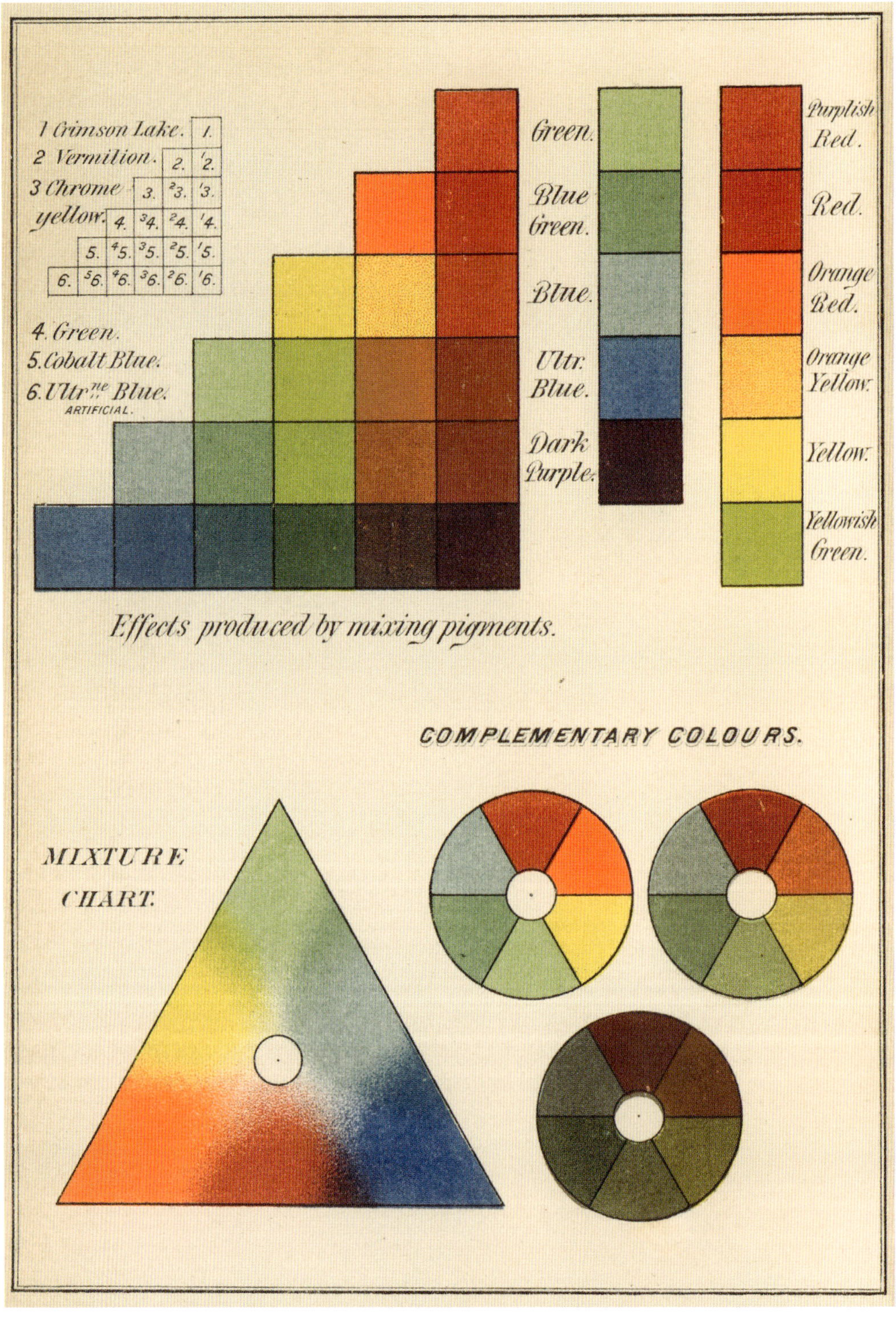
1 Crimson Lake.
2 Vermilion.
3 Chrome yellow.
4. Green.
5. Cobalt Blue.
6. Ultr.ne Blue.
ARTIFICIAL.
Green.
Blue Green.
Blue.
Ultr. Blue.
Dark Purple.
Purplish Red.
Red.
Orange Red.
Orange Yellow.
Yellow.
Yellowish Green.
Effects produced by mixing pigments.
COMPLEMENTARY COLOURS.
MIXTURE CHART.

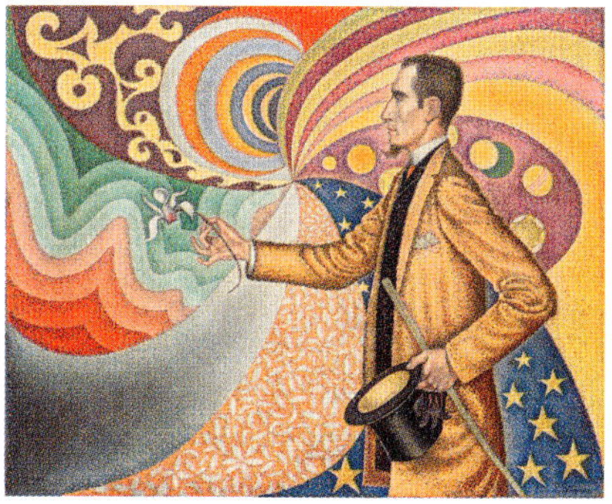

light (the technique was also known as chromo-luminarism) but in practice the intended effect is hard to perceive, relying on a particular distance between the viewer and the work—if the dots are too small, or the viewer too far away from the surface, the colors blend to a neutral gray and the effect can be desaturating.

As Edward L. Nichols noted in a biographical tribute to Rood published in 1909, his enthusiastic reception by his artist peers was "the more remarkable, since it has always been difficult to persuade those who use color as a medium of expression to master the real physics of their subject". Strangely, although the Neo-Impressionists embraced his ideas and embedded them in their practice, the admiration was not reciprocated. Rood's son, Roland, later recounted an exchange with his father about the extent of his influence on art. Roland had been studying in France and fallen under the spell of the highly chromatic practice of contemporary French painters, and entreated his father to offer his view of Monet, Pissarro, and associates. In an article for *The Scrip* (1902), a periodical, Roland later recalled the conversation as follows: "'What do you think of them?' I ventured. 'Awful! Awful!', he gasped. Then I told him what these painters said of his theories. This was too much for his composure. He threw up his hands in horror and indignation, and cried: 'If that is all I have done for art, I wish I had never written that book!'"

Ogden Rood's antipathy waned over time, however, and Roland hinted that his father later took a more measured view: "At times he seemed doubtful if he had not in fact endorsed impressionism; he seemed to feel that possibly while searching for truth in one direction he had also uncovered it elsewhere." This gnomic explanation could stand for many of the discoveries and progressions related to color in the nineteenth century, as happy accidents and purposeful study alike spurred advances in our understanding and ability to create an ever more colorful world. Color became a revelation and a tool: forced into being in test tubes, pressed into service by rapacious industry, analyzed for its inconsistency, and rehabilitated as a subject of scholarship. From Chevreul's investigations into fading blacks to Perkin's chance discovery of mauve, ever-increasing control of ever-wider color palettes was becoming possible, and color increasingly brought to heel. In the next century, things would only get brighter.

LEFT
This single color plate in Rood's Modern Chromatics *(1879) contains a table of squares to demonstrate a mixture of specific pigments. The triangle is similar to the models of immaterial color described by Young and Maxwell.*

ABOVE
The technique on display in Paul Signac's Portrait of Félix Fénéon *(1890) was inspired by the theory of optical mixing as expressed by Ogden Rood in* Modern Chromatics *(1879).*

6

THE COLOR OF

WELLNESS

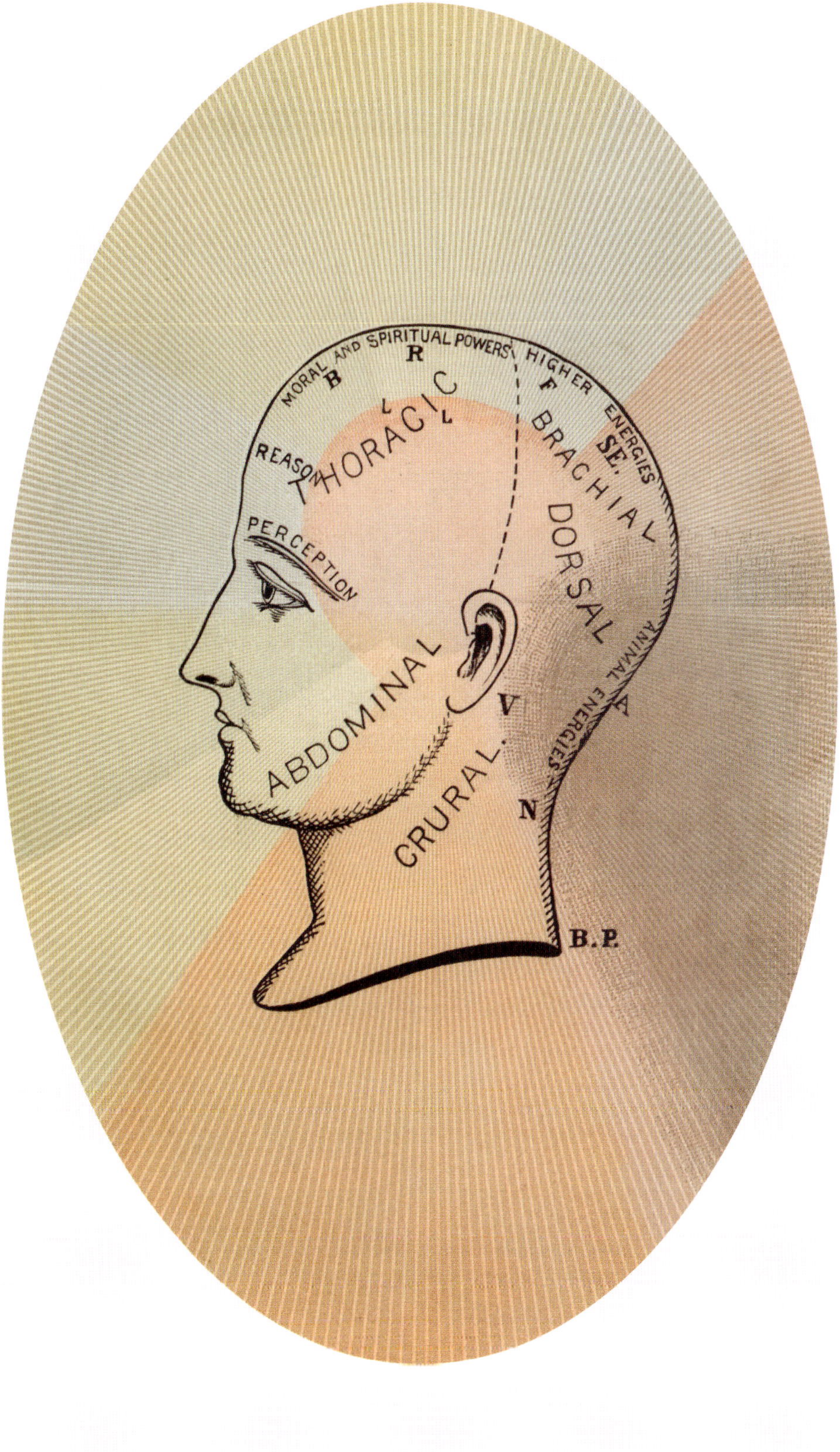
MORAL AND SPIRITUAL POWERS
HIGHER ENERGIES
B
R
F
L
L
SE.
REASON
THORACIC
BRACHIAL
PERCEPTION
DORSAL
ABDOMINAL
ANIMAL ENERGIES
A
V
CRURAL.
N
B.P.

Seemingly magical or even divine, it is little wonder color has historically been thought to possess healing properties. Some have touted it as a natural cure, drawn from the power of sunlight, but the world of so-called chromotherapy, the practice of attempting to cure illnesses with color, had links with the supernatural, too, and was often inspired by mystical beliefs in invisible forces (see p.26). From cure to quackery, both ends of the spectrum of color healing operated in a long tradition that linked specific colors to particular remedies, and endowed different wavelengths with particular therapeutic properties when applied to the body.

The popular image of the color healer, a profession that grew up in the late nineteenth century, is close to that of their contemporaries the mesmerist and the spiritualist. Influential texts on the healing power of colored light flourished at a time when interest in the occult was simmering away in respectable society, particularly in the English-speaking West. Not coincidentally, conventional science was then also probing "invisible" powers within mainstream physics, whether by harnessing electricity or analyzing the properties of the atom. But the relationship between color and health extends back far further than the Victorian era, all the way to the ancient Greek physician Hippocrates (*c.*460–*c.*370 BCE), who formulated a model of health and disease based on the four humours. These were a manifestation of the four elements in the form of bodily fluids—red blood, black bile, yellow bile, and white phlegm—each with a corresponding temperament. Those with an abundance of blood were sanguine, hearty types, while those with an excess of black bile were prone to melancholia. In the Middle Ages, it was even believed that a person's skin color was the result of their humoral composition. Illness was thought to arise wherever fluids were out of balance, and the aim of medicine was to restore their equilibrium, bringing the subject back to good health.

Color healing in antiquity involved the topical application of colored compounds with potentially therapeutic powers to the site of the ailment. Red cinnabar (a mineral medicine and pigment more theatrically known as dragon's blood) was helpful for healing sores but its color was a means of identifying its efficacy rather than the cause of it. The Tyrian purple dye manufactured by the Phoenicians from the boiled glands of murex sea snails, meanwhile, also proved remarkably effective as a calming treatment for boils with its active ingredient of calcium oxide.

Ibn Sina (Avicenna, 980–1037) identified a more central role for color as "an observable symptom of disease", described in his medical encyclopaedia *Canon of Medicine* (1025). The external coloration of the patient's skin, urine, eyes, and faeces should be closely observed, he advised, to identify their inner illness. A patient with yellowing skin, could, he rightly surmised, be suffering from liver disease. By medieval times, color scales of urine became a popular diagnostic tool. These hand-colored manuscripts provided a spectrum of possible pee, running from pale yellow to black-brown, that was used to identify infections and illnesses (diagnosticians became known as "pisse-prophets"). The inconsistent hand-coloration of the manuscripts, and the printed version that appeared in Ulrich Pinder's *Epiphanie medicorum* (1506), somewhat undermined their reliability, but as color printing and color measurement improved, standards of higher precision became available. Much later equivalents, including Vogel's Scale of Urine Tints, were still popular in urology textbooks of the nineteenth and twentieth centuries.

In 1915, meanwhile, Joseph Lovibond, inventor of the Tintometer color-measurement device for liquids, demonstrated how his equipment could be used to analyze a patient's blood for abnormalities. Originally devised to gauge the color of beer (Lovibond was a brewer by

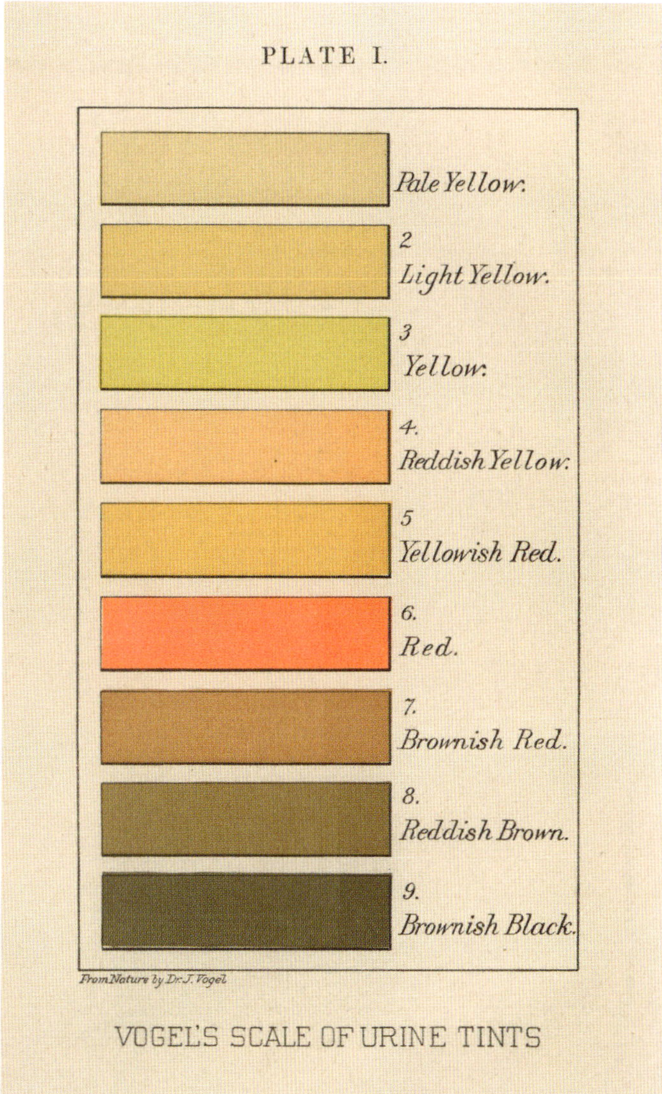

PREVIOUS PAGE
An image of color 'radiation' from the brain as included in Edwin Babbitt's *Principles of Light and Color* (1878). Babbitt's model resembled the pseudoscience of phrenology in which types of emotions and capabilities were associated with different portions of the brain. Babbitt went further and related these to particular invisible 'colors'. 'Animal energies' and 'sexual love' are represented at the base of the brain in a 'dingy red' colour, while the 'R' of religious feeling on the top of the head is a calm yellow.

LEFT
Dr J. Vogel's Scale of Urine Tints from *Practical Uranalysis and Urinary Diagnosis* (1898).

BELOW
A coloured woodcut depicting the analysis of a urine sample by hue to determine the patient's ailments. From Ulrich Pinder's *Epiphanie medicorum* (1506).

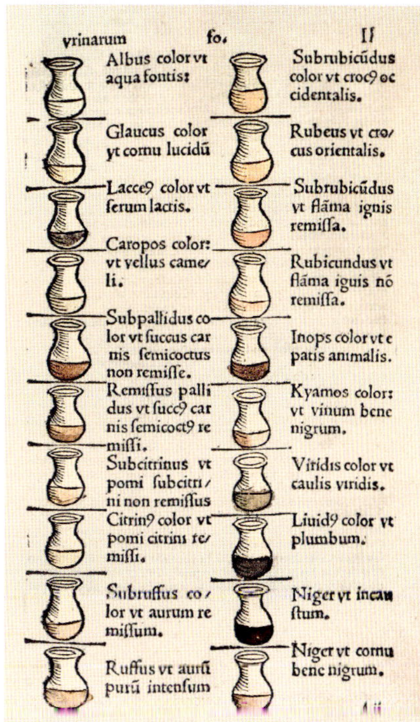

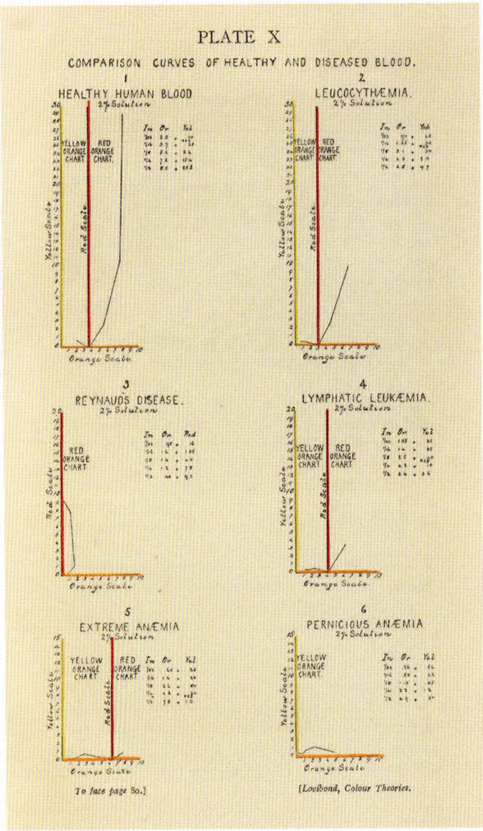

ABOVE
Graphs from Joseph Lovibond's *Light and Colour Theories* (1915) demonstrated the use of his Tintometer as a diagnostic tool in medicine. In this example, the color of a patient's blood sample could be analyzed to diagnose problems such as anaemia.

OPPOSITE
Two plates of color variants from the Japan Color Research Institute's published specification of the pigments of human skin. The colors were based on the Munsell system that allowed individual colors to be defined in terms of hue, value, and chroma.

trade), the Tintometer could also be used to diagnose lymphatic leukaemia, anaemia, and Reynaud's disease, and worked by matching the color of a sample through a combination of different colored filters of the device. The depth of redness of a patient's sample could be plotted and related to Lovibond's diagnostic charts included in his book *Light and Colour Theories* (1915).

Around the same time, a visual chart for direct comparison was published as *Tallqvist's Hamoglobin Scale* (*c.*1920). This contained detachable squares of blotting paper onto which blood samples could be dropped, and the color then compared with a scale of increasing redness, with holes to pass the sample beneath for a precise match.

Human skin has posed a particular challenge in the creation of standards. Every portrait painter understands the immense complexity and variety of colors involved, even within a single individual, or across a single face, and, in 1967, the Japan Color Research Institute produced a set of standards containing over 500 individual iterations of skin tones. Inspired by the Munsell system of color specification (see p.225), with accompanying striplike swatches (to be applied directly to the body of a patient for side-by-side comparison), the wide range of complex tints and shades helped achieve accurate matches for preparing skin grafts, and allowed for measurement of the progress of skin diseases. One of the contributors to the project, plastic surgeon E. Ito of the Keio University School of Medicine, plotted the range of the standard Munsell color variables hue, value, and chroma across a large number of people, and noted the particular difficulties of finding color matches when scar tissue discolored in various degrees in contrast to the undamaged skin around it.

If color had an obvious role to play in identifying both disease and cure, perhaps the richest yet most contested area in which it was applied to healing lay in the

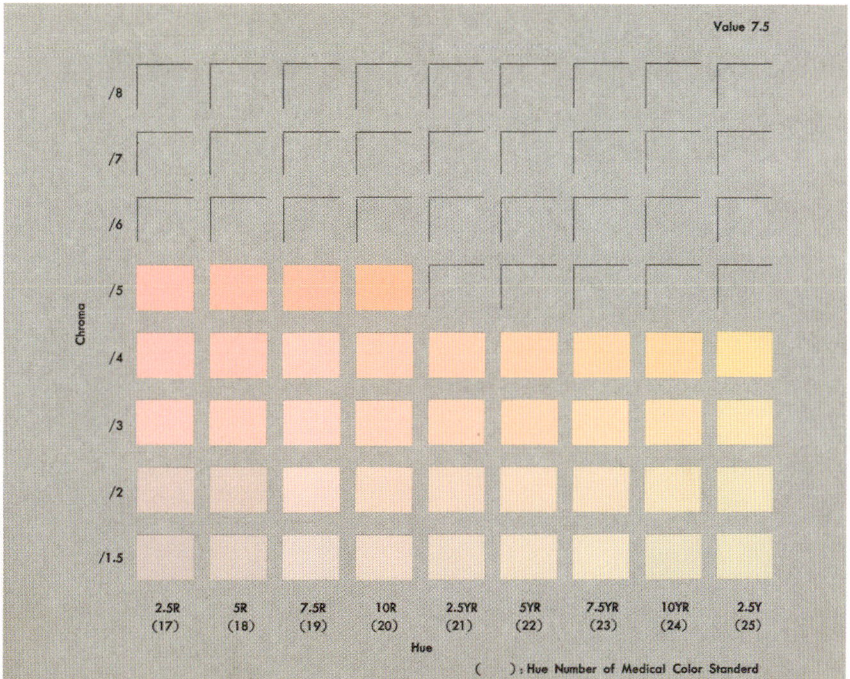

Chart 2

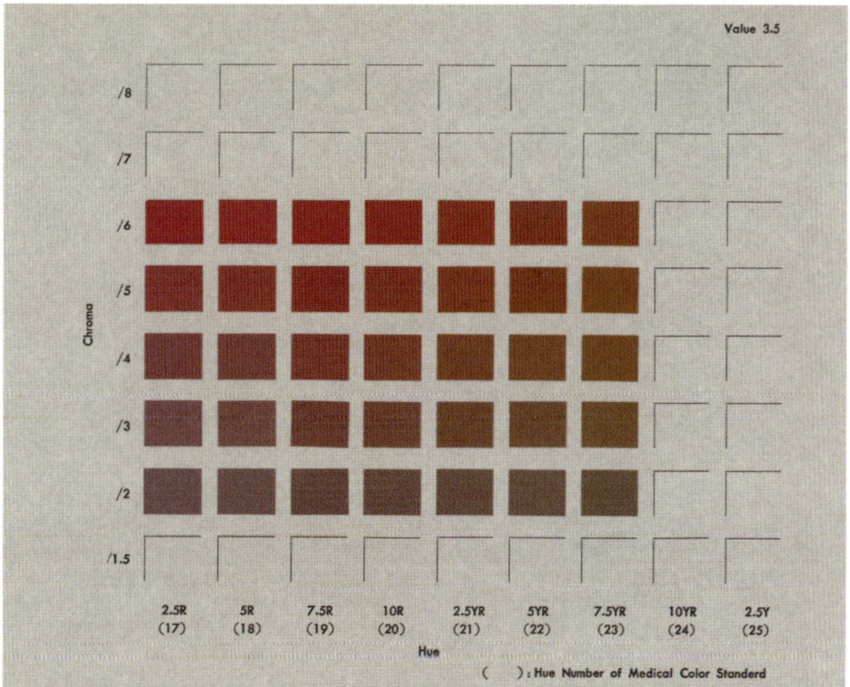

Chart 10

notion that "bathing" in colored light was inherently curative. Color itself as medicine, with the ability to spur bodily processes of rejuvenation as a physiological response to its wavelengths, again dates back to Ibn Sina, who coined one of the most enduring observations: that red light agitates the blood while blue light calms it. Centuries later, Seth Pancoast, an early member of the mystical and influential Theosophical Society and personal physician to its founder Madame Blavatsky (see p.30), wrote *Blue and Red Light, or Light and its Rays as Medicine* (1877) to promote what he believed to be the healing powers of colored rays. Printed in blue ink with a red border on every page, Pancoast believed that illness thrived where an individual was out of harmony, and argued that color therapy, particularly in the form of "sun baths" through colored glass, could restore equilibrium. The book was full of references to the Kabbalah, a school of thought within Jewish mysticism that believed light was a vessel of divinity and revelation. Pancoast supported this idea and maintained that visible light contained an invisible "celestial" light within it.

Of all the "chromopaths" in color literature, perhaps the most cited was the controversial self-described magnetist Edwin Babbitt (1828–1905), whose monolithic *Principles of Light and Color* appeared in 1878, just a year

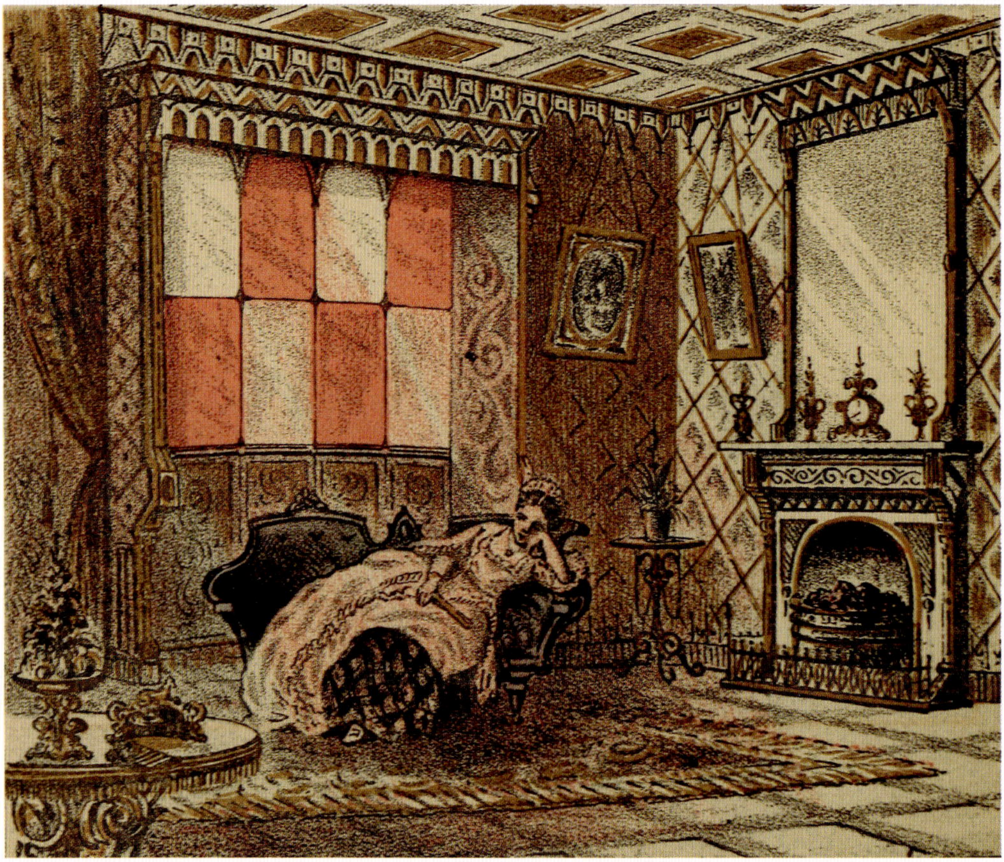

after Pancoast's work on blue and red light. Babbitt expanded Pancoast's effort substantially to prescribe a wide range of different treatments involving different colors for different ailments. Across 200,000 words, he expounded a complex theory of harmonic laws and unseen forces, believing color to be the product of atomic behavior and claiming light as the life-giver to all on both the micro and macro levels. Previously a stationer who sold ranges of pens, there is no evidence that Babbitt was a qualified doctor, but his work was persuasive enough to attract near-instant fame, an enormous readership, and the opprobrium of the conventional medical profession. *Scientific American*, reviewing the craze for light through blue glass, prescribed the following: "[B]lue glass, one part; faith, ten parts; mix thoroughly and stir well until all common sense evaporates."

Babbitt's color therapy was based on the spectral composition of different elements, which he analyzed through the use of a spectroscope, concluding that red, yellow, and blue had their elemental equivalents in hydrogen, carbon, and oxygen. He believed everyone emitted colored rays of energy just by being alive, and that a specialist could be trained to see distortions and imbalances in an individual's personal color field that could be corrected by supplying missing colors through a course of chromotherapy. Yellow light, for example, was a stimulant with emetic and purgative properties. "Cold, electrical" blue had anti-inflammatory effects. In his case studies, Babbitt cited testimonials from migraine sufferers who found relief bathing in sunlight refracted through blue glass, and he even claimed to have successfully treated tuberculosis with red light. Handily for the intrigued reader, he had a range of products for sale designed to deliver these same healing wavelengths through different vessels. Biggest and most impressive was a stained-glass window, the Chromolume, that could be installed in the south-facing wall of a patient's house, beneath which the sufferer could sit and soak up the rays of carefully juxtaposed colors. More portable was the Chromo-disk, a cone to which colored filters were applied so light could be trained on areas of concern, while the Chromo-lens was a colored flask to be filled with water and left in the sun. The patient drank the water once it had been infused with the light's vitality; a blue flask, he claimed, would concentrate copper and manganese in its contents.

The book contained countless moments to enrage medics and physicists alike. Sections on the mysterious power of "Odic light" and training in "chromo-mentalism", an extra-sensory vision to see colored "etherio-atomic forces", provided fuel for the sceptics. But Babbitt's frequent references to electricity and to the power and structure of the atom allowed him to relate his claims more persuasively: plainly there were invisibly powerful forces described in contemporary scientific discourse, so why should color and the electromagnetic spectrum not possess equal transformative energy? Although later readers would see clearly where the ideas in these books departed from accepted science, Pancoast and Babbitt were publishing at a time when occultism was

Illustration from Seth Pancoast's *Blue and Red Light, or Light and its Rays as Medicine* (1877). Pancoast recommended bathing in red light for its ability to "awaken all the dominant Vitality in the Nervous System". However, he also cautioned against overdoing it. In excess, red light "over-excites the Nervous System and may produce dangerous Fevers".

not always seen as its antithesis. To some, this was a novel, under-explored discipline that would eventually acquire enough of an evidence base to be accommodated within conventional wisdom. Pancoast, for example, was convinced that his remedies would be incorporated into standard medical practice in time.

A great many speculative works on color healing and color therapy continued to appear throughout the twentieth century, often tapping into historical color schemes related to chakras and auras. The belief in chakras as non-physical energy centers in the body dates back to the medieval era and its geographical origin in the Indian subcontinent. Much later, it was adopted by Western New Age philosophies of healing practices and colorized by relating each chakra to a color in the Newtonian spectrum. Many works about color healing also referred to auras, inspired by the belief in invisible energy fields around objects, including humans. In 1939, it appeared these had been detected in full-color photography by scientist Semyon Kirlian (1898–1978) and his wife Valentina (1904–71). The pair accidentally caught what looked like an emanation of energy fields on film after passing high voltage over objects to find they left an outline of mysterious colored bands on photographic paper. Although sceptics attributed this to interference caused by moisture, the striking and eerie results continued to persuade people that unseen forces were at work all around them, feeding the notion that there were more things in heaven and earth than were dreamt of in conventional science.

Not everything in the discipline of color healing in the last century was pseudoscience. Some practices had a strong evidential basis, including the use of blue light to treat jaundiced babies and skin disorders. Various studies, meanwhile, gathered evidence for the modest ability of different colored rooms and rays to raise or lower a subject's heart rate and blood pressure (the pituitary and pineal glands are affected by the reception of light and regulate the body's hormones accordingly). Outside of the visible spectrum, ultraviolet light has proven antibacterial and antiviral properties. Even with a paucity of evidence for chromotherapy's effectiveness, and the difficulty of distilling the science from the snake oil, its principles have never entirely gone away. The cheering, mood-enhancing power of color in different environments has benefits that may contribute to recovery in ways not easily measured by the physician. The placebo effect, after all, is a real phenomenon, and the road to wellness is never purely black and white.

OPPOSITE
In *The Principles of Light and Color* (1878), Edwin Babbitt related the spectral colors to the qualities of particular elements as described in the lower table. He then extrapolated further and identified portions of the spectrum as having specific curative or stimulant effects on the human body.

OVERLEAF, LEFT
Edwin Babbitt's interest in contrast and oppositional colors was inspired by the work of Chevreul. Yet he took those principles into the realm of pseudoscience by presenting each color as having a "chemical affinity" and particular effects on the body. In the outer ring of the lower circle, reproduced in his *Principles of Light and Color* (1878), he identified portions of the spectrum that are "animating to the nerves" and those that are "cooling to overheated blood".

OVERLEAF, RIGHT
These diagrams from *The Principles of Light and Color* (1878) reflected Edwin Babbitt's interest in invisible forces and their relationships to healing and the spectrum. The top wheel relates colours to the poles while the bottom colourises the effect of iron filings organised around horseshoe magnets. Babbitt speculated on the presence of 'Odic colours', both powerful and invisible to the naked eye.

BABBITT'S PRINCIPLES OF LIGHT AND COLOR.—PLATE I.

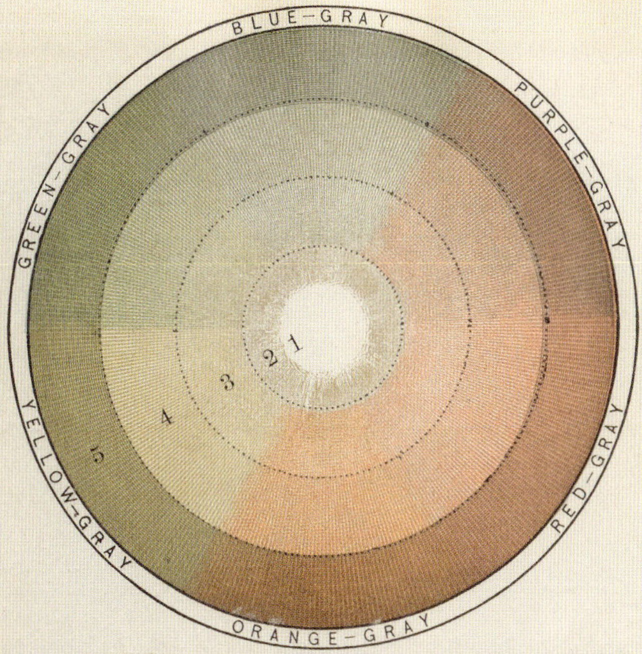

VARIOUS SHADES OF GRAY ARRANGED IN ANALOGICAL HARMONY.

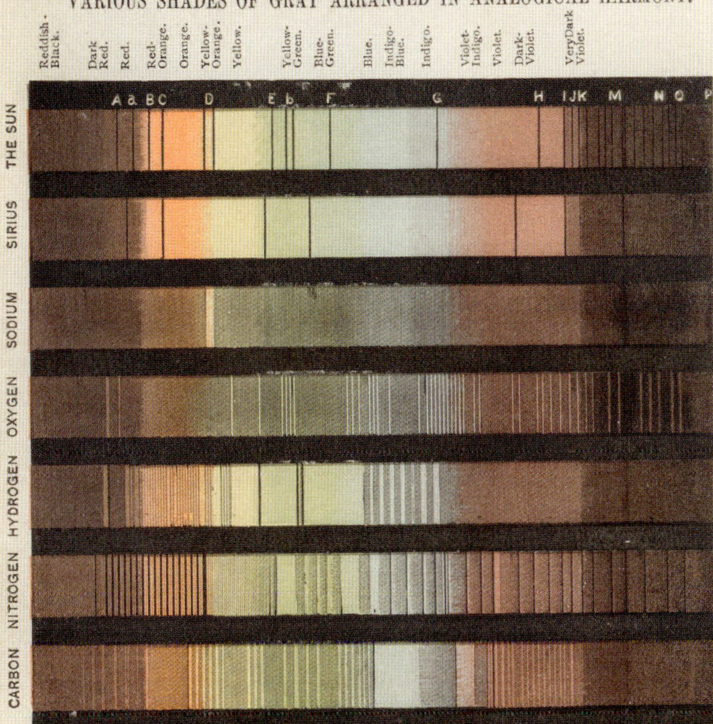

SPECTRA OF THE SUN, SIRIUS, AND SEVERAL ELEMENTS.

BABBITT'S PRINCIPLES OF LIGHT AND COLOR.—PLATE II.

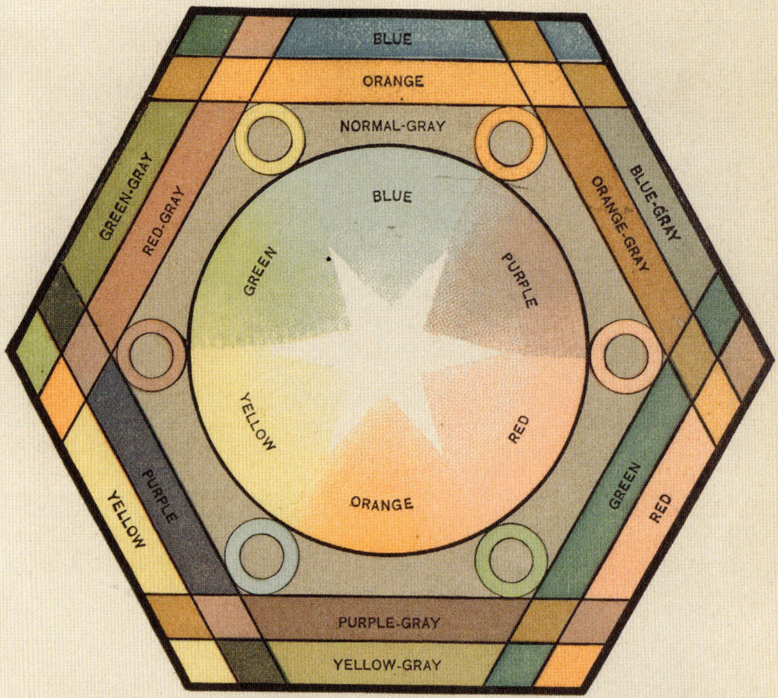

CHROMATIC HARMONY OF GRADATION AND CONTRAST.

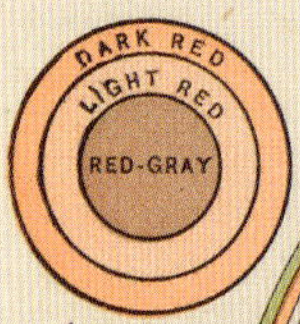

ANALOGICAL HARMONY

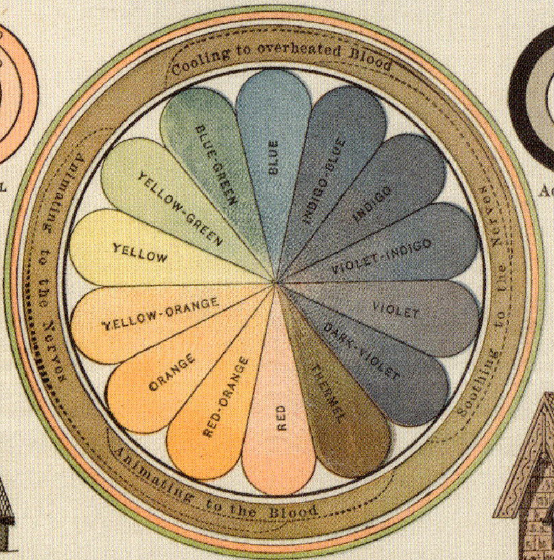

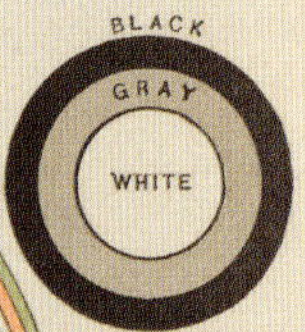

ACHROMATIC COLORS

5

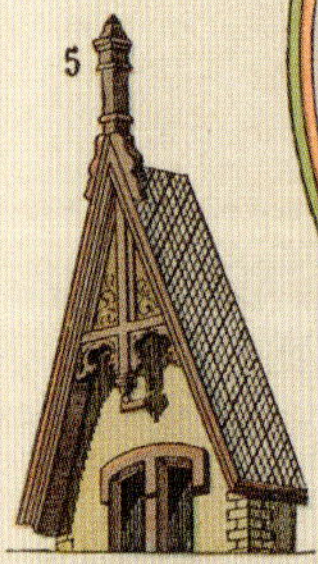
CONTRASTING HARMONY

CHROMATIC COLORS PLACED OPPOSITE THOSE WHICH FORM A CHEMICAL AFFINITY WITH THEM

6

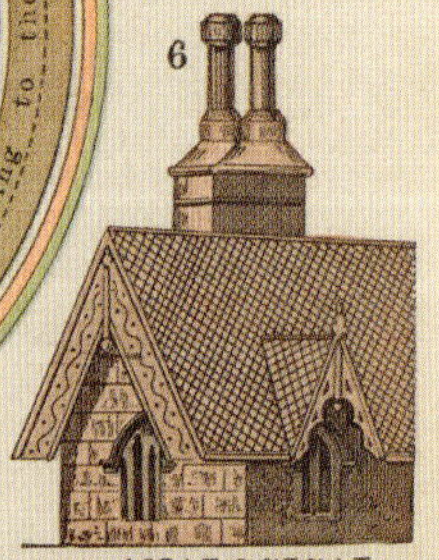
ANALOGICAL HARMONY

In the above elaborate combination of colors the artist has found it impossible to get every feature accurate, although he has many beautiful and pure tints. The grays on both plates I. and II. are not sufficiently subdued, the chromatic colors standing out too brilliantly, the red, for instance, in the house, fig. 6, being too strong, etc. For description of plates see pp. 63, 65, 66, 69, 71, etc. The spectra are described on p. 217.

BABBITT'S PRINCIPLES OF LIGHT AND COLOR.--PLATE III.

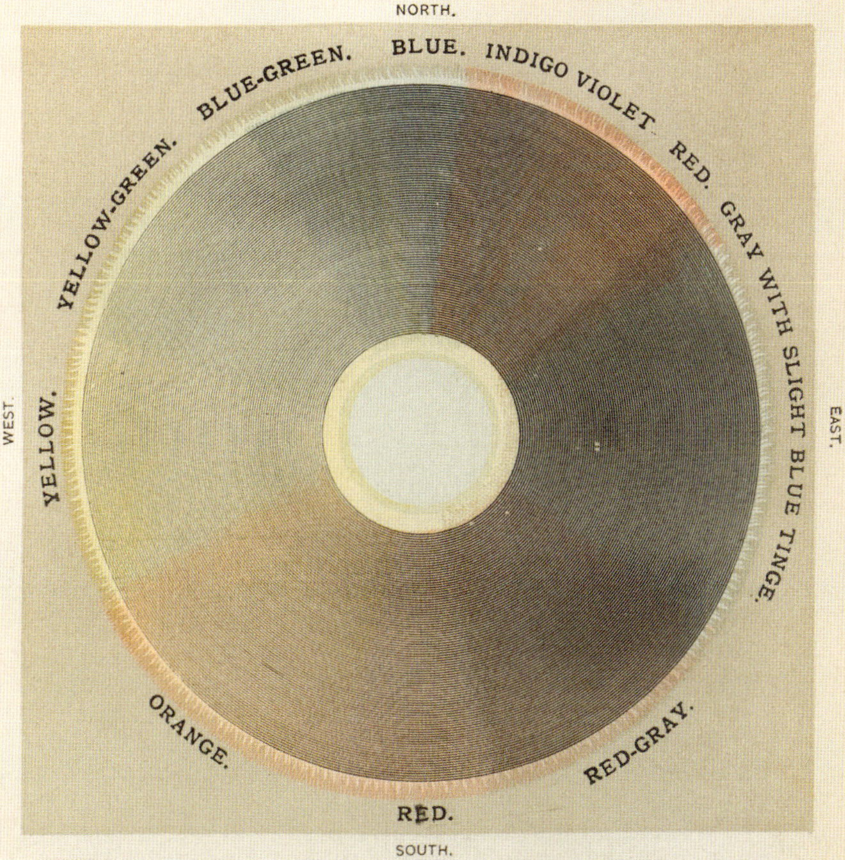

TERRESTRIAL DYNAMICS.—RADIATION OF ODIC LIGHTS AND COLORS.

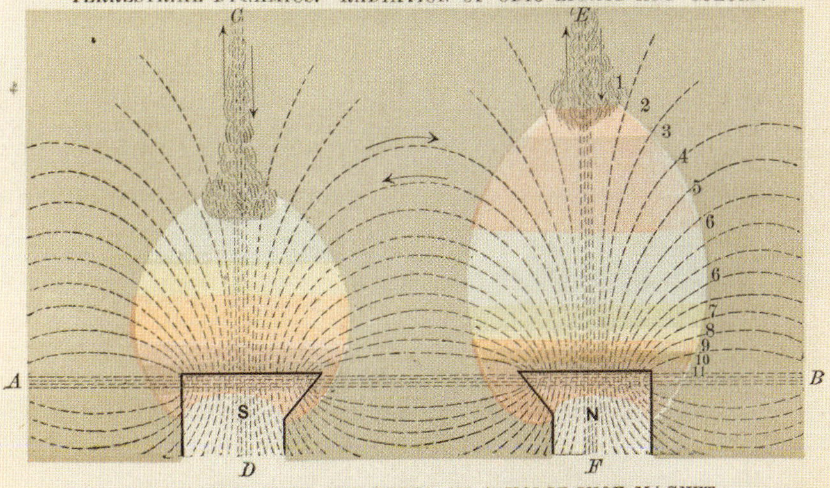

ODIC FLAMES FROM THE POLES OF A HORSE-SHOE MAGNET.

The colors are not put on very accurately nor blended properly in these magnets, but the reader can consult page 434, with which and these colors he may be able to gain a fair conception of the radiations.

7

THE COLOR OF

PRINTING

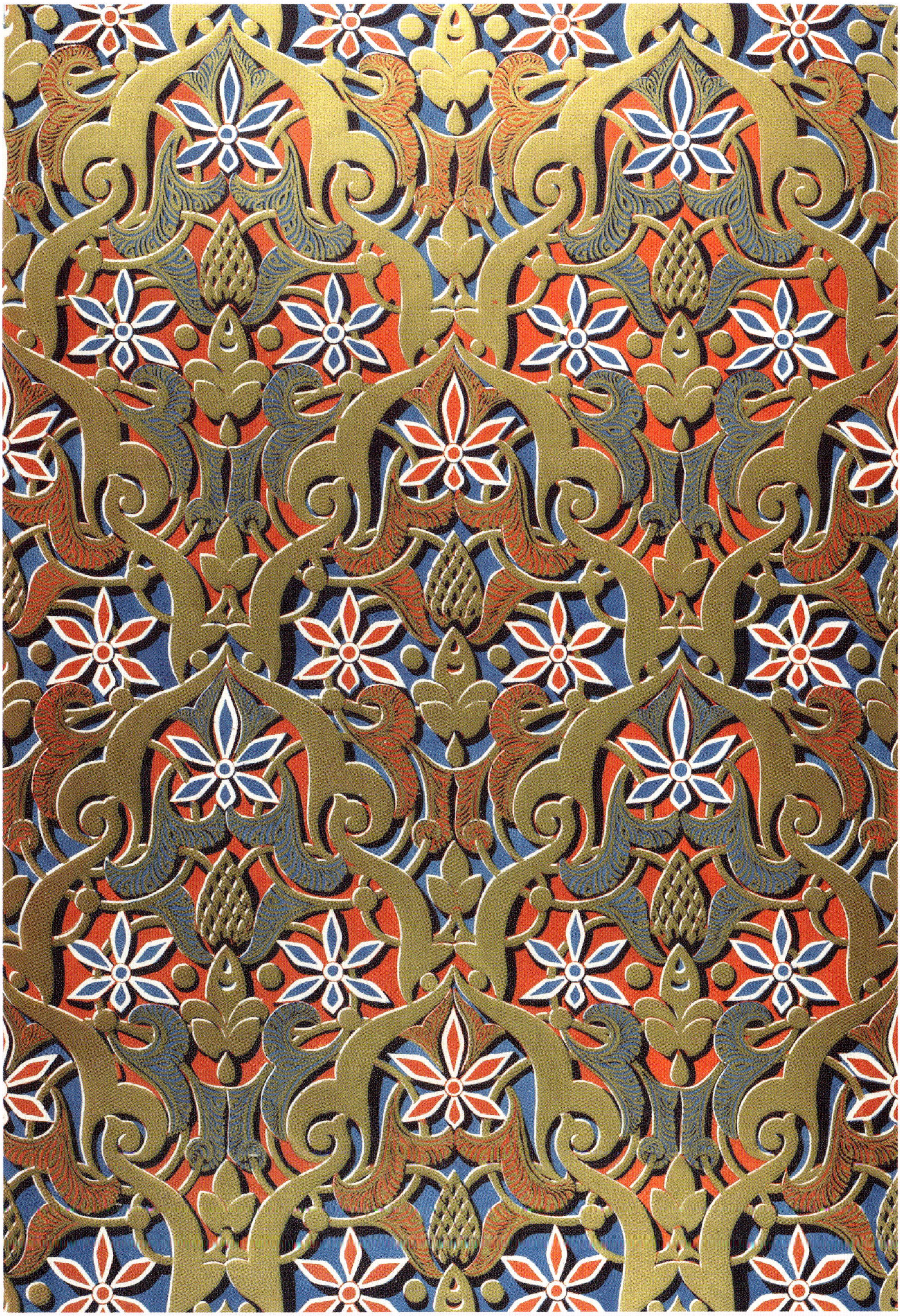

By necessity, books about color have always been in the vanguard of printing technology. The more accurately color images could be reproduced on the page, the better color theory could be illustrated with richly persuasive examples, but it took centuries to get there. After Johannes Gutenberg (*c.*1400–68) adapted Chinese printing technology and invented a printing press that used metal movable type rather than woodblocks, color drained from the page as books began to be reproduced mechanically. Where unique illuminated manuscripts had dazzled readers with plenteous use of carmine, ultramarine, and saffron in their hand-colored illustrations (the creator of the Lindisfarne Gospels of *c.*715 deployed around ninety different colors), printed books simply could not reproduce such complex color en masse. It was easy enough to ink up the type to print a solid block of text, and this could be done in one or more individual colors that combined on a single page. But the challenge of reconstituting the multiple and complex colors of an image, building translucent layers on the surface to blend on the page like paints on a palette, seemed insurmountable.

Printed color was initially all about initials. In early printed books solid colors were used for discrete, unbroken areas, with lead capital letters printed in a different color, mimetic of the manuscripts they were superseding. The Mainz Psalter of 1457, for example, only the second book to be printed after Gutenberg's Bible, used black, blue, and red ink. Red and blue capital letters at the start of each page were printed with separately inked woodblocks distinct from the movable type used for the body text. This was difficult to pull off, and the practice rarely appeared thereafter, but splashes of color still appeared intermittently over ensuing centuries: Newton's *Opticks* (1704), for example, included contrasting red type on its title page. Some books applied color more self-consciously, such as *Le livre de quatre couleurs* (1760), a satire of European society by the Marquis de Caraccioli. Each of its four sections was printed in a different colored ink—turquoise, brown, red, and yellow—to reflect, the author claimed, his eclectic readership. Caraccioli's analysis of the importance of the fan was printed in turquoise, while a section on the history of the lavatory appeared in brown ink. The author joked that the novelty of the different colors would inevitably seduce the reader, regardless of the quality of his prose: "I offer you the most beautiful of vermilions ... such that it finally shines on your magnificently and furiously illuminated faces".

Japanese woodblock prints from the seventeenth and eighteenth centuries exemplified the art of aligning a succession of colors, each printed on identical blocks. But reproducing complex multicolored illustrations in books in any way other than by hand-painting pre-printed engravings remained fiendishly difficult. The challenge was both physical and mental, requiring not only the mechanical means to blend and align primary printed colors perfectly but the perspicacity to work out which colors were required to begin with. Painter Jacob Christoph Le Blon (1667–1741) of Frankfurt had just that ability to see color in the world and then mentally unmix it into its primaries.

PREVIOUS PAGE
Plate XVIII from Jules Goury and Owen Jones's *Plans, Elevations and Sections of the Alhambra* (1845).

OPPOSITE
The title page and inner facing pages from the Marquis de Caraccioli's *Livre de quatre couleurs* (1760). The four-part satirical work used a different colored ink for each section with all four appearing together on the title page.

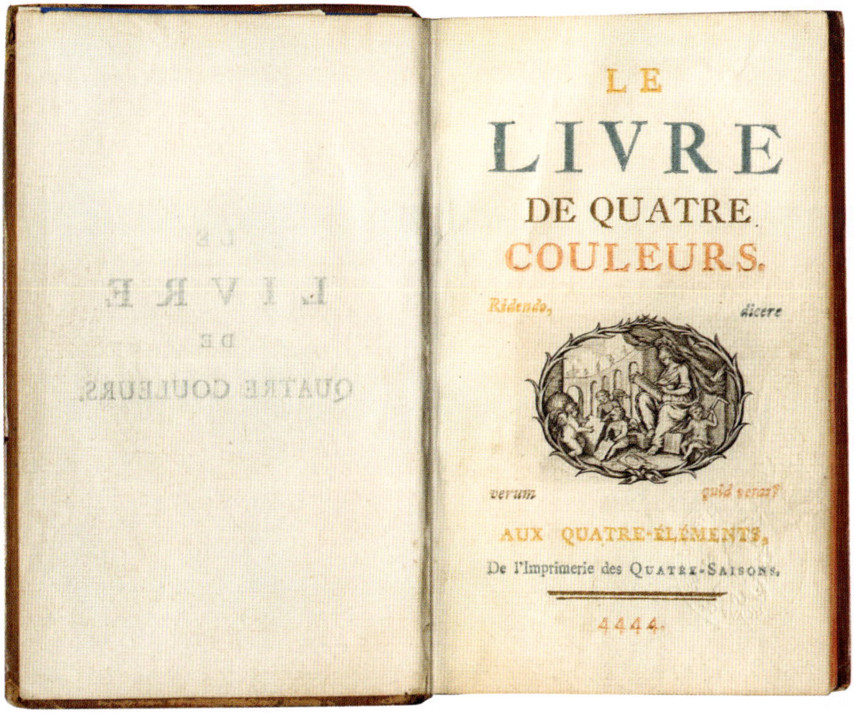

LE

LIVRE

DE QUATRE

COULEURS.

Ridendo, *dicere*

verum *quid vetat?*

AUX QUATRE-ÉLÉMENTS,

De l'Imprimerie des QUATRE-SAISONS.

4444.

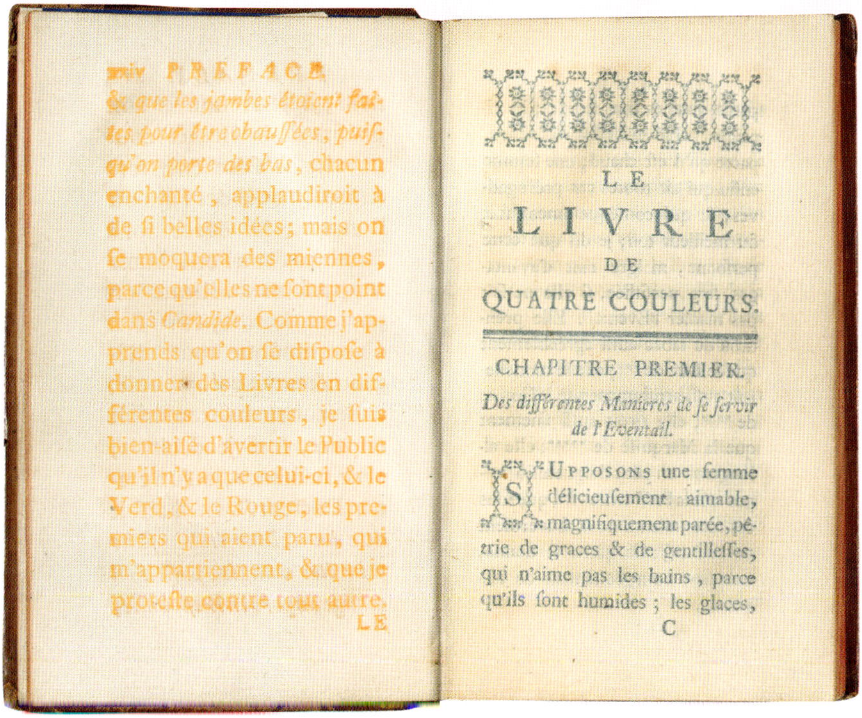

xiv PREFACE.

& que les jambes étoient faites pour être chauffées, puisqu'on porte des bas, chacun enchanté, applaudiroit à de si belles idées; mais on se moquera des miennes, parce qu'elles ne sont point dans *Candide*. Comme j'apprends qu'on se dispose à donner des Livres en différentes couleurs, je suis bien-aise d'avertir le Public qu'il n'y a que celui-ci, & le Verd, & le Rouge, les premiers qui aient paru, qui m'appartiennent, & que je proteste contre tous autre.

LE

LE

LIVRE

DE

QUATRE COULEURS.

CHAPITRE PREMIER.

Des différentes Manieres de se servir de l'Eventail.

SUPPOSONS une femme délicieusement aimable, magnifiquement parée, pêtrie de graces & de gentillesses, qui n'aime pas les bains, parce qu'ils sont humides; les glaces,

C

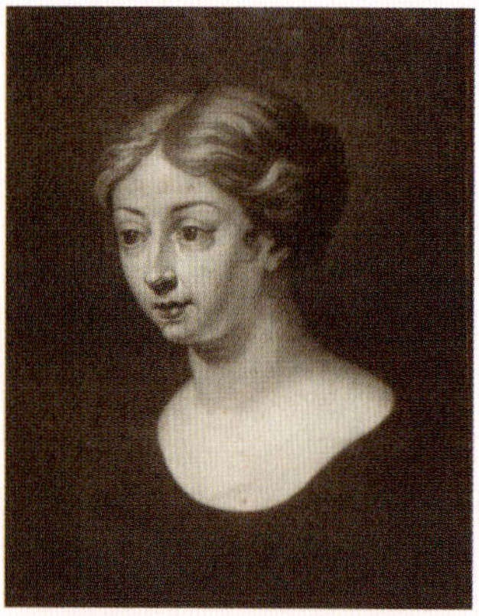

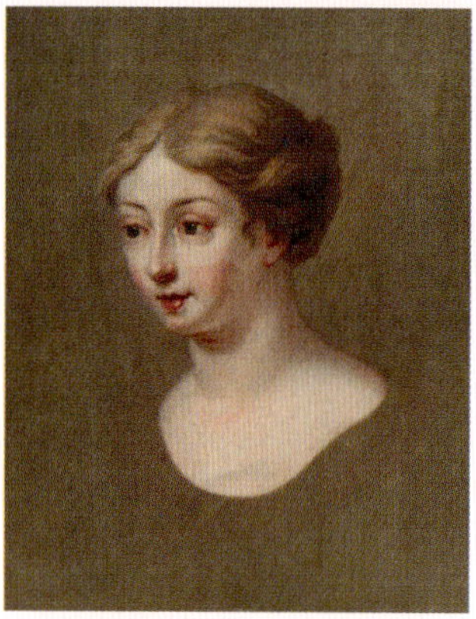

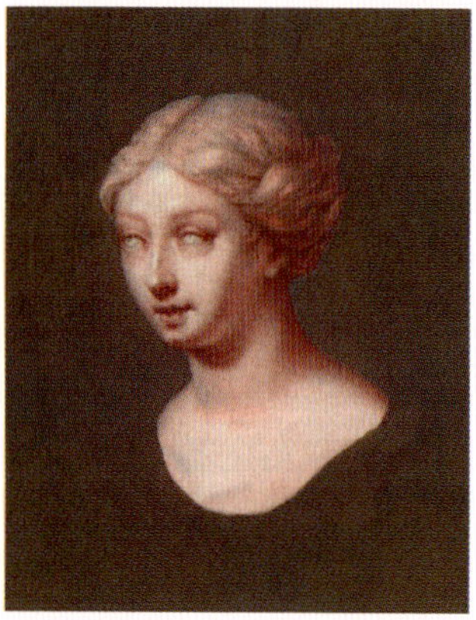

To refine his approach, he experimented with layering colored mezzotints, each printed with a different translucent primary-colored ink. An augmented edition of his painting manual *Coloritto* (*c*.1725) contained several color illustrations in which a portrait of a woman was reproduced in different states, with printed layers of black and red (and some judicious hand-coloring in parts) blending to add up to subtle porcelain skin tones. In this context, however, Le Blon was not attempting to show off the technological innovation so much as simply trying to show painters how to mix common skin tones in painting. Le Blon's primaries for printing were perfected through much trial and error. His eventual preferred blue was Prussian, a pigment only recently brought to market, while his optimal red was a cocktail of several different kinds. Le Blon then went into business to produce color reproductions of paintings, but misjudged the market and the whole enterprise foundered. Nevertheless, he was succeeded by his student Jacques Fabien Gautier d'Agoty (1717–85), who had more success producing colored prints of anatomical illustrations for subscribers; the glistening reds he achieved were perfect for rendering exposed viscera.

It took another century of development to refine Le Blon's invention. Lithography, in which marks drawn onto a limestone slab could be transferred to the page, was invented in 1796 by Alois Senefelder (1771–1834) and many of the monochrome book illustrations of the next century adopted his method. Color on paper began to thrive after 1837 when Godefroy Engelmann (1788–1839), a Franco-German printer, combined Le Blon's four-color process with Senefelder's lithography and patented the technique as "chromolithographie". In this method, different colors were layered in sequence but a separate stone was required for each. The more elaborately colorful the illustration, the greater the number of stones, with some advertisements and complex pictures requiring more than twenty. Over the rest of the century, the innovation spread far and wide, crossing the Atlantic with Prussian émigré Louis Prang, whose chromolithography workshop in the United States helped introduce the nation to cheap color in the form of posters, greetings cards, calendars, and other ephemera. By the 1890s, color pictures were cheaper and easier to produce and becoming conspicuous in the pages of periodicals in the form of attention-grabbing advertisements (see p.44).

Publishers were keen to innovate, producing opulent, folio-sized works at considerable expense (sometimes the authors' own). Architect Owen Jones (1809–74) published two masterworks that lifted the technology to new heights. His series of folios *Plans, Elevations, Sections and Details of the Alhambra* (1836–45) contained colorful illustrations of architectural details, tiles, and motifs from the great Islamic palace in Andalusia, and was the first major publication illustrated with chromolithographed plates. Jones researched the latest developments in printing to obtain the results he sought and oversaw much of the work himself. He is perhaps best known for *The Grammar of Ornament* (1856), another treasure box

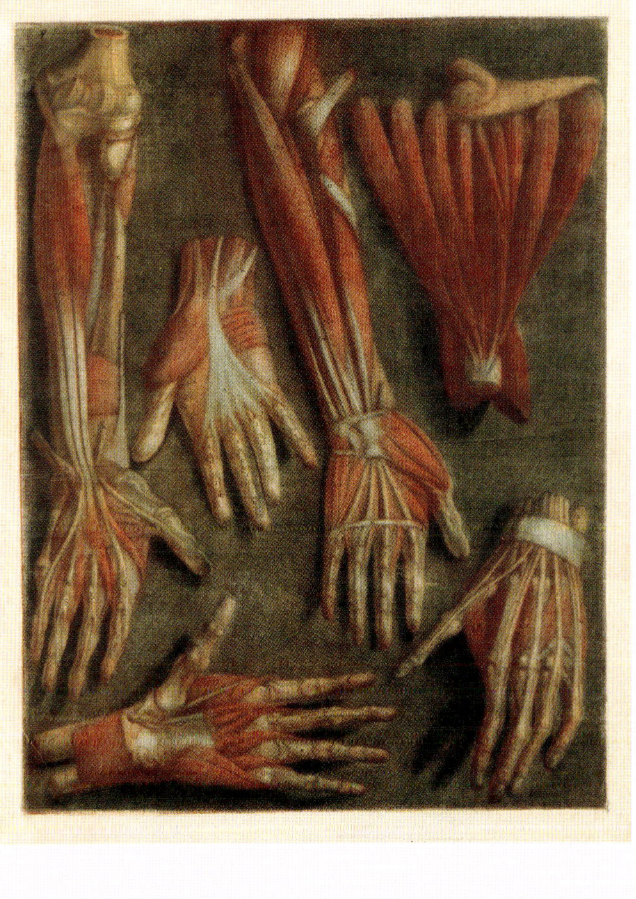

OPPOSITE
Different states of Jacob Christof Le Blon's layers of printed color in an illustration in his painting manual *Coloritto* (c.1725). These overlapped and aligned to create the skin tones in the subject's face, and were the result of careful calculation and experimentation.

RIGHT
Muscles of the hand and arm: six écorchés. Color mezzotint by J.F. Gautier d'Agoty after himself (1745–6). D'Agoty developed Le Blon's technology and had greater success producing anatomical prints in color.

OVERLEAF LEFT
A color plate from Owen Jones's *The Grammar of Ornament* (1856) depicting the intricate patterning and solid red of Turkish design. This particular example was copied from the Dome of the Tomb of Soliman (Suleiman) in Constantinople (Istanbul).

OVERLEAF RIGHT
A range of polychromatic colonnades from ancient Egypt, recorded in Owen Jones's *The Grammar of Ornament* (1856).

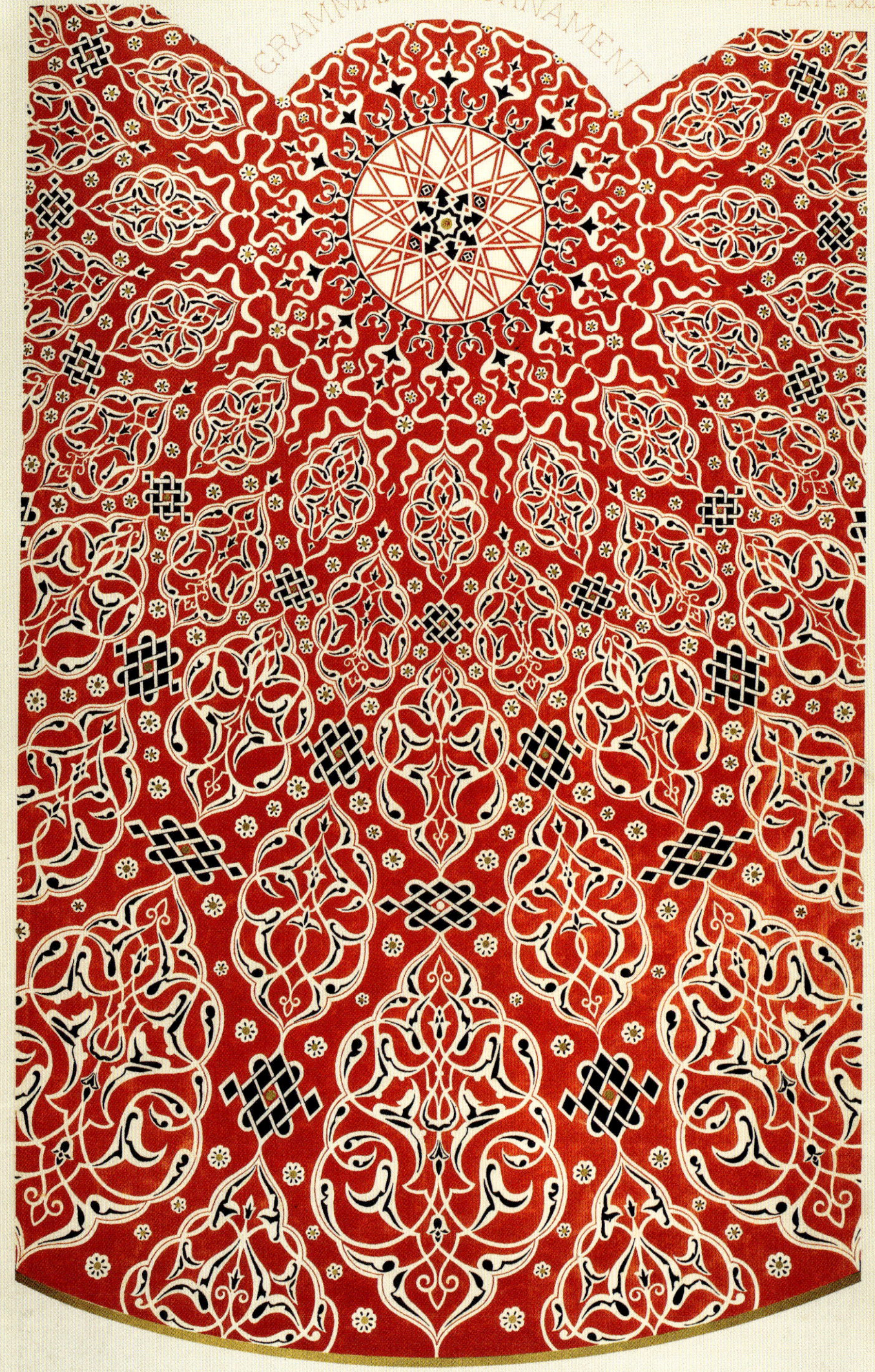

TURKISH Nº 3

FROM THE DOME OF THE TOMB OF SOLIMAN I. CONSTANTINOPLE

GRAMMAR OF ORNAMENT

PLATE VI

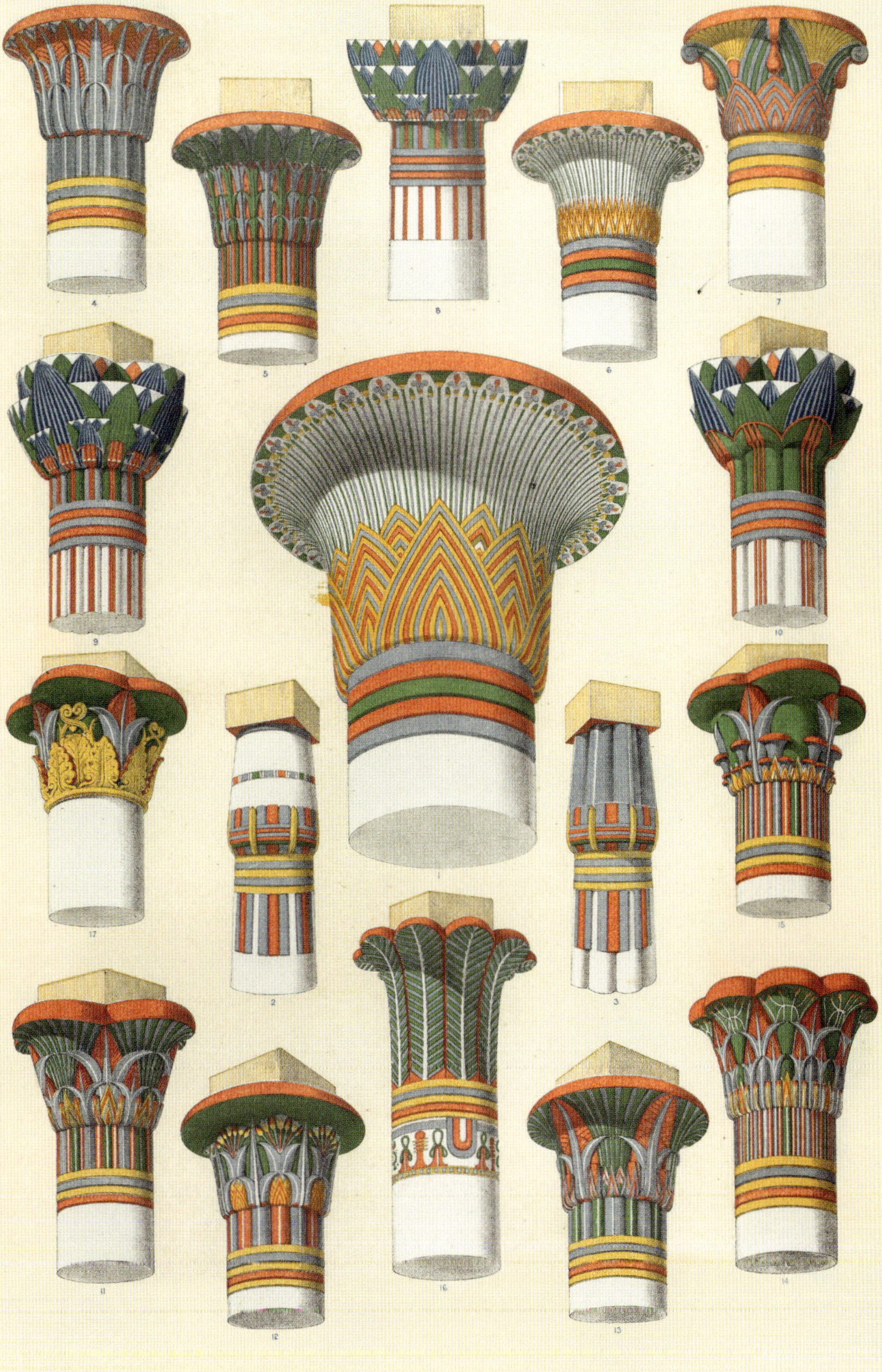

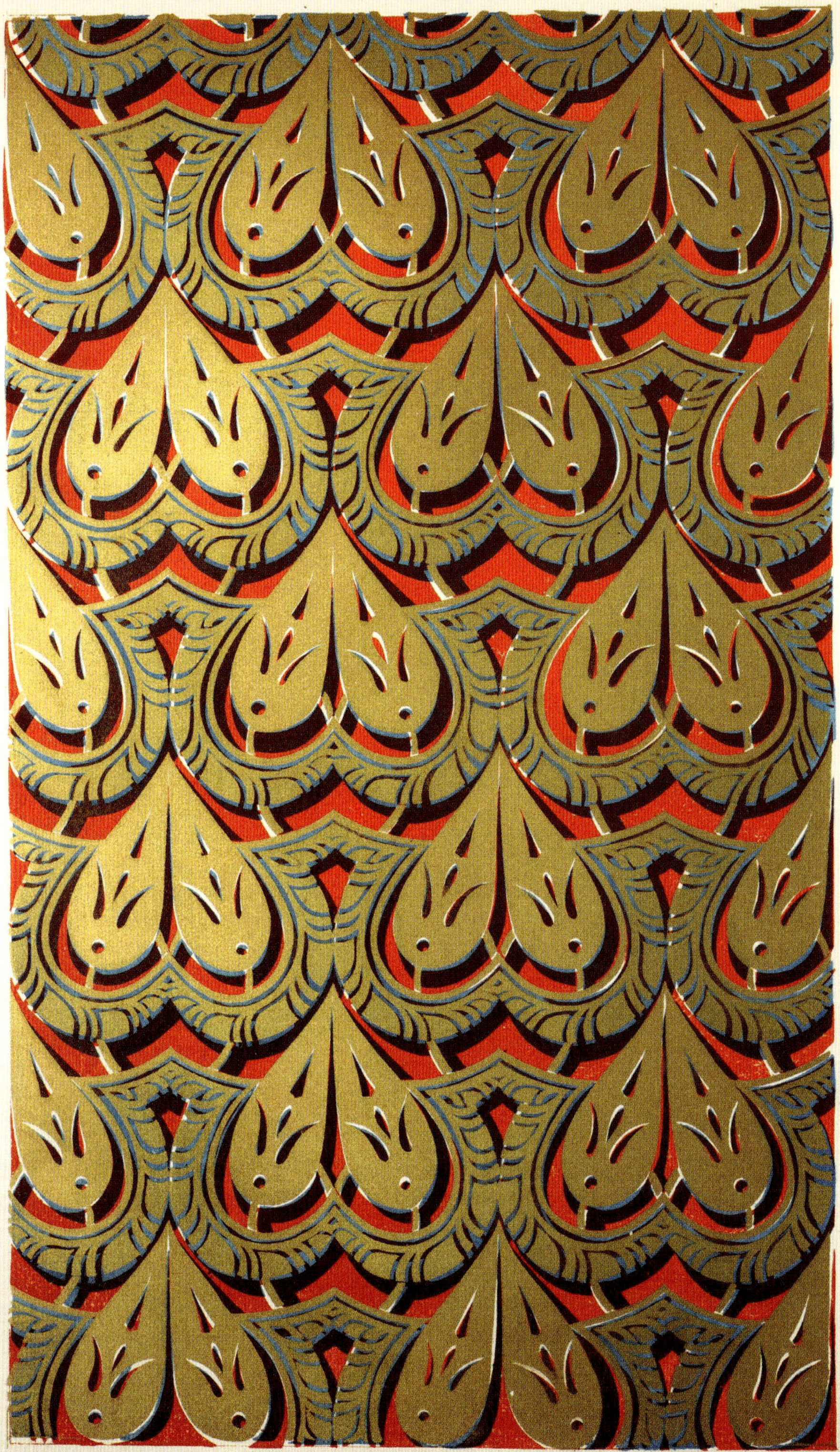

PL

Nº 26.

Published b

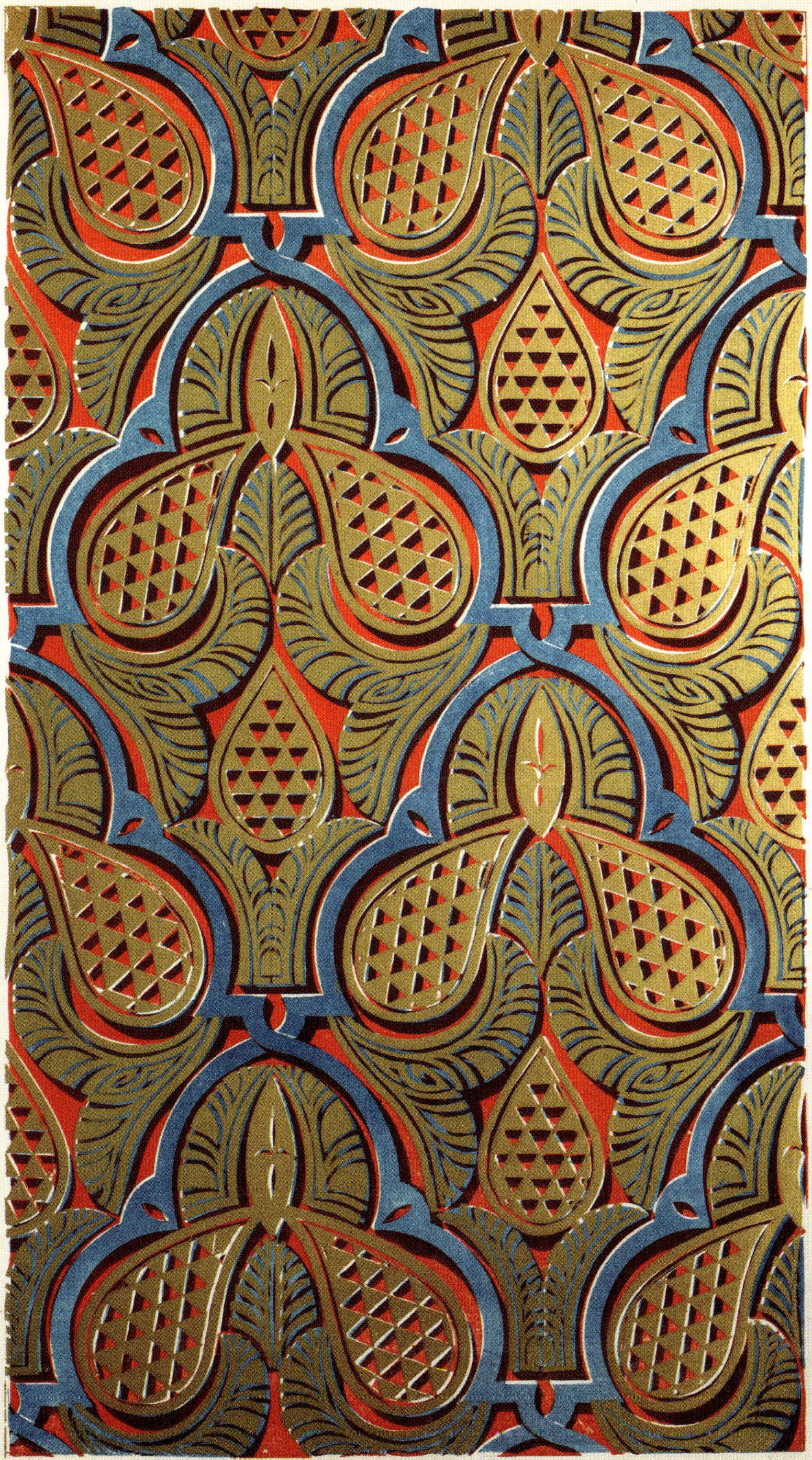

XV.

E.

ones, London 1841.

No. 27.

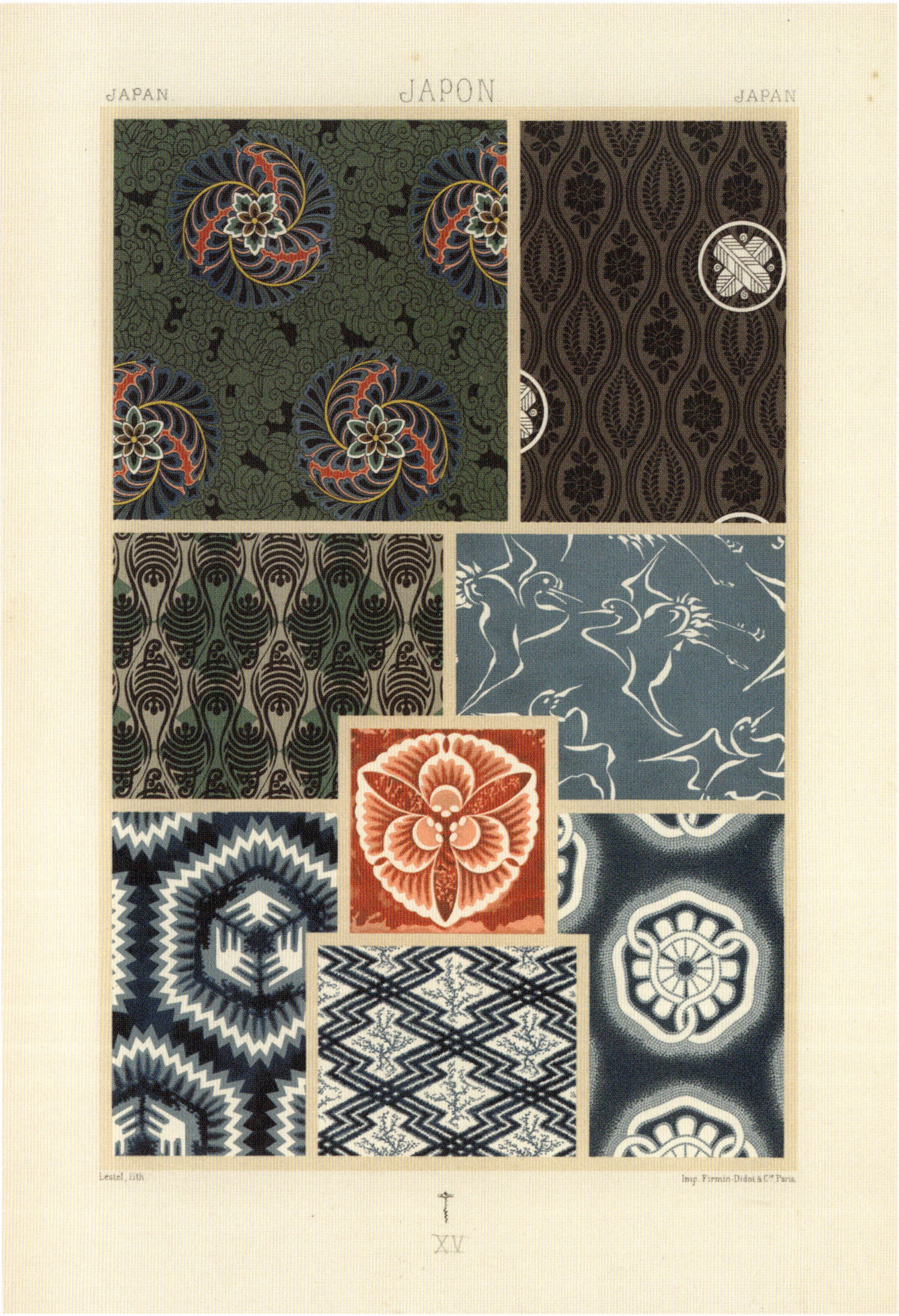
JAPAN
JAPON
JAPAN
Lestel, lith.
Imp. Firmin-Didot & Cie Paris.
XV

of global design, produced in the wake of the 1851 Great Exhibition in London, that compiled motifs from cultures around the world. Requiring up to twenty different lithography stones, Jones's printers conjured up coruscating color, and made copious use of gold ink. The result took readers around the world in a hundred plates, with stops to admire the historically radiant palettes of Turkey, India, and China.

These early milestones of color printing were driven by the symbiotic relationship between artistic ambition and technological possibility, as both human and machine elements pushed into new realms and set high standards for others to emulate. In 1869, a French answer to Jones's work, indebted to *Grammar*'s wildly colorful vision, was published as *L'ornement polychrome*. Compiled by Albert-Charles-Auguste Racinet, its different plates typically contained up to fourteen different inks, pre-mixed to match the correct colors as closely as possible, with less need for overprinting. Initially published as ten folios of a hundred plates between 1869 and 1873, covering the ancient world up to the eighteenth century, the work was so successful that a sequel was demanded, and a further set appeared in the 1880s, devoted to the nineteenth century. Racinet also filled in some gaps in Jones's work, most notably covering the decorative arts and color schemes of Japan.

Sometimes the evolving printing techniques directly influenced the theory under discussion. In *Répertoire chromatique* (1890), botanist Charles Lacouture (1832–1908) used detailed chromolithography to demonstrate his theories about how to mix colors successfully, and to represent his "*trilobe synoptique*", a three-lobed shape, one branch for each of the primary colors. By applying the color in specific places, with gaps or overlaps, intersections, and angles, he created in print the effects he described. He triggered the effects of optical mixing by leaving white spaces between overlaid colors and conjured shades with bands of black, like a cross-hatched drawing. Secondary colors were formed by over-printing different colors at right angles to the original, creating a visual blend on the page. This was not always successful and the designs were let down by muddy and dull areas. Lacouture also devised a "*rose synoptique*'—a color wheel interpreted as a flower, with each petal a different color. Yet for all his innovation, Lacouture's efforts were slightly out of time, pushing the established technology of chromolithography in a new direction just when it was running out of steam.

Eventually, American printer Frederic Eugene Ives (1856–1937) moved color printing on by combining Le Blon's inks with experiments in color photography conducted by physicist James Clerk Maxwell (see p.152). Maxwell successfully created a colored image by photographing it through three separate color filters, red, green, and blue, the primaries of immaterial color. Color images could be printed from the negatives of these, and Ives specified the ideal printing inks as "minus red" (a color that absorbed all the red in the spectrum), "minus green" and "minus blue". Ives also developed a kind of screening process (halftoning) where essential colors could be broken into dots and juxtaposed to give

PREVIOUS PAGES
Plate XV from Jules Goury and Owen Jones's *Plans, Elevations and Sections of the Alhambra* (1845). Originally issued as a series of folios, Jones's work was the first major publication illustrated with chromolithographed plates.

OPPOSITE
The second series of Albert Racinet's *L'ornement polychrome* (1885) included several prints of Japanese designs and palettes, filling a gap in Owen Jones's earlier survey in *The Grammar of Ornament* (1856).

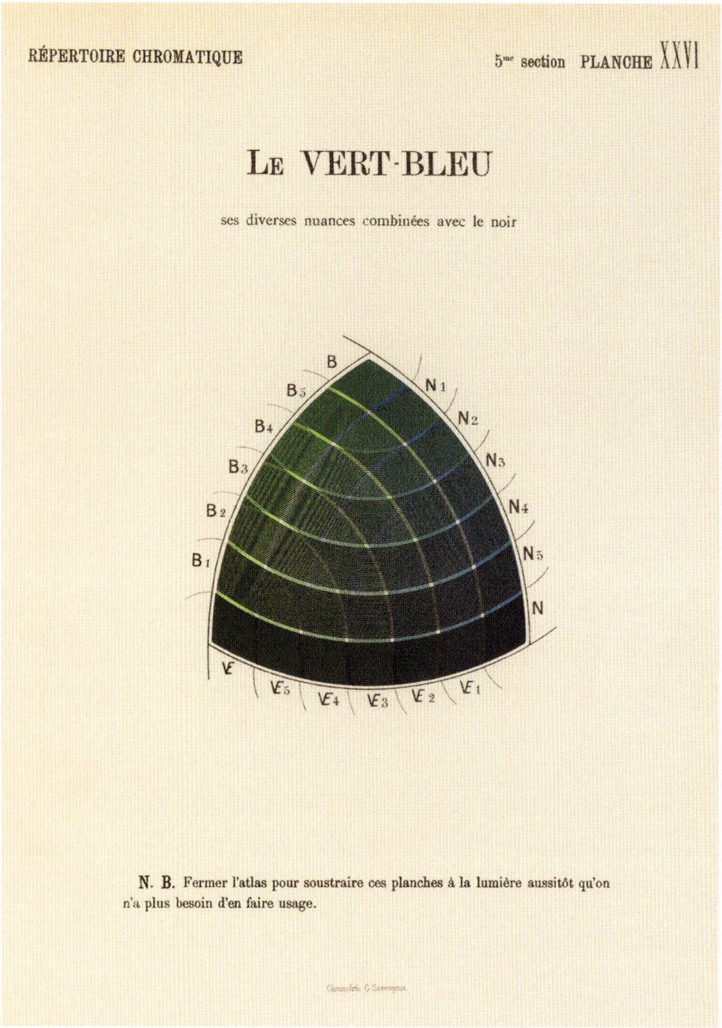

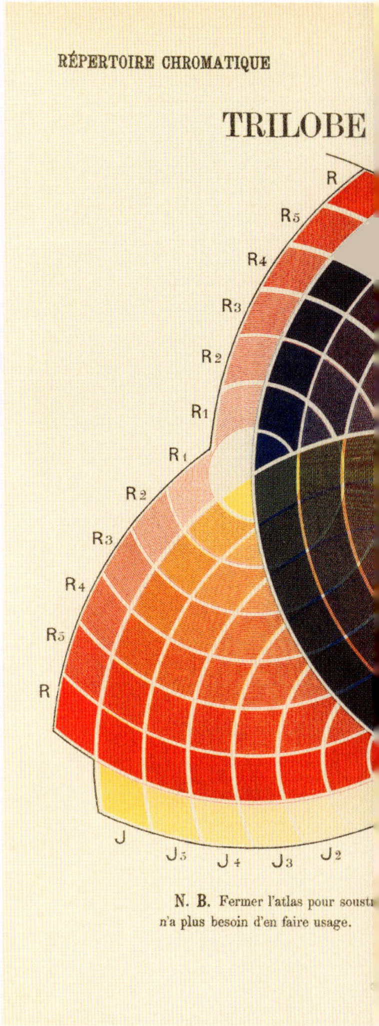

ABOVE LEFT
Charles Lacouture used chromolithography to explore the variants of colors and their blends on the page in his *Répertoire chromatique* (1890). Bands of overlapping color, with white spaces between, helped create tints and shades.

ABOVE CENTER
Répertoire chromatique (1890) also included Lacouture's design of the "*trilobe synoptique*", a three-pronged arrangement of the primary colors, with overlapping areas that created secondaries through layered inks and optical mixing.

ABOVE RIGHT
Lacouture created various color models using his system of complex chromolithography. His "*rose synoptique*" resembled a flower, with each color a different petal.

Frontispice PLANCHE I bis

OPTIQUE

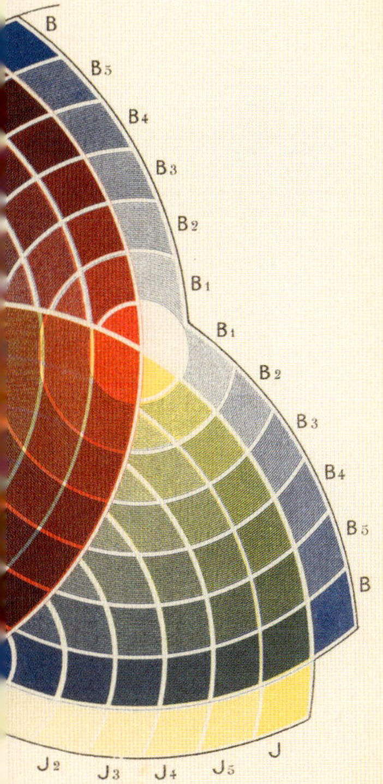

nches à la lumière aussitôt qu'on

Frontispice PLANCHE I

ROSE SYNOPTIQUE

N. B. Fermer l'atlas pour soustraire ces planches à la lumière aussitôt qu'on n'a plus besoin d'en faire usage.

Chromolith. G Severeyns

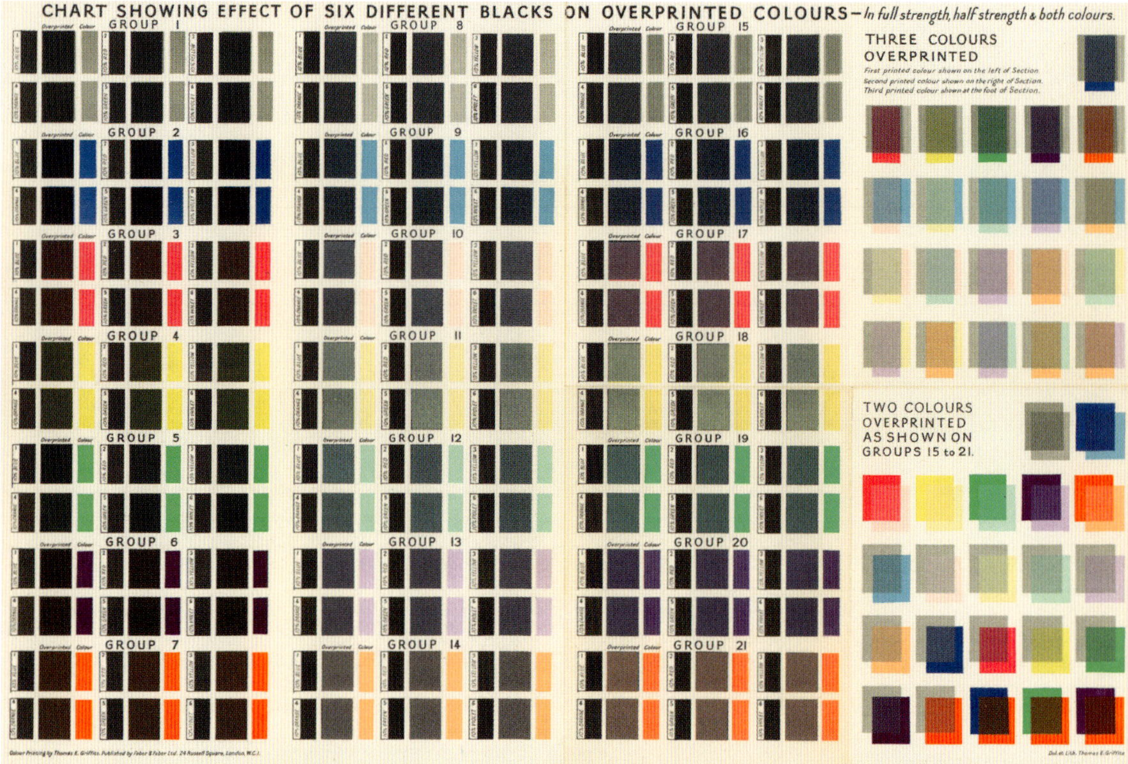

ABOVE
A chart from Thomas Griffits's *Colour Printing* (1948) demonstrating the effects of overprinting colors. Much of the sheet is devoted to the way six different types of black can modify the colors printed on top of them.

OPPOSITE ABOVE
In this fold-out sheet from Thomas Griffits's *Colour Printing* (1948), the same image is printed in a particular sequence of ink color: red, yellow, black, and blue.

OPPOSITE BELOW
This illustration from *Vogue* by Helen Dryden appeared in Albert Munsell's posthumous *Grammar of Color* (1921). In the two different colorways, Munsell's co-author Thomas Cleland demonstrated the difference between a balanced palette, in which all colors mixed to a neutral gray, and an unbalanced one.

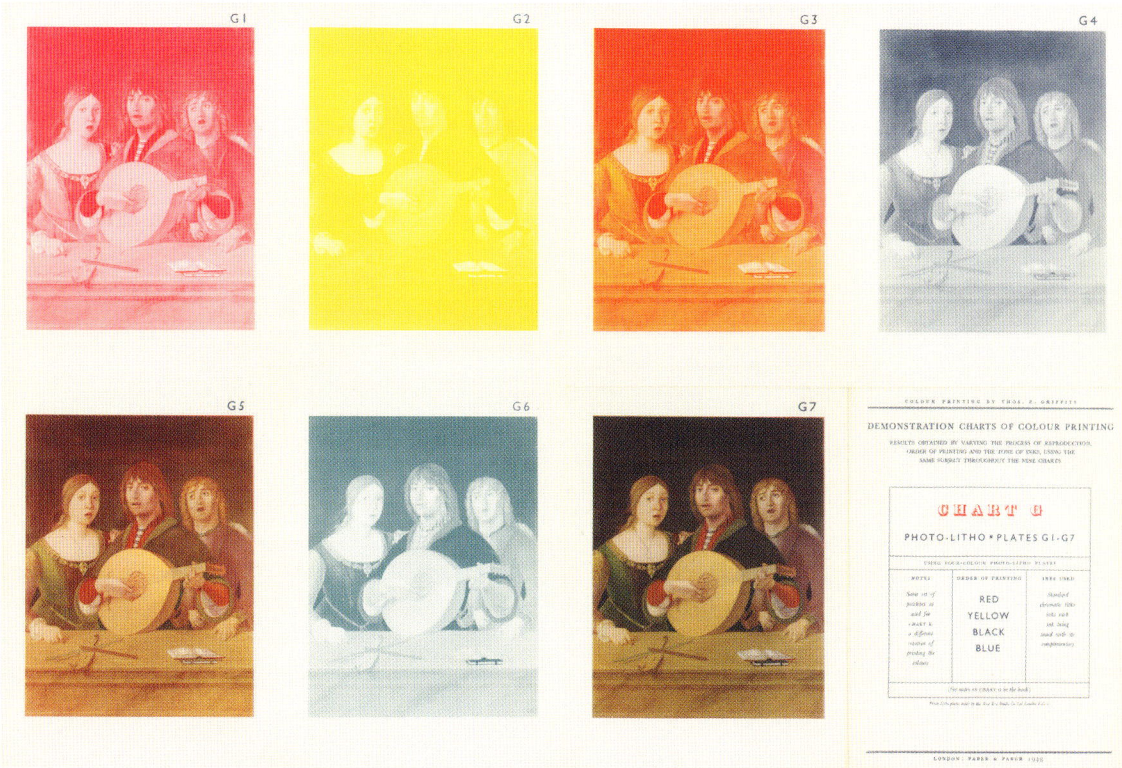

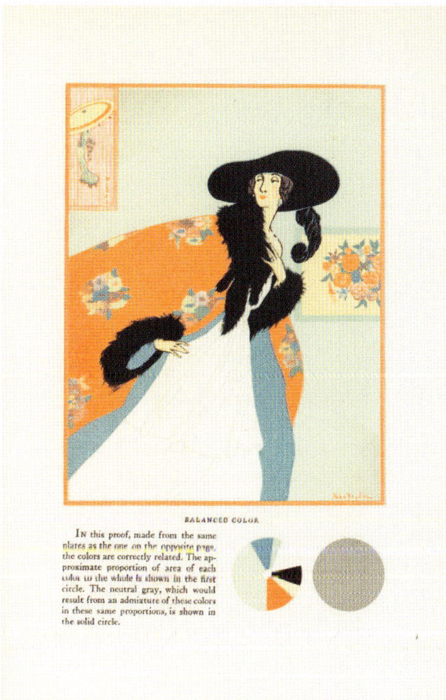

BALANCED COLOR

In this proof, made from the same plates as the one on the opposite page, the colors are correctly related. The approximate proportion of area of each color to the whole is shown in the first circle. The neutral gray, which would result from an admixture of these colors in these same proportions, is shown in the solid circle.

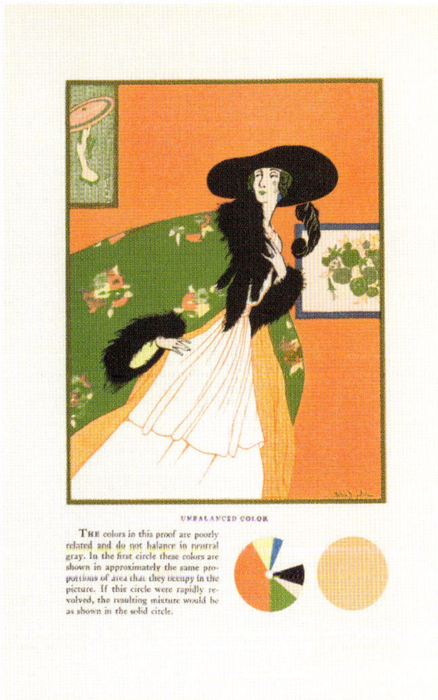

UNBALANCED COLOR

The colors in this proof are poorly related and do not balance in neutral gray. In the first circle these colors are shown in approximately the same proportions of area that they occupy in the picture. If this circle were rapidly revolved, the resulting mixture would be as shown in the solid circle.

the visual appearance of further colors, not entirely unlike the optical mixing of Pointillist paintings. Photographs could also be screened to be printed and reproduced in a format that was more light-fast and permanent than individual photographic prints. This methodical, mechanical process, which potentially yielded a large (if finite) number of colors from a set of three, evolved into the dominant "four-color" CMYK color printing process in the early twentieth century, composed of cyan (minus red), magenta (minus green), and yellow (minus blue), with the addition of black (K, standing for "key" plate).

As the results of color printing sharpened up in the early twentieth century, the practice featured in instruction manuals and commercial sample books. Albert Munsell's posthumously published work *A Grammar of Color* (1921), a collaboration with illustrator Thomas Cleland and the Strathmore Paper Company, demonstrated the perils of unbalanced color compositions. An illustration from *Vogue* by Helen Dryden was reprinted in two different colorways: one apparently balanced (where the different colors, in proportion, mixed to a neutral gray), the other, out of kilter and supposedly harsher to look at. Munsell, well-known for his aversion to bright color, recoiled from the gaudy appearance of much printed ephemera, declaiming: "The circus wagon and poster, although they yell successfully for our momentary attention, soon become so painful to the vision that we turn from them." His crotchety disdain for saturation was at odds with the overall charm of the book. *A Grammar of Color* was a lovely, tactile artefact, with eighteen pages of different-colored paper manufactured by Strathmore, each printed with five different-balanced color combinations. All the selections were appealingly dusky, if not wildly distinctive, muted in line with Munsell's prescriptions.

Thomas Griffits, an expert in lithographic reproductions of works of art, later produced practical and imaginatively realized guides to explain the printing process to artists. Just as the science of color printing was being honed, Griffits's *Colour Printing* (1948) encouraged the reader to smash the rules of established techniques, to try combining different processes or deliberately printing the colors in the "wrong" order. To illustrate the potential of this, he included ten fold-out sheets with the same image printed in different sequences to achieve different results. He also included a chart of the many possibilities afforded by overprinting, where colors could overlap, fuse and transform, and provided formulas for mixing different kinds of black with the same base color, with demonstrations of their behavior. The rules of the emerging technology were, it seemed, still up for grabs.

A rigorous but accessible system for specifying CMYK colors was devised by Alfred Hickethier (1903–67). A German painter with a keen interest in color photography, Hickethier knew how difficult it was to create "fool-proof color classification" through the halftone process, a problem he attempted to solve through his design of a 10 x 10 x 10 color cube. Each of its thousand little cubes was assigned a three-digit number expressing its unique proportions of yellow, magenta, and cyan, coded from pure white (000) to deepest black (999). The value of each was indicated by its position on the scale from 0 to 9. Pure magenta was 090, while the richest green, a combination of full-strength yellow and cyan, with no magenta content at all, was expressed as 909.

All Hickethier's work in progress, together with the plant where he was employed, was destroyed by an Allied bombing raid in 1943. With additional thinking time, he constructed a more refined version out of the smoking ruins of his nascent plan. This appeared as the *Hickethier Colour System*, published in English in 1956. In his accompanying commentary, he explored various tricks facilitated by the four-color process, including how to use secondary colors to darken primaries (a dash of orange in cyan) rather than resorting to black. Colors could be lightened if applied in dots with white space between, a common trick employed by publications of the time to maximize the available palette from the smallest number of inks. Although it used solid spot colors rather than blended CMYK inks, a typical example could be found in Dr Seuss's contemporaneous children's picture book *The Cat in the Hat* (1957), in which the anarchic feline's bright red bow tie and signature headwear were printed in identically colored ink to the salmon-pink fish he terrorized in the story. Comic books of the era also epitomized the technique. Simple CMYK printing was perfect for their fantastical tales: bold and bright yet flat, simple, and repetitive, like the morals of its primary-colored heroes.

The search for ever-refined color reproduction and accuracy was a quest for a surer representation of reality, for fidelity to things as they are, faithfully transplanted to the printed page. Books about color historically contain some of the most exhilarating displays of ink on paper, but also some of the most frustrating compromises and the most expensive fudges. From Le Blon's cocktails of red ink to the incremental details of Hickethier's cube, printed color in books moved only slowly from experimentation and opportunism to physical and mathematical precision. A lot of ink was spilled in the process.

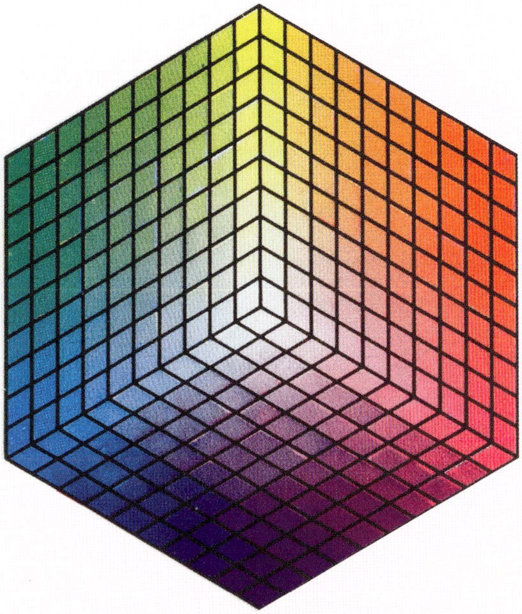

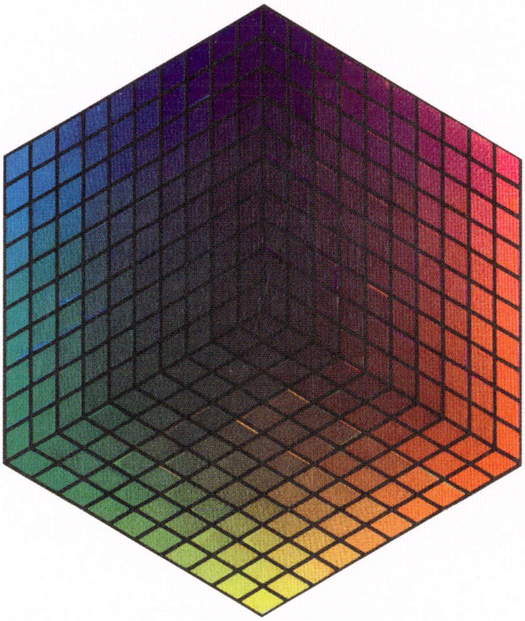

Alfred Hickethier's color cube from the *Hickethier Colour System* (1956) was designed for precise specification of proportions in CMYK printing. The 10 x 10 x 10 cube allows incremental variants as the ratios of cyan, magenta, and yellow are adjusted. Black and white, meanwhile, are located at opposite points on the cube.

8

THE COLOR OF

MUSIC

DIAGRAM II.

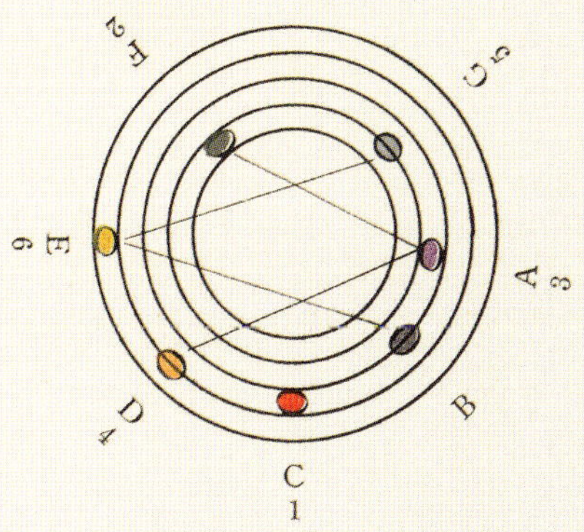

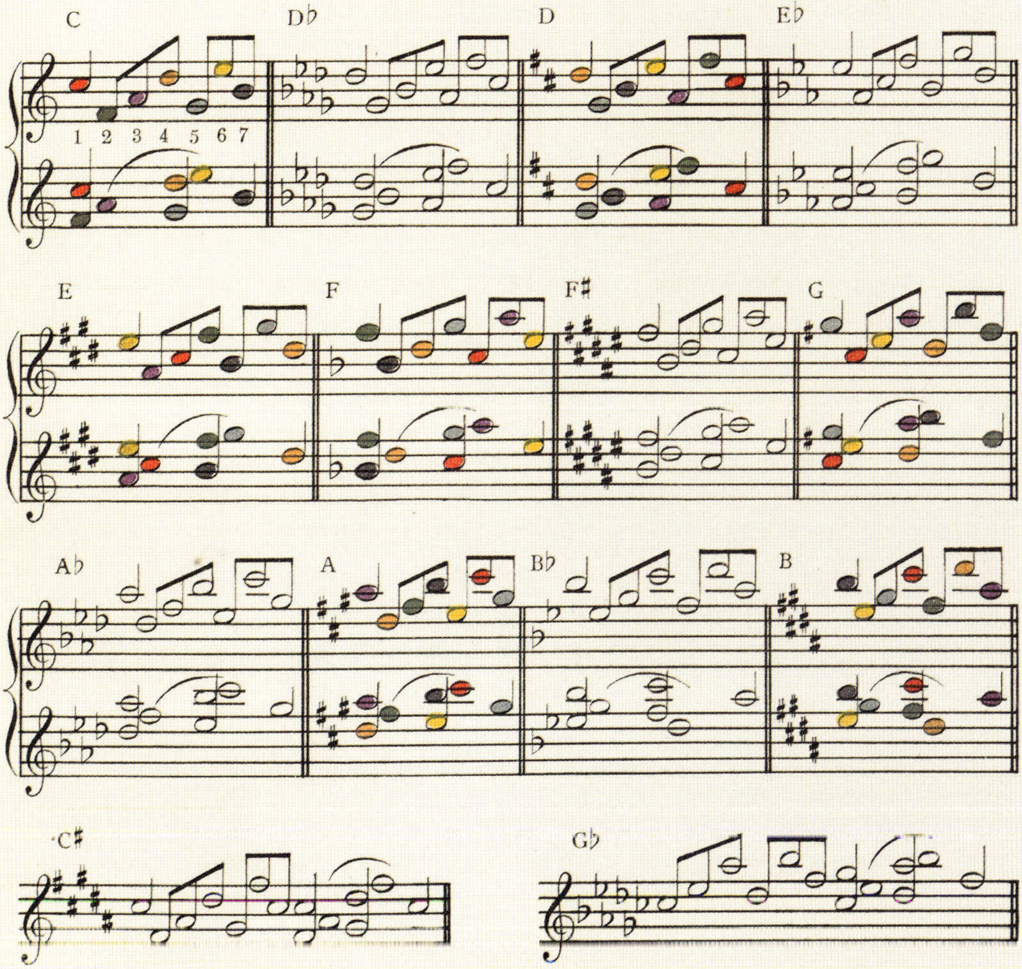

In the realm of the senses, with all its aesthetic pleasures, many have tried to divine a correlation between sound and color, trying to find a mystical link or natural order that relates the colors of the spectrum to notes in a musical scale. After all, the physics of light and sound are superficially similar. As color educator Albert Munsell explained in 1905: "the impulses of sound waves on the ear, like those of light waves on the eye ... are measured vibrations of the same ether." Both colors and notes can be arranged in relational scales, and combined in pairs and triads. Some color researchers, including Isaac Newton, attempted to identify a mathematical or physical basis for a link, but others preferred mystical speculation, looking for occult significance or evidence of cosmic laws. Yet another camp, one that included some of the greatest minds in color theory, dismissed any link as entirely fanciful. Munsell, in fact, cautioned against pursuing such thoughts, warning they could only lead to the "wildest vagaries".

Nevertheless, Aristotle himself was sure of a connection. He took the musical ratios first spotted by Pythagoras, that a plucked string will sound exactly one octave higher when halved in length, and applied them to color harmony. "Colors," he wrote, "may mutually relate like musical concords for their pleasantest arrangement." The bond was sealed many centuries later by Isaac Newton (see p.22). His revolutionary color circle artificially divided the spectrum into seven distinct colors precisely because Newton wanted to try to force an analogy with the diatonic musical scale and its so-called "white notes" running C-D-E-F-G-A-B. This resulted in his eccentric identification of seven separate colors in the rainbow, R-O-Y-G-B-I-V, an odd number and an odd arrangement. Nevertheless, Newton's divisions raised interesting questions around the fundamentals of harmony that warranted further exploration. Just as the essential musical triad in Western music consisted of a base note played with two other notes, evenly spaced, could color be combined in identical patterns?

The first known person to try to take the link between color and sound from theory to practice was Louis Bertrand Castel (1688–1757), a Jesuit mathematician. Castel invented several instruments designed to fuse the principles in experimental ways, including a modified harpsichord customized with sixty multicolored lanterns. These could be exposed individually and in combination when keys were struck. In reality, the design was more of a thought experiment and it is doubtful a working model was ever built. As he wrote: "The pressing of the keys would bring out the colors with their combinations and their chords; in one word, with all their harmony, which would correspond exactly to that of any kind of music." Using a triad of notes, arbitrarily linked to the primary colors—keynote C for blue, third E for yellow, fifth G for red—he worked out a full chromatic scale. He called his invention a "*clavecin pour les yeux*", or "ocular harpsichord".

Chemist and colorman George Field later tried a similar arrangement in his *Chromatics* (1817; revised edition 1845, see p.96), an exploration of the principles of color harmony, but he swapped the places of red and yellow in Castel's system. Field believed that many aspects of sensory experience were probably related in some intangible way, and that he could start to explore this by probing the relationship between color and music. He loved major chords and thought the intervals between the notes from which they were composed could translate into schemes of similarly spaced colors. Relating the primary colors blue, red, and yellow to the fundamentals of musical harmony, he started by connecting blue to C, explaining the centrality of this color as "the natural key, archeus or ruling tone, universally agreeable to the eye." *Chromatics* contained an attractive hand-colored musical scale, which he expanded and revised in the later edition.

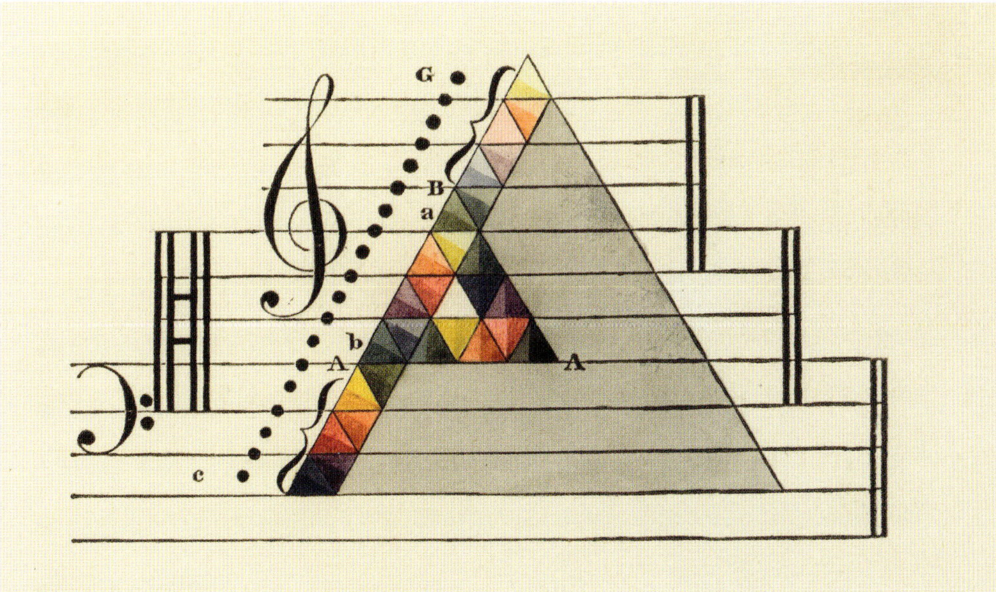

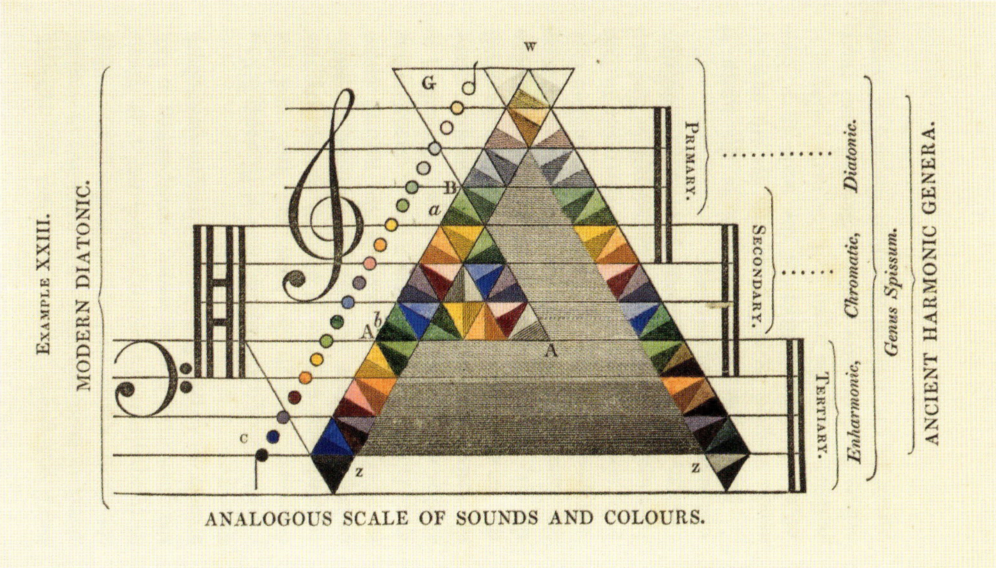

PREVIOUS PAGE

In the notation of Fitzgerald Hughes, the seven white notes of a keyed instrument are color coded. Intermediate tones, sharps, and flats, are left uncolored, but, if the scheme were fully realized, would become "intermediate tints".

ABOVE

Two versions of George Field's analogous scale of sounds and colors. The upper diagram is his first attempt in *Chromatics* (1817). Over time, Field worked out the scheme in more detail, and the expanded lower diagram was included in a later edition of 1845.

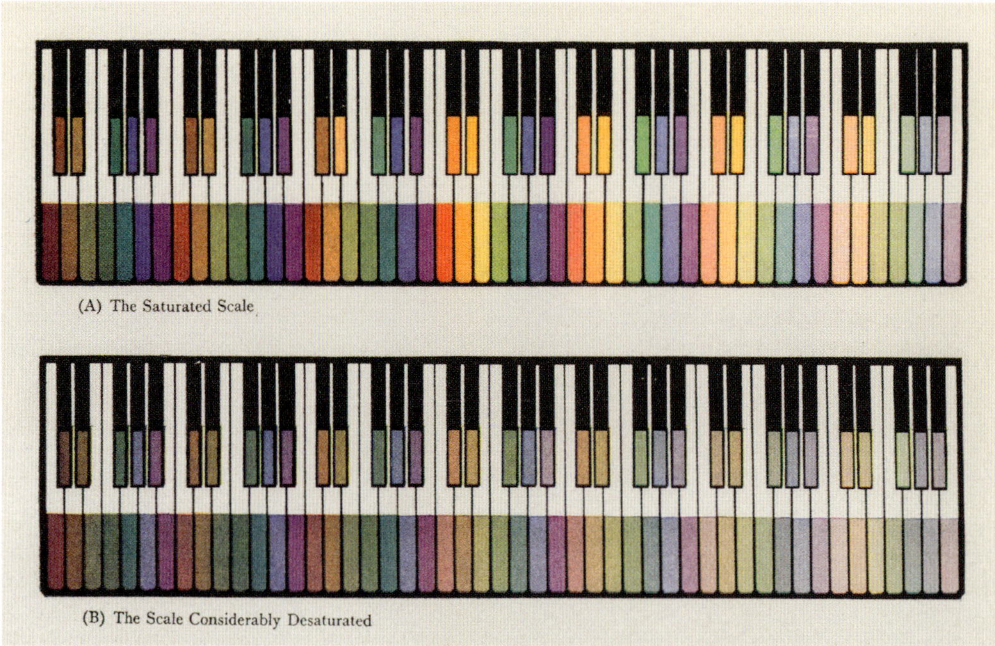

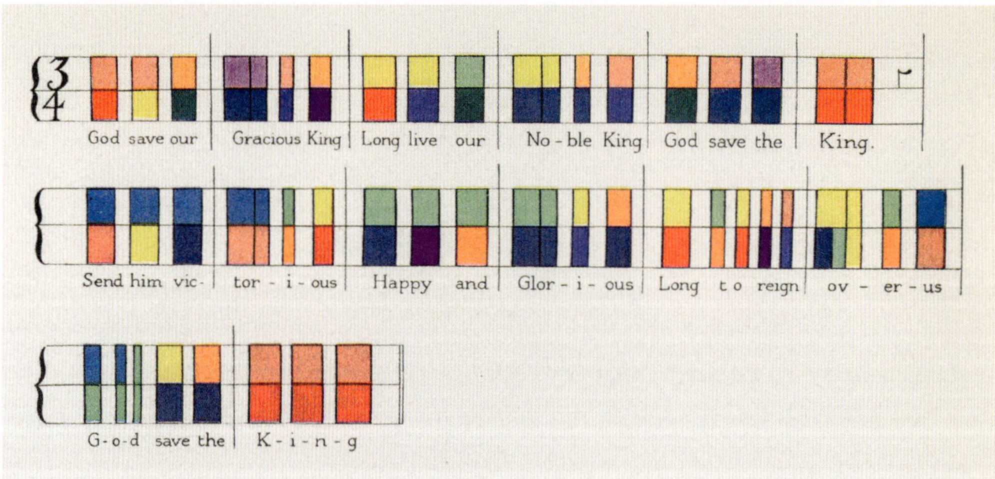

TOP
A.B. Klein's illustration of the possible analogy between the spectrum and the keyboard. The sequence of seven colors was shaded and desaturated in order that it could span multiple octaves.

ABOVE
A color-music schematic designed by E.G. Lind and reproduced by A.B. Klein. In this example, the tune of the United Kingdom's national anthem is visualized in a design in which the notes are represented by colors and the size of the color shapes reflects their duration.

Interior designer David Ramsay Hay (see p.147) attempted a similar analogy in his *Laws of Harmonious Colouring* (six editions, 1828–47). Unlike Field, who thought blue must provide the key, Hay believed all three primaries were equally capable of playing this role, "forming an archeus, or key, for an arrangement, to which all the other colors introduced must refer subordinately."

The fact that scholars could not agree which color went with which note was an early hint that all this was possibly far more arbitrary than its exponents were willing to admit. Different writers on the subject were all striving for evidence of some immutable laws of sensory harmony between sound and vision, yet they struggled to marry the two. Several tried to deepen the analogy by, for example, comparing the hue, value, and saturation of a color with the pitch, timbre and loudness of notes.

As well as exploring the mysteries of harmony, others followed Castel's innovation and created further color instruments to embody "color-music". These inventions usually took the form of keyboards that threw colored light on a wall when notes were played, and their creators had a common aim in mind: to create an entirely new immersive art form, fusing the principles and experiences of aural and visual harmony. One of the most successful was Alexander Wallace Rimington (1854–1918), whose "color organ" worked by channeling white light through prisms, projecting sections of the spectrum through slits onto a textured fabric screen. The sequencing and blending of colors was based on music theory, but could also be experienced soundlessly, as the shifting colors themselves were intended to express an innate musicality. In his book *Colour-Music: The Art of Mobile Colour* (1912), Rimington described the effect as a way to "see sound and hear colour". He hoped his performances would train the audience to develop a sharper color sense and believed that, by relying on immaterial color for the effect, he could create colors no one had ever seen before. The element of time was crucial to the experience. Colors were projected for different durations, just as musical notes were held for different lengths. Rimington gave numerous performances of his "mobile colour" experience, the first of which was in 1895 in the presence of an eclectic audience of special guests, including Sir Lawrence Alma-Tadema, the Duke of Norfolk, and Princess Hohenlohe of Austria.

All these works and many others were appraised by artist and writer Adrian Bernard Klein (1892–1969) in his wide-ranging survey *Colour-Music: The Art of Light* (1926). Like Rimington, Klein also devised an immersive performance of color projections but took a more critical and scholarly approach to the whole subject, and *Colour-Music* summarized his research. Alongside the detailed notation of his system and explanation of his instrument, Klein included a literature review of previous works on the subject, along with an overview of color-music equipment and instruments. Klein's tone was often combative, dismissing many of his peers. He analyzed the different models of defining harmony, alerting the reader to internal inconsistencies and limitations, but also expounded the clearest relationships, including a table that itemized the physical, physiological, and psychological analogies between sound and light. He took the emerging area of color psychology seriously and made the case for color-music's capacity to trigger certain moods. Among the book's appendices was part of the score for *Prometheus*, a work by the Russian composer Scriabin. This included perceptual parts "written for colour-organ" in response to Scriabin's interest in synaesthesia, a neurological phenomenon in which sensory inputs and responses are jumbled in the brain, often resulting in the experience of "seeing" colors in response to the sound of music. Klein himself wrote scores for performance "by six or twelve projectors".

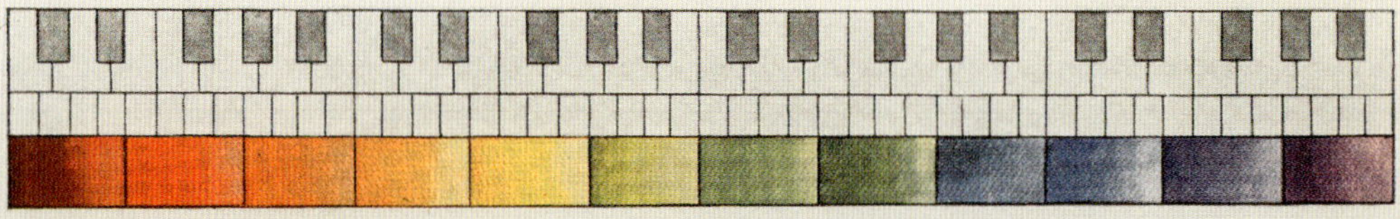

To shew division of colour scale when the spectrum is extended over the whole length of the key-board of the colour organ by spectrum stop.

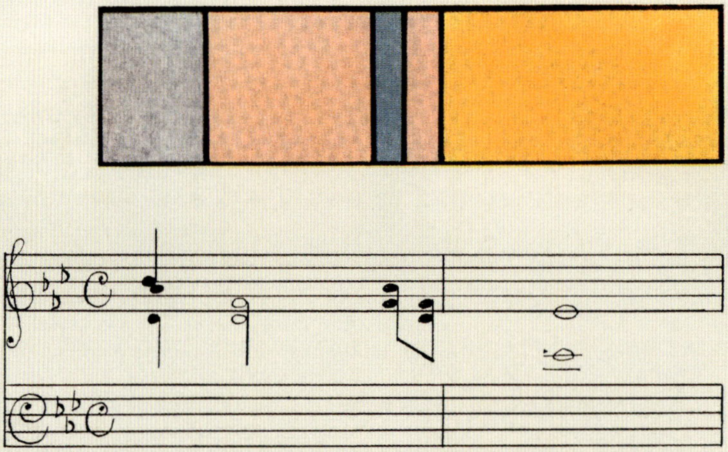

Diagram to illustrate introduction of the element of time into colour effects—the duration of the colour chords upon the screen corresponding to the musical notation.

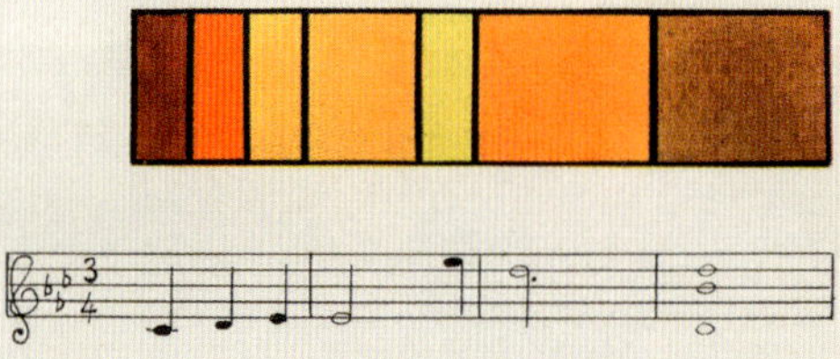

Example of a simple colour phrase in correspondence with musical notation.

NOTE.—It must be understood that the colours are merely diagramatic, and give little idea of their purity as actually seen upon the screen.

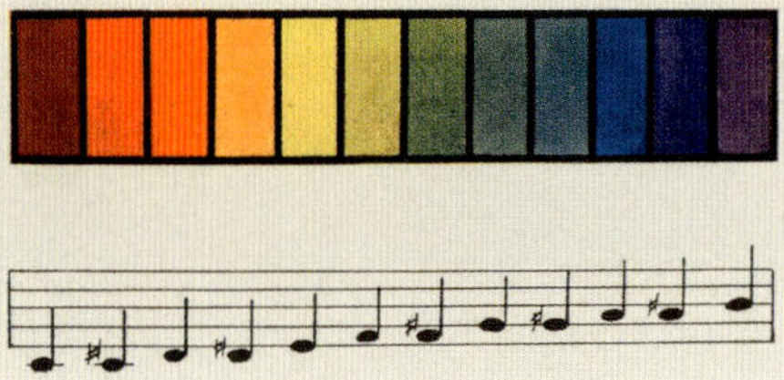

Chromatic scale in Music and Colour.
Shewing correspondence of intervals when C = lowest spectrum red.

Within his survey of previous publications on the subject, Klein drew attention to some merely to discredit them. These included a work by Navy surgeon John Denis Macdonald, whose *Analogy of Sound and Colour* (1869) compared the biological structure of the eye and the ear to help make his case. Rather eccentrically, Macdonald then proceeded to interpret the palette of various famous paintings as if they were musical compositions. Klein also considered a beautifully colored but conceptually baffling curio by Fitzgerald Hughes entitled *Harmonies of Tones and Colours Developed by Evolution* (1883). Hughes was Charles Darwin's cousin and her work tried not only to relate color and music but, rather more ambitiously, to reconcile her more successful relative's theory of evolution with her own Christian faith. In engaging with color, she wanted to show that "Complexities of Harmony are governed by the laws which are originated by the Creator", but this was a tall order, and the resulting work was quasi-mystical and often unintelligible. Klein himself dismissed it along similar lines. He also despaired of a scheme by the musician and composer Albert Lavignac that equated each instrument with a specific color, suggesting that the sound of a flute was inherently blue, while an oboe was green, and timpani were black. Klein believed such analogies were a dead end and that "an immense amount of nonsense has been uttered on these lines". But Lavignac's suggestions were not far removed from the popular ideas advanced by Wassily Kandinsky in his *Concerning the Spiritual in Art* (1912, see p. 236), in which he associated different depths of blue with different instruments, and insisted that music and color had equal power to stir the soul. No one, at least, could argue convincingly against that.

Klein also unearthed some gems, including an unpublished system held in the British Library and devised by one E.G. Lind of Baltimore. Lind had posited a relationship between music and color while a student at the Government School of Design in London but had never pursued his work further. His table compared seven colors and seven notes, each of which had a specified vibration that was also divisible by seven, and he devised a way of representing both speech and music through color. In this rendering, color represented the sound of a note while its size reflected its duration. Klein, taken with its ingenuity, reproduced two examples, including a visual representation of the national anthem.

OPPOSITE ABOVE
Alexander Wallace Rimington's attempt to stretch the seven parts of the spectrum across the full width of a keyboard in his work *Colour-Music* (1912).

OPPOSITE CENTER AND BELOW LEFT AND RIGHT
Rimington's notation for color-music projections in which the width of the color blocks reflect the duration of the immersive display.

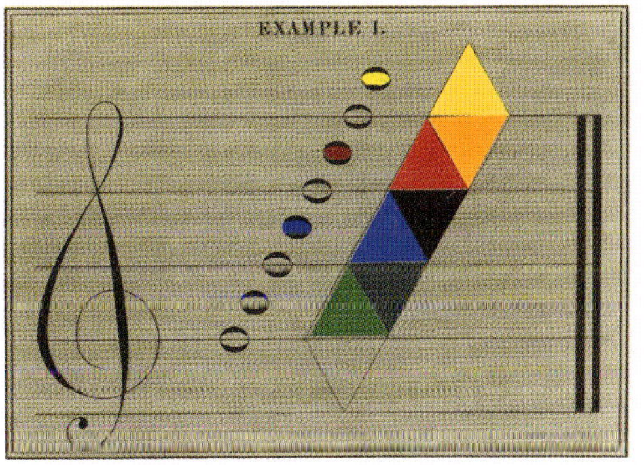

RIGHT
A diagram relating the spectrum to the musical scale as included in David Ramsay Hay's *Laws of Harmonious Colouring* (fifth edition, 1844). Hay attempted to find affinities between visual and aural harmony and to apply the principles that underlay both to design and decoration.

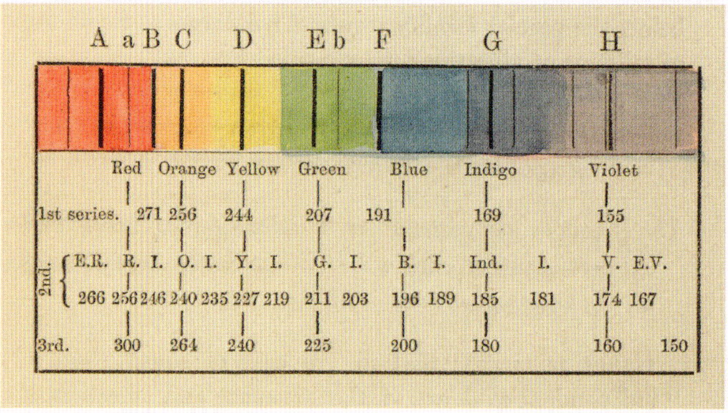

LEFT
In this diagram from *Analogy of Sound and Colour* (1869), John Denis Macdonald related the colors of the spectrum and their wavelengths to musical ratios and scales.

BELOW
Macdonald claimed opposite colors were "concords, standing in the double relation of fourths and fifths to each other".

OPPOSITE
Fitzgerald Hughes included multiple diagrams in her *Harmonies of Tones and Colours Developed by Evolution* (1883), a convoluted and quasi-mystical attempt to join the dots between sound and color.

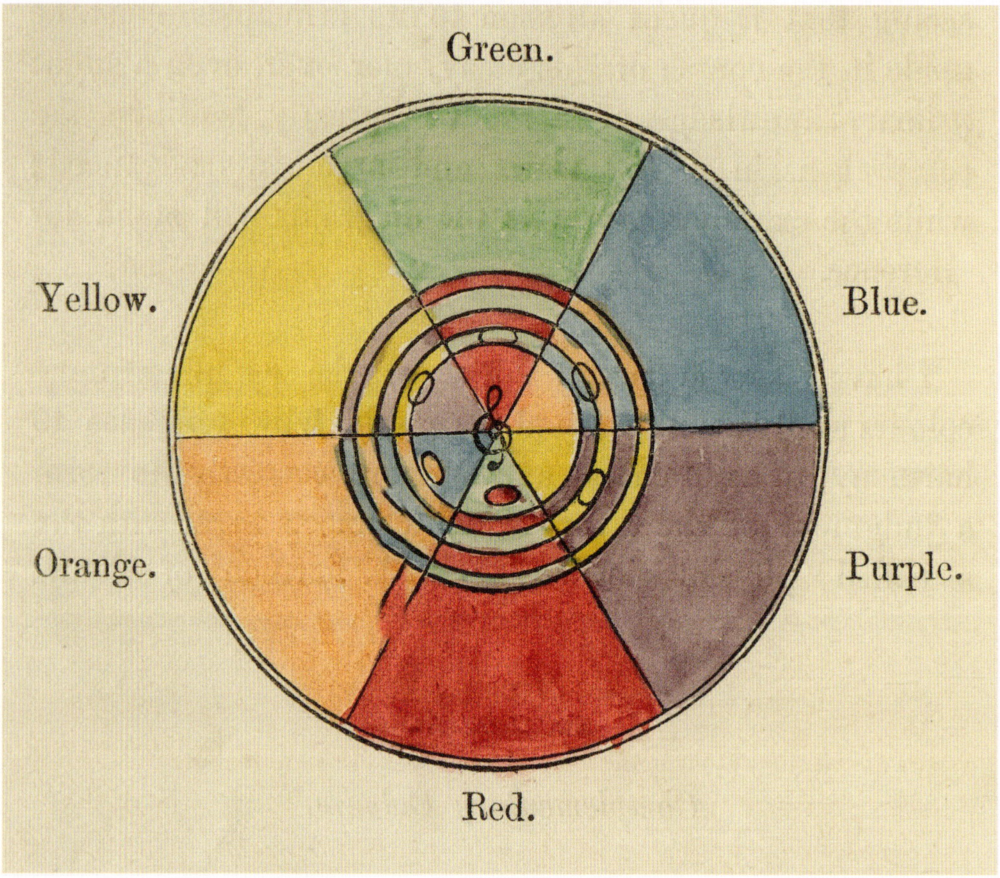

The numerous systems to lock color and sound together, to inch toward a unified theory of harmony, have generated profoundly attractive results, but many heavyweight detractors dismissed the notion of a meaningful link, including Thomas Young, Wilhelm von Bezold, Ogden Rood, and Albert Munsell. Goethe maintained that sound and color were two rivers that originated in the same mountain but then coursed through different landscapes. Rood, meanwhile, pointed out that although notes can be played together yet discerned individually by the listener, blends of colors cannot be visually unmixed into their separate components by the viewer, so the analogy faltered.

Nevertheless, the concept of color-music endured, tantalizing with its promises of multisensory harmony. It even played a role in psychological experiments, including the Auroratone films of British scientist Cecil Stokes, who devised an immersive color and music experience based on polarized light as a therapeutic balm for traumatized war veterans and those suffering from chronic depression or psychoses. Patients were brought in to sit in front of a film of moving colors accompanied by recorded organ music and a repertoire of songs crooned by Bing Crosby, including “Silent Night” and Schubert’s “Ave Maria”. The team studying the effects reported a clear sense of catharsis emerging among the participants.

Perhaps the best any advocates of color-music could hope for was for these explorations to result in aesthetically exciting harmonic experiences, achieved whether by accident or law. Klein, writing in 1926, noted that the spirit of the age was one of despair and irony in a post-war landscape full of broken places. In this context, he argued, the multidirectional sensory pleasures of color-music could be a force for good, even if “merely an aesthetic experiment; only another proposal for the diversion of tired senses”. Nevertheless, he concluded, “for the singularly few who enjoy loveliness, it might snatch one or two more gems from the chaos before the end.”

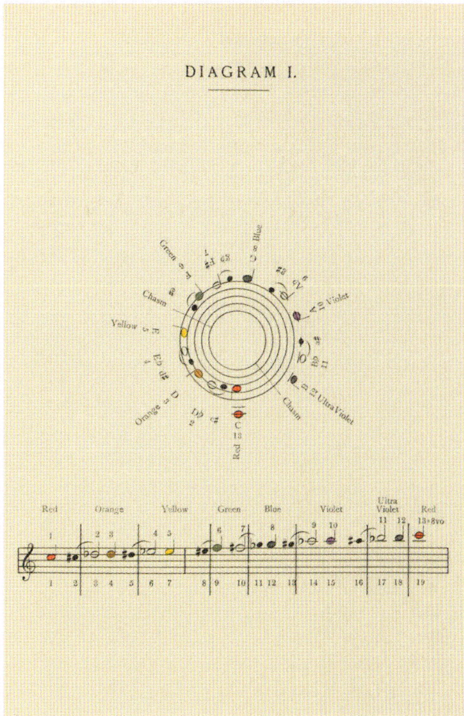

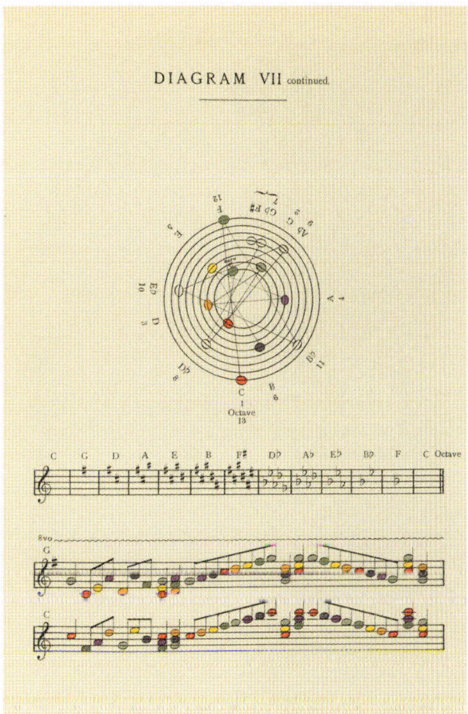

1901

present

CHROMATIC

TUNING

FORKS

In the twentieth century, color made a new world, seeping across page and screen, coating the mundane and the monochrome. It transformed black cars and white goods, sharpening the appeal of products by magicking them into rainbow ranges and maximizing profits in the process. Few areas were left untouched as the runaway forces of technology and capitalism fed the development of ever more showy palettes on the street and in the home.

More color meant more options and, in the early decades of a see-saw century, it was possible for the fizzing orange "Bizarre ware" of Clarice Cliff's ceramics and the radically bright primaries of Piet Mondrian's canvases to co-exist with the sober, naturalistic colors of the waning Arts and Crafts movement. As color provided new coatings to familiar objects, it also soaked into the public consciousness, and canny advertisers soon realized it could be marketed by linking it to a sense of personal choice (however illusory) and tapping into trends. As attitudes changed, so did the colorways. With each successive decade, the image became increasingly colorized, especially evident in mass-market entertainments from comic books and magazines to cinema and television. Once it became simple and affordable to change the color of an object, outfit, or living space, color became synonymous with change itself. In the West, the 1950s and its homely palettes of dusky pinks and eau de Nil were swiftly overpainted with the saffron yellow and deep purple of 1960s psychedelia, preferences that were as much a statement of societal and psychological revolutions as they were an evolution of taste. With improved air travel, the world was also becoming more global, and some of these colors were adopted by Western style gurus captivated by the confident palettes they encountered when visiting the Indian subcontinent. By the 1970s, color was fully inhabiting mass communications: television, coffee-table books, and Sunday newspaper supplements. But in order to reach this saturation point, it first needed to be precisely defined, specified with pinpoint accuracy, in a form that could be consistently reproduced. Color could capture a zeitgeist, once it had been captured itself.

The century's early decades were the golden age of standards, and proprietary or nationally regulated systems emerged to define commercially available color ranges (see p.44). If a client in Europe wanted to order fabric from Asia in salmon pink, both sides of the transaction needed to be sure it would be the right salmon pink, not a half-remembered hue with a misleading name, and definitely not *shrimp* pink. Reliable synthetic dyes spawned color systems, charts, and books of samples that offered try-before-you-buy reassurance in a universal visual language. After centuries of chromatologists apologizing for the inadequacy of print technology to fully represent the systems they had created, the shoe was now

OPPOSITE ABOVE LEFT
The left-hand column contains Ostwald's eight principal colors from Die Farbenfibel *(1917), displayed in a random arrangement. Ostwald believed that order equaled beauty, and demonstrated that humans would typically sort his colors into the natural-seeming sequence presented on the right. Note the isolation mask attached to a piece of string to screen off individual colors from distracting surrounds.*

OPPOSITE ABOVE RIGHT
In each row, a triad of equidistant colors is reduced to three pairs. Ostwald argued that any two parts of a triad made an equally pleasing combination.

OPPOSITE BELOW LEFT
Ostwald's circle of principal colors in Die Farbenfibel *(1917) contained eight evenly spaced full hues.*

OPPOSITE BELOW RIGHT
Ostwald expanded his original eight to a circle of twenty-four colors. This number allowed for the creation of harmonious combinations in a wide range of intervals: two, three, four, six, eight, or twelve spaces apart. In theory, the circle could be expanded further to a hundred equally spaced colors, calculated and fitted into the spaces between the numbered hues.

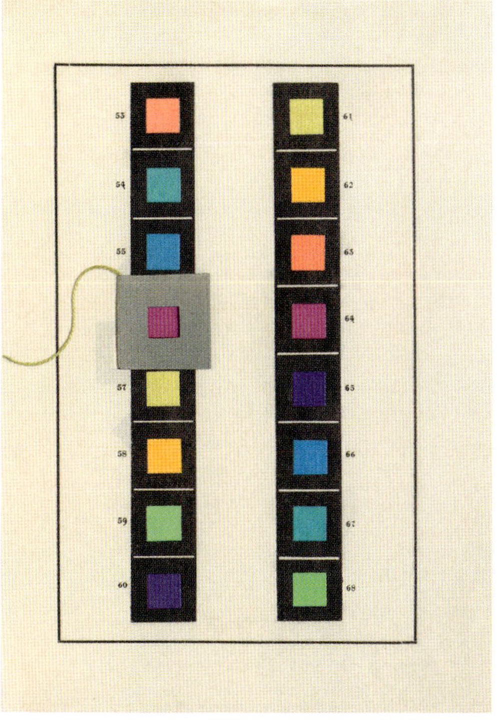

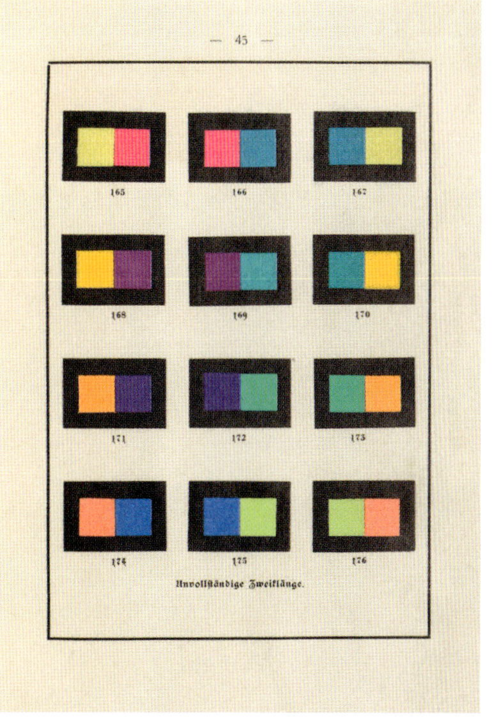
— 45 —

Unvollständige Zweiklänge.

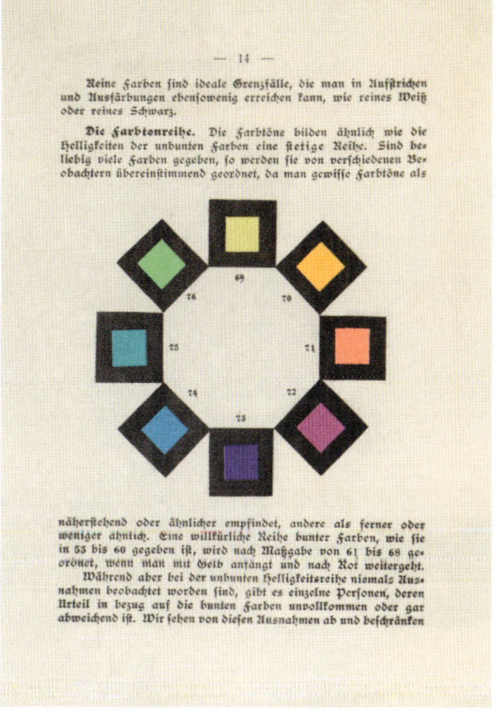
— 14 —

Reine Farben sind ideale Grenzfälle, die man in Aufstrichen und Ausfärbungen ebensowenig erreichen kann, wie reines Weiß oder reines Schwarz.

Die Farbtonreihe. Die Farbtöne bilden ähnlich wie die Helligkeiten der unbunten Farben eine stetige Reihe. Sind beliebig viele Farben gegeben, so werden sie von verschiedenen Beobachtern übereinstimmend geordnet, da man gewisse Farbtöne als

näherstehend oder ähnlicher empfindet, andere als ferner oder weniger ähnlich. Eine willkürliche Reihe bunter Farben, wie sie in 53 bis 60 gegeben ist, wird nach Maßgabe von 61 bis 68 geordnet, wenn man mit Gelb anfängt und nach Rot weitergeht.

Während aber bei der unbunten Helligkeitsreihe niemals Ausnahmen beobachtet worden sind, gibt es einzelne Personen, deren Urteil in bezug auf die bunten Farben unvollkommen oder gar abweichend ist. Wir sehen von diesen Ausnahmen ab und beschränken

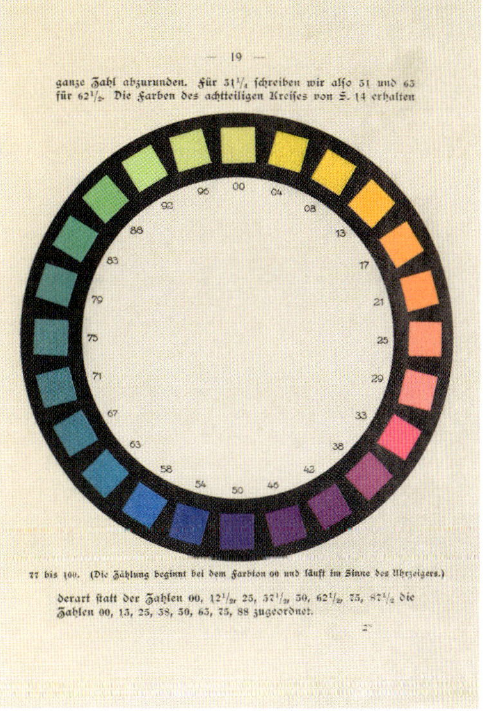
— 19 —

ganze Zahl abzurunden. Für $31\frac{1}{4}$ schreiben wir also 31 und 63 für $62\frac{1}{2}$. Die Farben des achtteiligen Kreises von S. 14 erhalten

77 bis 100. (Die Zählung beginnt bei dem Farbton 00 und läuft im Sinne des Uhrzeigers.)

derart statt der Zahlen 00, $12\frac{1}{2}$, 25, $37\frac{1}{2}$, 50, $62\frac{1}{2}$, 75, $87\frac{1}{2}$ die Zahlen 00, 13, 25, 38, 50, 63, 75, 88 zugeordnet.

2*

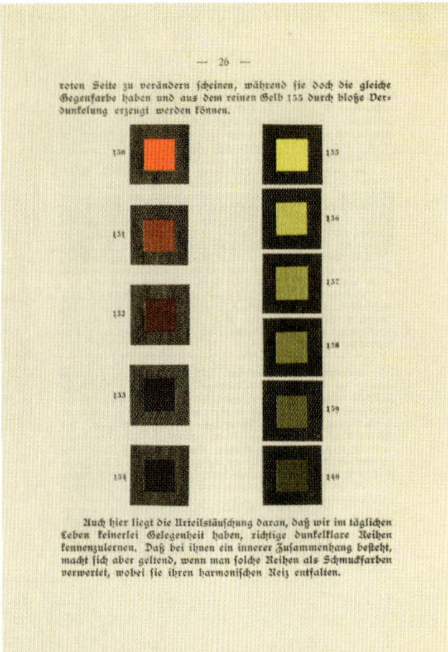
— 26 —

roten Seite zu verändern scheinen, während sie doch die gleiche Gegenfarbe haben und aus dem reinen Gelb 135 durch bloße Verdunkelung erzeugt werden können.

Auch hier liegt die Urteilstäuschung daran, daß wir im täglichen Leben keinerlei Gelegenheit haben, richtige dunkelklare Reihen kennenzulernen. Daß bei ihnen ein innerer Zusammenhang besteht, macht sich aber geltend, wenn man solche Reihen als Schmuckfarben verwertet, wobei sie ihren harmonischen Reiz entfalten.

ABOVE

Examples of Ostwald's "dark–clear" series from Die Farbenfibel *(1917) in which black is added to his full hues in increasing quantities.*

OPPOSITE

Four vertical sections through Ostwald's three-dimensional color model, which resembled a double cone. Grayscale forms the vertical spine, with colors radiating outward to the full hues. Ostwald called the smoky vertical color groupings the "shadow series". His "light–clear" series, in contrast, run along the top edges and more closely resemble pastels.

on the other foot. New schemes needed to be wide enough to fit in all the colors of the commercial world, and sufficiently elastic to accommodate new ones.

Early in the century, a tacit race began, played out on opposite sides of the Atlantic, between the Baltic German chemist Wilhelm Ostwald (1853–1932) and American art educator Albert Munsell (1858–1918), as both toiled to perfect a system of color specification that transcended the vagueness of subjective color names. As Munsell explained, "The terms used for a single hue, such as pea green, sea green, olive green, grass green, sage green, evergreen, [and] invisible green, are not to be trusted in ordering a piece of cloth. They invite mistakes and disappointment." Munsell planned to fix this with a system of notation, an alphanumeric code for each color "so that it cannot be mistaken for any other".

Ostwald, meanwhile, had won a Nobel prize for his research into the emerging area of catalysis, but color order was his private passion and one he pursued fully in retirement. He wanted his work to be useful to both art and industry, with the latter a more obviously lucrative realm. Ostwald hoped to establish a scientific rationale behind successful color combinations, why some pairings clashed and others sang. His answer lay in a color wheel, where each transitional step between the main elements—the compound colors where blue became green or red melted into yellow—were precisely calculated and evenly spaced. This "perceptual equalization" of the color wheel, he believed, allowed order to be definitively established, in turn providing a key to harmony. "Harmony = order" was a favorite mantra that guided his arrangement of colors and, for Ostwald, harmony and beauty were also synonymous.

The new system was articulated and illustrated in Ostwald's early important work *Die Farbenfibel* (*The Color Primer*, 1917). Embracing the color circle of Ewald Hering (see p.160) and its controversial four (rather than three) primaries of yellow, red, blue, and sea-green, Ostwald expanded its basis to eight colors with the addition of intermediates: orange, violet, turquoise, and leaf-green. He called the main colors *Vollfarben* or "full colors", each at an intense midpoint between black and white. Ostwald required these to be as pure as possible but used painted samples from the real world to keep his system from straying into the theoretical realm of idealized (and physically unattainable) pure color. The circle was arranged so that when any color was mixed with its direct opposite, it would produce a neutral gray. Once that gray was struck, it was evidence of a perfect pairing. The system could expand indefinitely with more intermediates, as long as they too could be shown to mix to that same gray when combined with their opposite. There was a precision and logic behind the arrangement more solid than simple aesthetics and Ostwald used his method to define a total of twenty-four base colors.

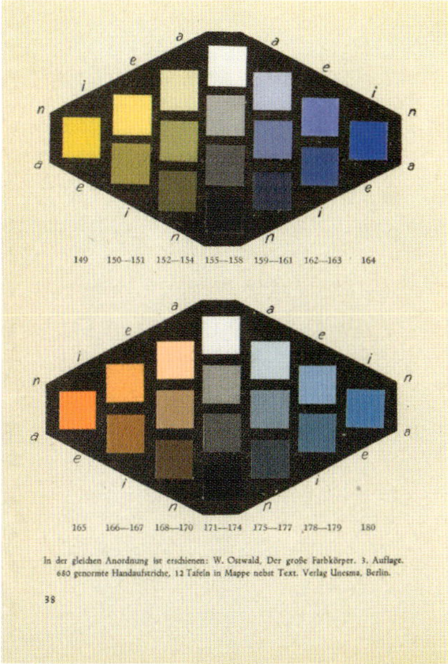

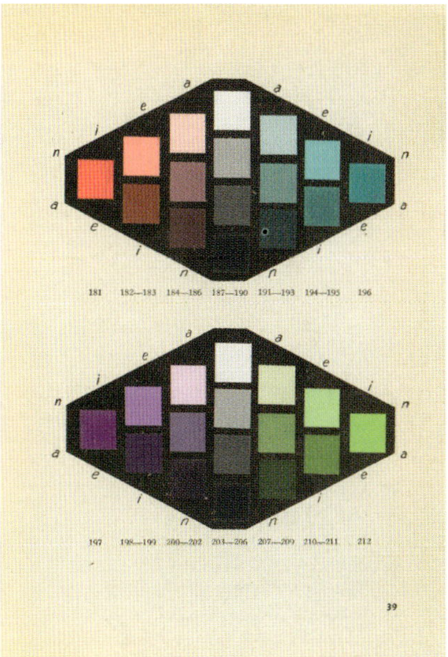

With this established, Ostwald then developed two further ranges of color moderated by additions of either white or black, series he called "light-clear" and "dark-clear", respectively. These fanned out from the circle's center in triangle formation, tapering to two points above and below, turning his two-dimensional circle into a three-dimensional double cone, rather like a spinning top or a UFO. Ostwald believed any color could be identified within this space. The fullest lay along the circumference where the cones met, with the top half reserved for lighter versions and the bottom for darker. These were linked through a central spine of grayscale values, moving from white to black through eight stages. As color educator Faber Birren pointed out decades later, the light-clear series, running along the upper sections, resembled pastel tints and Ostwald identified their inherent harmony, anticipating their enormous popularity in the years to come.

Any color within this double cone could be singled out and named with a code that combined a number from the wheel with letters that indicated the amount of black and white content. The genius of Ostwald's model was that it allowed ready identification of harmonious groups of colors yet multiple possibilities for discovering these. One could find beauty, or at least pleasing clusters of color, wherever one looked, simply by tracing a straight line in different directions and angles, encircling variants that fell at regular intervals, rather like drawing round the solutions to a word-search puzzle. Ostwald was especially pleased with his identification of what he called the "shadow series". This contained variants of hues that followed the vertical value scale, cleaving to its transition through various grays, creating smoky, sophisticated "shades-within-shades".

Ostwald's model was embraced by industry but also became a commercial enterprise in its own right. His models and books were subsumed under the branded umbrella of Ostwald Energie and his range of colors was brought to market as pigments, wool and paper. While industry took up his work, artists were less enamoured, with the notable exception of the tutors of the famous Bauhaus design school, who placed some of his color gadgetry on display in their institution's lobby, including a model of his double cone.

Although Ostwald's system appeared to have a fundamental basis, it suffered from the usual flaws: color simply resists being ordered in an overly schematic, uniform shape, and this one could not be expanded to keep pace with progress and the newly minted colors that industrial giants such as BASF and Bayer kept pushing onto the market. Ostwald's fix for the problem was unique: he advised that any color that did not fit should not be used. Just when industry was innovating with newer, brighter colors, the double-cone space was closed to new members. Nevertheless, his work was embedded in color education for several decades and embraced by the textile industry and the world of natural science.

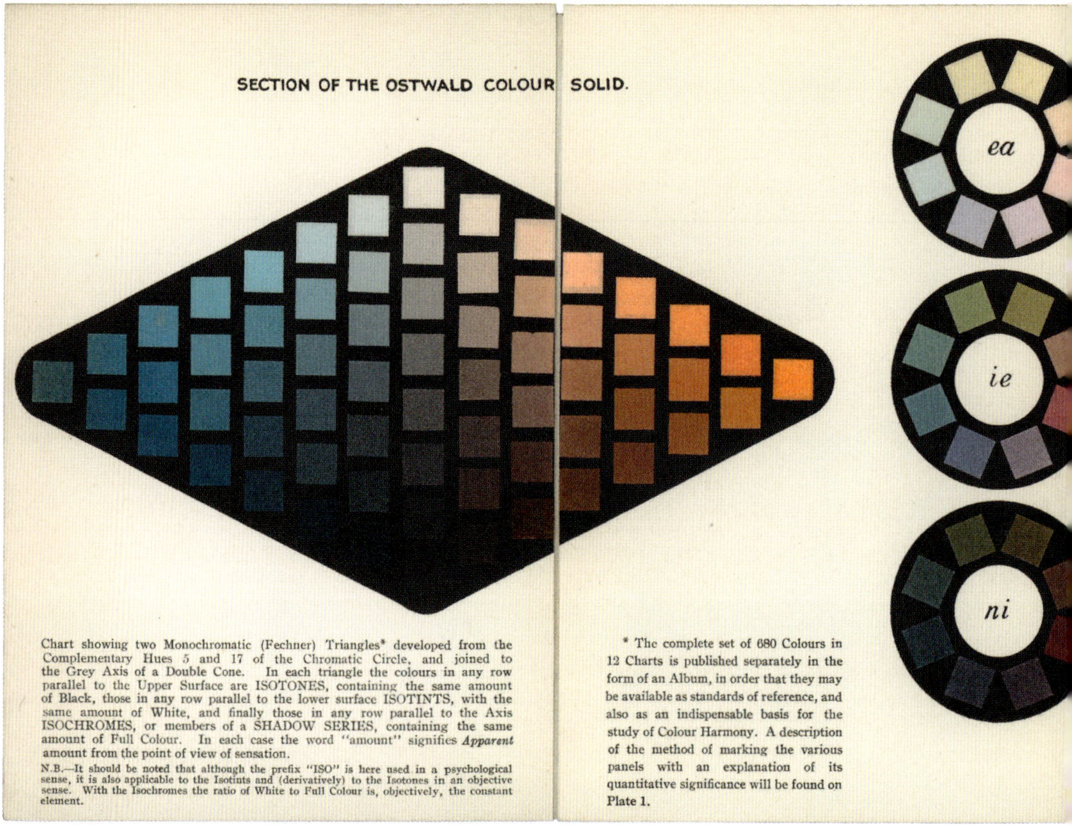

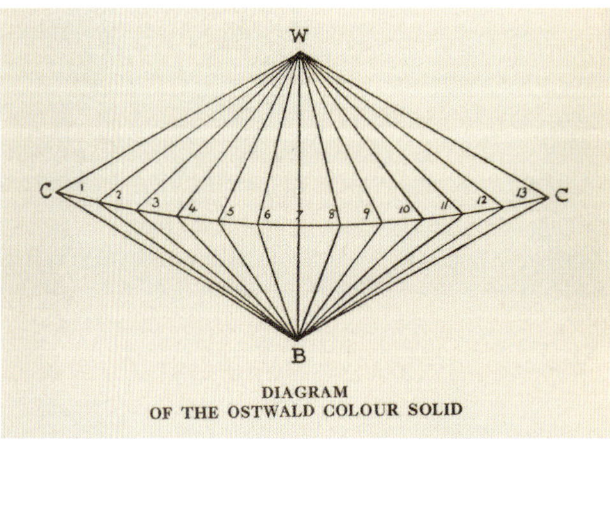

ABOVE

A fold-out card was included in a British translation of Ostwald's Color Science *by J. Scott Taylor and published by Winsor & Newton in 1931. The "isovalent" circles are naturally harmonious ranges of Ostwald's principal hues; each color in every circle contains the same amount of black or white as its seven neighbors. The dial, meanwhile, allows users to find the spectral composition of any pure hue. By pointing the arrow to its center, a semicircle of constituent "semichromes" is revealed.*

LEFT

A diagram of Ostwald's double cone "colour solid" as reproduced in Taylor's translation.

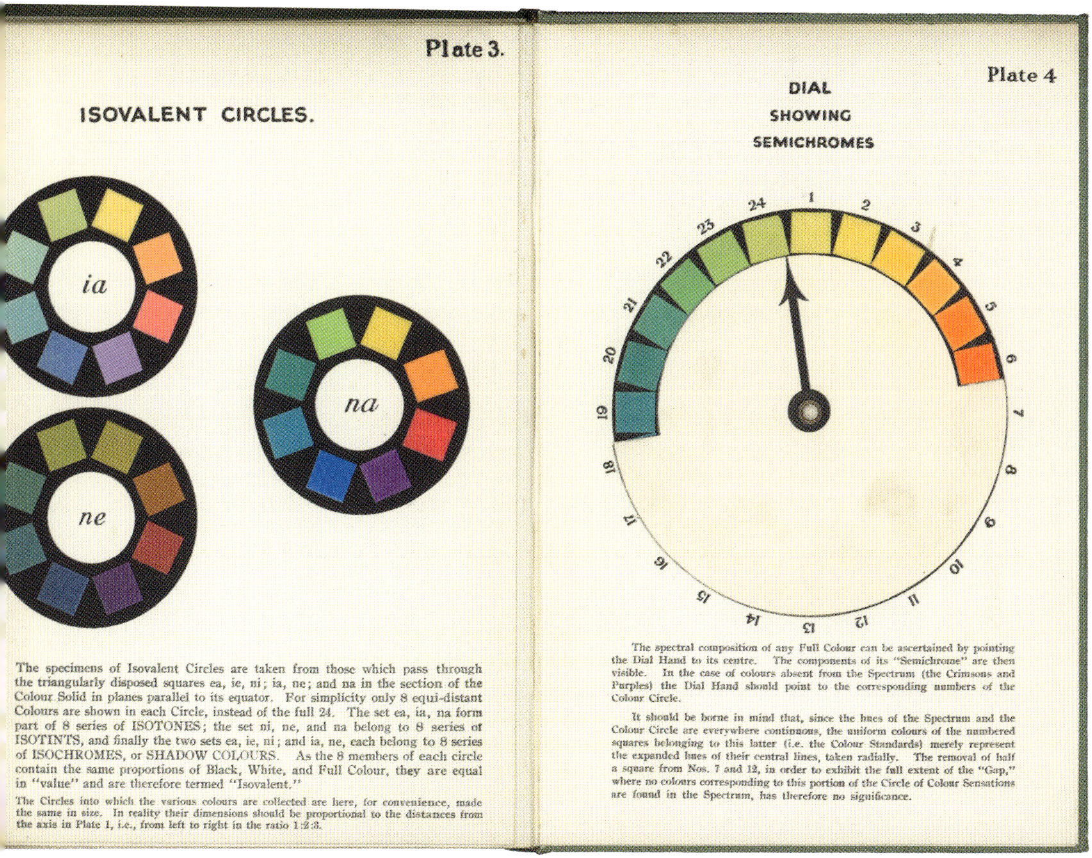

Though not immediately evident, the unspoken contest to create an optimal system for color specification was almost over before it began, as the limitations in Ostwald's system were already being anticipated by Albert Henry Munsell (1858–1918). An art educator and practicing artist, Munsell lectured at Boston's Normal Art School (later the Massachusetts College of Art and Design) in the 1890s. Like many color evangelists, he felt a profound affinity with nature, believing the palette of flowers and feathers, rocks, and leaves was so easy to appreciate that love for color was itself a natural state of being.

As his teaching developed, Munsell became interested in the problem of how to teach color relationships to students of all ages, from early-years schoolchildren upward. Understanding color and its workings should be easy and intuitive, he argued, much like the study of music, where a single note could be understood through its relationship to others. To aid comprehension, Munsell planned to create a system of color notation and specification that transcended language and communicated universally. Trying to define colors through descriptive and generic color names, he argued, was "foolish" and "misleading". Instead, he had a plan to create an order in which "color anarchy was replaced by systematic color description".

At the heart of his nascent model lay a reconceptualization of the very expression of color, a way of encoding, for example, the difference between a rich, deep blue and a pale, grayish-green. Munsell maintained these distinctions could only be adequately specified if three different variables were calculated for each color sample and he called these hue, value, and chroma. Hue was the specification of a particular color family: red, for example, or yellow. Value, as others had already explored, related to the amount of black or white in that color, whether it was a shade or a tint (Munsell likened this to the way colors might appear in a monochromatic photograph, reduced to a variety of grays of different depths). Many people could grasp these two distinctions intuitively, but Munsell's real innovation was to define a comprehensible third dimension that embodied what the others lacked. Intended to represent the strength, richness, or saturation of a color, Munsell struggled with the terminology for this quality at first, toying with calling it energy or purity. He finally settled on chroma.

With these three mandatory qualities outlined, Munsell needed next to establish base colors themselves and started with five "principal hues": yellow, red, purple, blue, and green. These were arranged equidistantly, each spaced in an equal

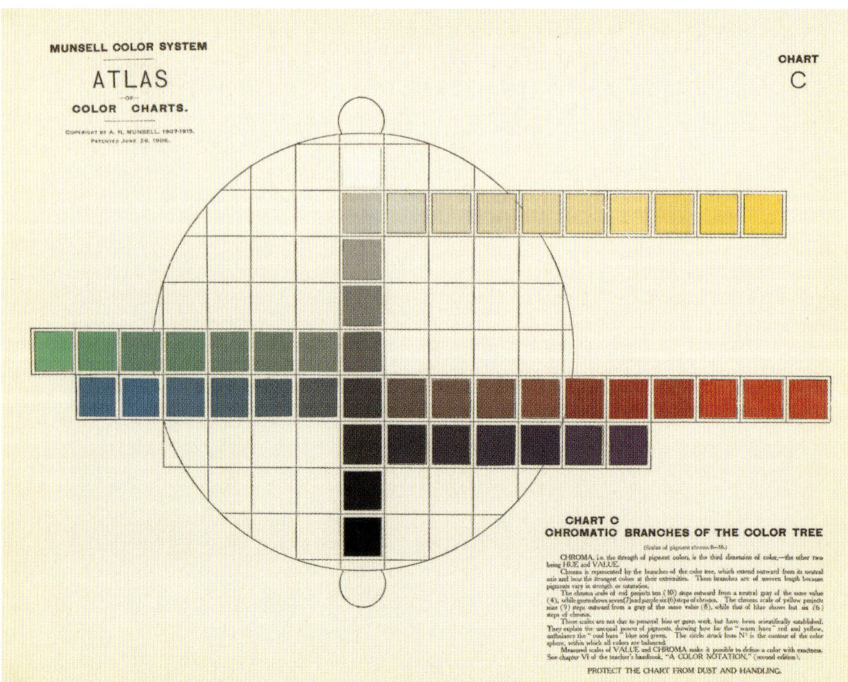

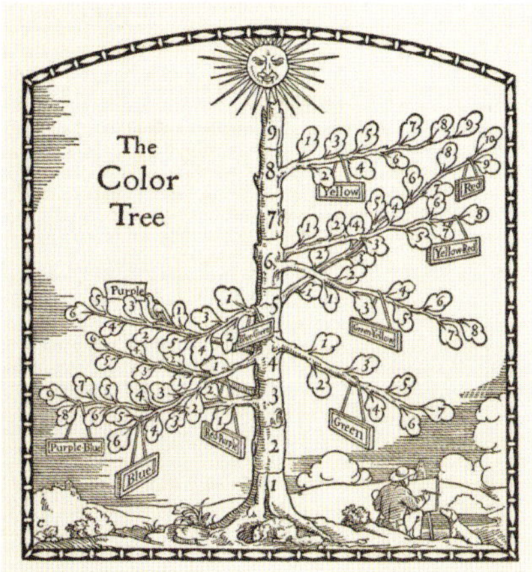

OPPOSITE

Chart C of the Atlas of the Munsell Color System *(1915) represented the "chroma" variable of the color-specification system. Munsell's five principal colors are included, their chroma (saturation) expressed by the variable length of their "branches".*

ABOVE

A woodcut of Munsell's three-dimensional Color Tree with its irregular branches. The numbered leaves represent the equal stages of increasing saturation. This image appeared in A Grammar of Color *(1921), Munsell's posthumous publication produced with illustrator Thomas Cleland. Note the artist at his easel, painting en plein air beside the tree.*

number of transitional steps from one another, the same distance from a midgray. He confirmed these by using spinning tops, similar to the color-combination discs perfected by James Clerk Maxwell (see p.152), to determine the relationship between the value and chroma of a given hue. Along the way, he even invented a photometer (the "Lumenometer") to measure the differences between the colors he was exploring. Munsell called his base colors a "chromatic tuning fork", because they provided a balanced starting point from which either more or less saturated versions could then be calculated. His five principal hues were combined into five further compounds, but Munsell took pains to omit any common names for these as this would defeat the purpose of his notation. In his world, the midpoint of yellow and red and the compound it created was just "YR" (yellow-red), an objective if prosaic term to replace a world of multiple, vague oranges.

These ideas coalesced into *A Color Notation* (1905), Munsell's initial explanation of his color model. Split into two parts, the first described color behaviors while the second outlined a color system and program of study for schools. His aim was simple and modest: to create a resource to train teachers. It was a self-confessed work in progress, a "fragmentary sketch" and a simple instruction manual, but it soon became obvious that it had the makings of something universal and potentially indispensable to the commercial world.

Everything in *A Color Notation* seemed to anticipate the question "How might children best understand this?", and the accessible approach extended even to complexities of harmony, described in simple terms from base principles. Like Charles Blanc (see p.162), Munsell noted how differently complementary colors behave depending on whether they are blended or juxtaposed: "each *enhances* the other when separate, but *destroys* the other when mixed". And he noted that simply using complementary colors in equal quantities was not an automatic recipe for success: the respective saturation of each color needed to be taken into account. "The true complement of the buttercup, then, is not the violet, which is too weak in chroma to balance [a strong yellow]." Readers were instructed to control the proportions of the contrasting colors, to "use more of the weaker color" or apply only small splashes of powerful color to balance out less dominant areas. The buttercup would only thrive on a lawn where a thousand violets bloomed.

In fact, for such an evangelical chromatologist, especially one trying to capture the imagination of children, Munsell had a surprising antipathy to bright and strong colors. He never missed an opportunity to disparage cheerleaders for cheerful color and the shift in register from enthusiastic teacher to scolding critic could be jarring. Disdain simmered beneath some of his judgements: "It is grotesque to watch a gaudily dressed person going into ecstasies over the delicate coloring of a Botticelli, when

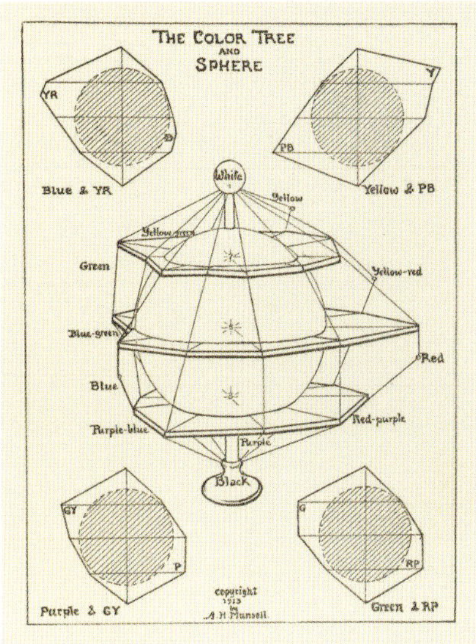

ABOVE
A diagram from the 1915 edition of A Color Notation. *This demonstrated how Munsell's uneven tree grew out of his original spherical design. The Color Sphere proved too perfect and regular to reflect the properties of different colors.*

OPPOSITE
An earlier pastel interpretation of the Color Sphere from Munsell's original Color Notation *(1905). The sphere is partially reflected in a mirror, hinting at the cooler colors on the other side.*

the internal as well as the external evidence is against them." Those who favored strong or bright color in their work were also likened to a shrieking boy who just needed to calm down. The fact that bright colors were now commercially available, Munsell often suggested, was no reason to actually use them; it was far better for practitioners to hover around the pleasing midtones. Fortunately for the history of art, many prominent painters of his era, from Gabriele Münter to André Derain, ignored the advice. So did Munsell's fellow teachers, some of whom complained about his prescriptive tone, warning he risked stifling children's innate love of bold color altogether.

A Color Notation introduced Munsell's first-draft color solid, a three-dimensional representation of the way his color variants came together as a sphere, similar to the one imagined by Philipp Otto Runge a century earlier (see p.91). In a ring around the equator of his globe, Munsell placed his five primaries and five compounds. These then progressed, from white at the north pole to black at the south, through a ten-step series of values, creating tints and shades, depending on whether they lay in the northern or southern hemisphere. So far, so familiar. However, once Munsell came to incorporate chroma, which started from the sphere's desaturated core and extended outward to reach peak saturation at the globe's surface, the scheme unraveled. With awkward timing, he realized the sphere was flawed almost immediately after he patented it, and allowed space in *A Color Notation* to face down some of its limitations and explore proposed refinements (later editions added a new diagram to visualize the differences between systems). The problem was that different colors reached their full saturation unevenly, in shorter or longer numbers of steps. Any convenient ten-stage scale that applied to all colors equally, the kind beloved of everyone from Schiffermüller (see p.80) to Chevreul (see p.135), was a sham. Yellow, for example, is brighter at its most saturated than red. Another problem was that colors arrived at their maximum chroma at different points on the value scale: yellow is also an inherently lighter color than blue or red, much nearer to the north pole than the equator or south pole. It was a physical impossibility for each hue to reach its maximum chroma at exactly the same equatorial point on the globe's surface. If this color solid really were a planet, some hues would protrude far above surface level, oversized mountains peaking beyond the atmosphere. Once again, a three-dimensional geometrical shape was ultimately too perfect to contain the messy irregularities of color.

While Munsell pressed on with the spherical model in *A Color Notation* for ease of comprehension (he also likened it to an orange segmented into five parts) his genius was to then find another metaphor that accommodated the physical differences between hues but still communicated them to a general audience: the Color Tree. Instead of black and white forming the poles of a globe, they now became the top and

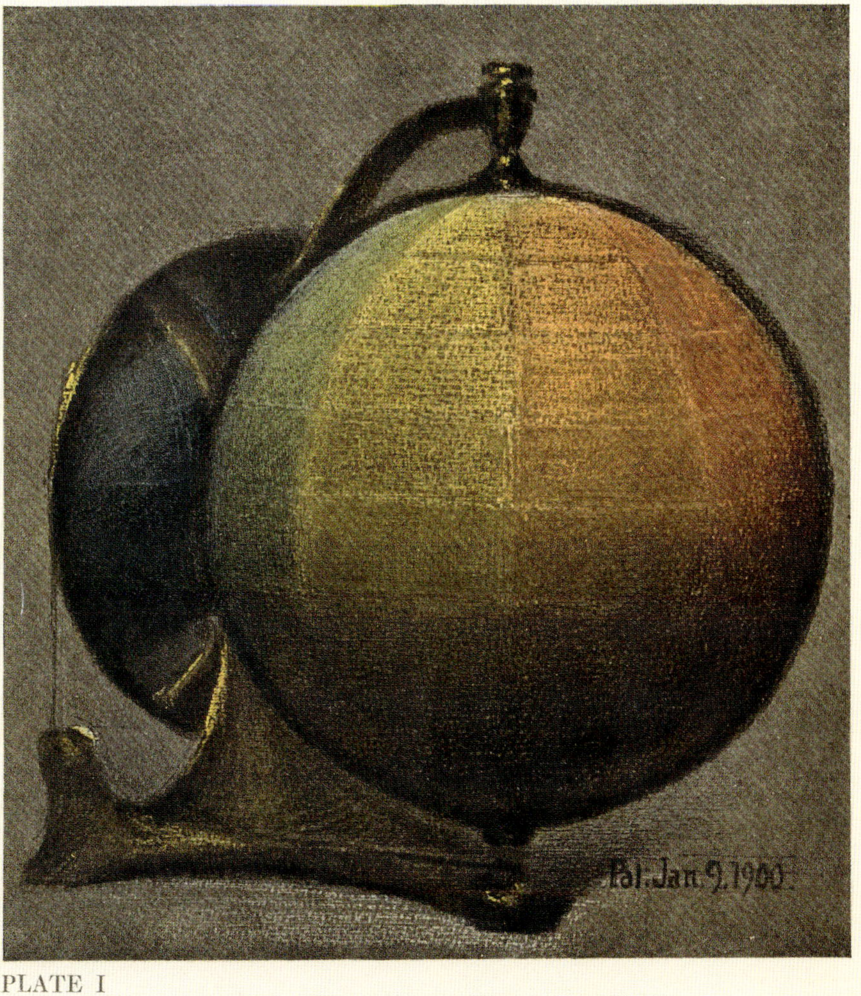

PLATE I

A BALANCED COLOR SPHERE

PASTEL SKETCH

bottom of a tree trunk from which branches of different hues grew horizontally outward, to different lengths (chroma) and at different heights (values). These branches could be as long or as short as each hue required, and could even carry on growing: "The branch ends represent the most powerful red, yellow, green, blue, and purple pigments which we now possess and could be lengthened should stronger chromas be discovered." The problem with Ostwald's closed-shop system, so at odds with the ambition and capacity of dye and pigment manufacturers, was solved at a stroke.

Munsell produced an attractive *Atlas of the Color Solid* in 1907, followed by an expanded version in 1915, to demonstrate the appearance and workings of his model, complete with cross-sections studded with rich and varied colored squares. In these grids, horizontal lines represented variants of equal value, while vertical groupings contained those of the same chroma. Each square was expressed through his unique system of notation, which took the form of Hue Value/Chroma. He observed, for example, that vermilion, a rich red-orange pigment, could be expressed as R 5/9, where R stood for the red of his principal hues, 5 was the middle value from light to dark, and 9 was close to the maximum saturation.

A Color Notation was a slimline twentieth-century classic. The book's commercial success spurred other ventures, and product lines including watercolor sets in "Munsell colors". Munsell left the Normal Art School in 1915 after his commercial ventures conflicted with his teaching. He wanted to bring his system to as many people as possible and undertook lecture tours of Europe with missionary zeal, in part to try to outpace Ostwald. After all, if the aim was to create a definitive color-specification system, any flourishing competition was an existential threat. Ostwald initially looked like the winner of the pair's unofficial duel. His system, with its mathematical basis, rose quickly and fell slowly, waning only as its limitations began to show. The Munsell system, on the other hand, based on visual judgement of the difference between colors, experience over calculation, had a long century ahead.

Munsell died in 1918 aged sixty, just after the formation of the Munsell Color Company, set up to manufacture related product lines of books, paints, and papers, but before it attained success. In 1942, the Munsell system was recommended by the American Standards Organization as the definitive means for specifying the surface color of objects. His labors never became widely embraced by artists and designers but remained fundamental to a range of disciplines, from archaeology to forensics, that required specification of the surface color of tangible materials.

Munsell's and Ostwald's systems jostled for primacy but the market was still wide open for other quantitative, if more idiosyncratic, approaches to color. Two Americans from different spheres, Robert Ridgway (1850–1929) and Emily Noyes Vanderpoel

(1842–1939), made compelling contributions to the field. Ridgway attempted to specify colors by tying them inseparably to particular names (over a thousand in his system), while Vanderpoel analyzed and quantified the relative proportions of color in inspiring objects of beauty, both natural and manufactured, to demonstrate sound principles of composition. The results of these appeared in her work *Color Problems: A Practical Manual for the Lay Student of Color* (1902), in which Vanderpoel broke down the constituent colors of each example and arranged them in a hundred-square grid to visualize the color palettes involved. This ready reference to successful combinations was a unique selling point amid her otherwise familiar text with its

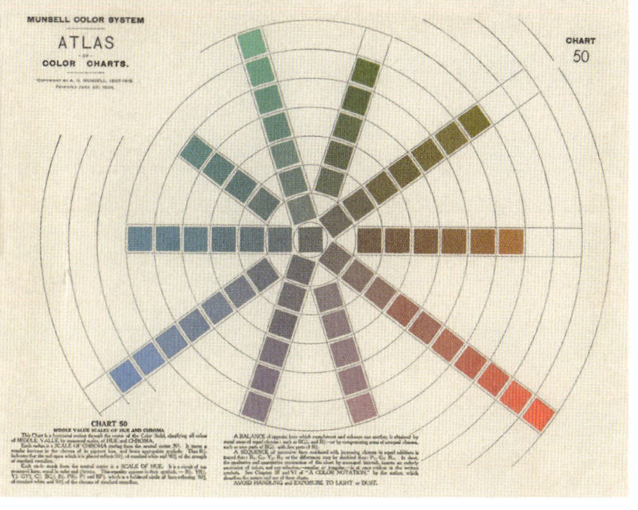

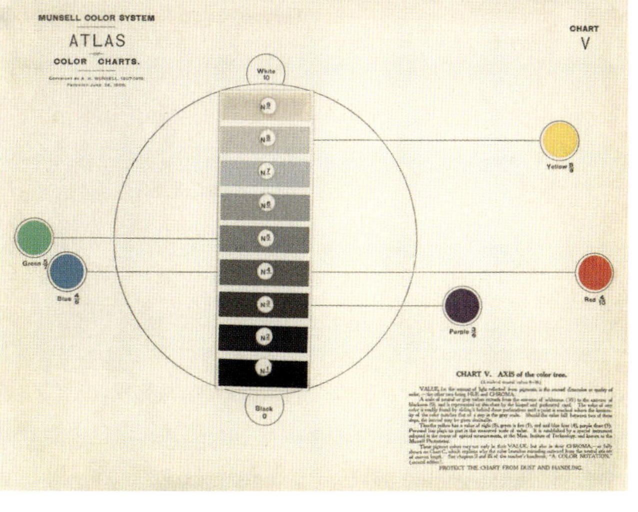

LEFT ABOVE

A horizontal section through the Color Tree, from the Atlas of the Munsell Color System *(1915). Chart 50 represented the ten hues in lighter values, as if they were reflecting 50 per cent of the surrounding light.*

LEFT

Chart V of the Atlas of the Munsell Color System *(1915) recorded the value (grayscale) quality from white (10) down to black (0). The nine-point interim values of different grays are printed on a flap with punched holes so that a color sample can be passed behind and its luminosity matched to a particular number. The chart notes the different values of principal hues, from Yellow (8) down to Purple (3).*

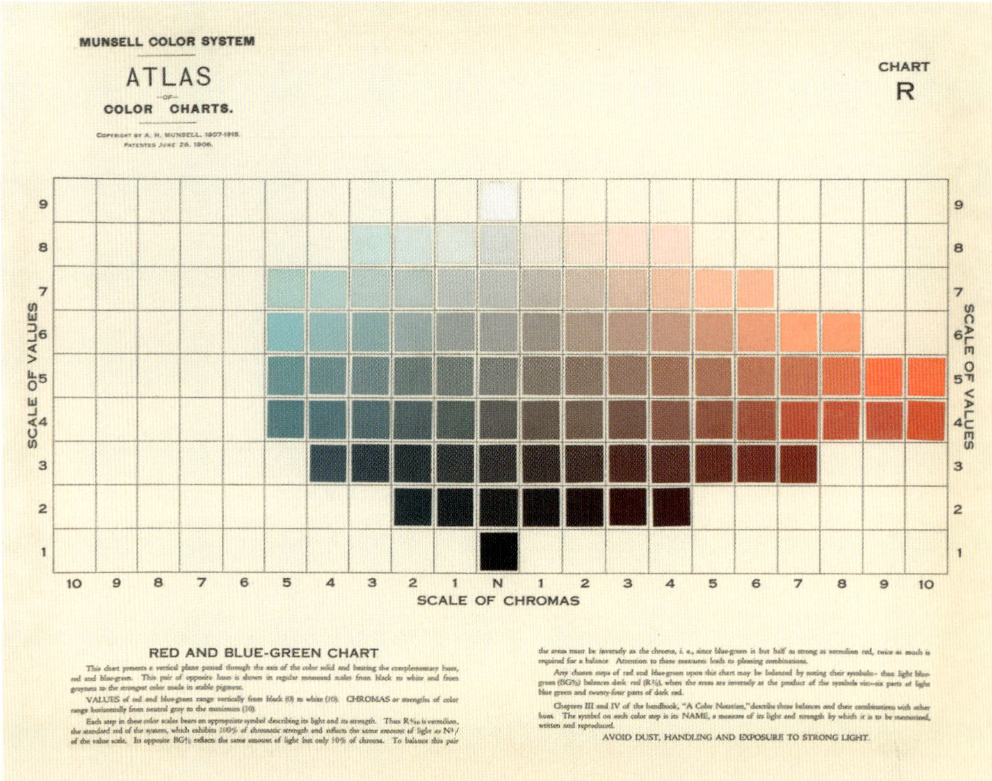
MUNSELL COLOR SYSTEM
ATLAS
—OF—
COLOR CHARTS.
COPYRIGHT BY A. H. MUNSELL. 1907-1915.
PATENTED JUNE 26, 1906.
CHART
R
SCALE OF VALUES
1 2 3 4 5 6 7 8 9
10 9 8 7 6 5 4 3 2 1 N 1 2 3 4 5 6 7 8 9 10
SCALE OF CHROMAS
RED AND BLUE-GREEN CHART
This chart presents a vertical plane passed through the axis of the color solid and bearing the complementary hues, red and blue-green. This pair of opposite hues is shown in regular measured scales from black to white and from grayness to the strongest color made in stable pigment.
VALUES of red and blue-green range vertically from black (0) to white (10). CHROMAS or strengths of color range horizontally from neutral gray to the maximum (10).
Each step in these color scales bears an appropriate symbol describing its light and its strength. Thus R 4/10 is vermilion, the standard red of the system, which exhibits 100% of chromatic strength and reflects the same amount of light as N 4/ of the value scale. Its opposite BG 4/5 reflects the same amount of light but only 50% of chroma. To balance this pair the areas must be inversely as the chroma, i. e., since blue-green is but half as strong as vermilion red, twice as much is required for a balance. Attention to these measures leads to pleasing combinations.
Any chosen steps of red and blue-green upon this chart may be balanced by noting their symbols— thus light blue-green (BG 7/3) balances dark red (R 3/4), when the areas are inversely as the product of the symbols viz:—six parts of light blue green and twenty-four parts of dark red.
Chapters III and IV of the handbook, "A Color Notation," describe these balances and their combinations with other hues. The symbol on each color step is its NAME, a measure of its light and strength by which it is to be memorized, written and reproduced.
AVOID DUST, HANDLING AND EXPOSURE TO STRONG LIGHT.

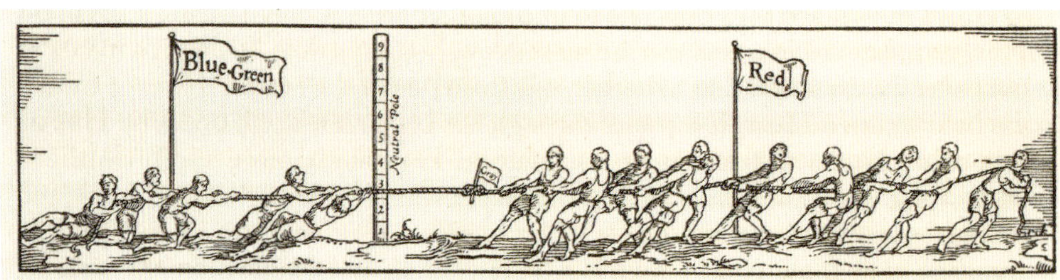
Blue-Green
Red
Neutral Pole
9
8
7
6
5
4
3
2
1

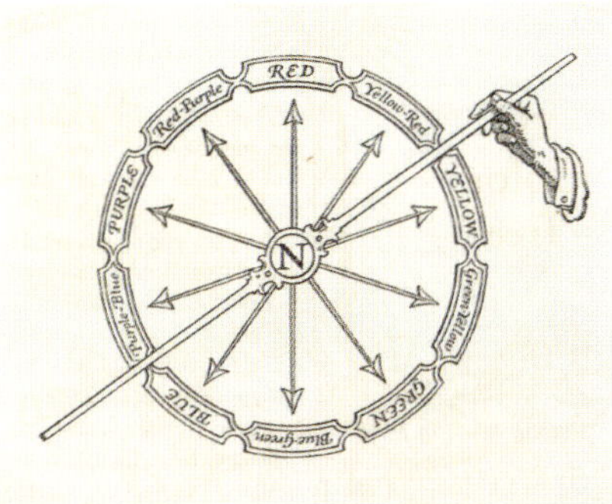

OPPOSITE ABOVE
A vertical section through the Color Tree of Munsell's Atlas *representing opposing colors Red and the hybrid Blue-Green. By incrementally adjusting the value and chroma of these two hues, seventy-eight variants are created on the page, with almost twice as many on the Red side as the cooler Blue-Green.*

OPPOSITE BELOW
A more folksy representation of the above disparity as interpreted by Thomas Cleland in A Grammar of Color *(1921). The two hues are presented as a one-sided tug of war with red unfairly overpowering its opponent. The metaphor explored the difficulties of balancing two colors of unequal strength in composition. To overcome this, Munsell recommended pairing a fully saturated Blue-Green with a less saturated Red.*

ABOVE
Munsell's basic color wheel of ten hues, five principal and five intermediate or hybrid colors, interpreted as a dial or compass by Thomas Cleland in A Grammar of Color *(1921). Complementary colors are found where the dial or hands cross both sides of the circle.*

re-statement of developments in color theory. Vanderpoel's taste was catholic, and her reference points global, with inspiration drawn from the cases of Egyptian mummies, Assyrian tiles, the Taj Mahal, and Japanese vases.

Vanderpoel was a somewhat conservative yet bohemian figure. She intended her book as a source of advice for students from different disciplines, including interior designers, and lithographers, and attempted to demystify color for practitioners. She fervently believed that nature itself provided perfect palettes of inherent harmony, and encouraged the reader to draw inspiration from it always.

As a collector of Japanese art, including textiles and wood carvings, Vanderpoel's passion shone through in her examples of perfect color balance. Oriental rugs, she argued, were especially beautiful for being hand-made, because of their inherent inconsistencies in color and finish, "far finer than the even monotony of a perfectly matched surface". The best examples of color in arts and crafts were Japanese, and Vanderpoel judged those dating from when the country was a "shut-in nation" particularly outstanding because the designs were not qualified by any need to pander to Western markets.

In exploring color behavior, Vanderpoel observed how the surface of objects affected their underlying color, citing red sealing wax as an example. She also described structural color, or "interference", where the polychromatic appearance of peacock feathers and soap bubbles arose not through their inherent pigments but as a result of white light diffraction when hitting a particularly complex surface. Crucially, Vanderpoel also paid due consideration to how color behaves differently under artificial light, noting its heightened appearance under the then recent innovation of electric light compared with daylight.

Outlining seven rules for using contrast, Vanderpoel stressed the importance of balancing the proportions of colors used in any design. This was better illustrated through an anecdote than a diagram and she recounted the famous story of how J.M.W. Turner once submitted a green-gray roiling seascape, *Helvoetsluys* (1817), to the Summer Exhibition at the Royal Academy of Arts in London. Just before opening, he spontaneously added a small scarlet buoy, bobbing in the foreground, in an attempt to outshine John Constable, whose domineering work hung alongside. The shock of the contrast from a simple flash of red brought Turner's painting to life. Although Vanderpoel did not include this detail, Turner's stroke of genius was reportedly to his rival's chagrin. "He has been here and fired a gun," concluded the wounded Constable.

One of the most striking moments in the book arose when Vanderpoel touched on the growing importance of color as a means of personal expression, or at least acknowledged the role it had to play in keeping up appearances. Her prescription was conspicuously gendered: "[N]o art is finer or higher for a woman however placed than that of being a harmonious whole

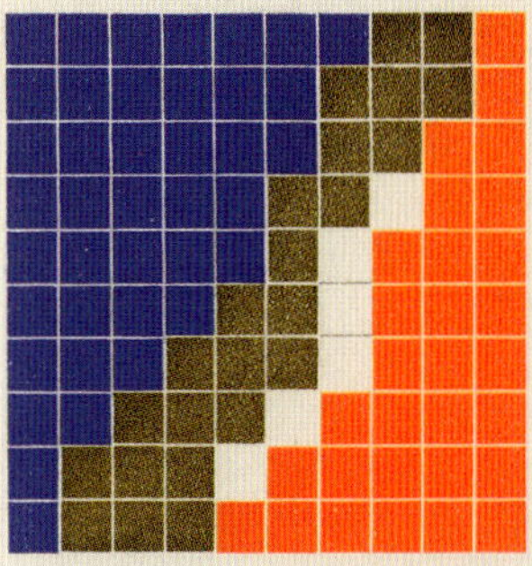

COLOR ANALYSIS FROM A PANEL OF THE ALHAMBRA

Blue	40
Red	30
Gold	24
White	6
	100

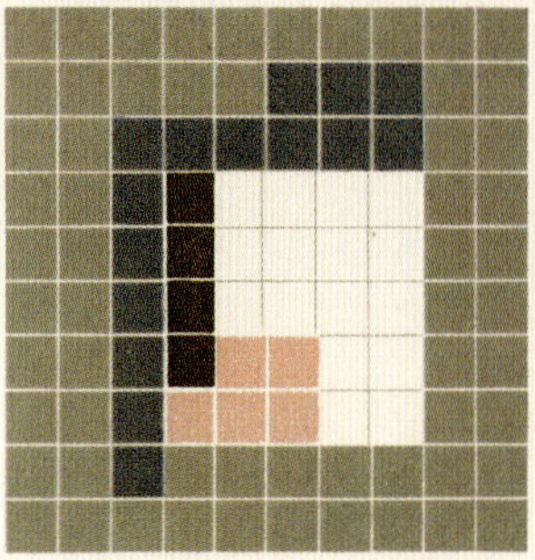

COLOR ANALYSIS FROM JAPANESE SILK BROCADE

Yellow-Gray Ground	60
Blue-Gray Leaves	15
White Daisies	16
Pink Tips to Daisies	5
Gold Veins to Leaves and Centres to Daisies	4
	100

Quantitative color analysis by Emily Noyes Vanderpoel in Color Problems *(1902). Vanderpoel reduced the constituent colors of different designs to a hundred-square grid in order to visualize their relative proportions. This analysis of a panel of the Alhambra includes gold ink. The color palette is remarkably consistent with the books of Owen Jones's record of designs from the Alhambra published decades earlier (see p.195).*

herself, and of making or adding to a harmonious home." Her assessment anticipated the coming decades in which women, almost exclusively, would be targeted by predominantly male advertisers as a lucrative market for colorful product ranges.

In the story of color, the personal profile of Vanderpoel's contemporary Robert Ridgway almost fits better into the late eighteenth or early nineteenth centuries, when the quest for optimal color ranges and systems was driven by a sense of discovery and a need to capture the kaleidoscopic natural world. Ridgway was a globe-trotting American ornithologist and botanist whose life and scholarship revolved around birds; he even named his son Audubon, after the canonical author of *Birds of America* (1827–38). An avid birdwatcher from a young age, Ridgway drew the specimens he observed and enlivened his drawings with hand-blended colors created from leftover chemicals supplied by his pharmacist father. His consuming passion eventually led to his appointment, aged thirty, as Curator of Birds at the United States National Museum (a forerunner of the Smithsonian), a post he held until his death. Ridgway published widely and authoritatively on the taxonomy of birds, producing eight volumes of *Birds of North and Middle America* throughout the early twentieth century. Contemporaneous accounts suggest he was methodical and devoted to his work yet ill at ease with the publicity it drew.

Among his works on color, Ridgway is best remembered for *Color Standards and Color Nomenclature* (1912), an attempt to provide a visual reference and a language of color for identifying natural specimens (avian particularly, of course). Compiling over a thousand different variants spread across fifty-three plates, this was his second, more successful attempt at creating a definitive guide after the dry run of *Nomenclature of Colors for Naturalists* (1886).

All the 1,115 variants in the later work sprang from an essential set of thirty-six colors (twelve full spectrum and twenty-four intermediate hues), established, once again, with Maxwell's discs (see p.152). Arranging colors in nine rows on each plate, he placed his first thirty-six on the middle rows, with tints above and shades below. Ridgway asked the reader to picture each plate as a piece of woven fabric with two interlocking scales: the warp of the color cloth was a horizontal chromatic scale; the vertical weft was its luminosity. Subsequent series of plates then explored how these colors appeared when mixed with varying shades of gray, the so-called broken colors. These, he argued, were far more prevalent in nature than the spectrum hues, and included russet, citrine, and olive.

Ridgway's essential colors were in themselves nothing particularly new. His more distinctive contribution to the color systems of the time was anchored in language rather than hue. Each rectangular color sample in the book was appended with a unique, definitive name as Ridgway attempted to fuse them to a proper noun or descriptive phrase, terms that stuck to

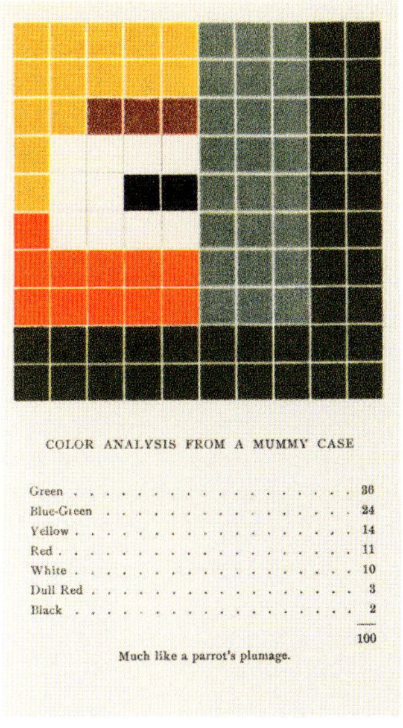

COLOR ANALYSIS FROM A MUMMY CASE

Green	36
Blue-Green	24
Yellow	14
Red	11
White	10
Dull Red	3
Black	2
	100

Much like a parrot's plumage.

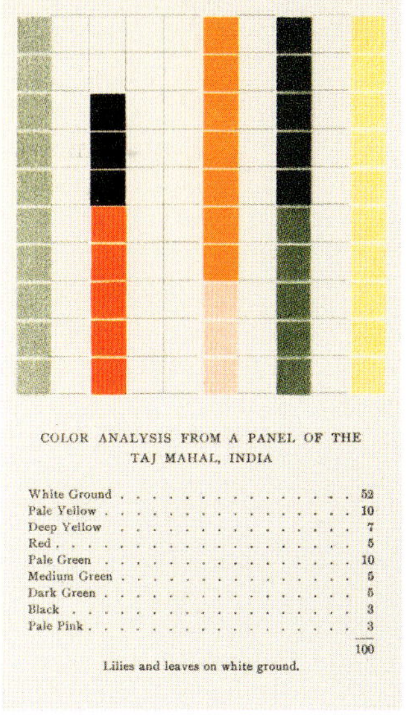

COLOR ANALYSIS FROM A PANEL OF THE TAJ MAHAL, INDIA

White Ground	52
Pale Yellow	10
Deep Yellow	7
Red	5
Pale Green	10
Medium Green	5
Dark Green	5
Black	3
Pale Pink	3
	100

Lilies and leaves on white ground.

Vanderpoel's color analysis of a "mummy case". Her quantification of color proportions was strictly geometrical and easy to interpret. In the top example, the "dull red" occupies three squares, or three per cent of the surface design. Note Vanderpoel's footnote observation that the palette of the mummy case is "much like a parrot's plumage".

specific colors just as samples of those colors were glued into place. As he explained, the book's motivation was to ensure that when naturalists, or indeed anyone, wrote of a color, "there need be no question as to what particular tint, shade, or degree of grayness, of any color or hue is meant". There had to be an independent, authoritative reference that erased the "personal equation" when defining colors, otherwise it would never be possible for anyone to agree where to draw the line between purple and violet (a perennially tricky distinction). And no color should remain nameless: science demanded an agreed term for all observable hues. "Without standardization, even if arbitrary, color nomenclature must, necessarily, remain in its present condition of absolute chaos," was Ridgway's doomy conclusion. His work, he claimed, would instead weave a common thread through divergent specialisms, a unification of color to speak equally to "the zoologist, the botanist, the pathologist, or the mineralogist".

But how, then, should a color sample be matched to a name, "even if arbitrary"? Compiling a nomenclature was tricky, and established starting points and existing authorities could not be trusted. Just look, Ridgway instructed the reader, at different commercially available paint tubes of Van Dyke brown, and see how no two manufacturers' offerings of that name match. To begin the process of standardization, he scoured the literature for samples in existing works, including *Werner's Nomenclature of Colours* (1814, see p.109), the publications of David Ramsay Hay (see p.147), the horticultural color guide *Répertoire de couleurs* (see p.65) and a work to aid the identification of plants entitled *Chromotaxia* (1894) by Pier Andrea Saccardo (see p.110). Ridgway gathered numerous physical samples and historical references, creating a card-based index to cross-reference. Exploring differences between published samples of colors with the same name, he intended to establish definitive versions and end quibbling over where one color ended and another began. Was royal blue darker or lighter than Prussian? How did apple, leaf, and turtle green relate, if at all? Ridgway's *Color Nomenclature* tried to place all possibilities between its covers to help readers decide with confidence. If you could name it, you could tame it.

The color terms in Ridgway's previous book were largely descriptive and prosaic, but for the revised and improved work, his imagination took flight. While Ridgway labeled many of his colors with familiar terms—teal, for example, or mauve—his large number of samples quickly soaked these up, and he was left to improvise with some arbitrary, or playfully referential descriptions. In the small world of color, there was space for nods toward some of his inspirations and peers: [Charles] Blanc's blue, [David Ramsay] Hay's brown, and [Ogden] Rood's lavender were all present, while Emily Noyes Vanderpoel (whose *Color Problems* Ridgway praised as an "excellent work", see p.231) lent her name to variants of blue, green, and violet.

Color Standards and Color Nomenclature had a troubled gestation. After a failed attempt to publish it in collaboration with the Smithsonian, Ridgway ended up issuing the work himself. He personally oversaw the production of the individual color samples, each printed separately on large sheets then cut down to individual rectangles and pasted into every one of the book's 5,000 copies. This was essential to guarantee consistency between any two copies of the book, to ensure that the "Light Amparo Blue" on Plate IX in a copy in Boston would match exactly the sample of the same color in a different copy that had made its way to San Francisco. Ridgway's efforts were appreciated by the ornithological community but the book's appeal was not limited to his own professional world. It was enthusiastically adopted in some eclectic fields, including mycology, wallpaper manufacture, and food coloring.

While color can seem like a universal and timeless phenomenon, attempts to master it are always framed by the spirit of the age: the cultural reference points, the needs of commerce, the opportunities of technology. Munsell, Ostwald, and Ridgway had tried to disperse the ambiguity around color communication by labeling its iterations. But every time objectivity seemed to prevail, others stepped in to approach the subject through a more personal lens and the qualitative nature of color kept reasserting itself, returning it to the eye of the beholder.

Leading the way was a pantheon of twentieth-century artists clustered around the Bauhaus school of design in 1920s Weimar Germany. All approached color with a mixture of curiosity and awe, re-emphasizing the human response and glorying in its contradictions, its numinous essence. For Paul Klee, Wassily Kandinsky, Johannes Itten, and Josef Albers, color could be viewed anthropomorphically: full of personality, it swirled with energy and agency. "Color has taken possession of me," wrote Klee in his diary, after a revelatory visit to sunlit Tunisia for a working holiday in 1914. "I know that it has hold of me for ever [...] Color and I are one." Klee's Bauhaus colleagues Kandinsky, Itten, and Albers also embraced dimensions of color that were both spiritual and human-focused. At the heart of their teaching and beyond, they centered the experiential nature of color, its effects on people, in ways that felt indelible and true.

Klee and Kandinsky perceived an inextricable relationship between color and form. Klee used colored rectangles as building blocks to aid composition, combining them in multiple ways to find haphazard inspiration. Kandinsky, working with an intensely chromatic palette as a founding member of Der Blaue Reiter group, was more radical. Lyrically outlined in his short work *Über das Geistige in der Kunst insbesondere in der Malerei* (1912), often translated as *Concerning the Spiritual in Art*, he described the "psychic shocks" color could inflict on the viewer: "Color is the keyboard, the eyes are the hammers, the soul is the piano with many strings. The artist is the hand which plays, touching one key or another, to cause vibrations in the soul."

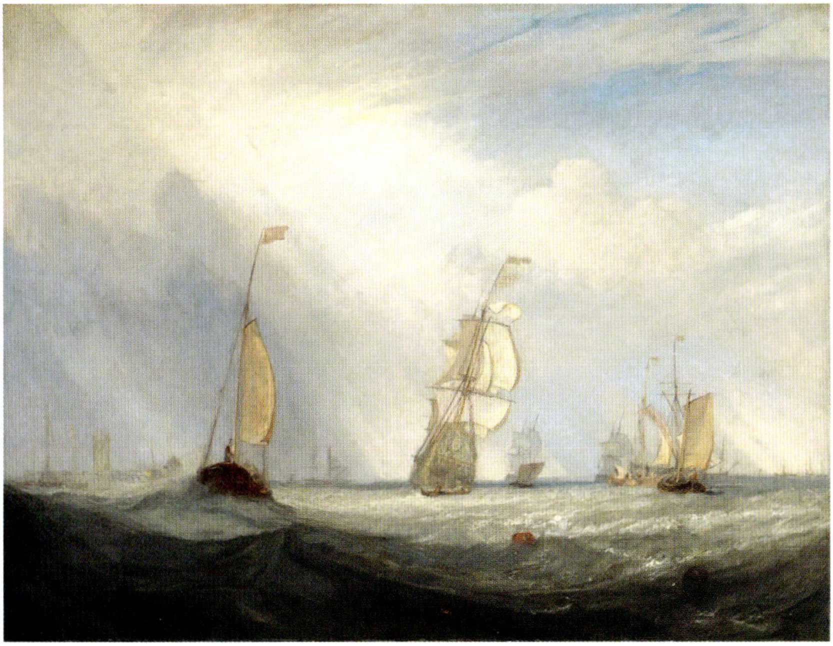

J.M.W. Turner's painting Helvoetsluys; the City of Utrecht, 64, Going to Sea *(1832) was cited in Vanderpoel's text as a particularly effective example of red-green contrast. Turner's last-minute addition of a red buoy added a shot of drama and a point of focus.*

The mere act of looking, therefore, was a creative process in its own right, or at least a transmutation of energy. Many had argued that color was a sensory stimulation akin to taste and sound, but Kandinsky thought this undersold its unique force that hummed with an "inner resonance" in touch with the human soul, capable even of triggering a spiritual awakening. He believed its inherent power could be properly tapped if the artist approached the relationship between color and form with an urgent radicalism. But while form could stand alone, he explained, color was indecipherable without shape to contain it. Pushed further, the argument led inevitably to abstraction, and experimental modes of expression that both fused color and form and asserted the primacy of form over subject. Kandinsky practiced what he preached, and had largely abandoned figurative representation (including richly chromatic landscapes) by the time his book appeared in print. His high-minded writing made clear the distinction between an art that represented reality and another kind that aspired to a higher plane.

To explore whether there was a universal link between shape and color, Kandinsky issued a questionnaire to his students asking them to match three different shapes, a circle, a square, and a triangle, to whichever primary color the participant believed it most resembled in spirit. He thought the natural order was to identify a yellow triangle, a red square, and a blue circle, and, though the results of his survey were mixed, plenty seemed to agree with him. All this was hardly science, of course, and

Kandinsky's whims and convictions floated on the mystical end of a spectrum of rationality, as if drawn from a collective unconscious of color symbolism.

In an early example of color psychology, Kandinsky devoted part of his book to a consideration of each of the main colors in turn and ascribed personalities, behaviors, and resonances to each. He believed blue and yellow were fundamentally in opposition, for example, in a model that acknowledged both Goethe's theory (see p.92) and Hering's four-color opponent process (see p.160) as antecedents. Kandinsky endowed colors with mood and character. Yellow advanced toward the viewer while blue receded, "like a snail, retreating into its shell"—the former, harsh and unruly; the latter, calm and spiritual. But Kandinsky acknowledged that there were different types embodied within a single color family and that contradictory behaviors were possible: not all yellows behaved alike. A lemon yellow, for example, "hurts the eye in time as a prolonged and shrill trumpet note the ear". Blue was "the typically heavenly color [... but] when it sinks almost to black, it echoes a grief that is hardly human". In contrast, white was "not a dead silence but one pregnant with possibilities". The allusions to life cycles, birth, and death, were unlikely to be coincidental, and acknowledged the elemental dimensions of color, its significance in the mystery of existence.

Concerning the Spiritual in Art was fluid and persuasive, however esoteric and unscientific its underlying model of color behavior. Kandinsky elevated the role of color in art to a compositional element possessed of an almost supernatural energy while humanizing the colors themselves. His book asserted the value of color for its own sake, a subject and an end in itself, unmoored from quotidian representation and earthly constraints.

Kandinsky's colleague, the Swiss-born expressionist painter Johannes Itten (1888–1967), provided a more earth-bound and structured component to the Bauhaus's teaching of color. Itten taught color theory and application within his rounded preliminary course of foundational principles in art and design, a series of lessons he devised with his own teacher, Adolf Hölzel. Itten's time at the Bauhaus—1920 to 1923—was relatively short, but he cut a dramatic and inspiring figure while there. With shaven head and mandarin collar, he followed Mazdaznan, a Zoroastrian cult, and was a strict vegetarian in an environment when this was almost unknown. A gentle soul, Itten likened teachers to gardeners whose role was to create the right conditions for plants to grow. Accounts of his teaching style noted that he never criticized a student directly, preferring to speak to the whole class about general errors in the hope that individuals would quietly recognize mistakes in their work without feeling publicly shamed. Itten's concern for the individual did not survive changes in the Bauhaus's ethos, and he left when he felt the pedagogy moving away from personal expression and toward consistency of production at scale.

A range of plates from Robert Ridgway's Color Standards and Color Nomenclature *(1912), a work that provided names for 1,115 different varieties of color. Ridgway asked the reader to imagine each plate as woven cloth with a warp and weft, two axes to represent increases in chroma and luminosity. These plates also include examples of colorful terminology, including Dragon's-blood Red and Shrimp Pink.*

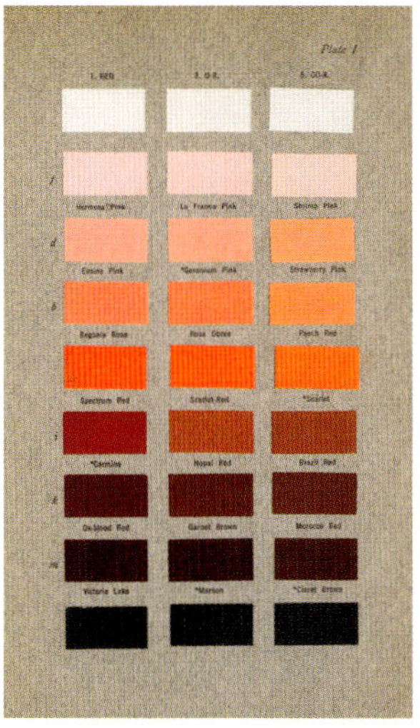
Plate I
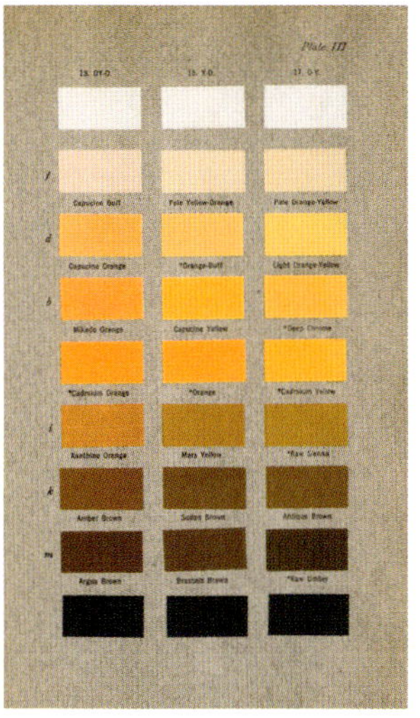
Plate III
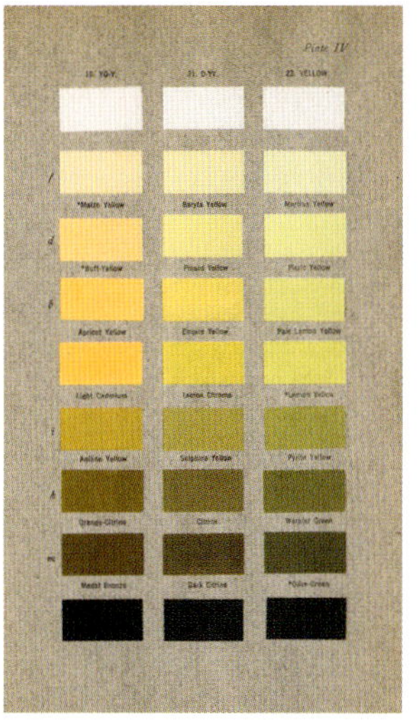
Plate IV
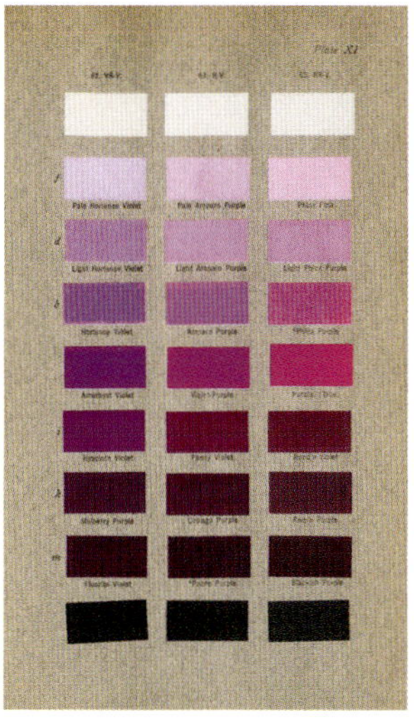
Plate XI
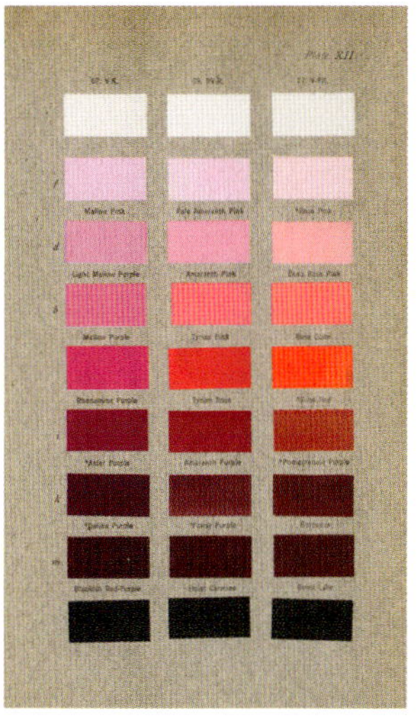
Plate XII
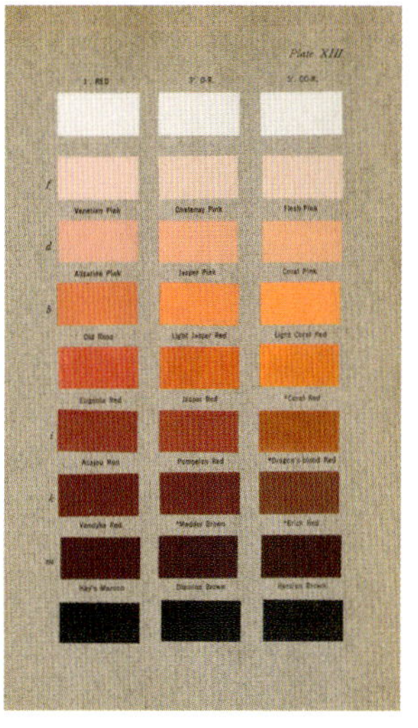
Plate XIII
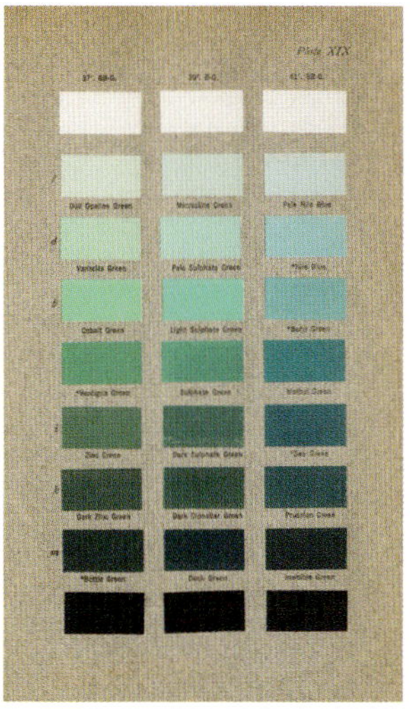
Plate XIX
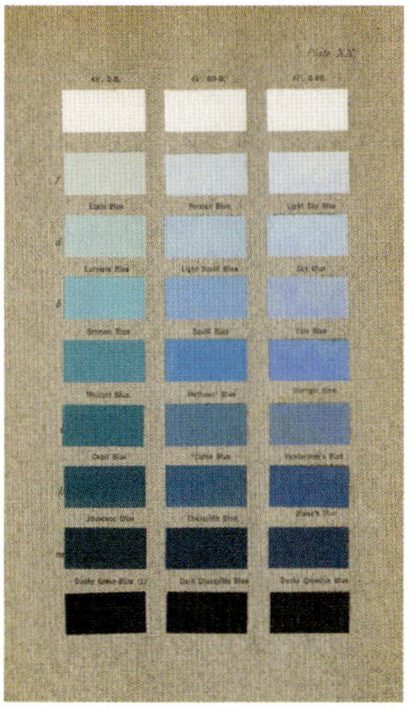
Plate XX
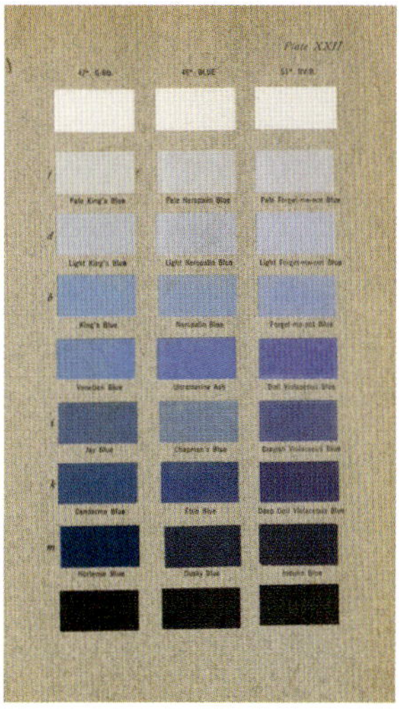
Plate XXII

BELOW
Wassily Kandinsky's Murnau Street with Women *(1908). Before embracing abstraction, Kandinsky's paintings used intense color to heighten the representation of the landscape around him and to charge familiar scenes with a highly saturated chromatic power.*

OPPOSITE ABOVE
The cover of Kandinsky's classic work Über das Geistige in der Kunst *(1911) on the power of color and the artist's responsibility to harness it. The text was translated into English as* Concerning the Spiritual in Art.

OPPOSITE BELOW
Kandinsky endowed color with personalities that were key to their effects. In this diagram, yellow is lively and outgoing, while chilly blue retreats into its shell.

Itten's anatomization of color was influenced by Runge, Goethe, Bezold, Chevreul, and Hölzel. Although his theories—which included a model of a star shape to organize color relationships—were fully formed at the Bauhaus and well rehearsed in subsequent teaching posts, he did not publish his definitive work on the subject until retirement. In 1961 his *Kunst der Farbe* (*The Art of Color*) appeared in Germany, when Itten was in his seventies. It was a remarkable meeting of theory and practice, historical and contemporary references. Like many far-reaching books on color, it needed to push the technological limits of printing of the time to realize its arguments. Color illustrations were printed separately and pasted into the correct position on the page, like a scrapbook. At the book's heart was a lively description, bursting with examples, of Itten's typology of contrast, which he believed to be fundamental to successful composition and mastery of hue. He objected to Ostwald's maxim of "harmony = order" because he felt it over-simplified, failing to take into account the manifold and complicated effects of these different modes of color behavior.

In his analysis, Itten (like Vanderpoel) identified no fewer than seven different types of contrast, including "light—dark" and "cold—warm". He included Chevreul's simultaneous and successive contrasts (the latter was related to after-images), and also explored complementary contrast and the contrast of saturation. While the granularity of his subdivisions looked like splitting hairs, Itten maintained that every type was a different proposition, with its own rules and peculiarities. Each received

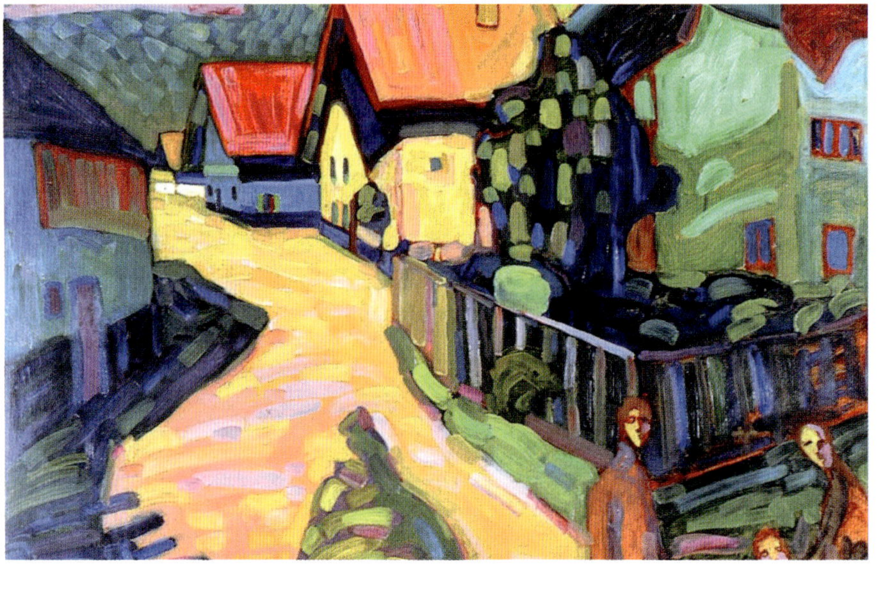

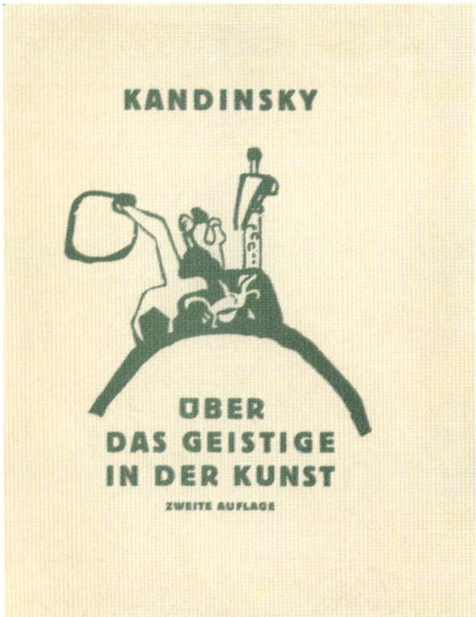

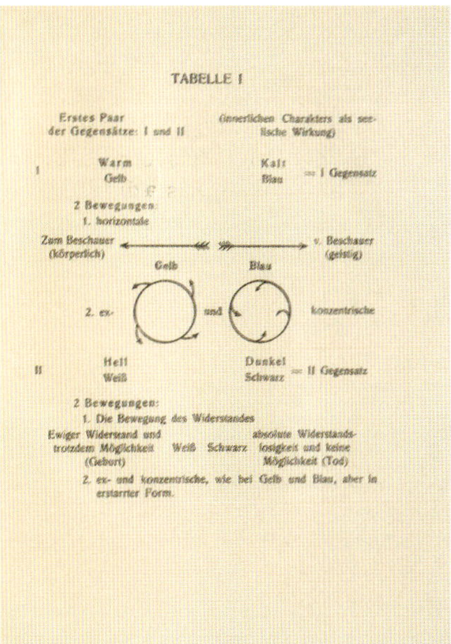

its own chapter, illustrated with examples of the effects in practice through history, from Renaissance paintings to modern masterpieces, to demonstrate the timelessness and universality of his observations. In describing "contrasts of hue" for example, where three very different primary or secondary colors are arranged to play off against one another, Itten called as evidence everything from folk art and illuminated manuscripts to the paintings of Matisse and Mondrian. Turning to "light–dark" contrast, Itten praised the "outstanding example" of Chinese and Japanese ink drawing, and noted that it was also the basis of entire techniques such as woodcuts and etching. The masters of "cold–warm" contrast, meanwhile, were the Impressionists, with their porous boundaries between warm sunlight and cool shadows. This type of contrast, he asserted, "provides the possibility of representing the music of the spheres in colors". Itten's final type, contrast of extension, helpfully considered different effects depending on the relative surface areas of a pair of contrasting colors. Inspired by Goethe's scale of color intensities, where the German playwright scored individual hues to denote their comparative luminosity (see p.93), Itten outlined the proportions of each required to maximize the impact of the contrast. A blue-orange combination worked best if blue occupied two-thirds of the space with orange taking up the remaining third. The most powerful red-green combination, meanwhile, required a fifty-fifty split across the surface.

Itten's enduring contribution to the world of color schematics was a twelve-pointed color star, in fact a template of a three-dimensional model that could be cut out along its outline and wrapped around another Runge-inspired globe (see p.92). In a world where color standards and ranges were growing, Itten insisted that twelve distinct hues were ample, and that the larger schemes were becoming ridiculous in their level of detail: "Can any painter, unaided, visualize Color No. 83 of a 100-hue circle?" (Those who had ploughed through all of Ridgway's thousand-odd samples may have felt a flicker of sympathy.) Itten's main colors could be enclosed in a circle in which one could place an equilateral or isosceles triangle, a square or a rectangle. On rotation of this inner shape, wherever its points touched the ring of colors, harmonic groupings of two, three, or four colors (dyads, triads, and tetrads) could be pinpointed automatically. He was fastidious about the hues allowed into his system, singling out particular pigments for key placement, including cinnabar and ultramarine. He linked colors to seasons, and related individuals' personal coloring (skin tone, hair color) to their own embrace of color in creative practice and self-expression.

Writing at the dawn of the 1960s, Itten knew he was living in supersaturated times. He noted the growing interest in color spurred by advances in color photography and fashion trends, but remained unconvinced this was progress. All that commercial color, he argued, took no account of the "intellectual or emotional" human response it could trigger. It remained "a superficial, external toying with metaphysical forces".

The Art of Color was a successful and accessible attempt to integrate different ways of thinking about the subject, deftly blending a mathematical approach to color with elements of psychology, symbolism, and cultural history. By calling famous works from the history of art as witnesses, he built an evidence base for enduring and instructive principles that had been followed through time, consciously or otherwise. The book was so immediately successful that an American edition was rushed into publication within the year. Its enduring popularity can be in part attributed to Itten's long career tending his garden of student saplings, and his natural skills as a communicator of both the theory of color and the energy of its effects.

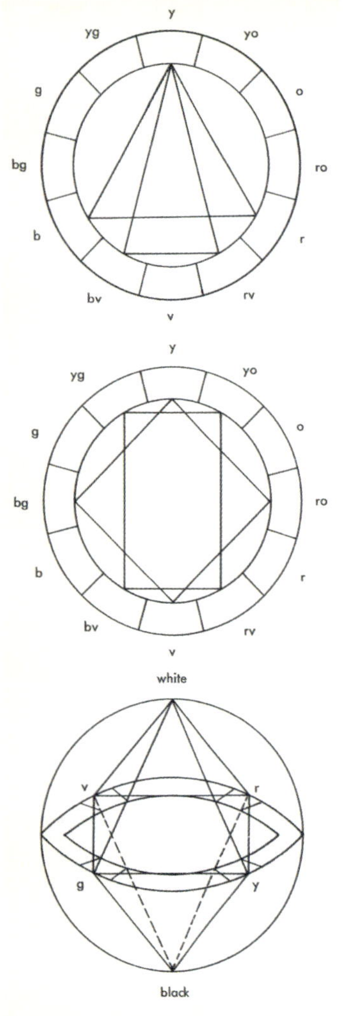

Shortly after the success of *The Art of Color*, another Bauhaus alumnus, Josef Albers (1888–1976), produced *Interaction of Color* (1963), one of the most immersive and enduring books on the subject to appear in the twentieth century, and, like Itten's work, inspired by a lifetime of working with students. Albers had been both student and teacher at the Bauhaus until its closure by the Nazis in 1933. His second act unfolded in the United States, when he and his wife, Anni, an accomplished textile artist, were poached by Black Mountain College in North Carolina. In 1950, Josef took up a post at Yale, where he led the design school until his retirement in 1958. Like so many colorists, Albers's creative impulses flowed in different directions: he made furniture, worked with experimental typography, and designed album sleeves for the sonically experimental Command Records label. From 1950 until his death in 1976, he worked on *Homage to the Square*, a lengthy series of paintings of nested squares set out in energetic color combinations with hard edges. The colors in these had an unadulterated power derived from prosaic origins: unmixed paint from tubes spread straight on to a primed Masonite surface by palette knife, "the way I smear butter on pumpernickel," as Albers himself put it.

Albers was fascinated by the context-dependent and ultimately misleading behavior of color, the "discrepancy between physical fact and psychic event". *Interaction of Color* helped the reader-viewer attune to color's volatility through a series of visual exercises, "seeing color action as well as feeling color relationships" by studying an accompanying set of gorgeously screen-printed plates. Philosophically this all felt a little like a descendant of Michel Eugène Chevreul's pioneering work on simultaneous contrast (see p.137), but the French chemist went unmentioned in Albers's text and had fallen out of print by the time of *Interaction*'s publication. And Albers's approach could not have been more different from Chevreul's. His method was experiential not explicatory, sensory rather than descriptive. As if wearied by the repetition of many established works on color, Albers announced in the introduction that this was not going to be a science lecture: "[T]he book does not begin with optics and

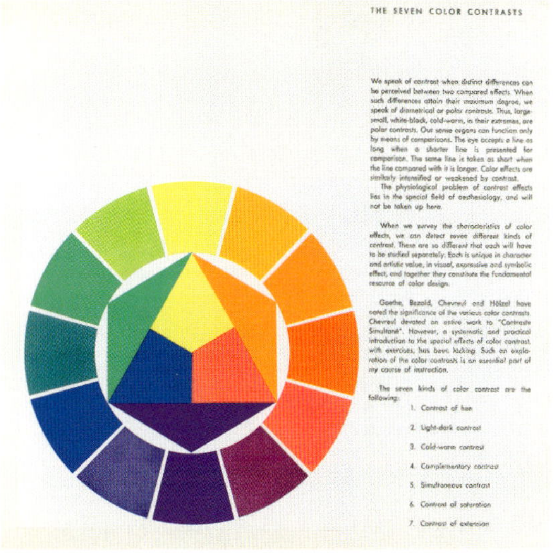

THE SEVEN COLOR CONTRASTS

We speak of contrast when distinct differences can be perceived between two compared effects. When such differences attain their maximum degree, we speak of diametrical or polar contrasts. Thus, large-small, white-black, cold-warm, in their extremes, are polar contrasts. Our sense organs can function only by means of comparisons. The eye accepts a line as long when a shorter line is presented for comparison. The same line is taken as short when the line compared with it is longer. Color effects are similarly intensified or weakened by contrast.

The physiological problem of contrast effects lies in the special field of aesthesiology, and will not be taken up here.

When we survey the characteristics of color effects, we can detect seven different kinds of contrast. These are so different that each will have to be studied separately. Each is unique in character and artistic value, in visual, expressive and symbolic effect, and together they constitute the fundamental resource of color design.

Goethe, Bezold, Chevreul and Hölzel have noted the significance of the various color contrasts. Chevreul devoted an entire work to "Contraste Simultané". However, a systematic and practical introduction to the special effects of color contrast, with exercises, has been lacking. Such an exploration of the color contrasts is an essential part of my course of instruction.

The seven kinds of color contrast are the following:

1. Contrast of hue
2. Light-dark contrast
3. Cold-warm contrast
4. Complementary contrast
5. Simultaneous contrast
6. Contrast of saturation
7. Contrast of extension

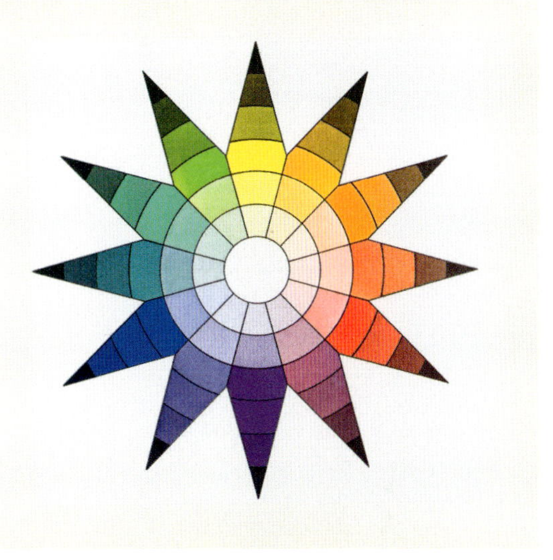

OPPOSITE
Johannes Itten's diagrams from The Art of Color *(1961) for establishing harmonies between different colors by inserting geometrical shapes within his color circle and rotating them. Whichever colors are touched by the three or four points of the inner shape should harmonize in a satisfying and coherent manner.*

ABOVE LEFT
Itten's "twelve-hue color circle" from The Art of Color *(1961). At the center is an equilateral triangle of primary colors, "defined with the greatest possible accuracy". A surrounding hexagon adds the secondary colors.*

ABOVE RIGHT
Itten's "color star" moved his circle into three dimensions. In theory, the star could be cut out and wrapped around a sphere to embody different values of the main colors.

physiology of visual perception, nor with any presentation of the physics of light and wave length." This refreshing approach was barely the start of the book's unconventionality.

The largest and heaviest book Yale University Press had ever published, *Interaction of Color* was a spectacle of book arts, deconstructed pages and multiple components—not exactly a book, yet almost something more. Limited to a print run of 2,000 copies, its presentation box (itself inside a slipcase) included eighty numbered folders that opened up to reveal screen-printed plates, each ablaze with energetic color combinations, relative temperatures and optical illusions. Nestling alongside were two publications: a hardback book providing context and instruction—each section tied to the corresponding numbered plates—and a further booklet of commentary to invite further reflection, after experiencing the visual effects of the color plates. There was a kind of logic to the sequence: set up; observe; reflect. But the multiformat package allowed readers to weave their own paths through the exercises, physically shuffling the components and moving between instruction, sensation, explanation, and reflection, in or out of order. Whatever the approach, the vivacious color bursts in those folders remained central. Each was a work of art in its own right under plain cover. Some plates involved paper engineering: flaps to be lifted to reveal the changing appearance of the underlying colors; masks to isolate sections and note the differences between hues. Many of the plates were designed by participants in Albers's workshops, and the

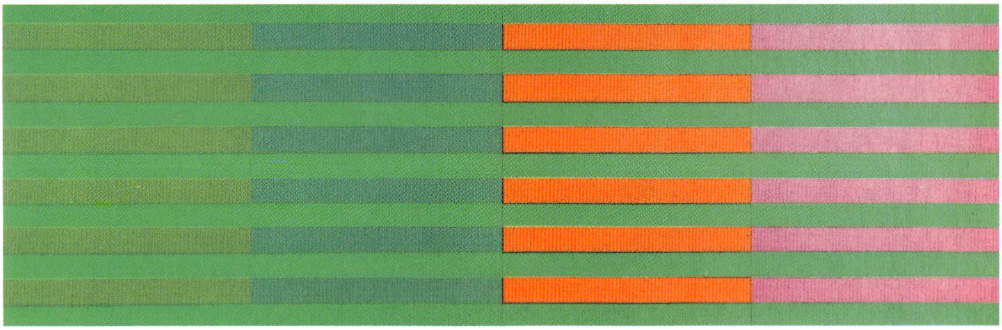

ABOVE
These horizontal bands of color accompanied Itten's advice on the juxtaposition of two colors in any composition. Itten stressed that color only made sense in the context of its surroundings. In the upper example, the pale orange is "completely inactive" against the yellow. In the lower example, the red forms the strongest contrast with green.

OPPOSITE
Itten's diagram to demonstrate his "contrast of extension" and his rule that the pairing of any two complementary colors should always be undertaken in the correct proportions. The precise ratio differs depending on the colors involved, as represented by the unequal divisions between these classic combinations.

selection in *Interaction* included the work of his notable former students, among them sculptor Eva Hesse and poet Mark Strand. Readers were encouraged to recreate the experiments at home but Albers recommended the use of shop-bought colored paper over home-made painted strips, which could be inconsistent, with distracting brushmarks. The purity of the sensation of color was essential to its effects.

Even the typographical arrangement of the accompanying texts compounded the sense of *Interaction* as an immersive rather than theoretical experience. It superficially resembled free verse or imagist poetry, with a stanzalike layout and eccentric line breaks. Albers's language was accessible and he used simple metaphors to convey the complexities of working with color. He was particularly fond of food-based imagery, likening color combinations to cooking up a stew, and to adjustments in mixtures as a kind of seasoning. Unlike almost all of the other writers on color so far considered, he was never concerned with the best or most harmonious combinations, only in examining the behavior of color in these pairings. In any case, he did not believe the classic combinations of complementaries and triads were universally correct, or even useful, calling time on ready-made combinations: "they are worn out".

Interaction of Color quickly sold out, but was succeeded by several different editions, which varied widely in format. A mass-market conventional book appeared in 1971, with most of the screen-printed color plates omitted and those that made the cut reproduced by duller offset printing. A heavily compromised version compared with the original, its existence nevertheless delighted Albers, who correctly believed a portable, affordable edition would reach a far wider audience. An electronic *Interaction* became available as an app for tablet devices in 2013. Using digital additive color rather than the subtractive color of the printed page, it reproduced the text but added video demonstrations and colored versions of the plates, allowing users to drag elements around on screen to see colors change against different backgrounds in real time. *Interaction* had become truly interactive. As the tablet technology relied on screen-based colored light, it allowed the manipulation of combinations of immaterial color, away from pigments and back, in a way, to where it all began, with Ibn al-Haytham, Isaac Newton, and intangible beams of light.

Taste and technology encouraged the twentieth century to undergo numerous costume changes and it went out looking a lot more colorful than it came in. Color bloomed throughout the decades, and around the world: on cinema screens, on magazine racks, and on clothes hangers, as technology captured ever more of the visible spectrum and commerce set it to work. Color-specification systems became especially important, striving for authority and exclusivity, each claiming ownership of their own defined colors. Yet any purportedly definitive color model in art or commerce underestimated its subject: isolating colors in a system, arraying them in grids and glueing them into place only turned them into something else: dead specimens, pinned butterflies. The twentieth century's artists, on the other hand, had color's number: they knew it could be a trickster or an ally. The same color could be a very different beast depending on who was wrestling with it.

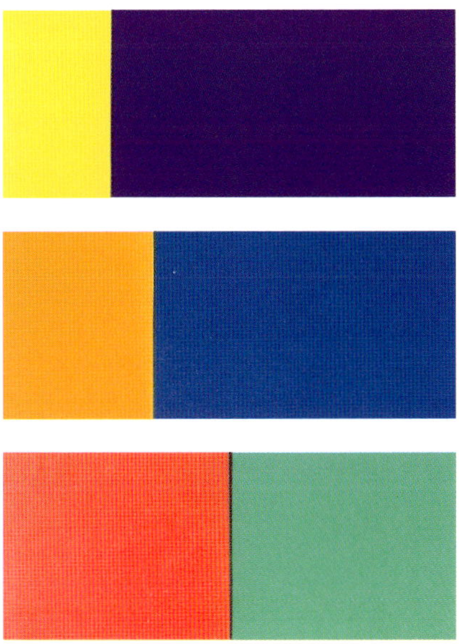

This survey has attempted to balance some of the many contradictions of color, even if they cannot be reconciled. As a subject and a phenomenon, color embodies all kinds of duality: it is infinite and constrained, subjective and objective, measurable and ineffable. It can be expressed through art and explained by science, or the other way around. And yet it has often been a Cinderella subject, for so long regarded by artists as subordinate to line and form. In science, it was frequently a footnote, something explored as a by-product of another line of enquiry, usually an investigation into light itself. Many advances in our understanding of color, or the technology we developed to exploit it, arose through pure happenstance. For all their contributions to the science, the most notable figures in the history of color are usually remembered first

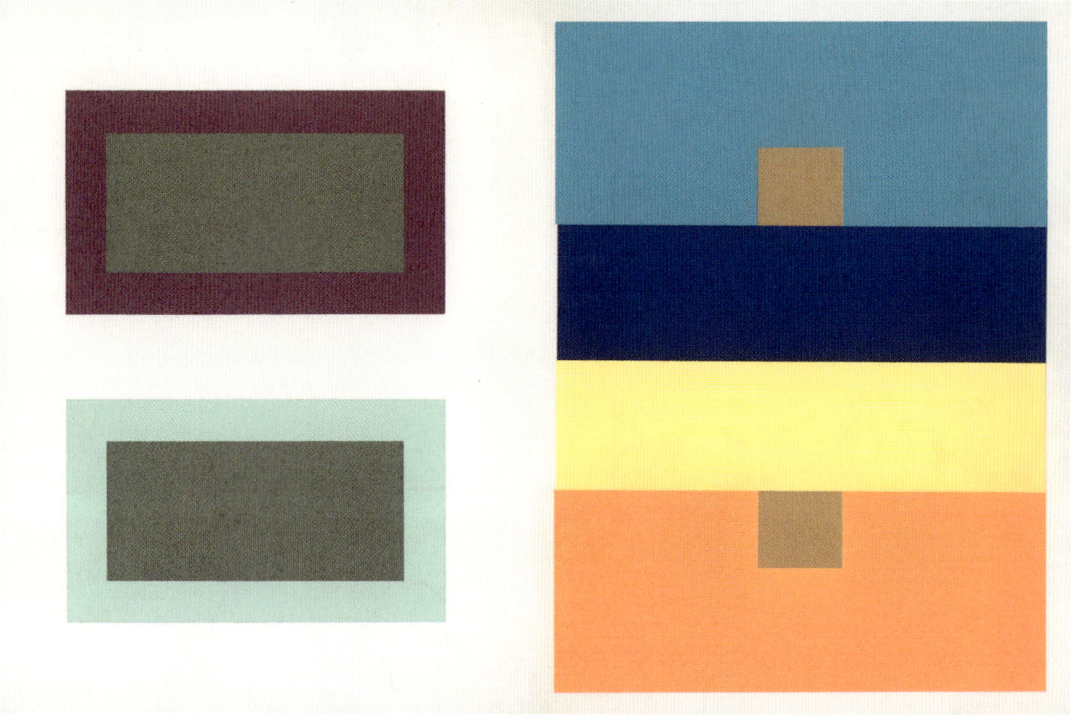

ABOVE
The opening plate of Josef Albers's Interaction of Color *(1963) provides two dramatic optical illusions in which a single color can appear to change against different backgrounds. In the left-hand example, the olive color appears darker in the lower rectangle than the upper. On the right-hand side, the upper brown square appears a few tints lighter than the bottom.*

for other, unrelated, achievements, and this is true even of Newton, Goethe, and Maxwell. It is remarkable how often the authors of some of the greatest works described in the preceding pages tackled the subject only in retirement, as a leisure activity, or indulgent hobby.

Nevertheless, the signs and systems devised to organize color remain beautiful and often moving works in their execution and their ambition. Most endure for their aesthetic delights more than their accuracy or comprehensiveness. Indeed, many thought they had arrived at a definitive model only to be supplanted within a few years by a rival system, or a technological leap. The history of color is the journey of a subject in flux, endlessly reconceived but always hard to pin down. Even when perfectly analyzed through the technology of colorimetry (objective color measurement), which reached a point of remarkable precision in the twentieth century, the symbolic and psychological dimensions of the full palette can never be fully charted. So elusive is the subject that it recalls Christian Dior's famous observation about fashion: even when there are no more secrets, it remains a mystery.

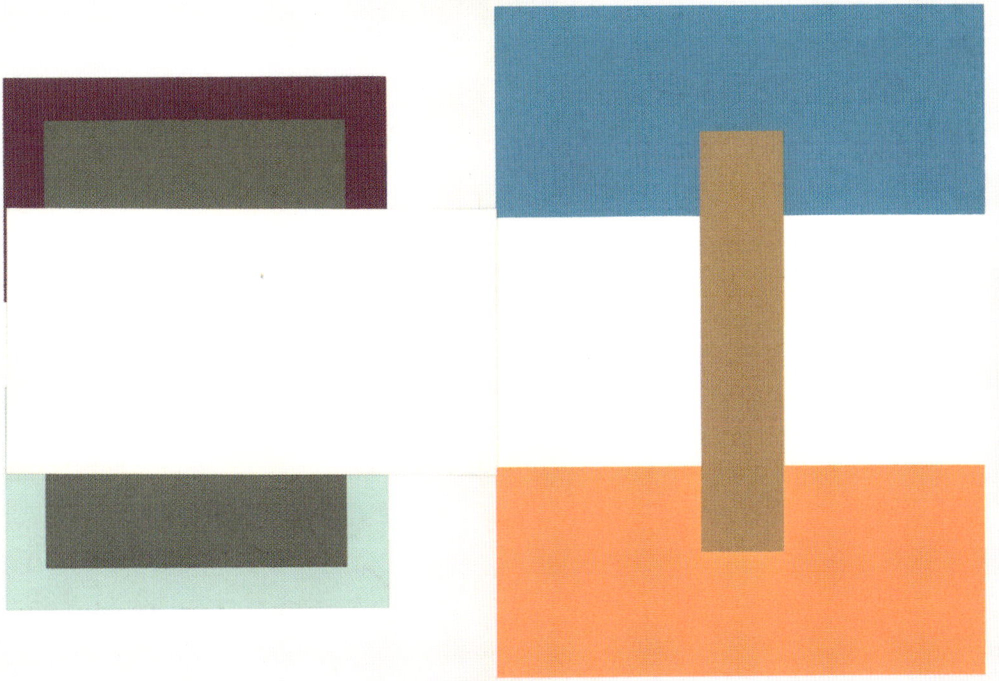

ABOVE
The plate contains a hinged card flap of dark blue and yellow that can be folded back to reveal the two brown squares to be composed of the same color in a continuous bar. The quality of the original plates, each individually screen printed, gives them a power that comes from the purity and solidity of its hues.

OVERLEAF
In this plate, Albers and his students explored assumptions around color temperature and challenged the belief that red colors are always warm while blue ones are inevitably cool. In these particular versions, Albers wrote, "a reading of all the left halves as warmer than the paired right is not unreasonable".

If color is a moving target, it is no wonder that many of the physical books covered in this volume are often not quite books at all, their execution demanding unconventional formats. The fold-out attachments, tipped-in sheets, multiple book blocks, portfolios, and paper engineering were all deployed to try to distil color onto the page, to contain it. The fluidity of color can also be sensed in the three-dimensional models of color spaces that scholars devised. Rotating spheres, pivoting cubes, and spinning double cones all invite us to think of color as something in flux and on the move, manipulable in space. Nevertheless, after centuries of complex geometrical arrangement, perhaps the simplest two-dimensional color wheel of Isaac Newton's invention has endured for good reason. A circle might well be the most appropriate metaphorical embodiment of the elusive magic of color itself: cyclical and ordered, transitional yet eternal. All the historical attempts to place boundaries around color only help us catch it for a second, before it wriggles free and moves on. Color is always just within our grasp and we are ever in pursuit.

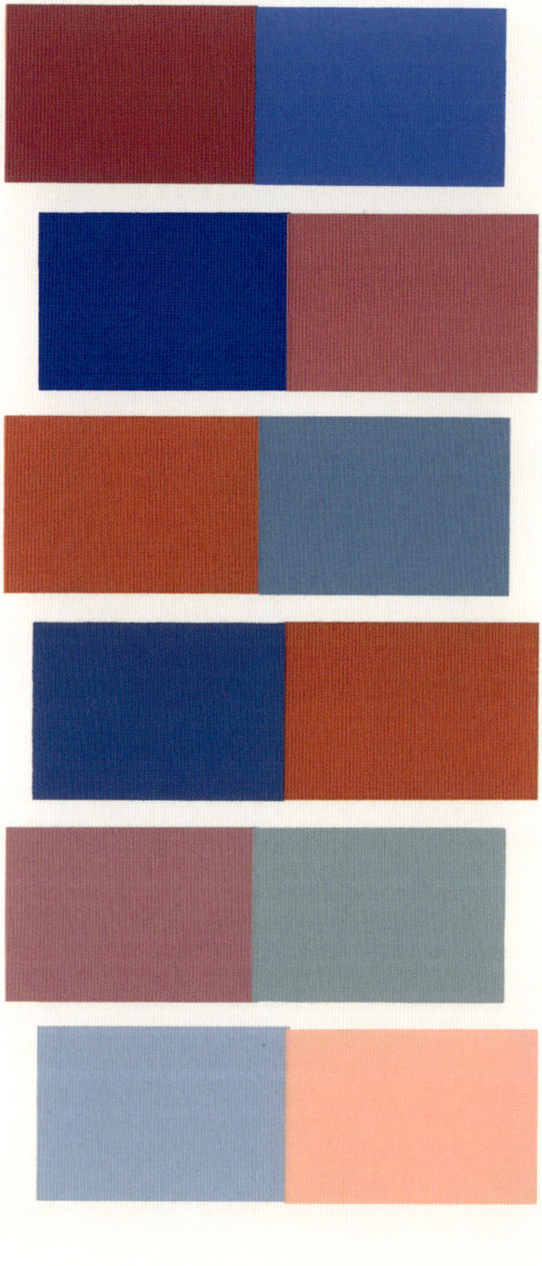

APPENDIX

Page numbers in *italics* refer to illustrations

PICTURE CREDITS

All images are reproduced courtesy of the Colour Reference Library, Royal College of Art (photographer Sarah Mercer), with the exception of:

Maxwell Ashby Armfield/Bridgeman images 41
Artokoloro/Alamy Stock Photo 81
Courtesy of Alexandra Loske (photograph by Clive Boursnell): 105
Bibliothèque nationale de France/ Creative Commons 194
Bridgeman Images: 92
© British Library Board. All Rights Reserved/Bridgeman Images: 73, 80
Heritage Library, Creative Commons: 45
Keith Corrigan/Alamy Stock Photo 104
Kunsthaus Zürich, Creative Commons: 134
Library of Congress/Creative Commons 184
Linda Hall Library, Creative Commons: 108
Metropolitan Museum of Modern Art, New York, Creative Commons: 177
Private collection: 39, 57, 59, 60–1, 62–3, 118–19, 127, 129 below, 131, 163, 183, 204, 205 above, 207, 224–5
The New York Public Library, Astor, Lenox and Tilden Foundations, Creative Commons: 104
Sascha Grusche (2015), Creative Commons: 23
Courtesy of Science History Institute, Philadelphia: 47, 48–9, 51, 125, 126, 128, 129 below, 130, 146–7, 149, 181 above
Smithsonian Institution Libraries, Creative Commons: 111
Solomon R. Guggenheim Museum, New York City, Creative Commons: 38
Svintage Archive/Alamy Stock Photo 85
Tokyo Fuji Art Museum, Creative Commons 237
Wellcome Collection, Creative Commons: 112–13, 181 right, 195
Wikimedia Commons 240
Yale University Press: 103, 122 above, 123, 246, 247, 248

Every effort has been made to provide correct atributions. Any inadvertent errors or omissions will be corrected in subsequent editions.

Although this is a book about books, its bibliography does not itemize the main publications already discussed in the main text. Instead, this list acknowledges the secondary sources and annotated editions that greatly illuminated all those primary works.

GENERAL

Abel, Adrian, 'The History of Dyes and Pigments: From Natural Dyes to High-Performance Pigments', in Janet Best (ed.), *Colour Design: Theories and Applications* (Woodhead Publishing, 2012)

Al-Khalili, Jim, *Pathfinders: The Golden Age of Arabic Science* (Penguin, 2012)

Aldersey-Williams, Hugh, *Periodic Tales: The Curious Lives of the Elements* (Penguin, 2012)

Ball, Philip, 'Colour, Art and Science: Notes for a Talk Delivered at the Victoria & Albert Museum, London' (20 October 2002), https://www.philipball.co.uk/articles/colour/51-colour-and-art

Ball, Philip, 'The Invention of Colour', *Interfaces* 33 (2012), https://www.holycross.edu/interfaces/interfaces-volume-33

Ball, Phillip, Mark Clarke and Carinna Parriman, *Colour in the Making: from Old Wisdom to New Brilliance* (Black Dog, 2013)

Baty, Patrick, *The Anatomy of Colour: The Story of Heritage Paints and Pigments* (Thames & Hudson, 2017)

Baty, Patrick, 'The Quest for Colour Standards in 20th-Century Britain', in *La Conservazione delle policromie nell'architettura del XX secolo* (Conservation of Colour in 20th-Century Architecture) (Nardini Editore, 2013)

Biggam, CP, and Kirsten Wolf (eds), *A Cultural History of Color: In the Medieval Age* (Bloomsbury, 2021)

Biggam, CP, and Kirsten Wolf (eds), *A Cultural History of Color: In the Age of Enlightenment* (Bloomsbury, 2021)

Birren, Faber (ed.), *Ostwald, The Color Primer: A Basic Treatise on the Color System of Wilhelm Ostwald* (Van Nostrand Reinhold Co., c.1969)

Birren, Faber (ed.), *The Elements of Color: A Treatise Based on the Color System of Johannes Itten Based on His Book The Art of Color* (Van Nostrand Reinhold Co., 1970)

Buono, Amy, and Sven Dupré (eds), *A Cultural History of Color: In the Renaissance* (Bloomsbury, 2021)

Burchett, Kenneth E, *A Bibliographical History of the Study and Use of Color from Aristotle to Kandinsky* (Edwin Mellen Press, 2005)

Douma, Michael (curator), *Pigments through the Ages* (2008) www.webexhibits.org/pigments

Eckstut, Arielle, and Joann Eckstut, *What is Color?: 50 Questions and Answers on the Science of Color* (Abrams, 2020)

Fehrman, Kenneth, and Cherie Fehrman, *Color: The Secret Influence* (Prentice Hall, 2004, 2nd edn)

Feisner, Edith Anderson, *Colour: How to Use Colour in Art and Design* (Laurence King, 2006, 2nd edn)

Gage, John, 'A Romantic Colourman: George Field and British Art', The *63rd Volume of the Walpole Society* (The Walpole Society, 2001)

Goethe, Johann Wolfgang von, *Goethe's Color Theory, Arranged and Edited by Rupprecht Matthaei* (Van Nostrand Reinhold, 1971)

Healey, Declan (dir.), *Scotland's Einstein: James Clerk Maxwell - The Man Who Changed the World* (BBC Four, 2015)

Hutchings, John B, 'Symbolic use of color in ritual, tradition and folklore', in Andrew J Elliot, Mark D Fairchild and Anna Franklin (eds), *The Handbook of Color Psychology* (Cambridge University Press, 2015)

Kuehni, Rolf G, and Andreas Schwarz, *Color Ordered: A Survey of Color Order Systems from Antiquity to the Present* (Oxford University Press, 2008)

Loske, Alexandra, *Colour: A Visual History* (Ilex, 2019)

Loske, Alexandra (ed), *A Cultural History of Color: In the Age of Industry* (Bloomsbury, 2021)

Lowengard, Sarah, *The Creation of Color in Eighteenth-Century Europe* (Gutenberg-e/Columbia University Press, 2006) http://www.gutenberg-e.org/lowengard/

Nichols, Edward L, *National Academy Biographical Memoirs Vol VI - Ogden Nicholas Rood* (National Academy of Sciences, 1909)

Osborne, Roy, 'The History of Colour Theory in Art, Design and Science', in Janet Best (ed.), *Colour Design: Theories and Applications* (Woodhead Publishing, 2012)

Osborne, Roy, *Books on Colour 1495–2015: History and Bibliography* (Lulu, 2015)

Pastoureau, Michel, *The Colours of Our Memories* (trans. Janet Lloyd) (Polity, 2012)

Peruzzi, Giulio, and Valentina Roberti, 'The Color Top and the Distinction Between Additive and Subtractive Color Mixing', *IEEE Antennas & Propagation Magazine* (IEEE Antennas and Propagation Society, 4 October 2019)

Rood, Ogden, *Modern Chromatics with a Preface, Introduction and Commentary by Faber Birren* (Van Nostrand Reinhold Co., c.1973)

Roque, Georges, *Chevreul's Colour Theory and its Consequences for Artists* (Colour Group (Great Britain), 2011)

Sabel, Clare, *Colour Science*, Whipple Library Exhibitions and Displays (University of Cambridge, 2015-16) https://www.whipplelib.hps.cam.ac.uk/special/exhibitions-and-displays/colour-science

Shires, Linda M, 'On Color Theory, 1835: George Field's *Chromatography*', *BRANCH: Britain, Representation and Nineteenth-Century History: 1775-1925* (2012) https://branchcollective.org/?ps_articles=linda-m-shires-on-color-theory-1835-george-fields-chromatography

Silvestrini, Narcisco, and Ernst Peter Fischer, *Color Systems in Art and Science: Catalogue* I (Color Klaus Stromer, 1996)

Spillmann, Werner, 'Color Order Systems', in Harold Linton, *Color Consulting: A Survey of International Color Design* (Van Nostrand Reinhold Co., 1991)

Steinvall, Anders, and Sarah Street (eds), *A Cultural History of Color: In the Modern Age* (Bloomsbury, 2021)

Turner, Jeremy (dir.), *Light Fantastic: Let There Be Light* (BBC Four, 2004)

Varley, Helen (ed), *Colour* (Mitchell Beazley, 1980)

Wharton, David (ed), *A Cultural History of Color: In Antiquity* (Bloomsbury, 2021)

Wurmfeld, Sanford, Mary S. Duffy, Nancy Littlejohn Gray, et al, *Color Documents: A Presentational Theory: Plates from Treatises Published 18th Century to the Present* (Hunter College Art Gallery, 1985)

Usborne, Tim (dir.), *Science and Islam, The Empire of Reason* (BBC Four, 2009)

BELIEF

Breen, Benjamin, 'Victorian Occultism and the Art of Synesthesia', *Public Domain Review* (19 March 2014) https://publicdomainreview.org/essay/victorian-occultism-and-the-art-

of-synesthesia
Janes, Dominic, 'The Wordless Book: Visual and Material Culture of Evangelism in Victorian Britain', *Material Religion* volume 12, issue 1 (Taylor & Francis, 2016)
Sympathetic Vibratory Physics Wiki (SVPWiki.com)

COMMERCE

Birren, Faber. *Selling with Colour* (McGraw-Hill, 1945)
Blaszczyk, Regina Lee, *The Color Revolution* (The MIT Press, 2012)
Dymock, Charlotte, 'A Colourful History: The Textile Colour Card Association of the United States', *Tuppence Ha'penny* (24 January 2019) https://www.tuppence hapenny.com/blog/textile-colour-card-association

LANGUAGE

Deutscher, Guy, *Through the Language Glass: How Words Colour Your World* (Picador, 2010)
Hardin, C L, 'Berlin and Kay Theory', *Encyclopedia of Color Science and Technology* (Springer New York, NY, 2013)
Sassi, Maria Michela, 'The Sea was Never Blue', Aeon (31 July 2017) https://aeon.co/essays/can-we-hope-to-understand-how-the-greeks-saw-their-world
Scott, Tom. 'All the Colours, Including Grue: How Languages See Colours Differently', tomscott.com (7 June 2013) https://www.youtube.com/watch?v=2TtnD4jmCDQ
Yglasias, Matt, 'The Bizarre Myth that Ancient Greeks Couldn't See Blue', *Slow Boring* (4 April 2022) https://www.slowboring.com/p/greeks-blue

NATURE

Ayers, Elaine, 'Coded Colours: Botanical Histories of Colour Standardization', *The Site Magazine* (30 April 2020), https://www.thesitemagazine.com/read/codedcolours
Baty, Patrick et al, Nature's Palette: *A Colour Reference System from the Natural World* (Thames & Hudson, 2021)
Beddard, Honor, Tim Dee, and Wellcome Collection, *Animal. Vegetable. Mineral: Organising Nature: A Picture Album* (Wellcome Collection, 2016)
Cooperman, Jeannette, 'He Turned Birds into Pantone Colours', *The Common Reader: A Journal of the Essay* (19 May 2021) https://commonreader.wustl.edu/he-turned-birds-into-pantone-colors/
Lewis, Daniel, 'How Red is Dragon's Blood?', *Smithsonian Magazine* (24 June 2014) https://www.smithsonianmag.com/arts-culture /how-red-dragons-blood-180951822/
Meier, Allison, 'The Bird-Based Colour System that Eventually Became Pantone', *Hyperallergic* (22 September 2016) https://hyperallergic.com/283388/the-bird-based-color-system-that-eventually-became-pantone/

FOOD

Berube, Chris (prod.), 'I Can't Believe it's Pink Margarine', *99% Invisible* (podcast, episode 462) (19 October 2021) https://99percentinvisible.org/episode/i-cant-believe-its-pink-margarine/
Finch, Vincent, 'Food and Visual Culture', *Victorian Visual Culture* (12 December 2020) https://victorianvisualculture.blog/2020/12/12/food-and-visual-culture/
Hisano, Ai, 'The Rise of Synthetic Colors in the American Food Industry, 1870–1940', *Business History Review*, vol. 90, no. 3 (Cambridge University Press, 2016)
Hisano, Ai. *Visualizing Taste: How Business Changed the Look of What you Eat* (Harvard University Press, 2019)
Hutchings, J B. 'Colour in food', in Janet Best (ed.), *Colour Design: Theories and Applications* (Woodhead Publishing, 2012)
Spence, Charles, 'Eating with Our Eyes: On the Color of Flavor', in Andrew J Elliot, Mark D Fairchild and Anna Franklin (eds), *The Handbook of Color Psychology* (Cambridge University Press, 2015)

WELLNESS

Alter, Adam, *Drunk Tank Pink: The Subconscious Forces That Shape How We Think, Feel and Behave* (Penguin, 2013)
Chajes, Julie, 'Seth Pancoast and the Kabbalah: Medical Pluralism and the Reception of Physics in Late-Nineteenth Century Philadelphia', *Kabbalah: Journal for the Study of Jewish Mystical Texts* (Cherub Press, 2018)
Karliczek, André, 'One for All? Werner's Nomenclature of Colours as a General Standard of Colour and its Particular Use in Medicine', in Baty et al, *Nature's Palette* (Thames & Hudson, 2021)
Mahnke, Frank, *Color, Environment and Human Response* (Van Nostrand Reinhold Co., 1996)
Turner, Christopher, 'The Kingpin of Fakers: Colonel Dinshah P Ghadiali and the Spectro-Chrome', *Cabinet Magazine*, 18 (Immaterial Incorporated, Summer 2005)

PRINTING

Hugues, 'Des Livres à l'honneur: Les "Livre à la Mode" de Caraccioli', *Le Blog du Bibliophile* (23 November 2007), https://bibliophilie.blogspot.com/2007/11/des-livres-lhonneur-les-livre-la-mode.html
Twyman, Michael, *A History of Chromolithography: Printed Colour for All* (British Library, 2013)
Parraman, Carinna, 'Colour Printing Techniques', in Janet Best (ed.), *Colour Design: Theories and applications* (Woodhead Publishing, 2012)
Stijnman, Ad, 'Ink and Light: Le Blon's Coloritto and Newton's Opticks', *Thinking 3D* (University of St Andrews, 2017) https://www.thinking3d.ac.uk/LeBlon1725/
Public Domain Review, 'Albert Racinet's L'Ornement Polychrome, 1869-73', *Public Domain Review* (5 July 2018) https://publicdomainreview.org/collection/albert-racinet-s-l-ornement-polychrome-1869-73

MUSIC

Ferreira, Becky, 'Behold the Ocular Harpsichord: the Laser Light Show of the 18th Century', Vice (16 November 2015) https://www.vice.com/en/article/kb7qzn/behold-the-ocular-harpsichord-the-laser-light-show-of-the-18th-century
Raz, Carmel, 'Music of the Spheres: David Ramsay Hay and the Reinvention of Pythagorean Aesthetics', *Public Domain Review* (16 May 2019) https://publicdomainreview.org/essay/music-of-the-squares-david-ramsay-hay-and-the-reinvention-of-pythagorean-aesthetics
Special Collections, Princeton University, 'Analogy and Harmony of Colors', Graphic Arts Collection, Firestone Library, Princeton University (28 January 2020) https://graphicarts.princeton.edu/2020/01/28/analogy-and-harmony-of-colours/

I am grateful to all at Frances Lincoln who steered this project into the light. Particular thanks to Philip Cooper for the original suggestion, and for the faith in me to carry it out, and also to Nicki Davis and Michael Brunström for patient support and guidance in the earlier and later stages, respectively. Thanks to Sam Wolfson, for her thoughtful and elegant design and for finding the loveliest patterns among the kaleidoscopic sources.

For their interest, encouragement and sensible advice along the way, I am grateful to Christopher Holt, Cathy Johns, Jill McGivering, Ewen Moore and Dawn Parkinson. For kind hospitality while I worked on the final draft, my thanks to Nancy Kessick and Sarah Kessick.

This book owes a debt to the vision and legacy of Stuart Durant and Don Pavey, the Colour Reference Library's core founders, and I am mindful of their past generosity and willingness to share their knowledge with me. Every week I get to work with the many brilliant users of the CRL, including so many talented students and staff of the Royal College of Art, and they make the collection what it is. Among the external users, I reserve a single category for Alexandra Loske (much like Sol did for the colour white) in recognition of her enduring friendship, enthusiasm and erudition.

I am lucky to be supported by two exceptional RCA colleagues who helped me get this book over the line. Thank you to Darlene Maxwell for her support, trust and kindness. Without Sarah Mercer, who digitized many of the works herein with such care and respect for the originals, this book would be a shadow of its potential self, and much grayer. I am also indebted to Peter Hassell for appointing me to run the College's special collections in the first place, and for backing me all the way during his RCA tenure.

I also wish to acknowledge the unsung librarians, cataloguers, curators and technicians who freely provide so many valuable materials online through such resources as the Science History Institute, the Internet Archive, the Linda Hall Library, the Wellcome Collection and the Public Domain Review.

Finally, and above all, thanks to my domestic support team: to Rosalind Parkinson for her rainbow-hued cheerleading, and to Elizabeth Kessick, the orange to my blue, for plenty of pep talks, for patiently wading through multiple drafts, and for sound judgement in all dilemmas. In my universe, these two are phenomenal.

NEIL PARKINSON is Archives and Collections Manager at the Royal College of Art, London, where his responsibilities include development of the renowned Colour Reference Library. He has presented widely on the subject of color to audiences from schoolchildren to chemists.

Quarto

First published in 2023
by Frances Lincoln,
an imprint of
The Quarto Group.
One Triptych Place,
London,
SE1 9SH
United Kingdom
(0)20 7700 6700
www.Quarto.com

A catalogue record for this book is available from the British Library.

ISBN 978-0-7112-8884-3
Ebook ISBN 978-0-7112-8966-6

Edited by Michael Brunström
Design by BLOK design
Printed and bound in China

10 9 8 7 6 5 4 3 2

FSC www.fsc.org MIX Paper | Supporting responsible forestry FSC® C016973